Personal Relationships. 4:

Dissolving Personal Relationships

Personal Relationships. 4:

Dissolving Personal Relationships

edited by

STEVE DUCK

Department of Psychology
University of Lancaster, England

1982

ACADEMIC PRESS
A Subsidiary of Harcourt Brace, Jovanovich, Publishers
London   New York
Paris   San Diego   San Francisco
São Paulo   Sydney   Tokyo   Toronto

ACADEMIC PRESS INC. (LONDON) LTD.
24/28 Oval Road,
London NW1

United States Edition published by
ACADEMIC PRESS INC.
111 Fifth Avenue
New York, New York 10003

British Library Cataloguing in Publication Data

Personal relationships.
Vol. 4: Dissolving personal relationships
1. Interpersonal relations
I. Duck, Steve
302 (expanded)   HM132
ISBN 0-12-222804-9

Filmset in 10/12pt Times by
Reproduction Drawings Ltd., Sutton, Surrey

Printed in Great Britain by
T. J. Press (Padstow) Ltd, Padstow, Cornwall

Contributors

FRAN DICKSON-MARKMAN, Department of Speech Communication, Utah State University, Logan, Utah, USA

STEVE DUCK, Department of Psychology, Fylde College, University of Lancaster, Lancaster, UK

FRANK FLOYD, Department of Psychology, Bowling Green State University, Bowling Green, Ohio, USA

WILLIAM G. GRAZIANO, Department of Psychology, University of Georgia, Athens, Georgia, USA

GUNHILD O. HAGESTAD, Division of Individual and Family Studies, The Pennsylvania State University, University Park, Pennsylvania, USA

JOHN H. HARVEY, (Chapter written from Educational Affairs, APA, Washington, DC) now at: Department of Psychology, Texas Tech University, Lubbock, Texas, USA

MICHAEL P. JOHNSON, Department of Sociology, The Pennsylvania State University, University Park, Pennsylvania, USA

JOHN J. LA GAIPA, Department of Psychology, University of Windsor, Windsor, Ontario, Canada

HOWARD J. MARKMAN, Department of Psychology, University of Denver, Denver, Colorado, USA

LYNN MATHER MUSSER, Department of Psychology, University of Georgia, Athens, Georgia, USA

GEORGE J. McCALL, Department of Sociology, University of Missouri, St. Louis, Missouri, USA

GERALD R. MILLER, Department of Communication, Michigan State University, East Lansing, Michigan, USA

MALCOLM R. PARKS, Department of Speech Communication, University of Washington, Seattle, Washington, USA

MIRIAM J. RODIN, Department of Psychology, San Diego State University, San Diego, California, USA

MICHAEL A. SMYER, Division of Individual and Family Studies, The Pennsylvania State University, University Park, Pennsylvania, USA

BONNIE E. STEWART, Department of Psychology, Vanderbilt University, Nashville, Tennessee, USA

ANN L. WEBER, Department of Psychology, University of North Carolina, Asheville, North Carolina, USA

KERRY L. YARKIN, Department of Psychology, Vanderbilt University, Nashville, Tennessee, USA

Preface

The dissolution of a close personal relationship is a significant and usually a stressful occurrence in most people's lives. For all that psychologists, sociologists and anthropologists have recognized and acknowledged this fact, they have not, as yet, any widely accepted general models of relationship termination. The present volume attempts to identify and address the key issues that face researchers in coming to terms with this state of affairs, and hence to contribute to the development and testing of effective programmes of relationship counselling and assistance. The writers in this volume are all keenly aware of the value of research-based suggestions for counselling of relational turbulence and helping people to resolve the relational conflicts. Some of them also take the novel position that we should also attend to the creation of research-based programmes for *extricating* persons from unsatisfactory relationships in the way least damaging psychologically.

The volume as a whole gives detailed attention to the view that relationship dissolution represents not an event but a process, composed of many constituent elements, each of which must be clearly understood and clearly related to the other components, if we are to obtain the most useful total picture. The contributors provide a thorough consideration of a significant and often painful part of the human enterprise which, in this case, is one with wide medical, social and practical significance. Relationship loss increases risk of illness, both physical and psychological, increases the likelihood of alcoholism and suicide attempts, and even makes it more likely that the person will be the victim of a fatal traffic accident or a homicidal assault!

We are perhaps more familiar with the lesser forms of pain, disturbance and stress that also stem from dissolving personal relationship. Both professional and informal counsellors and confidants know that these result from friendship loss as well as from loss of a spouse. The present volume, however, represents the first attempt to depict *general* relationship dissolution rather than marital dissolution in particular. It also reflects the style of the earlier volumes in the series (see below), by drawing together eminent scholars from a variety of disciplines and schools of thought. It also prepares the way for the last of the series (Personal Relationships 5: Repairing Personal Relationships, S. W. Duck, editor, Academic Press, London), which will consider both the ways in which relationships can be repaired and the ways in which they repair and protect the people involved in them. Earlier volumes in the series have covered the nature of relationships and the best means of studying them (Personal Relationships 1: Studying Personal Relationships, S. W. Duck and R. Gilmour, editors, Academic Press, 1981); have given detailed attention to issues in the normal development and growth of relationships (Personal Relationships 2: Developing Personal Relationships, S. W. Duck and R. Gilmour, editors, Academic Press, 1981); and, finally, looked at relationship problems and disturbances (Personal Relationships 3: Personal Relationships in Disorder, S. W. Duck and R. Gilmour, editors, Academic Press, 1981). The present volume takes us to the next stage: how people get out of relationships, the decisions involved, the pressures that they must face, the social actions that must be completed, and the psychological and social consequences of all of this.

The chapters are ordered in a way that reflects the progress of relationship dissolution. Duck, Rodin and Johnson present, in the first three chapters, general discussions of the process of relationship dissolution, of "non-starter" relationships, and of the reduction of personal forms of commitment to the relationship. In the next three chapters, the authors consider the impact of the starting and maintenance of relationships upon their dissolution (Graziano and Mather Musser), of beliefs and attributions upon dissolution (Harvey, Weber, Yarkin and Stewart) and of the communication of intents that takes place at both a verbal and non-verbal level of analysis (Miller and Parks). These lively and challenging chapters represent unique contributions to the relationship literature, in each case dealing with aspects of the problem that have been given no consideration by researchers so far. The next three chapters give attention to the social forms of relationship dissolution, the social impact of its occurrence, and the social management of its consequences. Relationship dissolution does not simply occur in a vacuum: it has to be managed and presented to the partner and to the surrounding social network. Hagestad and Smyer give attention to the nature of transitions in social life, and take the special case of divorce as the basis of their thinking; La Gaipa considers the rules that apply to disengagement, the role of gossip in upholding them, and the activities of other persons in the social environment; McCall details the ways in which people cope with the spoiling of a relationship's identity, the manner of their mourning of its loss, and the means by which they construct socially acceptable stories of the relationship's demise. The final chapter, by Markman, Floyd and Dickson-Markman, leads us to the primary task of preventing marital and family distress and dissolution. Their detailed, scholarly and incisive proposals contain many insights with practical value in the years to come, when research on dissolution begins to make a stronger contribution to the work of repairing unsatisfactory relationships.

In completing work on the book I have been able to draw on the support of a most valuable network myself. Colin Brydon, Dorothy Miell, David Miell and Martin Lea have made untold contributions to my thinking about the field. John La Gaipa has patiently assisted me to clarify my thoughts and has given me many insights. Helen Lea, Anne Parker, Hazel Satterthwaite and Sylvia Sumner have provided prodigious feats of secretarial work. To all of these people I am most grateful. Finally, I am grateful to my wife Sandra and daughter Christina (and the, at time of writing, 2/3 of a sibling shortly to join her): I am particularly appreciative of the sacrifices that they made that allowed me to disappear frequently and unexpectedly, often returning covered in ink and in a mood that would have dissolved most relationships. Their support made the book possible.

Lancaster, March 1982   Steve Duck

Contents

CHAPTER 1

A Topography of Relationship Disengagement and Dissolution

Steve Duck

This chapter is about relationship dissolution and yet is not the traditional form of research review that an editor's chapter habitually embodies. Since the present volume presumes to take us on a journey to something of a New World rather than on a tour of already very familiar and well-mapped territory, the need is rather for a forward-looking but basic orientation towards key areas of the topic. This would localize and orient us towards those existing careful analyses that seek to provide insights into specific topics and aspects of the ending of relationships (e.g. Albert and Kessler, 1978; Altman and Taylor, 1973; Knapp, 1978; Lanei, 1978; Salts, 1979; Scott and Powers, 1978). What is presently lacking, however, is a framework for locating and understanding such mini-maps; for showing whether relationship growth relates to disengagement; indicating where communication processes fit in, how attribution ties in, and so on. The present volume as a whole sets out to do this job, and within that context the present chapter attempts to give a general sketch to "place" the concerns of such analyses in a general picture of the dissolution of relationships. Its purpose is thus to separate issues that are sometimes confused, and hence to prepare the way for the coming chapters which again take up detailed but specific themes in the analysis.

1

I will begin my task by considering some essential, if familiar, points about the nature and character of relationship dissolution, and by then going on to consider the relevance of present theoretical formulations about interpersonal *attraction* for understanding its opposite, namely, relationship decline. Finally, I will propose a general mapping for the topics in the area. A map is only implicitly a theory and this chapter does not propose an explicit theory of relationship dissolution—but it does, I hope, indicate the potential interest and the range of research challenges that lie in the area of future workers for a range of academic and applied research disciplines.

In discussing relationship dissolution I will adopt here (and have imposed throughout the present volume) a consistent terminology. Following Duck (1981), I will use the terms "dissolution" and "termination" to refer to the permanent dismemberment of an existing relationship, as distinct from "breakdown" which refers to such turbulence or disorder in a relationship that may or may not lead to dissolution. I will adopt the term "decline" to refer to reduction of intimacy without actual physical withdrawal from relationship and hence decline encompasses those instances that involve the restructuring or reformulating of a close relationship as a less intimate and more distanced one (e.g. when a couple get divorced but remain friends). I use the term "disengagement" to cover the processes of withdrawing from a relationship that constitute most of the subject matter for the present chapter and others in this volume—such processes as the negotiation of the dissolution of the relationship, reducing commitment, and restructuring social networks. Finally, I will refer to the "Person" as the active dissolver of the relationship and to the "Partner" as the other individual involved.

Throughout any discussion of relationship disengagement and dissolution it must be clearly noted that many different sorts of relationship termination can be identified both at the dyadic and at the network level. Davis (1973) led the way here, drawing useful distinctions between dissolution of formalized and of informal relationships; pointing out the psychological and theoretical relevance of the duration of a relationship prior to its dissolution; noting the significance of the type of relationship before disengagement (whether a casual acquaintance, a close friendship or a romantic attachment); finally, and most usefully, drawing attention to the importance of the expectations of the partners concerning the post-dissolution relationship state.

Nevertheless, in my view the most important observation for research is that we must avoid the risk of seeing relationship dissolution as an event. On the contrary, it is a process, and an extended one with many facets: affective, behavioural, cognitive; intra-individual, dyadic and social. Dissolution usually occurs after the relationship breaks down, but breakdown and dissolution are psychologically distinct. Similarly we have learned to distinguish "liking" and "relationship formation": liking for someone is a common basis for making a relationship but is not enough on its own. In the case of "liking" and "relationship" it took some 20 years to clarify the links between the one and the other (Hinde, 1979; 1981). In the case of "breakdown" and "dissolution" the present major research issues concern precisely the mechanisms and the processes through which the one leads into the other and why, sometimes, it does not.

We must also plainly acknowledge that the activity leading to relationship dissolution is not necessarily consciously "driven", even if we can cite instances where "strategic deletion of a relationship" is indeed a person's goal (Baxter, 1980). It is undesirable to assume that disengagement is necessarily orderly, predictable and certain. Most often it is messy, uncontrolled and uncertain (Duck and Miell, 1981). Neither should we assume that relationship dissolution represents a choice completely unlimited by other constraints such as network pressures, peer-group influences, and management of social "face". A strictly intra-psychic or strictly dyadic model of relationship dissolution is an inadequate single explanation of all the observable processes: people do not always in reality have the freedom of choice that they appear to have in theory. We are all subject to the normative social and cultural constraints that apply to relationship conduct. Finally, we should not assume that all relationship dissolution is necessarily undesired or necessarily a bad thing, meriting management, correction, or therapy. For one thing some relationships stifle the individuals' growth and their dissolution can be a creative act of rejuvenation, full of promise and freedom. For another thing not all relationships "matter" in deep psychological or personal ways such that, for instance, the dissolution of a temporary working partnership is not usually a powerful psychological experience. Furthermore, as Rodin observes in Chapter 2, some relationships are non-starters, because of dislike, or through realistic acknowledgement of circumstantial constraints, or through difficulty of maintaining the relationship. Equally, some relationships are socially distanced anyway, whether in the sense of formal and cool or in Harré's (1977a) sense of working negative social relationships (*Feindschaft*). Workers in this field therefore could usefully follow the suggestion (Graziano and Mather Musser, Chapter 4, this volume) that style of opening and intent behind a relationship are as relevant to its dissolution as are its conduct and development. To do this, however, is to cut across most existing simple models of relationships which assume open-ended steady intimacy growth to be the norm for personal relationships.

Interpersonal Attraction and Relationship Dissolution

Because interpersonal attraction and communication researchers have hitherto been much , more attentive to the beginning and successful progression or conduct of relationships, studies of breakdown and ending of relationships are relatively scarce and make reference to growth and development of relationships only as a source of analogy or of inspiration. Altman and Taylor (1973), for instance, proposed that disengagement is a reversal of relationship growth ("like a film shown in reverse" in their elegant analogy). Albert and Kessler (1978), on the other hand, analogize from the ending of social encounters to the ending of relationships, pointing out the commonalities between parting rituals after social encounters and those that inhere in dissolution of relationships. Such analogies are very useful first guides to the understanding of specific components of the whole process. Indeed, their strength lies in their recognition that disengagement and dissolution represent not so much a single act as a process created from sequences of actions. Unfortunately, they are also very limited in scope and lack empirical support or have actually been challenged (Baxter, 1981). Other analyses contend that reversal of relationship growth simply cannot be what occurs in relationship dissolution. Duck and Lea (1982), for instance, argue that partners' information about one another does not decline as a relationship dies, but is simply gathered in different ways, with different intents, or from different perspectives; intimacy decline carries different meanings from those carried by intimacy growth; liking does not decline in steady linear fashion; self disclosure changes in form as well as decreasing in scope. In short, a reversal analogy is logically suspect as well as empirically unsupported.

Four latent models of dissolution

Perhaps, then, we have not made the best use of existing work on intimacy growth, preferring to use the study of beginning and development of relationship merely as a steady source of insight and analogy about relationship dissolution without any attempt to integrate it theoretically. It is, indeed, astonishing that theoretical and empirical work on interpersonal attraction and relationship development has not brought its contribution to bear on the questions of relationship dissolution. Yet even at first sight there are many simple research-based observations that seem to apply. For instance, if theorists argue that relationship growth is caused by attitude similarity or personality variables, then one would expect explanations of relational failure and dissolution to be cast in such terms also. There are enough of such explanations available in the interpersonal attraction literation, after all (see, e.g., Duck, 1977, or Berscheid and Walster, 1978, for a hint of the range of factors that could provide possible accounts). I will pick on three that are already latent in such literature ("Pre-existing Doom" ideas; "Mechanical Failure"; "Process Loss") and one which is peculiar to dissolution ("Sudden Death"). My intent is to indicate that they can each shed some light on the parts of the whole process but that some overarching view of the total enterprise is also needed.

Pre-existing Doom. Several theories of initial attraction and/or relationship growth imply quite unambiguously that certain inherent features of individuals necessarily enhance their chances of a satisfactory relationship. Thus we can readily find the suggestion that physical attractiveness or extraversion promotes liking (e.g. Perrin, 1921; Hendrick and Brown, 1971). More subtly, others have shown that IQ similarity enhances attraction (Austin and Thompson, 1948) or that socioeconomic similarity does so (Byrne *et al.,* 1966). Other even more complex proposals suggest that discovery of attitude similarity (Byrne, 1971) or of different depths and types of personality similarity (Duck, 1977) will emerge to enhance attraction. It ought to follow then, that pairs of individuals lacking such characteristics, or failing to demonstrate them, will be likely to dissolve relationships or will fail to engage. But where are the studies of physical attractiveness and breakdown, of extraversion and disengagement, of IQ and dissolution, of socioeconomic status and dissolution, of attitudes and dissolution, or of personality matching and dissolution? I know of only one single study (i.e. Duck and Allison, 1978) that has so far investigated the personality matching of pairs of friends who formed a relationship which they later dissolved. It was found, as would be predicted, that pairs who had originally selected one another from the available pool were more similar than those who had not; but within this set, those who subsequently fell out were less similar than those who stayed together. The results thus seem to be consistent with present theoretical notions about relationship growth, but this one study really is a rather inadequate basis for firm propositions along those lines. Whilst such studies are of limited value to the overall picture about relationship dissolution, they are of value none the less and merit amplification. This would help us to establish the extent to which failure of relationships can be predicted independently of process within the relationship—by using knowledge of the pre-existing characteristics of the partners that are predictive of their match (un)suitability.

Mechanical Failure. Several recent suggestions about termination of relationships (e.g. Baxter and Philpott, 1980; Hatfield and Traupmann, 1981) have urged that the poor conduct of the relationship by one or both partners is the ultimate cause of dissolution. Thus iniquitous or inequitable conduct of interactions or failures to communicate with one another satisfactorily may bring the partnership to a tottering collapse. The selfishness and thoughtlessness of a partner are indeed frequently-cited reasons for dissolving personal relationships, as seems intuitively obvious (Levinger, 1979). Such occurrences and such theories presuppose that partners are, in all other respects, suited to each other; yet it seems to the present author at least plausible that *some* "mechanical failures" actually reflect the partners' inherent unsuitability to each other. For instance, partners' pre-existing value structures may make it effectively impossible for a given pair of partners to negotiate satisfactory role-relations between them during the gradual development of the relationship. This would store up trouble for the future and vitiate the prospect that partners could later develop or conduct the partnership in a concerted and mutually satisfactory manner (a possibility derivable from Murstein's, 1977, SVR model, at least). Until such possibilities are studied effectively, we just won't know.

"Process Loss". A subtler version of the foregoing point derives from consideration of research on group problem-solving. Steiner (1972) noted that human resources are rarely optimally employed and actual productivity invariably falls short of potential productivity through faulty process ("process loss"). It would be surprising if this general human tendency were not observable in the context of personal relationships. We would expect that some partners would fail to develop a relationship to its theoretically optimal level and so become dissatisfied with it to the extent that they may even wish to terminate the relationship. At present, many theories of interpersonal attraction contain the unstated assumption that if individuals possess or share a given characteristic (e.g., physical attractiveness or attitude similarity) they will be able to "use" it to further their relationships. A slightly different assumption is that all individuals not only possess but can effectively use the skills that are necessary to maximise a relationship's potential. Thus for instance, it might seem plausible to assume that if attitude similarity is attractive it is so because people can detect it in life to the same degree and with the same significance as they do in the laboratory. Yet Duck (1977, pp. 153–156) and Byrne (in Baron *et al.*, 1974, pp. 43–45) have shown why such an assumption is unwarranted. For instance, partners may be unsuccessful in their attempts to reveal such similarity to one another, or the opportunity for doing so may be allowed to slip by, or they may fail to recognize subtle instances of similarity when they arise. In such a case, faulty process would prevent the potential influence of attitude similarity being successfully realized in subjective terms and it cannot therefore be assumed in such cases to have its full effect on attraction levels. Such process loss would predictably lead to the failure to

reach a satisfactory level of relationship and hence may create dissatisfaction with the relationship and lead to its ultimate dissolution.

Research on such a possibility is, in my view, an indispensable means of discovering the true lifesome significance of the factors unearthed in the past 20 years' research on interpersonal attraction. It is a subtler version of the frequent complaint that factors found to be influential in laboratory study are not necessarily significant to the same extent in real life. However, as readers will readily detect, it places the origin of the difference *in the two interacting partners* rather than in some undefined (as it usually is) metaphysical difference between "laboratory" and "real life" (which is usually left crucially undefined also, Duck, 1980b). At least this version of the point makes it researchable—whilst also relating dissolution and growth of relationships to the same theoretical propositions.

Sudden Death. A relatively obvious proposition in the context of relationship dissolution, yet which has little connection with relationship growth, is that new, surprising, and significant negatively charged information about a partner can hasten the relationship's death. Discovery of a partner's adultery, betrayal of trust, or deception, and instances of personal renunciation or simple ratting on the relationship are obvious examples of such inputs that are likely to bring a sudden end to a relationship. The interpretation and explanation of their effects is, however, problematic for two reasons. In the first place, they do not invariably and inevitably lead to dissolution of the relationship. As Hagestad and Smyer (this volume, Chapter 7) report in detail, some marriages survive repeated discoveries of partner's adultery, betrayal, deceit, brutality, and perversion. So there is no *psychological* necessity that such things do indeed cause the sudden death of the relationship: if they do, then they have to be "allowed" to do so, or "identified" as causes; but they may simply cause the intimacy or relationship level to be "cranked back a notch", as when partners remain friends after divorce. In the second place, many adulterous, deceitful rats would claim that their negatively loaded acts *followed* rather than caused dissolution, and represented not the true ending of the relationship but their redressing of the balance once it had, in effect, already ended for them.

It is with the recognition of such familiar points that we begin to find even more clearly thrust into the foreground the inadequacy of single-focus intra-individual models of relationship dissolution. It is necessary to consider and account for the persuasive influence of such factors as probability of entering a satisfactory alternative relationship, probability of being able to create a publicly acceptable "story" about the break-up, fear of partner (as in, for example, the case of battered wives, who may be afraid to leave a rebarbative spouse), guilt or anxiety about consequences to other parties (e.g. children)—and a host of other psychological influences.

A general model of relationship dissolution

The problem is not that the above models (or "straw models", perhaps!) are incorrect but that they have only local or limited concern with some small part of the jigsaw puzzle. Each of the four proposes something about relationship dissolution that seems to contain an element of truth or an element of observable fit with reality. Each of them describes something that is an intuitively plausible contender for the prize of Dissolution Cause: partners' individual qualities, poor conduct of the relationship, inability to realize relationship potential, or impulsive selfish acts all seem likely to contribute to a relationship's demise. Yet their inadequacy as explanations of relationship disengagement and dissolution is made apparent through their magnification of some single element of a process that, in our more reflective moments, we know just cannot be that simple nor so radically different and disjunctive from normal relationship activity. In the first place, negative information about the partner or the relationship has no simple mechanistic results any more than other information has upon the relationship: instead it has to be processed by the individuals involved, has to be larded with personal significance, and has to lead to a desire to withdraw. It does not invariably do so and, indeed, in the normal course of relationship development some sorts of negative information often have very little effect at all. Yet research has so far failed to clarify the psychological algebra involved in such decisions and why it is that partners often tolerate "objectively" unacceptable partners. The first problem, then, is one for cognitive social psychologists. The second problem is different in scope, however. It is that relationship dissolution not only has to happen but has to be managed and dealt with in a teeming social context. Real friends, real relatives, real social institutions may have to be informed about the dissolution and, if the relationship was a significant one, these social entities will probably have a strong view about the whole thing. Partners who otherwise intend to dissolve their relationship may be cowed into inactivity by anticipations of such reactions from the social network.

One of the theoretical problems that confronts us at this stage, then, is the issue of how such "local" components of the broader canvas should be placed. How does dissolution relate to relationship growth? What similarities and differences are there between the two cases? What *is* the relationship between partners' individual qualities and relationship conduct in the dissolution equation? At what point(s) in the process are they each considered and balanced out in the partners' minds? When do individuals weigh up their desire to withdraw against their guesses about the likely responses of significant outsiders? In essence these research problems can be represented as hinging on the difficult judgement of the relative weights of cognitive and social elements in relationship dissolution at different points in the process.

This topographical problem actually takes us to the roots and confronts us with the inadequacies of predominant research styles in the general area of interpersonal attraction research. It implicitly points to weaknesses in research styles that require remedy: four examples only will be given here.

First, predominant theoretical models in social psychology at present stress the rational judgements that individuals make and they underplay the social pressures that confront the person intending to consider or execute such decisions. In the present context we can asume that persons are strongly driven by emotions and feelings—or, at the very least, that their decisions create emotion and feelings that have to be dealt with when they arise. My argument in the rest of the chapter will thus be essentially contextualist: that any "rational" judgements must be seen in the context of the social constraints upon executing them; that cognitive activity, on the other hand, represents a context for dealing with social pressures (e.g. when individuals create rational accounts of their relationship dissolution in order to satisfy relatives or to justify themselves publicly).

A second weakness in present research is the assumption that individuals conduct their relationships in each other's presence, and until recently there has been too little account taken of the evaluative, reflective, fantasizing, assessment work that people do in the absence of their partner (Duck, 1980a).

A third dominant impression is that most of our interpersonal attraction or social intercourse is directed towards strangers, but Wheeler and Nezlek (1977) have gathered data to indicate the balance of people's actual social participation, and Duck and Miell (1981, 1982) have used diary records to study the frequency and type of encounter with friends as they develop in natural settings over ten and twenty week periods. From this it is clear that individuals, quite unexpectedly, are very tentative and uncertain about even their deep, long-lasting relationships. They are continually reviewing and assessing their friendships—even when these are "objectively" stable and are reported as deep, constant and satisfying. People are still, none the less, evidently insecure and vigilant—perpetually re-evaluating both their developing and even their well-established friendships.

Fourthly, and most important, Emler (1981) has questioned the implication in interpersonal attraction research that people sit and discuss their attitudes, personality characteristics, traits, and so on. On the contrary, he finds that in real-life encounters people discuss other people and gossip—particularly about personal events rather than attitudes or states. Clearly a general approach to relationships—and particularly relationship-dissolution processes—will need to be based on a more accurate assessment of what people actually do in dissolving relationships. In preliminary work, Duck and Miell (in preparation) and Duck and Palmer (in preparation) have made a modest start by recording the amounts of time spent in given activities before, during, and after relationship dissolution. The change of activity patterns may itself be one of the first indicators that the relationship is faltering and it seems an intuitively plausible idea that patterns of interaction change in systematic ways as the relationship deteriorates. For instance, Duck and Miell and Duck and Palmer find that persons report a change in the location of meeting with partners in distressed relationships (from private accommodation to public social places) and that the initiator of interactions is more likely to be the other person when things go badly but mutual when they are going well. It is important that other more significant dimensions of social participation rates and characteristics be explored in future research. We need a data base and we need to avoid the footsteps of researchers into interpersonal attraction who for too long ignored, or failed to first gather data about, people's actual relationship behaviour, and merely isolated particular interaction or encounter "packages" for experimental study.

Such points, then, bring us inexorably to another theoretical issue that also arises here. It has its simplest expression in the form of a query about how relationship growth relates to decline and dissolution— or, more accurately, how *what we know about* relationship growth relates to *what we know about* decline and dissolution of relationships. It is naive to assume a sudden catastrophe-like switch from relationship development to relationship dissolution: real social life just is not like that most of the time. However, neither am I convinced that decline is the reversal of growth, any more than ageing is the reversal of child development: indeed, it makes far more sense to see one as a continuation of the processes characterizing the other rather than simply its reverse (Duck, 1981; Duck and Lea, 1982; Duck and Miell, 1982). The contention here is that we must start to regard dissolution as the end point of a series of psychological processes which have some overlap and similarity with those that also produce relationship growth: it is largely the products which differ, not the processes. I will propose here that relationship partners continually review the state of their relationship in an attempt to achieve or negotiate a mutually acceptable form of involvement. They do this when the relationship is developing *and* when it is deteriorating; when it is starting *and* when it is ending. During the early formative stages of a relationship this activity is naturally both necessary and frequent (cf. Graziano and Mather Musser, this volume). It can yield crystallization of the relationship, intimacy growth, or containment and decline of involvement depending on partners' intentions. During later stages of a relationship's life it becomes necessary less frequently and resurges only in times of conflict or transition (e.g. relocation, marriage, birth of children). Such activity is proposed to be largely conscious, private, evaluative and concerned with consideration of the present form of the relationship apropos of its likely future form (see Fig. 1).

Importantly, then, a proposal like this does not view decline and growth as the reversal of one another: rather each is the contrary product of the same generative process of evaluation and assessment. *Ultimately* the two diverge (see Fig. 1) but they start from the same place. Clearly evaluations of partner, attribution, communication and consideration of social consequences are not occurring only in dissolution: they run through "relationshipping" as a whole, both when it is going well and when it is not. Accordingly, in Fig. One I present a sketch of some of the processes and decisions taken in the course of formulating and dealing with the problem of creating a satisfactory form for an established close relationship. It can be seen that I emphasize the similarities of process between relationship building and early phases of relationship demolition, merely contending that the intermediate products and the final stages are different in kind.

Whilst previous speculations about relationship ending have contrasted affective processes with the social barriers that contain their effects (e.g. Levinger, 1979), the present proposals will argue that the two are psychologically linked through an intermediate, dyadic, phase. It will be suggested that early points of disengagement are marked by predominantly intra-psychic, individualistic processes; that these merge slowly into dyadic processes, where the two partners begin to face up to, and deal with, the fact that one of them wishes to close the relationship; and that the final phase is a social, or network, phase where the partners together or separately negotiate the "public presentation" of the relationship dissolution. A post-dissolution phase is also proposed: here partners clean up the picture and tidy the last resting place of the memories associated with the relationship (see Fig. 2, page 16).

Such a proposal is based on the belief that there are several non-exclusive ways to depict the process of relationship disengagement. For instance, there is a model implicit in the comments made in the foregoing section: namely, that the partners' characteristic qualities influence their conduct of

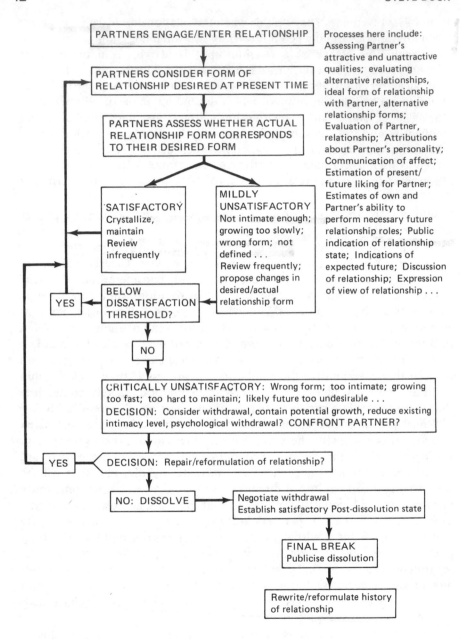

FIG. 1   Some steps and decisions in relationship development and decline.

the relationship in a way that produces process loss until a critical cataclysmic event or discovery finally creates the public grounds on which to terminate the relationship. Alternatively, the structure of chapter organization in the present volume offers another implicit system for conceptualizing the process of relationship dissolution. It can be seen that this stresses the public conduct of the wish to terminate and deals with issues surrounding social management of the dissolution. Such a model emphasizes the expression and conduct of dissolution rather than its inherent causes.

These two ways of conceptualizing relationship dissolution are not necessarily incompatible: they are merely different perspectives. Likewise, the third possibility which I am about to consider in detail simply represents a further different viewpoint over the phenomena. It begins with an emphasis on the private decisions that must be faced by a person wishing to foreclose on a relationship, goes on to discuss communicative and strategic matters within the dyad, focuses on the social negotiations that follow, and finally addresses the issue of publicly accounting for the break. In short it proposes four broad phases to relationship dissolution, each one requiring the person and the partner to focus on different issues, make different decisions, contemplate different sorts of behavioural-strategic questions, and make different social responses from those faced in the other phases. The forces and emotions that press upon the two persons at different points of the process of dissolution must be seen to differ and change as things proceed. They do not remain constant nor of a single type throughout, and at each new point there is a requirement for extended psychological and behavioural energy—one psychologically important reason why fatigue and stress are often reported to attach to persons who attempt to dissolve established close relationships (Bloom *et al.*, 1978).

The relevant forces pressing upon the persons at each point will be proposed here to be problems of the social management of each stage of the process. Thus once one decides that one's partner is no longer liked, one is faced with the social management problem of telling them so; once one wishes to withdraw from the relationship, one is faced with the social management problem of negotiating disengagement; once one has reached a satisfactory stage in the negotiation, one is faced with the social management problem of letting the social network know that one of its constituent pairings is dissolved; once it is dissolved one must face up to explaining what happened. Accordingly the person is faced with a range of at least four strategic problems. *First*, the person who wishes to leave must first find a plausible (private) justification for doing so. I contend that Persons do this by an attempt to assess and evaluate Partner's alleged inadequacies, faults, and incompetences. They thus face the strategic issues of how best to cope with a defaulting Partner, and whether to confront Partner about these negative discoveries or avoid confrontation. *Second,* the two partners who know that at least one of them wants to change the relationship are faced with a range of strategic choices centred on the questions "Should we attempt to repair or to dissolve the relationship?" The management and negotiation of the repair or dissolution are complex social processes. *Third,* a final range of behavioural strategic choices faces two partners who have agreed upon, agreed to accept, or are confronted with a unilateral demand for, dissolution. At this stage the choices concern the best or most effective way of managing the impending dissolution and communicating it to the immediate social network— how to arrive at the desired post-dissolution state. *Finally,* and most important, partners must choose how and where to attribute the blame for the dissolution after it has occurred. So the model suggests that the four broad stages, each with its consequent focus of attention for Person and with its accompanying behavioural manifestations, are as follows: first, an intra-psychic stage where Person focuses on Partner and Partner's behaviour, the result being a private evaluation of Partner's performance; second, a dyadic phase where the partners jointly focus on the relationship, its merits and provisions, its chances of repair— the result being discussions about the future of the relationship; third, a social phase focusing on management of the consequences of the desired dissolution; last, a grave-dressing phase that tidies up the relationship's last resting place and puts up public markers of its ending.

Mapping Relationship Disengagement and Dissolution

Perhaps it reflects well on psychologists that we are too prone to assume that people are nice (cf. Moscovici, 1972) and that their niceness pours over to flood their behaviour in relationship disengagement and dissolution. We assume that people will feel guilty about hurting their partner; we assume that they will control outbursts of negative feelings; we assume that they will handle disengagement—at least in the beginning—in a covert, indirect, defused, sanitized and socially packaged way. Thus several workers have noted the tendency, in turbulent relationships, for partners to prefer avoidance styles to confrontational ones (e.g. Kaplan, 1976). Studies of communication in turbulent relationships assume that there will be only "leakage" at the early stages of withdrawal rather than straightforward nastiness (Duck, 1980c); studies of behavioural strategy choice assume initial unwillingness to confront the partner once a negative view of partner is being formed (Baxter, 1980).

Tacitly assumed in all such approaches is the belief that partners wish to avoid, and struggle to prevent, public demonstration of disaffection. Following from that is the assumption that such forms of ambivalence, indecision and oscillation as have been identified are partly due to social pressures and strains coming into sharp conflict with personal, emotional ones. Yet it is surprising that at present there are no explicit studies of argument, insult, recrimination, negative exchange, the whips and scorns of growing hostility and "the spurns that patient merit of the unworthy takes" (Shakespeare, 1599/1951). It is true that there are *subsequent* well-recognized social constraints on the open expression of a desire to withdraw once it is formed, but these are due not so much to inherent niceness as to the partners' realistic recognition of the social sanctioning power of surrounding social networks—indeed persons often adopt indirect means of withdrawal and simultaneously regret doing so (Baxter, 1979b). Also there are general social consequences of "being negative". To say derogatory things about a partner is to open oneself to the charge of being a negative or disloyal person; if the dissolving relationship was a close one, then the public display of strongly negative views of the formerly close partner opens one to a charge of capriciousness or earlier bad judgement. Ambivalence, uncertainty and plain cowardice are hard to distinguish, in this context, from social and cultural pressures to uphold the ideal values of friendship and one's own public "face" (see La Gaipa's chapter, this volume).

Nevertheless, researchers must recognize that there are several separable forms of decision and indecision that surround the transformation of a private relational disturbance into a publicly acknowledged relational failure—and "niceness" does not create them. For instance, there may be genuine ambivalence or doubt about the Partner as well as unwillingness to accept the implications of a negative view of Partner. Furthermore, ambivalence, inconsistency and oscillation can be due to indecision whether to adopt an expressive or repressive coping style with the growing disaffection with Partner (Kaplan, 1976) or a confrontational or avoidance style once one has accepted one's negative view of Partner (Baxter, 1979b). Finally there is the kind of oscillation noted by Altman and Taylor (1973), where partners have confronted and accepted the issues that are separating them, but oscillate between withdrawal and intense reconciliations. These oscillations continue until the point where the ideal post-dissolution state is achieved, at which point the dissolution is set in social concrete. Equally one must note the different sorts of strategic choice that confront Person at each point, and the several psychological and social thresholds that have to be crossed (see Fig. Two). It is the proposal of the present model that several such thresholds are arranged in a sequential manner, beginning with the creation of one's own private justification for wishing to withdraw and

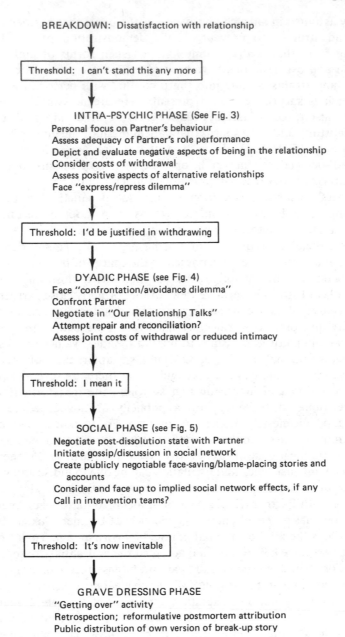

BREAKDOWN: Dissatisfaction with relationship

Threshold: I can't stand this any more

INTRA-PSYCHIC PHASE (See Fig. 3)
Personal focus on Partner's behaviour
Assess adequacy of Partner's role performance
Depict and evaluate negative aspects of being in the relationship
Consider costs of withdrawal
Assess positive aspects of alternative relationships
Face "express/repress dilemma"

Threshold: I'd be justified in withdrawing

DYADIC PHASE (see Fig. 4)
Face "confrontation/avoidance dilemma"
Confront Partner
Negotiate in "Our Relationship Talks"
Attempt repair and reconciliation?
Assess joint costs of withdrawal or reduced intimacy

Threshold: I mean it

SOCIAL PHASE (see Fig. 5)
Negotiate post-dissolution state with Partner
Initiate gossip/discussion in social network
Create publicly negotiable face-saving/blame-placing stories and
    accounts
Consider and face up to implied social network effects, if any
Call in intervention teams?

Threshold: It's now inevitable

GRAVE DRESSING PHASE
"Getting over" activity
Retrospection; reformulative postmortem attribution
Public distribution of own version of break-up story

FIG. 2   A sketch of the main phases of dissolving personal relationships.

ending with the public presentation of a termination agreed or accepted by both partners themselves.

Figure 2 gives a schematic depiction of the major concepts at each stage or phase of the dissolution process and each phase is further elaborated in a subsequent figure. It can be seen from Fig. Two that the emphasis of the early phases of the model is conceived to be a cognitive one, especially focused on evaluation and decision-making. Later phases are the times where the actions consequent upon such evaluation and decision-making are executed. At these stages the Person is faced with real behavioural, strategic choices about the best ways for socially managing and executing the growing intent to dissolve the relationship.

Perhaps it needs to be reiterated that although the first stress of the present map falls on cognitive activity, this is not primarily a cognitive model. I simply wish to analyse the dissolution process and, by doing so, to illustrate that different research techniques are needed to illuminate the full richness of each phase. Thus self-report techniques would be most suitable at one phase (cf. Harvey *et al.,* this volume), communication analysis would be better in another (cf. Miller and Parks, this volume), and social process analysis in yet another (cf. Johnson, La Gaipa, McCall, this volume).

The subsequent discussion deals with the four phases suggested as primary foci for future research. In so doing, the discussion assumes that for at least one partner the threshold of Unbearable Dissatisfaction with the state of the relationship has been crossed, i.e. that the relationship is, for that person, in the process of breakdown or turbulence. This person is supposed in the present scheme to begin to seek and consider active grounds for withdrawing from the relationship as the first step towards dissolution of the relationship in its previous form or its renegotiation into a less intimate form. Accordingly, the first phase of the present model focuses on the intra-psychic activity that the person produces in seeking a justification for withdrawing from the relationship. This is seen as a bridging phase between breakdown and dissolution: Person doesn't yet know which of the two possibilities will actually result.

Intra-psychic phase: focus on partner

Researchers have been reluctant to study relational turbulence for fear that this may itself generate dissolution of the relationship. Studies, on the whole, are either retrospective in character (e.g. Hill *et al.,* 1976) or tend to deal with hypothetical relationships (e.g. Baxter, 1980) and they look for evidence of a reducing satisfaction with the relationship or an increase in the difficulty of maintaining it. They assume, therefore, that partners have passed a stage where they have begun to reflect on the relationship negatively and that they are concerned to negotiate disengagement. In contrast, I suspect that there are a few psychological stages before partners get to this point. The present model assumes that an early stage towards dissolution involves a strong evaluative focus on the Partner, not on the relationship as such, and that such a focus is used to create a justification for dissatisfied feelings, for psychological withdrawal, or even for leaving— a justification that satisfies oneself privately and will be used as the basis for subsequently confronting the Partner when and if that occurs.

Traditional psychological explanations that might be used to explore the creation of such justifications have been couched in terms of Equity and Exchange, but not explicitly in connection with the formation in one partner's mind of such a justification of withdrawal. My point is that such a consideration of Equity and Exchange is necessary but not by any means sufficient for relationship extinction. In my view it merely sets in train a set of other psychological processes as outlined in the model (Fig. 3) and subsequent subsections of this chapter. Equity and Exchange evaluation does not, of itself and without other *social* processes, such as consulting confidants, create more than a groundplan for dissolution.

Goals: Identifying causes of dissatisfaction with Partner
 Identifying problems with present form of relationship
Adjusting Partner's behaviour
Increasing satisfaction with Partner
Increasing satisfaction with relationship

Major specific concerns	Researchable manifestations and consequences
To weigh up Partner's behaviour	Hostility, vigilance, evaluation, increased personal attribution
To assess internal dynamics of relationship	Equity/Exchange Focus
To express discomfort (but not directly to Partner)	Consultation with confidants; "Leakage"
To question one's relationship judgements	Self Doubts; Recrimination; Negativity in personal descriptions of Self and Partner and "Life"
To find ways to modify Partner's behaviour and to change relationship outcomes	Changes in communication style and communication focus within the relationship
To convince oneself that leaving could be better than staying	Anxiety, stress, guilt, indecision, brooding

Final outcome: The resolve to confront Partner

FIG. 3   Intra-Psychic Phase of Relationship Dissolution.

Furthermore, there are several sides to the evaluation of Equity and Exchange since merely noticing imbalance and actually taking action about it are different psychological activities with different relational consequences. The mere noticing of Inequity is a cause of dissatisfaction personally, but doing something about it makes the problem a dyadic, not an intra-psychic, individual one. I would speculate that once a person has formulated the view that relationship Equity or Exchange is significantly out of kilter, the consequence is *not* immediate confrontation with the Partner but instead, on the individual level, some brooding recriminative response, or a social consultation with a confidant and a general private sense of discomfort. I am claiming, then, that such a process is *essentially* private, or one that is not immediately communicated directly to the offending Partner. Although private in the normal way, such processes are none the less accessible to researchers using self-report and interview techniques to study individuals, as well as to Equity researchers studying couples. But we may be unjustified in assuming that proper calculation of actual Exchange is the only way in which such decisions get taken. There is too little research in social psychology, and in this area too, on errors and misjudgements (but cf. Backman and Secord, 1962). Mismatched perceptions, mistakes, and misunderstandings are frequent causes of relational turbulence and these can occur outside or inside the interactions that make up a relationship. Brooding outside an interaction is quite as powerful a cause of relational disaffection as is misconduct within one. Deep, private contemplation about the desired and achieved course of a relationship; perpetual, normal monitoring of relationships; the actual build-up towards dissolution, planning and organizing it are all private events that are not necessarily communicated to the Partner. Much happens *outside* the vital encounters composing relationships, such as fantasy, recapitulation, planning, evaluation and quiet assessment of Partner, Self and the relationship (Duck, 1980a). When one comes to consider the first moves in breakdown or dissolving of personal relationships, then, it is even clearer that such activity must be counted into the formulae. Revenge, planning, stressful anxiety and many other such actions and thoughts just might exert a great initial influence on relationship decline and the psychological algebra occurring in it.

In sum, the essential focus of this intra-psychic stage is hypothesized to concern vigilance about Partner's behaviour, sifting and assessment of relevant evidence, worries over Equity and Exchange, and the weighing up of the internal dynamics of the relationship. It is essentially cognitive activity, and is essentially private, leaking to Partner undramatically and unintentionally. In this respect, then, it is importantly different from what occurs in the next (dyadic) phase. In the intra-psychic phase, choices are hypothesized to be strictly related to these issues above, but will have non-cognitive effects (e.g. "leakage" of disaffection by means of non-verbal behaviour; communicative changes and reduced display of intimacy or relatedness). During the process of deciding that one might be justified in withdrawing from the relationship the Person will probably be focusing attention first on means of coping with the Partner and attempting to modify Partner's faulty behaviour. One would expect the Person to become hostile to the Partner, to recriminate about the relationship, to feel discomfort and vigilance in interactions and perhaps to undergo some changes in attitudes to self and life—all of which are measurable. Additionally one might expect to find changes in behaviour, such as increasing consultation with confidants or other outsiders to unburden and clarify the festering negativity felt about Partner: "My wife doesn't understand me" is a characteristic style of this phase of the enterprise.

The Person may indeed press on no further than minimal psychological withdrawal or resentment, or may go as far as half-hearted involvement in other parallel relationships such as affairs. At this point it seems uncertain that a Person will be convinced that the relationship is over, and hopes of improvement are primary. The choice of strategic action at this phase is presumably centred on the way to cope with one's feelings of negativity towards Partner, but a secondary component concerns choices of method to set Partner aright and an evaluation of whether it is in fact possible ever to do so. If the Person concludes that Partner's faults are inherently unalterable only then is a different coping strategy needed. Such a conclusion by the Person is thus a likely first step on the path to actual withdrawal and turns private dissatisfaction into a more active phase of dissolution with different concerns.

At some point the Person undoubtedly considers the desirability of the relationship in the context of alternatives (Thibaut and Kelley, 1959), as a separate issue that goes beyond mere dissatisfaction with the Partner. Such private calculations need not yet involve the Partner: they are personal judgemental problems requiring decisions whether leaving is better than staying, whether the negative aspects of Partner really do outweigh the positive values of the relationship. Considerations of Comparison Levels for Alternatives (Thibaut and Kelley, 1959) would be likely to arise here, but not for the last time, and evaluation of the costs of leaving have to be pitted against the costs of staying. To have formed the opinion that one is justified in leaving, the Person must have concluded that enough areas of the relationship are irredeemably dissatisfactory or that the positive aspects of none of them outweigh the disadvantages of the remainder. Researchers should be able to identify and distinguish two sorts of ambivalence or oscillation in the Person at this phase. First, the Person in such straits is likely to be genuinely undecided about the future of the relationship and hence to show the agitation, stress and ambivalence that characterize people making any major decisions. Secondly, the Person is now faced with major social issues: whether or not to confront the Partner with the decision; when and how to do so. Such decisions will have to be based on personal knowledge of the Partner's likely response. The Miller and Parks (Chapter 6, this volume) compliance-gaining strategy model fits best here (although it is more complex than this): Persons will need to refer to their store of knowledge about their erstwhile Partner in order to know how best to effect their desire to redefine the relationship. At this stage researchers investigating the relationship are likely to detect oscillation between desires to confront Partner and desires to avoid confrontation (Baxter, 1980), but it is psychologically and focally a different sort of oscillation from the agitated indecision about the Partner noted previously.

Once such issues of confrontation and negotiation with Partner begin to appear, and once, effectively, the decision is taken to redefine the relationship, the Person enters a different phase and the focal concerns shift towards dyadic issues; that is, away from personal, private, intrapsychic issues towards those directly involving *both* partners.

Dyadic phase: focus on the relationship

Perhaps, by now, the relationship is so turbulent that both partners start to reassess it. But if not, a unilateral decision to reveal one's dissatisfaction with and to the Partner inevitably confuses things. The Person intending to redefine the relationship will now have his or her resolve questioned, will have to give reasons, will have to present a case that satisfies other people not just themselves, will be presented with alternative explanations of events that they had regarded as critical to their decision ... and so on. Alternatively, the announcement of the wish to redefine the relationship might be dismissed by the Partner as a mere power ploy. Or the response of the Partner may be extreme or unpredicted. The costs of going ahead with disengagement may now seem underestimated. The personal costs to Partner may now appear to be much greater than had been initially supposed. In short, an additional series of psychological forces comes into play, not least of which will be negotiation about the Person's reasons for wanting to redefine the relationship, about explanations for conflict, and about attributions.

The present model delineates this phase as beginning with the Person's consideration of the most effective strategy to renegotiate the relationship (see Fig. Four). Accordingly, it would predict that the Person is essentially

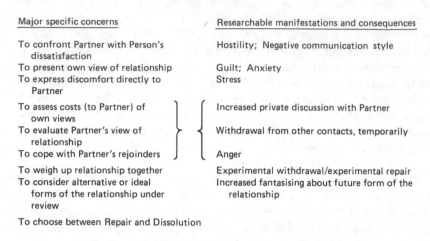

Goals: Confronting Partner
         Gaining compliance from Partner
         Redefining relationship
         Repairing/Dissolving relationship

Major specific concerns	Researchable manifestations and consequences
To confront Partner with Person's dissatisfaction	Hostility; Negative communication style
To present own view of relationship	Guilt; Anxiety
To express discomfort directly to Partner	Stress
To assess costs (to Partner) of own views	Increased private discussion with Partner
To evaluate Partner's view of relationship	Withdrawal from other contacts, temporarily
To cope with Partner's rejoinders	Anger
To weigh up relationship together	Experimental withdrawal/experimental repair
To consider alternative or ideal forms of the relationship under review	Increased fantasising about future form of the relationship
To choose between Repair and Dissolution	

Final outcome: Resolve to dissolve/repair the relationship

FIG. 4   Dyadic Phase of Relationship Dissolution.

aggrieved and hostile, in such a way that attitudes to the Partner are extremely negative. Negativity about Partner and decision-generated stress are demonstrable through the non-verbal and verbal channels of social communication and the reader is referred to the chapter by Miller and Parks (Chapter 6). My point here is that any such communicative changes reflect private turmoil, and that they reflect oscillations and ambivalence about how to approach the Partner rather than about the relationship and its dissolution management. These latter appear later on in the sequence and are distinct, different sorts of turmoil.

Once discussions begin, however, the Person is going to be confronted with other issues than those which concern his/her own private judgements about Partner's behaviour. These are likely to begin with the implications—for the *Partner*—of the Person's negative evaluation of them. Partners themselves, if the Person does not, will be likely to point out their own costs in the relationship in its present form, the consequent costs of discussing redefinition of the relationship, the costs of actually disengaging, and the costs of managing the disengagement in public (that is, for other members of the network).

A Person's resolve can be shaken at this stage by several things. For instance, such stress may be caused to Partner by such discussions that the Person may decide not to go through with it after all. Or Partner's claims to be able and willing to put matters right may effectively block off the Person's intent to redefine or dissolve the relationship.

At this stage, then, an intent to redefine or dissolve the relationship can be (temporarily) abandoned; or processes of repair, focused on amending Partner's behaviour and/or the Person's expectations, can be initiated. This merely reflects the beginnings of that sort of oscillation within the relationship noted by Altman and Taylor (1973) where partners do not agree about dissolution and so go through counterpoised phases of intense reconciliation and of withdrawal. Such oscillations are consequently about something psychologically different from those noted earlier and hence must not be confused with them in theory and research.

Even if the partners agree to redefine or dissolve the relationship, their problems are not over. They must turn to discussing, for instance, the distribution of shared goods and face up to the job of "presenting" the disengagement to other people as well as to actually conducting it satisfactorily. Again, the real implications of doing so may strike partners for the first time and cause slowing down of the disengagement or else may promote vigorous attempts at repair of the flagging relationship. If such repair attempts are unrealistic, however, the focus must, at some stage, turn away from individuals' behaviour *in* a relationship, and towards the nature of the relationship itself and its theoretical potential *as a working social relationship* if both partners were to act ideally.

Next, then the partners start to explore what the relationship *ought* to be like—its ideal state—rather than focus on how they have actually conducted it. Partners presumably ask themselves a number of crucial questions. Is it realistic to expect the relationship to work? Is it the right sort of relationship? Is it, perhaps, unduly stifling or constraining to the partners, such that they would be better out of it after all? Researchers who discover indecision or oscillation here are picking up fluctuations between experimental withdrawal from the partnership and experimental repair of it. Likely scenarios for disengagement and for a patched-up relationship can be proposed, replayed, considered. The partners' costs if they reveal, manage, or confirm the breakdown of relationship need at this stage to be realistically stressed and evaluated against the alternatives of redress and repair.

At this stage the partners are concerned, then, with the issue of Repair versus Dissolution. Oscillations reflect their attempts to achieve the ideal or desired scenario in the light of discussions in this phase (cf. Altman and Taylor's, 1973, discussion of attempts to achieve the desired post-dissolution state). My point is that at this stage the partners may oscillate both about the ideal post-disengagement state and also about the post-*discussion* state, which may not in fact be dissolution. Some partners may genuinely decide to repair the relationship rather than to dissolve it. However, the ambivalence about dissolution is probably genuine: we need not assume that partners are always crystal clear about their intentions and so they may communicate about them confusingly.

Where repair of the relationship is rejected as a possibility, the final steps in this phase involve preparation for the post-dissolution state: essentially this means starting to create the "public story" about the causes and course of the disengagement. We should note that there are presently no generally developed understandings of the social systems and psychological mechanisms that are used to indicate graduated withdrawals from relationships. However, it is clear that those things that are indicators of disaffection are also the means of registering intent and of conducting disengagement. Thus changes in communicative styles are part of a complex social process for indicating withdrawal from a relationship as well as being ways of "leaking" intent (see Miller and Parks, this volume). However, in momentarily stressing communicative changes that take place we have not attended fully enough to the self-relevant or personal effects that occur within the individual: the need to escape blame or to serve one's own self-interest which may "drive" the processes of negotiation of withdrawal from the relationship and the searching for scapegoats. The present model assumes that such scapegoating becomes a major focus of the next two phases.

Social phase: facing the public consequences

Assuming that the negotiated push towards dissolution is accepted as a reality by both partners, the final phase represents a working out of the social and public consequences of executing and publicizing the decision (see Fig. 5). At this stage, for certain, the partners are faced with constraining forces of a social kind—ones that are not strictly affective. Borrowing Lewin's ideas, Levinger (1979) has referred to "Barrier Forces" that help to hold a relationship together or prevent it coming apart—above and beyond its emotional cement. Such things as network pressure, sanctioning powers of social groupings, the implied loss of status consequent on disengagement, the legal powers of social institutions, and so on, are such Barrier Forces that may hold together an emotionally decayed relationship. [La Gaipa (1981a, and Chapter 8 here) has given fuller consideration to the power of such factors in the relationship conduct and the disengagement processes, respectively.] Perhaps they should be

Goals: To dissolve the relationship
To have the dissolution recognized and accredited by
the relevant social network(s)
To come out of it all socially and psychologically intact

Major specific concerns	Researchable manifestations and consequences
To create agreed post-dissolution state of relationship	Oscillation between reconciliation and withdrawal
To create acceptable post-dissolution state for partners	Doubts and anxieties about own future
To consider implied status changes	Trial repair *vs* trial withdrawal
To evaluate consequences of dissolution	Stress, mourning, fear of "loss"
To place blame	Gossip
To save face	Scapegoating
To create and distribute public stories about the relationship dissolution	Attributing blame
	Seeking causal explanation for break
To obtain public sanction for the dissolution	Marketing versions and accounts of the break

Final outcomes: Publicly acknowledged dissolution of the relationship
Move to grave-dressing

GRAVE-DRESSING PHASE:

Goal: To get over it all and put it behind one
Concerns: To create an acceptable personal story for the course of the
relationship, its beginning and its end
To tidy up the memories associated with it
Manifestations and consequences: Reinterpretative attributional work
concerned with "getting over it" (i.e. redressing and reconceptualizing
the relationship path and significance: distinct from attributing blame
for the break).

FIG. 5   Social Phase of Relationship Dissolution.

regarded as forces that prevent *rapid* dissolution rather than as forces that
prevent dissolution altogether. However that may be, it is in this phase that
a simple individual or dyadic model of relationships is least useful: the
social network is the significant base and background for the dissolving
relationship in this phase. Accordingly, parts of the negotiation and
evaluation processes that occur here will undoubtedly be concerned with
what to tell the neighbours and friends, but also with how to handle and
cope with partners in the network after disengagement or dissolution, i.e.

whether the relationship is merely much reduced in intimacy or actually terminated.

There are thus at least three separate issues for research at this phase:

First, a major problem for the disengaging pair is the personal issue of how to handle their own status change (probably a status loss). In a society where "couplehood" is valued, normative, and expected, the sudden return to singlehood is a major problem for dissolving marital or courtship partners (Bohannon, 1970b). Not only are there unattractive implications of relationship loss, in terms of labels of failure and consequent lowered social values, there are also social problems. Much of our society's life is based on the assumption that people are paired: pairs of people are invited to dinner parties; it is even true that pairs of people are usually the socially negotiable unit that is invited to play tennis and bridge! A single person, one without an appropriate partner, is thus something of a difficulty for *other people* to manage in a vibrant social environment (cf. Johnson's chapter, this volume).

The second issue for research and analysis, currently a focus of sociological and anthropological enquiry, concerns the means by which the network adjusts to the loss of a previously acknowledged constituent pairing. The problem is as much an adjustment problem for the network as it is one for the pair themselves within the network. For instance, difficulties for others in the social network stem from the fact that since both members of the dissolved pair were members of the network also, the network probably continues to see both of them, at least in the beginning. They are thus faced with the awkward problem of taking sides in the dispute, managing the disturbance, and generally facing up to a relationship that now has a spoiled identity. Fears of such social consequences and awareness of such social pressures operate as major restraints on Persons' freedom of action in these circumstances. Both in their own imagination and, perhaps, also through actions by a Partner unwilling to accede to disengagement, Persons can be restrained even at this point from carrying out a wish to withdraw. They may decide to stay physically in a hollow marriage, for instance, and yet withdraw psychologically.

As a third research topic, most in sympathy with present styles in social psychological research, we need to attend carefully to the attribution processes and "ordinary explanation" work that partners undertake in order to prepare their own public story about the relationship dissolution and help themselves to get over the relationship loss. The chapters by Harvey *et al.,* and McCall (this volume, Chapters 5 and 9) represent innovative and pioneering attempts to shape up the literature on this matter and to point out directions for future enquiry. It is also important to note, as La Gaipa (this volume) urges, that accounts of the dissolution have to be socially valid at this stage, not merely personally valid. An individual must create a public account that accords with prevailing cultural myths. Equally, as McCall (this volume) indicates, the precise nature of the negotiated account will depend on the nature of the spoiling of the relationship and the stage reached in the disengagement. However, partners have the problem of accounting to themselves individually and to each other for the disengagement as well as accounting to others. Thus, they must have valid accounts which apply *whilst the relationship is still undissolved*—and those *after* the dissolution may be different in style and functions (see next section).

These three areas constitute separable research issues and present new, different problems. The stresses that they create for partners are also separable from those observable in other phases: by this stage the partners have accepted the break and have to face up to it. Physical and psychological stresses are thus going to be consequent on a sense of loss (Bowlby, 1979), status change (Bloom *et al.,* 1978) and bereavement (McCall, Chapter 9, this volume)—i.e., consequent on doubt about their personal future rather than on doubt, ambiguity or ambivalence about the future of the relationship (see above).

Grave-dressing phase: tidying up the accounts

Once the main psychological "work" of dissolving a personal relationship is over, the problem remains of what to do with the memories associated with it. The processes here remind me of grave-dressing: the attempt to neaten up the last resting place of the corpse and to erect public statements of its form, contribution, and importance. Much of the activity of getting over a relationship concerns simplification, rationalization and beautification of the course, themes, and outcomes of the relationship when it still flourished (cf. McCall's chapter, this volume). Furthermore, as Harvey *et al.* (this volume, Chapter 5) observe, there is a considerable amount of *post mortem* attributional activity to be accomplished, in terms of retrospective accounting and analysis for both the relationship and the break.

This neglected aspect of relationship dissolution is an important one, nevertheless, and it is recognized tacitly in the objections that are sometimes raised against retrospective reports of relationship dissolution. It is noted that such accounts may reflect bias, idealization, self-interest, and so on. What is missed is the fact that such processes are not mere accidents or psychological epiphenomena: they are probably psychologically crucial to the persons coming to terms with the relationship dissolution. Noting that they are different from attributions about a relationship that still has a chance of surviving, we should examine them vigorously to explore their underlying dynamics and to find out what they tell us about the serious business of grave-dressing a dead relationship.

Concluding Observations: Practical Consequences

Again let me reiterate the cartographic nature of this model. I have laid things out in relation to one another in a way that seems to suggest that the process is slow and deliberate or that only one person does all the deciding. I do this for analytic convenience only, since we do not yet know for instance, whether it is this slow, nor whether all disengagements begin at Phase 1 so explicitly, nor whether (as seems likely) it is naive to assume it is all one-sided. I have given little emphasis to the mechanisms by which relationship dissolution is avoided, or by which repair is effected [but see Volume 5 in this series (Duck, in preparation)]. Studies of dissolution of relationships are sorely needed so that we can tell if these are separate issues.

None the less, some general thoughts about this empirically neglected area of dissolving personal relationships arise to summarize the intent of the present chapter specifically and the volume as a whole. First, the area of interpersonal attraction research has not yet given proper general weight to the deserving problems of relationship termination. Nor do its theoretical emphases adequately address the dissolution of relationships. Secondly, parallels between entry and withdrawal; between growth and dissolution; and between ending of encounters and ending of relationships have not been adequately tested. Thirdly, the phases in the process of dissolution need extended analysis and research attention: disengagement and dissolution are not simple events but complex processes.

The problems of dissolving personal relationships, however, are not simply intellectual, theoretical exercises. There are practical implications of a growing understanding of the process, both in terms of improved ability to recognize relationships that would be best dissolved and also since it would produce a useful input to the *prevention* of dissolution and to the *repair* of relationships where this is desirable. There are two distinct aims and two kinds of product here: first, we should aim to explore and validate techniques to prevent dissolution and to promote repair of relationships where partners wish it (cf. Markman *et al.,* Chapter 10, this volume); secondly, we should attend to the contrary side that would tell people how to unhitch without nearly dying—namely, we should investigate techniques and constructive advisory programs to facilitate withdrawal and stress-free disengagement where it is desired. In short, it would be an error to assume that our only applications of research in this area would be to give advice to counsellors wishing to repair relationships. Repair of persons can sometimes mean dissolution of destructive relationships, yet persons do not always have an effective set of strategies and skills for so doing. We are, after all, socialized to *preserve* relationships, not to get out of them neatly. As McCall (this volume) suggests, therapists can usefully aid in the construction of mutually acceptable accounts of relationship dissolution. My argument is that we can help them to go further.

As part of a move towards fulfilling both of these intentions, we can note that the present model proposes that there are many parallel and sequential processes of decision and strategy choice. The handling of these different "crisis nodes" requires different skills in disengaging partners and techniques in counsellors which have yet to be fully depicted. Strategy choice can concern the general nature of behaviour in the dyad (openly hostile, subtly manipulative, regretful, accepting, etc.). It can also, on the contrary, concern considerations of complementarity of strategy (tacit acceptance of partner's withdrawal, tacit or open resistance, counterstrategy to withdraw first oneself, etc.). Strategy choice in Phase 1 concerns focus on (re)establishing exchange equality within the relationship or on alternative relationships. In other phases, different sorts of choice have been identified and discussed. Each of these strategic possibilities has different therapeutic implications and requires entirely different sorts of decisions and actions by the Person and his or her Partner. The trick for present research is to explicate the dissolution process in ways that help us maximize input to therapeutic, counselling and guidance program.

Understanding relationship dissolution is a problem in its own right. Nevertheless, parsimonious explanation of growth and decline in intimacy, starts and endings, development and dissolution of relationships can only be a Good Thing for personal relationships research. It will better equip us to deal with the pressing practical issues such as prevention of dissolution and repair of relationships. If I do not miss my guess, these will be prime issues in society during the coming years.

Acknowledgements

I am grateful to the following for their constructive critical discussion of a first presentation of some of the ideas in this chapter: Charles Antaki, Leslie A. Baxter, Colin Brydon, Robin Gilmour, Diane Lowenstein, and David K. Miell. Further, I am very appreciative of the extensive time and trouble taken by John La Gaipa, Martin Lea and Dot Miell in prolonged discussions about the chapter and in giving a detailed review of the first and second drafts.

In the light of their comments on the earlier versions—albeit kindly expressed—I hope that they find this version unrecognizable.

CHAPTER 2

Non-engagement, Failure to Engage, and Disengagement

Miriam J. Rodin

Although the rest of this book concerns the dissolution of established relationships, this chapter will explore the failure to establish relationships as well as the failure to maintain them, once established. The present chapter will develop and extend a discussion of liking and disliking which I first presented in Rodin (1978). This latter work assumed a model in which the criteria for liking and disliking are not complementary, as is usually supposed, but are completely distinct from one another. The model proposes two other central hypotheses: that friendship choices are made from a set of eligibles on the basis of "liking" criteria; and that there are two exclusion judgments—dislike and disregard—by which we eliminate people from the set of eligibles. With persons who meet our exclusion criteria we simply do not proceed beyond the point of initial judgment and no form of relationship is entered. The present chapter's section on "Non-engagement" deals with these initial exclusions. A second concern of the chapter is with the fact that even when people appear to meet our liking criteria we sometimes fail to explore matters further. This is likely to happen when the risks and costs of following up seem too high. The section on "Failure to Engage" deals with these lapsed opportunities for friendship. The final section on "Disengagement" is about some of the conditions that lead to dissolution of established relationships. Disengagement is the theme of this volume; non-engagement and failure to engage may be seen as special cases if one is willing to stretch the concept just a little and think of them as the dissolution of potential relationships.

I will use the term "friendship" to cover all relationships that have an attitudinal component of liking: those in which the other's company is in itself a source of pleasure. I mean to exclude by this definition those relationships, such as being friendly with a teacher for a grade, that we enter into cynically, as a way of getting something we want. Of course our friends also give us things we want. The important difference is that at least some of those things are intrinsic to their person. I believe that in most instances the difference between the two kinds of relationship is clear. One can think of problem instances, but every distinction is blurred by intermediate cases. Friendship covers that subset of relationships for which liking is a necessary condition. It thus includes relationships at all levels of intimacy, from weekly tennis partner to spouse. Most of the examples I use will come from the lower end of the intimacy range, but the principles they illustrate are intended to apply along the whole of it. One caveat is in order. Statements about the genus mammals are informative in a context of arthropods and amphibians but they do not tell us about differences between spider monkeys and chimpanzees, and the same limitation applies here. Because the discussion is generic it will be relatively uninformative about the conditions for establishing and dissolving relationships that are specific to different levels of intimacy.

Non-engagement—Initial Dislike and Disregard

We select our friends from a set of eligibles. [The term "set of eligibles" is meant to designate the set of non-excluded people; it is not coincident with the term "field of eligibles" introduced by Winch (1958).] People are rejected from the set of eligibles on the basis of dislike and disregard criteria. Those who meet our dislike criteria engage both our attention and emotion whilst those who meet our disregard criteria tend to engage neither.

Dislike

In an earlier paper I argued the case for regarding dislike criteria as being entirely distinct from liking criteria. Dislike criteria are grounds for rejecting people from the set of eligibles from which we select our friends.

We never like people who meet our dislike criteria regardless of what likeable qualities they may also possess. The point is clearly demonstrated in the following simple experiment (the data have been collected from experimental subjects, but readers may as readily perform it on themselves, for everyone responds alike). First, think of someone you like very much, and state the one or two things you like best about that person. You might come up with qualities like "warm" and "sensitive". If you now ask yourself whether you can think of someone you don't like who is "warm", and someone you don't like who is "sensitive", the answer is almost always affirmative. The occasional negative occurs because people sometimes characterize the same sort of behavior differently when it occurs in someone they like than when it occurs in someone they dislike, as, for example, when the behavior(s) that signify "scholarly" in a friend are, in someone one dislikes, evidence of pedantry. Thus the occasional negative is really a delayed affirmative; it appears when the person is asked to make the characterization behavioral and concrete. Next in this little experiment is the inverse procedure: think of someone you dislike and note the one or two qualities you most dislike about that person. Now ask yourself whether you can think of anyone you like who has those qualities. The answer is invariably negative.

The experiment shows an asymmetry in liking and disliking judgments— disliked others may have likeable qualities but liked others seem never to have disliked qualities. The important implication of this finding is that interpersonal attraction is the result of sequential judgments: first exclusion judgments, then inclusion judgments. Friendship choices are made from among those who pass the screening. Those who fail to pass, whether or not they also have likeable qualities, are not included in the set of eligibles. Dislike is one of the exclusion judgments. (Disregard, the other exclusion judgment, will be discussed in a later section.)

One's dislike criteria are defined, at least partially, by what is most disliked about the person(s) one dislikes. However, our experiment tended to reveal generalized (characterological) dislike criteria. There are also context-specific dislike critera, such as physical unattractiveness, for example. If Aunt Martha is unattractive, it doesn't much matter, but if a potential date is unattractive, little else seems to matter (Walster, *et al.,* 1966). The experiment showed that physical unattractiveness is a dislike criterion for a potential date and the subjects responded as the model would predict. Once a potential date had been excluded from the eligible set, their other likeable qualities didn't count.

We do not like everyone whom we do not dislike because the criteria for liking and disliking are distinct. Although we like only persons in the eligible set, we do not like everyone in the eligible set. The fact that liking and disliking are separate (rather than unidimensional) judgments is obscured by the linguistic convention that leads speakers of English to use the term "like" for both those in the eligible set and those they have chosen from the eligible set. It is simply that there is no special term to designate those people whom one neither likes nor dislikes. Thus, a positive answer to the question "Do you like your boss?" may really mean one does, but it may also just be a denial that one dislikes him. The asymmetry of liking-disliking judgments is not a special case. Rokeach (1960) has suggested that all belief systems are asymmetric in precisely the same way, that is, composed of belief and disbelief systems. The structure of beliefs about personal relationships is, if we accept his formulation, no different from the structure of other beliefs.

Nothing in the above argument is meant to suggest that all negative information provides grounds for disliking. Since it is part and parcel of the human condition that the people we like are not perfect, it is important to distinguish among different kinds of negative information. Negative information may be relevant to the dislike criteria, to the liking criteria, or to neither, and only the first two have a heavy weight in evaluation judgments. Negative information relevant to the dislike criteria excludes a person from the set of eligibles. Negative information relevant to the liking criteria lessens our liking for a person. It is information of the third sort that we have in abundance about the people we like.

Aspects of others which we value negatively but which don't affect our liking for them will be called "disfavored". The term is introduced because the terms "not liked" and "disliked" tend to be used interchangeably in ordinary English. Let "distress" be the umbrella term for all those disagreeable feelings whose locus of origin is in another person; feelings such as jealousy, resentment, annoyance, guilt, and so on. Ambivalence is the complex of feelings we have towards those liked people whose disfavored qualities cause us distress. Distress is part of the cost of the relationship, but is independent of liking. Indeed the very existence of ambivalence is evidence that disfavored qualities coexist with liking rather than being averaged in with it. There is further evidence in the fact that although the lessening of a disfavored quality may reduce distress, it does not *ipso facto* increase liking. Consider your response to a friend who gives up the irritating habit of filling each pause in his speech with an "uh". Your irritation level goes down, but you do not like him correspondingly more because your liking is based on quite other factors than his speech habits. The independent coexistence of disfavored qualities and liking holds true in more intimate relationships as well; even though annoyance decreases when a spouse begins to squeeze the toothpaste tube from the bottom instead of the middle, liking does not take a corresponding leap forward.

We have a lot of disfavored information about ourselves—qualities to which we would give a negative rating but which don't affect our self-concept. "I'm no good at maths" is for most people a confession of something that doesn't count: though negative, it is irrelevant to self-liking criteria. Disfavored qualities in others are regarded in much the same way as disfavored qualities in ourselves. They are simply there in the person one likes. The presence of the odd disfavored quality may even be endearing (Aronson, *et al.*, 1966). "Too perfect" is not a compliment.

Disregard

Disregard is the second kind of exclusion judgment. Disregard cues function as unsuitability markers. They signify that the person will not meet our liking criteria, thus letting us "know" at once that the person would not suit us as a friend. We do not dislike the people we disregard. We fix them in a formulated phrase and simply fail to notice them further. To regard something (or someone) is to look attentively at it and the term "disregard" is meant to describe precisely the opposite response. People who meet our disregard criteria are not disambiguated beyond the point at which the disregard cue is discovered. They are in this sense invisible to us. As Ellison (1952), who codified the notion of invisibility, pointed out, our inability to see beyond the disregard cue is a literal as well as figurative truth. A good behavioral test for disregard is failure on a subsequent occasion to immediately recognize the person as someone you have met before. Of course the invisibility will fade with repeated exposure.

Disregard is a cognitive response. I am not speaking of disregard in the behavioral sense since the behavior and the judgment may or may not co-occur. We don't necessarily ignore people who meet our disregard criteria. In ordinary social situations we may treat them quite courteously, and even interact with them at some length, since it is generally considered a gross breach of social propriety to let people know that they meet our disregard criteria. The point is rather that the interaction is ritual and carried out with glazed attention.

Disregard cues may be personal or situational. Though it is the personal ones that concern us here, I will discuss the situational cues briefly, for they are familiar to us and may help to clarify the point. Role interactions are a common disregard cue and uniforms are a standard means of role identification. Our dealings with people in uniform are usually role interactions and it is a sociological truism that uniforms tend to render their wearers invisible. The uniform is not a necessary condition for role-determined invisibility, however. Whenever you deal with someone on a purely functional level, be it paying a salesperson or asking a corner policeman for directions, you are very likely to disregard them. The test is whether, even just a few minutes later, you could pick them out of an identity parade. The odds are that you would be unable to do so, even though the conversation and/or interaction may have lasted for a longish time. The phenomenon is particularly commonplace in restaurants: one has looked at the waiter, spoken to him, perhaps consulted with him over choices, yet when looking around the room to catch his attention, one is often quite unable to tell which of several likely candidates he is.

It is obvious that there are huge individual differences in disregard criteria. The set of personal disregard cues seems almost indefinitely large. There are, nevertheless, some cues we tend to hold in common. In general, granting individual variations on the pattern, we tend to disregard people who do not meet minimum acceptability standards for a relationship such as those of race, educational background, socioeconomic status, and intelligence. Age discrepancy is another common disregard cue, although the variations on it are numerous. Many of us disregard the very young and the very old (Griffitt *et al.*, 1972); young men tend to disregard women discernibly older than they are; some of us disregard people N years discrepant in age, with the direction of the discrepancy contingent on the sex of the person. For many people, the occupation "housewife" is a disregard cue, and wives sometimes fail to elicit any sign of recognition from a spouse's colleague they have met before— an occurrence far less likely to be suffered by a husband in the same position. Mode of dress and grooming are another fertile source of disregard cues. Imagine, for example, the fate of a woman in a polyester trouser suit at a gathering of the fashionably dressed. Such behavioral cues as mode of sitting, moving, eating, talking can also all function as disregard cues and so can the book one is carrying. The examples are endless. It is important to note, however, that disregard cues are not generalized cues. They tend to be context-specific because our liking criteria are context-specific. One looks for different qualities in a bridge partner and a drinking companion and the disregard cues vary accordingly; middle age in a woman may be a disregard cue at a party, but it is irrelevant at the bridge club.

Disregard cues are not in themselves aversive but are important because of their signification. We can understand how they signify by going back to the notion of implicit personality theory (see Schneider *et al.*, 1979 for an excellent review of this topic). A person's implicit personality theory is that person's idea, as differentiated or complicated as you please, of what people are like. Psychologists have traditionally described implicit personality theory as a set of expected (believed-to-be-true) correlations among personality traits, for example, "people who are punctual are likely to be warm and unlikely to be intelligent". However, there is plenty of evidence, experimental as well as introspective, to suggest that this definition is too limited. Implicit personality theory includes more than expectancies about relations among personality traits; it includes expectancies about relations among personality traits, behaviors, appearance, possessions, tastes and accomplishments (e.g. Darley and Cooper, 1972; Dion *et al.,* 1972; Gibbins, 1969; McKee and Sheriffs, 1957; Mussen and Barker, 1944). The reason that any of these can function as disregard cues is then easy to see: according to the individual's implicit personality theory they are negatively correlated with operative liking criteria. The use of such cues is not quixotic. Clearly, personality traits, appearance, tastes, possessions, occupation, accomplishments, etc. do cluster in the world. Of course, an individual's implicit personality theory may be a more or less accurate representation of these relations.

Disregard cues enable us to operate on actuarial or "best-guess" strategies so that our energy and attention are not expended fruitlessly on people we are unlikely to like. Imagine for the moment that you're with a group of people you don't know. It is entirely possible that the woman over there is someone you would like very much, but let us assume for the sake of our example that your past experience with people who adopt a like mode of dress suggests that this is improbable. You formulate her as "the woman in the polyester trouser suit" and, having affixed the label and left her wriggling on the pin, you direct your attention elsewhere.

Our "best guess" strategies are pretty much self-validating since one consequence of acting in accord with them is that we rarely encounter disconfirming instances. However, it sometimes happens that we are inadvertently faced with a disconfirming instance, as when we discover what would have been a disregard cue in someone we have already come to like. You learn, for instance, that the neighbor of whom you have grown quite fond favors the guillotine as the solution for overcrowding in prisons. Had you learned that early on you would not have disliked him, but you would have "known" that he was someone you could not like. After many shared Thursday suppers, however, the information probably falls into the disfavored category. Whether we modify our disregard criteria or regard him as the exception is moot (Abelson, 1959; Festinger, 1957; Schneider *et al.,* 1979, pp. 175–187).

I have discussed at some length the disregard judgment which renders others invisible at the initial stages of a potential relationship. A final word seems in order about the experience of being invisible to someone else— something that has happened to all of us. We are generally invisible to bureaucrats, for example, for they function precisely by fixing us in a category so that they may invoke the appropriate rule; no recital of special circumstances is likely to free us from the imposed anonymity of "just another person who wants a permit/licence/passport in a hurry". One is more or less armored against disregard in institutional settings. It is harder to bear in social situations (Fromkin, 1972), though equally difficult to remedy.

In this section it has been argued that initial liking and disliking are independent judgments, based on different criteria. Initial attraction is a two-phase process: first we make exclusion judgments which eliminate the disliked and the invisible from the set of eligibles; then we make inclusion judgments on those who are left to determine which of them meet our liking criteria. The next section deals with the decision about whether to pursue acquaintance with a person we think we will like.

Failure to Engage—Lapsed Opportunities

I discussed in the preceding section dislike and disregard—the two exclusion judgments by which we eliminate people from the set of eligibles. We choose our friends from among those who are left, but there are several stages to acquiring a friend and at each of these there is the possibility that the potential relationship will abort. First, there is the initial attraction, the sense of possibility. Then there is the reconnaissance dance, the set of exploratory moves which allow one to sample the other's company on what might be thought of as trial occasions. Experience with false positives (people we think we will like but who prove disappointing in some way) are commonplace and the trial occasions give us an opportunity to see whether the person really does meet our liking criteria. Finally, there is the decision about whether the other person is accepted as a friend, and this decision depends not only on liking but also on our assessment of the likely cost of the relationship. It is clear that between attraction and friendship may fall any number of shadows. The focus here will be on lapsed opportunities— failures at the juncture between attraction and reconnaissance. I will explore some of the reasons that people sometimes decline to follow up the possibility of friendship with someone they think they would like.

The meaning of attraction and liking, as I will use these terms, is implicit in the foregoing paragraphs. Both are tied to the notion of affiliation. Attraction is the initial positive response to someone met (or regarded) for the first time whom you would like to see more of. Liking is a delayed response which follows when you find that the person does in fact meet your liking criteria. The model assumes a setting for the initial attraction such that, unless a reconnaissance move is made, there is little likelihood that the other person will be seen again. Often at gatherings we find congenial people and have a perfectly pleasant time in their company, yet have no particular desire to see them again. We feel amicably towards them but are not, in the way I am using the term, attracted to them. Amicable feelings are ipsative "liking", what we feel towards the people whom we prefer of those who are available on a particular occasion. (This distinction is not unlike Kerckhoff's distinction between available and desirable others, although the context of application is completely different; he refers to indefinitely large sets of people in the world whereas I refer to the limited group of others present on a given occasion [Kerckhoff, 1964].)

I feel it is important to be clear about what I mean by "liking" and "attraction". Not only are these terms often used interchangeably, they have also been given countless different meanings in the research literature (this point is discussed and documented in detail in both Duck, 1977, and Huston, 1974). Our concern here is with people met (or regarded) for the first time who seem sufficiently likely to meet our operative liking criteria that we consider pursuing the acquaintance. Neither the existing literature on the evaluation of hypothetical strangers nor that on the evaluation of others after brief encounters seem to bear on the issue. This is true for several reasons. There is, of course, the standard objection that the evaluation of unmet strangers from fixed (and fragmentary) information may have little to do with how we evaluate strangers in the flesh, since in the latter instance we can note and/or elicit the particular information we deem relevant. There is good reason to suppose wide individual differences in the information people deem relevant, even when the judgment criterion is held constant (Kelly, 1955; Rodin, 1975). Secondly, the liking measures have not been related to measures of subsequent affiliation so that it is indeterminate whether they measure "not disliking", "amicable feeling", or "attraction" (in the senses in which I have defined these terms). Finally, the meaning of the measures is also in question because the judgment criteria (viz. liking for what) are almost never specified; since the anticipated context(s) of interaction determine the qualities we seek in a person, the failure to tell judges what evaluation criterion to use is far more likely to yield uninterpretable responses than global liking measures (see Rodin, 1978, for a further discussion of this point).

The familiar model of a cost/benefit calculation is the basis for decisions about whether to make reconnaissance moves towards those people to whom one is attracted. I will discuss three factors that influence the decision: the subject variable of receptivity, the known-in-advance costs of a friendship, and the costs of exploration. It is well known that there are wide individual differences in the readiness to seek friends (see Duck, 1977, pp. 77–82). Less commonly noted, though probably equally important, are the intra-individual differences. I think we are all aware of a variable receptivity factor in ourselves. Sometimes we are not conscious of any gap in our lives: we are busy, our days are full, we are content with things as they are, and we don't really have room for someone else. At those times we are far less open to opportunities for friendship. The explanation can be formulated very naturally in terms of cost, since a new friendship exacts a double cost from those whose lives are full. There are the ordinary costs of reconnaissance and friendship, but to these must be added a further cost which is reckoned in terms of the activities and people that would have to be given up or foregone. Sometimes there is a transient prevailing affect, such as sadness or sourness, that makes us unreceptive to others. Here the natural explanation is not in terms of escalated cost, but in terms of radically decreased reward value.

Let us assume that an individual is receptive to the prospect of making a friend. What are the factors that deter further exploration of a person to whom one is attracted? In the first place, we are likely to forego reconnaissance when we can tell ahead of time that a friendship with the person would prove too costly. The obvious costs are well known. The person may live at too great a distance, for example, or there may be balance theory considerations if the friendship would have an adverse effect on our other relationships (e.g. "J.D. would be upset if I started playing tennis on weekend mornings"). But even when there are no *a priori* reasons to forego further exploration, the individual may be discouraged by the costs of the reconnaissance process itself. The peripheral costs of reconnaissance, such as discordant schedules, difficult arrangements, or inconvenient distances, can be sufficiently large that further exploration simply seems like too much trouble.

The reconnaissance cost we wish to avoid most, however, is probably rebuff, which exacts a sufficiently serious toll of face and pride that most of us will not risk this cost unless the perceived probability of incurring it is near zero. We tend to respond negatively to people who don't like us (see Mettee and Aronson, 1974), but "not being disliked" is rarely adequate. Most of us will not initiate reconnaissance unless we feel that the other person is attracted to us. Unfortunately, it is not always easy to tell whether the other person is attracted to us, merely feels amicably towards us, or is camouflaging disregard under a veneer of friendliness, particularly since polite behavior sanctions a behavioral blurring of the difference. Success in avoiding rebuff depends on making an accurate correspondent inference about the other person's feelings of attraction; both gaining in the other's esteem and observing the other's selective friendliness permit such an inference. People prefer extroverts to introverts (Hendrick and Brown,

1971), and it is easy to see that universally high levels of initial friendliness in others would be preferred in self-limiting situations, such as working with people on a single occasion or interacting with them in a psychology experiment. It is equally easy to see that they might be less preferred when accuracy of correspondent inference is a relevant concern.

Finally, there are the costs related to the size of the reconnaissance moves. The moves may be large or small. The apparent size of a move depends partly on the expectations of the perceiver and the social *mores* to which he or she is accustomed. When we are sufficiently attracted by someone that we seek to explore the possibilities of friendship further, we at the same time usually wish to reserve the option of painlessly abandoning the enterprise should it not turn out as we hoped. In other words, we try to explore without committing ourselves. In small moves, the getting together occasions are relatively short, and do not necessarily imply further occasions. Getting together for a drink is a small move. In large moves, on the other hand, the getting together occasions are of longer duration and do tend to imply further occasions. Having someone over (or going to someone's home) for dinner is a large move because of the implicit reciprocation cycle.

Since the social and personal costs of breaking a reciprocation cycle can be non-trivial, we may, when the move offered by someone is too large, let the opportunity lapse rather than risk a series of unwanted and escalating occasions. We may also let the opportunity lapse when the move offered is smaller than we were ready to offer, or than we think is warranted. Moves that are too large are threatening, those that are too small are insulting. Negotiating the size of moves is a very delicate matter. It is rather flattering, for instance, when a larger move is counter-offered for a smaller one; but the counter-offer of a smaller move for a larger one ("I can't make it for dinner at your house but could we get together for a quick drink on Thursday.") is usually acceptable only when there is a mutually acknowledged power differential as might be the case, for example, when one person has more interest than the other in further exploration.

There are many similarities between the process of making reconnaissance moves and the self-disclosure process: the negative reactions of others to self-disclosures that are too large (Rubin, 1975) or too small (Cozby, 1973); the requirement for proper pacing of self-disclosure (Altman and Taylor, 1973); the fact that there is negotiation concerning level of disclosure (Davis, 1976); and the asymmetry in self-disclosure that obtains between unequal pairs such as patient and therapist, or child and adult, for example. It might be useful to think of reconnaissance moves as a form of self-disclosure; the size of the move is a disclosure of how much eagerness one feels, or is willing to show, about pursuing the possibility of relationship.

Disengagement — The Dissolution of Established Relationships

In the preceding sections I discussed dislike and disregard—the exclusion judgments that eliminate people from the set of those eligible for friendship. I touched also on some of the conditions which keep us from following up on the possibilities of a relationship with people we think we might like to have as friends. In this section I will consider the dissolution of relationships that have already been established. One has risked rebuff, got over the initial awkwardness, and found the pleasure in the other's company to be a nice balance for whatever effort or trouble is involved in obtaining it. Still, most friendships prove impermanent. Sometimes, of course, we disengage because we meet someone new who provides us a pleasure/cost ratio nearer the ideal point. Our focus here, however, will be on dissolution that occurs because there is a shift in the pleasure/cost balance: the value of the friend diminishes or the cost of the relationship escalates beyond our willingness to pay.

Liking

Before discussing disengagement conditions in more detail, it will be useful to first examine some of the bases on which we value our friends. The research literature seems to indicate that similarity is the main determinant of liking, although there is some disagreement about exactly why this is so (Ajzen, 1977; Lott and Lott, 1974; Wheeler, 1974). Almost any kind of similarity will do apparently; correspondence of interests, attitudes, personality characteristics, socioeconomic status, even level of physical attractiveness, have all been found to be associated with liking (Duck, 1977 has an excellent review of the relevant literature). There are obvious counterexamples to the similarity effect. We are not, for example, attracted to a mental patient, similar attitudes notwithstanding (Novak and Lerner, 1968). (I would note in passing that this is precisely the finding my model would predict given the plausible assumption that mental derangement is a dislike criterion for most people; once a dislike criterion has been met, otherwise likeable qualities, such as similarity, cease to matter.)

Even if we leave aside this class of counterexamples, however, it is clear that similarity, even on dimensions that might be considered the more central or important ones, is not a sufficient condition for liking; we can all retrieve examples of people similar to us on the above dimensions whom we don't particularly like. One reason that it is impossible to find similarity dimensions that are sufficient conditions for liking is that our liking criteria are at least partly context-specific (Rodin, 1978). Friends are associated with a particular context— a characteristic set of activities and settings which form the background of our interactions with them. It follows that similarity on any given dimension is likely to be important only if it is relevant to the interaction context. This does not deny the possibility that there are trans-contextual liking criteria which must be met by everyone we like. The point is simply that interaction contexts carry their own additional imperatives.

Though we like all our friends, we don't value them equally. There is an ordering such that some friends are more precious to us than others. There are at least three important factors that underlie the ordering: our valuing of a friend depends on the importance of the liking criteria satisfied, the substitutability of the friend, and the pleasure/cost ratio of the friendship. Our liking criteria are clearly ordered on an importance-to-our-lives dimension, and the friends who fulfil them are ordered accordingly. Importance has to do with the amount of time we spend in, or the amount of interest we attach to, the context(s) with which the friend is associated. If one plays tennis only irregularly but is passionately devoted to bridge, then clearly the friend(s) associated with the latter context will be valued more highly.

Substitutability is also important and, as in the marketplace, ease of replacement is a yardstick of value. People who have difficulty in meeting others, because of shyness, immobility, intractable gaucherie, or whatever, may feel none of their friends is "easily" replaceable, and value them more highly on that account. This individual difference dimension aside, there are two criterion-related conditions that determine substitutability. Some criteria are inherently harder to fulfil than others: for example, we value our friendship with the only other chess player within 50 miles who can give us a decent game. Probably more important is the number of liking criteria that the friend meets. There are some people whose company we seek in restricted contexts (e.g. only for chess) and some whose company we enjoy over many different contexts. The greater the variety of contexts, the more we see of the friend, the harder it is to replace him or her, and the more integral he or she is to our life. As people see more of each other, the shared occasions themselves enhance liking. This may be due partly to a familiarity effect (Zajonc, 1968), and partly to the easy communication that develops when there is a common frame of reference. Whatever the reasons, there is undeniably cement in a common history of occasions.

We value more those friends for whom the pleasure/cost ratio falls near the ideal point. All exchange theorists seem to agree that for a given amount of reward, the value of the relationship approaches the ideal point as the cost approaches zero. (A brief overview of exchange theories may be found in La Gaipa, 1977b and Huston, 1974.) I want to modify this formulation and suggest that the cost can be too small as well as too large. When the cost is too large the relationship ceases to be worth it, and when the cost is too small the perceived value of the friend diminishes. We do not value most those friends who maximize our reward/cost ratio by giving us much and demanding nothing in return. On the contrary, friends like that tend to be described in unflattering terms (like "doormat", for example), and though we may value them cynically, they do not generally have our respect. The explanation is straightforward— someone who permits us to exploit him must, on a "just-world" rationale, be the sort of unworthy person who deserves it. There is a marketplace analogue. We don't place much value on what we acquire too cheaply or easily. We value something rather more when it is acquired at some cost; perhaps, as Aronson and Mills (1959) have suggested, we enhance its value by way of justifying the cost.

There is a well-known experiment (Walster et al., 1973) which is often cited as a refutation of my line of argument. The experiment seems to show that people like others who are selectively easy for them to get rather than those who are hard for them to get. I will explain why the results of this study are not the counterinstance they appear to be. In the first place, the argument is not that the attribute of being "hard-to-get" of itself increases value, but that the attribute of being "hard-to-get" increases the value of something (or someone) initially desired. The experiment tests the former proposition, which seems on its face to be false—most of us would not like to have plutonium, a capybara, or friendship with a mass murderer even though all of them are rather hard to come by. Secondly, the experimental operations do not bear directly on liking. The significant results of the experiment deal with the subject's choice of girl for a first meeting. The choice was among five girls— one (hard-to-get) who didn't especially want to meet someone like the subject (or anyone else on the available list for that matter, though it is not clear that this influenced the subjects' choice), one (easy-to-get) who wanted to meet everyone on the available list, one (selectively easy-to-get) who wanted to meet someone like the subject but not like any of the others on the available list, and two (control) about whose preferences the subjects had no information. The subjects' choice is presumably their best guess about which of the dates is most likely to prove successful. The overwhelming majority of subjects chose the third girl, and their choice is not at all surprising. A date with someone who doesn't especially want to meet someone like you is rather unlikely to be successful (Huston, 1973). The odds are in your favor if you choose a girl you know wants to meet someone like you, rather than a girl whose preferences are unknown. Of the two girls who wanted to meet someone like the subjects, one wanted to meet everyone, and, as the authors point out, the inference drawn about such a person is likely to be negative, e.g. "she's desperate" The remaining girl was clearly the best bet.

I would also argue that liking (or attraction) was not the genuine issue in this experiment. The only information the subject had on the girls, besides their dating choices, was stereotypic information like age, religion, position on the political spectrum, year in school, and so forth. Liking (or attraction) is usually thought of as a response to a known and particularized person. Stereotypic information gives us an actuarial basis for predicting liking, but it certainly does not guarantee it.

Finally, I would like to make a parenthetical observation about the minority of subjects (29 out of 71) who did not choose the "selectively easy" girl. They are not commented on in the article itself, but it is tempting to see their otherwise inexplicable choices as support for my proposition that exclusion judgments come first; for these subjects the fact that the girl was, for example, Jewish or Catholic or "right of center" or whatever, happened to meet their dislike criterion, and after that nothing else counted.

Similar observations about the role of acquisition and maintenance costs are embodied in all the folk wisdom concerning the future of a relationship in which one person is too easily acquired or comes to be taken for granted. In an intentional comment on human relationships, St. Exupéry (1943) noted that one cares more for the rose one must water thrice daily than for those that require less attention. His intriguing corollary hypothesis was that, given the initial liking, one comes to care more deeply for the rose *because* one waters it rather than the other way about. Of course this effect cannot be pushed too far—only to the vicinity of the ideal point. Beyond that, the relationship ceases to be worth it. There is support for a weaker version of his hypothesis in the findings that people come to like more those people to whom they have been kind or for whom they have done a favor (Jecker and Landy, 1969; Lerner and Simmons, 1966; Schopler and Compere, 1972). The effect has been explained as a self-attribution of liking based on the observation of one's own behavior (Tedeschi, 1974).

Disengagement

The conditions for disengagement are implicit in what has been said so far. Dislike criteria may be belatedly met—either our ordinary dislike criteria or the sort that become operative only in the context of an ongoing friendship. One's liking criteria may change, or the friend may change and no longer meet them. A better candidate may displace the current person—someone who meets more criteria, or meets the same ones better. Finally, the pleasure/cost ratio may shift too far in either direction from the ideal point.

It is rare that someone we have come to like belatedly meets our ordinary dislike criteria. We may find that our erstwhile friend enjoyed meals of roast dog during his travels in the Orient, or that his particular sexual pleasures correspond with our notion of the perverse, or that he cheats on line calls at tennis. A more common occurrence is for the person to meet the dislike criterion that applies only in established relationships—a criterion we might call "behavior egregious in a friend". Our expectancies are different for our friends than for others (La Gaipa, 1977a). Thus it is not behavior *per se* that constitutes betrayal or rejection, but behavior relative to expectancy. The point is obvious really. Someone's failure to invite us to a party is egregious only if we expected to be invited.

Sometimes our liking criteria change in kind. A friendship may not survive if we cease participating in the context which supported it, because the reward value of the friend will decline when, for example, we give up tennis or move to another office. Our liking criteria may also change in the direction of greater stringency. Disengagement is likely to follow if a friend cannot meet the stricter criterion—if, for example, you improve so much more quickly at tennis that your friend can no longer give you a decent game. The expression "outgrowing someone" is used to describe the same sort of stringency change in more intimate relationships. An alternative explanation of "outgrowing someone" in terms of diminishing similarity (of interests, accomplishments, what have you) doesn't really work. Diminished similarity is a reasonable description of "growing apart", but not of a spouse who has become faintly embarrassing.

There is a range of tolerance in liking criteria so that people who meet them may nevertheless meet them more or less well. Displacement of a friend by someone else can occur when one meets a new person who meets the same liking criterion better. Displacement may also occur when a new person meets more of our liking criteria; we like those friends better with whom we share a greater breadth of contexts. Displacement of our friends by others whom we find more rewarding is far from automatic since we are usually quite happy to have a range of friends. Displacement is most likely to occur when time (or other) constraints force us to a choice.

The likelihood of displacing friends seems to exist as an important individual difference dimension. It is tied to different friendship-seeking strategies which might be called meeting minimal criteria v. maximizing. The same difference in strategy can be seen in shopping behavior. Some people are content to buy a suit that looks good while others will not buy until they have (quasi)exhausted the domain of all suits that look good so that they may choose the best among them. The important difference between shopping for friends and for suits is that there are no people stores one can go to. One cannot exhaust the domain *before* choosing in the same way—new possibilities present themselves all the time. Those people who apply a maximizing strategy to relationships will obviously change them more often. The price of maximizing is probably paid in intimacy coin.

Disengagement occurs when the pleasure/cost ratio deviates too far from the ideal point. This occurs when pleasure diminishes, or when the cost shifts radically in either direction. Perhaps the commonest reason for diminishing pleasure in the absence of a criterion change is boredom. Since novelty is in itself a source of pleasure, the security–novelty tension is a constant in our lives (Maslow, 1970). Sometimes we have simply had a surfeit of people whom we like but with whom our interactions have become overly predictable. This might be the explanation for relationships that have a cyclic pattern—those in which we see someone regularly, don't see them for a while, then begin to see them again.

Costs, physical or psychic, may increase past the breakeven point. Physical costs increase when, for example, the friend moves or changes schedule so that arranging to get together, or getting together itself, is more difficult. With a sufficient increase in time, money, or trouble, the friendship will no longer seem worth it. An unacceptable increase in psychic costs usually arises from disfavored qualities that by their nature do not emerge until a relationship has been established. When a friend becomes overly demanding, possessive, or intrusive, this adds to the cost of the relationship. As is true with other disfavored qualities, these do not get averaged in with liking. Liking does not diminish, but the price measured in negative feelings (e.g. irritation, guilt, jealousy) may raise the cost of the relationship to an unacceptable level. Finally, the relationship may also come to deviate from the ideal point in the direction of lowered cost, with the result that the friend comes to seem less valuable. (People valued on cynical grounds are not a counterinstance because they do not meet the definition of friends.) Friends who are overly complaisant, or never request that we water them, are likely to be seen as unimportant precisely for the reason that they cost us no effort on their behalf. As friends fall lower in the value ordering, there is a corresponding increase in the probability of disengagement.

Summary

In this chapter I have discussed non-engagement, failure to engage, and disengagement. Attraction and liking were distinguished from "not disliking", and from "amicable feeling", which is ipsative liking unrelated to desire for further contact. Attraction to another person was defined as the expectation that he or she would meet one's liking criteria, and liking was tied to affiliation. The underlying assumptions were that disliking and liking are distinct judgments made on different criteria, and that interpersonal attraction is a sequential process in which persons are first excluded from the set of eligibles and liked others are then chosen from those who are left. An important consequence of the fact that our liking and disliking criteria are different is that we do not feel attraction towards all those who are not excluded.

People who meet our (sometimes context-specific) dislike criteria are excluded from consideration regardless of what other likeable qualities they may have. We all have negative information about our friends, and a careful distinction was made between "disfavored" qualities which coexist independently of liking although they may increase the cost of a relationship, and negative information relevant to liking and disliking judgments. Also excluded from consideration are those others we disregard, fail to really notice, as it were, beyond the disregard cue. It was stressed that disregard is a cognitive response to another person, not rude disregarding behavior towards him, and that the relevant behavioral test is failure to recognize the disregarded person on a subsequent occasion.

The section on lapsed opportunities dealt with our failure to follow up on people to whom we are attracted. It was noted that between attraction and liking there is usually a series of reconnaissance moves which allow people to determine whether they really want to affiliate. The analysis of lapsed opportunities was in terms of the familiar reward/cost framework. It was noted that we allow opportunities to lapse when we can tell ahead of time that the costs of a friendship would be too high, and also when the costs, both feared and actual, of the reconnaissance process itself discourage us. An important part of the reconnaissance process is the size of the move(s) one is willing to offer or accept. It was suggested that the business of transacting moves is akin to the process of self-disclosure in dyads.

The section on disengagement, using a reward/cost framework and the liking/disliking model discussed above, considered some of the conditions leading to the dissolution of established relationships. A modification was introduced to the usual exchange-theory formulation that our ideal point for the valuing of a friend is maximum reward at minimum cost. It was argued that relationships deviate from the ideal point when reward gets too low, and when cost becomes either too high or too low. Our friends are on a value ordering determined by their substitutability, by how well, within the range of acceptability, they fulfil our liking criteria, by the importance to us of the interaction context(s) in which we see them, and by the breadth of contexts in which we see them; these are measures of their reward value and as these decline the probability of disengagement increases. Besides our ordinary dislike criteria there is a class of dislike criteria relevant only to established relationships, and if a friend is found to meet either, dissolution is likely to follow. Just as there are dislike criteria that apply only to friends, there are disfavored qualities that emerge only in friends. An increase in such psychic costs and/or a negative change in the peripheral costs of maintaining contact may make the relationship no longer seem "worth it". When the cost of a relationship declines too far there is the paradoxical effect that the reward value of the person also declines, again sometimes to the point that the relationship no longer seems "worth it".

CHAPTER 3

Social and Cognitive Features of the Dissolution of Commitment to Relationships

Michael P. Johnson

In modern, industrialized, urban societies with their high rates of geographic and social mobility, most relationships end before the death of one of the partners. Of course, many of these relationships are not expected to last; they are role relationships entered into for pragmatic purposes, involving people, hardly known to each other as individuals, who expect the relationship to end as soon as immediate goals are accomplished. Yet other relationships do involve considerable interdependence and involvement with the other person as a unique individual (Kelley, 1979): even such personal relationships are likely to end. A survey of men living in the Detroit metropolitan area found that even among one's three closest friends, only 23% were friends that had lasted since before the age of 18, and, of course, this figure decreases as one becomes older such that for men aged 50–64 only 9% of their closest friends were friends that they had kept from their youth (estimated from Stueve and Gerson, 1977). Equally 45% of young Boston couples involved in serious romantic relationships had broken up by the end of two years (Hill *et al.*, 1976). Finally, to go one step further in relationship depth, recent data suggest that in the United States

30–40% of the marriages entered into in the 1970s will end in divorce (Glick, 1975; Norton and Glick, 1979).

Although most of one's relationships are therefore likely to end, the social and cognitive impact of these relationship dissolutions will vary tremendously. The loss of one's schoolbus driver is hardly noticed, and the loss of a favorite grammar school teacher, though more difficult, is easy to handle. But the loss of a lover or best friend may result in a major disruption of one's thoughts and behavior, and the loss of a spouse may involve personal and social trauma which last a lifetime. The present chapter argues that the major source of these differences in the social and cognitive impact of relationship dissolution is the depth of one's commitment to the relationship.

This chapter is organized into three sections, each dealing with one of three dimensions of relationship dissolution (viz. commitment, social aspects, cognitive aspects). I will treat each one independently of the other two, although I shall ultimately conclude, as above, that the processes are inextricably intertwined. The first section, focusing on *commitment*, hinges upon the distinction between personal and structural commitment, between a personal dedication to the maintenance of a relationship and those features of social life that make it more or less difficult for one to dissolve a relationship to which one is no longer personally committed. The second major section of the paper draws upon the recent developments in the network perspective on social life (e.g., Boissevain, 1974) in order to describe the *social features* of relationship dissolution. The final major section of this paper concerns the *cognitive aspects* of relationship dissolution. It takes a phenomenological approach, the basic assumption of which perspective is that one's ideas regarding both oneself and one's environment are socially constructed: that is, developed through an interpersonal process of interpretation which draws upon culturally given schemes of typification.

One final note of introduction concerns the type of relationsnips covered in this paper. First, since this book is focused on *personal* relationships, my discussion does not deal with purely secondary role relationships. Secondly, although an attempt is made to deal with a broad range of personal relationships, most previous considerations of relationship dissolution have focused on *marital* separation, and my choice of illustrations for the processes discussed is therefore similarly biased.

Commitment to Relationships

People stay in relationships for two major reasons: because they want to;

and because they have to. Accordingly, social psychological explanations of relationship dissolution traditionally argue that relationships break up when partners wish to leave or when the constraints upon them are reduced (Levinger, 1965, 1976). The discussion of commitment which follows here acknowledges these dual determinants of relationship dissolution, but emphasizes the role of constraint over that of choice for three major reasons. First, changes in relationship satisfaction are more closely related to the breakdown of relationships (Duck, 1981; Duck and Gilmour, 1981c), while the operation of constraint is intimately related to the process of dissolution which is the focus of the present volume. The second reason is the tremendous imbalance in the literature in favor of "dissatisfaction" determinants of relationship dissolution. Third, it is illusory that quality explains more variance than constraint—simply because, in most studies of dissolution, constraint does not vary dramatically. The typical social psychological study of relationship dissolution investigates one type of relationship in one social location at one point in history. It seems to make perfect sense that personal inclinations rather than structural constraints apparently explain all the variance that is explained. However, one needs to ask why friendships end more often than kin relationships, why casual dating relationships end more often than engagements, why divorce rates vary dramatically among different countries, social classes, and states, and at different times in history. One might try to argue that we like our friends less than our kin, our fiancé(e)s more than our dates, and so on. Nevertheless, the more plausible interpretations of such variations emphasize changes in constraints and argue that it is these that produce the most dramatic effects on the social and cognitive impact of dissolution.

The concept of commitment has always carried two distinct meanings in both common speech and social science writing (Johnson, 1969; 1973; 1978). One is a reference to an individual's dedication to the maintenance of a line of action, as in "She is committed to the development of a feminist consciousness". This meaning carries with it a sense of determination to continue in the face of adversity or temptations to deviate, a determination which results from strong personal attachments to the line of action. This will be referred to here as "personal commitment". The second basic meaning of the term "commitment" is captured by the expression "I can't back out now, I'm committed to writing this paper". The connotation is one of external constraints which come into play as a consequence of the initiation of the line of action and which make it difficult to discontinue should one's sense of personal commitment decline. Since, in the case of commitment to relationships, these constraints are closely tied to aspects of the social structure in which the relationship is embedded, they will be referred to as "structural commitment".

Personal commitment to relationships

The major component of personal commitment is the satisfaction with the relationship which grows out of the personal rewards and costs involved, comparison with other relationships with which one is familiar, and perhaps some sense of the relative payoffs for self and other (e.g., Ajzen, 1977; Thibaut and Kelley, 1959; Kelley and Thibaut, 1978; Hatfield and Traupmann, 1981). A second aspect of personal commitment is definition of self in terms of relationship. As Goffman (1961) put it (although he used the term "attachment"),

> "The self image available for anyone entering a particular position is one of which he may become affectively and cognitively enamored, desiring, and expecting to see himself in terms of the enactment of the role and the self-identification emerging from this enactment." (p. 89)

The final component of personal commitment is an internalized sense of moral commitment to the maintenance of the relationship. This may be derived either from a general belief that one ought to finish what one starts, from moral strictures focused on the maintenance of specific types of relationships, or perhaps from a perception of the relationship as involving an implicit contract, obligating one to its maintenance even in the face of declining satisfaction. While the first two components of personal commitment will generally be perceived by the individual as internal matters of personal preference, this third component may frequently involve a sense of internal constraint on the attainment of one's own wishes.

The aspects of relationship quality discussed by Lewis and Spanier (1979) and the processes of relationship disorder addressed in Volume 3 of this series (Duck and Gilmour, 1981c) result in a decline of personal commitment. Once the individual has decided that he or she is no longer satisfied with the relationship, does not wish to have his or her self wrapped up in it, and has no moral obligation to maintain it, the process of relationship dissolution becomes salient and the social and cognitive consequences of the dissolution of structural commitments must be faced.

Structural commitment to relationships

Structural commitments are events or conditions which constrain the individual to continue a line of action once it has been initiated, regardless of personal commitment to it. The various kinds of structural commitments which may be engaged in once one enters a relationship may be conveniently classified into four general types: irretrievable investments, social pressures, available alternatives, and termination procedures.

Irretrievable Investments. The development and maintenance of a relationship necessitates at the very least the investment of some time and energy (Marks, 1977), and potentially involves the investment of emotions, money, or other possibly irretrievable resources. The person faced with the end of a relationship may fully consider whether these investments have been wasted in the pursuit of intangibles—which may no longer appear to have been important once the relationship comes to an end. The strength of this sense of loss will, of course, vary as a function of the length and intensity of the relationship, and the extent to which the relationship is defined (culturally or personally) as one in which the major payoffs for investments have not as yet been realized. The short-term pragmatic relationship with a tennis partner at school involves investments which are paid off immediately in the play itself; when one graduates and the relationship ends, there is no sense of lost investment. Even very close same-sex friendships have as their major payoff the immediate experience of the relationship in the present. On the other hand, our attitude towards romantic relationships in this culture is such that they are defined as failures, as wasted efforts, if they do not last a lifetime. Our romantic involvements are imbued with a future orientation that leads us to react to our investment as lost if the future is not realized. So, for this aspect of irretrievable investments, the work of neutralizing commitment here involves primarily a cognitive effort to define the perceived loss as an acceptable loss.

In addition to these sorts of direct investments in the relationship, the individual considering dissolution will also be faced with the consequences of having forgone a variety of alternative possibilities for investment. Relationships certainly differ dramatically in the extent to which they require the forgoing of alternatives. The maintenance of a mere acquaintanceship takes little time from other relationships and is culturally defined to allow one wide latitude in the application of resources to activities outside the relationship. A marriage, on the other hand, may require strict monogamy, the abrogation of all other romantic involvements and even friendships. Many wives effectively eliminate attractive potential career possibilities by investing themselves in their marriage, through childbearing and childrearing, during periods of their lives which are crucial for the development of a viable career line.

The work involved in the neutralization of loss through forgone alternatives will involve both cognitive and social features. Forgone alternatives which have faded into the background of an ongoing relationship once again become salient; one then has to make sense of them and refit them into one's biography, either by suffering with them, redefining and minimizing their importance, or opting to restore them through the reconstruction of one's life. Since the forgone alternatives of relationship commitment are largely social alternatives, such as personal relationships or socialization for alternative roles, the reconstruction will be largely social: it will center around entering networks which restore access to forgone alternatives. In the case of personal relationships, this may mean beginning to date again or joining the social world of the formerly married (Weiss, 1975). In the case of forgone preparation for roles, the reconstruction may involve either a retraining process or entering a network of social service relationships which can provide the rewards which would have been available from the lost career (Weiss, 1973).

Social Pressures. Every personal relationship is embedded in a network consisting of the other relationships of the partners (see McCall and Simmons, 1978); the couple's relationship is often important to these other people. It is usually the case that once we begin a romantic relationship, the people around us develop expectations that we will continue it. To some extent these expectations, one source of network discouragement of dissolution, are based on normative themes regarding the morality of relationship dissolution, so these moral reactions will differ as a function of cultural definitions of the relationship in question (see La Gaipa, this volume). The expectation surrounding the marital relationship in the United States is that one must struggle to maintain it in the face of adversity. Other relationships, such as dating relationships or friendships, may come and go, within limits, without critical social reaction. The limits have less to do with the morality of dissolution than with the second major source of network resistance to relationship dissolution: the effects of the dissolution on the lives of such third parties. Members of the partners' networks build patterns of behavior around the partners' lines of action, and relationships differ dramatically in the extent to which their dissolution will alter lines of action upon which other people depend for the making of their own plans. To take a trivial example, a pair of friends may have acquaintances with whom they frequently play doubles tennis and the dissolution of the friendship will force the acquaintances to either play singles or engage in a search for a new pair of tennis partners. More seriously, the children of a married couple may have their total life pattern disrupted by the dissolution of their parents' relationship.

As a consequence of these cultural definitions and behavioral interdependencies, the members of partners' networks will develop more or less strong feelings regarding the dissolution of the relationship. The variability of such network commitments across various types of relationships is exemplified in the Penn State data I have collected on dating relationships of young couples. A random sample of university students $(N = 428)$ filled out questionnaires regarding the dating relationships in which they were currently involved. The relationships included, in ascending order of involvement: occasional dating, regular dating, exclusive dating, engagement, and marriage. Each respondent was asked to construct a list of "those people whose opinions of your personal life are important to you", and was asked how each of the persons listed would feel if the relationship in which the respondent was involved were to end. The mean percentages of the network who would disapprove of relationship dissolution for each of the ordered stages of relationship involvement were 19%, 50%, 63%, and 86%, respectively. Disapproval of dissolution is clearly related to level of involvement. The prospect of dealing with these individuals' reactions to dissolution can be a major structural commitment, either contributing to the maintenance of a relationship long after personal commitment has seriously declined, or requiring some form of interpersonal work to make the dissolution socially bearable.

Available Alternatives. One of the cornerstones of Thibaut and Kelley's (1959) exchange theory is the Comparison Level for Alternatives, a concept which makes explicit the process of comparison which is involved in decisions about ending relationships. Individuals are structurally committed to a relationship to the extent that reasonably available alternatives are unattractive. The individual who is casually dating someone on an American university campus may dissolve the relationship with the full knowledge that there are 10 000 other potential partners standing in the wings. On the other hand, the forty-five-year-old mother of four children who has given up her career for her family must think much more carefully about the alternatives available to her following a divorce. Of course, the issue of alternatives is not really merely one of substitution for the particular relationship dissolved. The question is a more general one regarding the general impact of being without the relationship, and whether the quality of one's life will be noticeably altered by the dissolution. It is certainly not unreasonable to expect that the cognitive and social impact of dissolution is intimately related to this component of structural commitment, although in an interesting way. The operationalization of this component involves asking people to report the ways in which their lives would change if they were to end their relationship, then following up with a question about how they would feel about the anticipated changes. High structural commitment corresponds to a great many negative changes, low structural commitment corresponds to few changes or a neutral balance of changes, while individuals who expect positive changes would experience *extremely* low commitment or what we might call structural temptation. The cognitive and social impact of dissolution would be high at either end of the continuum of attractiveness of alternatives.

Termination Procedures. The specific steps which have to be taken to end a relationship differ from situation to situation, and the difficulty of those procedures is a major component of structural commitment. To end an acquaintanceship one might need only to refrain from calling one's acquaintance again. To end a marriage may require tedious explanations to kin, legal difficulties, and all of the problems of changing residences. In the aforementioned project at Penn State, we asked respondents to identify steps they would have to take to end their relationship; a few examples should suffice to illustrate the variability in the termination procedures involved across the various stages of romantic involvement. Only 43% of the students who were occasionally dating their partner reported that they would have to explain the break-up to their parents, as compared with 80% of the married respondents. The comparable figures for students explaining to their partner's parents were 29% and 77%. Only 10% of the occasionally dating couples would have to look for a new place to live, while 92% of the married students would have to move. Only 14% of those occasionally dating would have to make some decisions about splitting up possessions; the figure is 98% for married respondents. Thirteen per cent of the occasionally dating respondents would look for a job if they broke up; the figure is 54% for married respondents. Finally, of course, none of the occasional daters would have to go through a legal divorce process. The difficulties involved in each of these aspects of termination proceedings commit the partners to the maintenance of their relationship, and they also ensure that the process will require considerable social and cognitive work.

Social Features of Relationship Dissolution

Of course, the most immediate and obvious social aspect of a relationship dissolution is the elimination of the relationship itself from the lives of the former partners. But dyadic relationships are embedded in a wider social context, a network of other relationships which may make significant contributions to the process of dissolution itself and will in turn be affected by its progress (cf. La Gaipa, this volume). While the network has this important impact on the dissolution process, I have chosen to spend my limited space focusing on the dissolution consequences for networks. The discussion is accordingly organized into two sections, the first being a brief description of the network perspective, illustrated through two exemplary network projects. The second section will address the basic processes involved in network change, with illustrative discussion of processes of change in various sectors of the network.

The network perspective

"The social relations in which every individual is embedded may be viewed as a network. This social network may, at one level of abstraction, be looked upon as a scattering of points connected by lines. The points, of course, are persons, and the lines are social relations. Each person can thus be viewed as a star from which lines radiate to points, some of which are connected to each other."

(Boissevain, 1974, 24)

This perspective on social life has recently spawned a tremendous burst of activity in sociology and social anthropology (e.g., Fischer, 1977; Mitchell, 1974) and alternative means of approaching the analysis of networks provide access to varieties of information which are almost overwhelming. These include purely structural properties of networks, such as size, density, and multiplexity, as well as the results of elaborate formal mathematical procedures for analyzing the patterns of interconnection in the graphs of networks (Feger, 1981). What I would like to do at this point is to describe two recent studies, one on marital and the other on dating relationships, which deal specifically with the effects of relationship dissolution on social networks.

Marriage. Marylyn Rands' (1980) study of social aspects of divorce utilized a retrospective version of network identification procedures developed by Fischer and his colleagues (McAllister-Jones and Fischer, 1978). She interviewed twenty men and twenty women who had recently been divorced and asked them to identify people with whom they had various kinds of interaction (e.g., sharing activities or discussing personal problems). Data were collected for the present and retrospectively for a subjectively identified point before the divorce when the marriage still had a high likelihood of continuation. This procedure thus provided two lists of individuals for each respondent about whom one could then ask a series of other questions. Rands collected data regarding characteristics of network members and their relationships with the respondent. She also utilized another important methodological tactic in collecting more specific relational information for a selected subset of the network than she could feasibly have collected for the total network.

On the average, 42% of the respondents' marital network members had been dropped after separation. Spouses' kin were frequently dropped and replaced with friends and coworkers. Persons known to the spouse first and those closer to the spouse than to the respondent were especially likely to be dropped, as were opposite sex associates and married friends. Although many of the dropped network members were "replaced", networks were on the average 14% smaller after separation than they were during the marriage. The information on the eight closest members of each network suggests a decrease in density or interconnectedness, and a widening of the contexts from which the network members were chosen. After separation, self-disclosure, physical contact, sharing feelings, and participation in joint activities with each non-spouse member of the closest part of the network was higher than it had been during marriage. It should be kept in mind, however, that total extent of joint activity and physical contact was reduced, due to the loss of the spousal relationship.

Some of the *differences* in network change which Rands identifies are also interesting. For example, 70% of the men were likely to be involved in a steady heterosexual relationship at the time of the interview, as compared with 40% of the women, even though the women had on the average been separated 10 months longer than the men. Even with respect to friendship, men had more cross-sex relationships; after separation men's eight closest relationships were equally divided among males and females, while the women's closest relationships were predominantly with other females. As one might expect, parental status was another crucial determinant of network change. Parents' networks were generally more stable than non-parents' and they were more likely to continue to interact with kin after separation. This effect was particularly striking for custodial fathers.

Dating. The second study to be presented here (Milardo, 1982) provides informative contrasts with the Rands study. First, the research focuses on premarital relationships. Second, it is longitudinal in design rather than restrospective. Third, and most importantly, the network identification is based on daily records of social interaction (as originally developed by Wheeler and Nezlek, 1977).

Network data were collected from 63 university students who were involved in dating relationships which included casual dating, regular dating, exclusive dating, and engagement. Milardo asked respondents to report on face-to-face or telephone interaction of ten minutes or more in length during a ten-day period. The collected information included length of interaction, participants in the interaction and their relationships to the respondent and his/her partner, satisfaction with the encounter, its intimacy and importance, and the topics of conversation. Data were collected at two points in time, roughly three months apart. Although the research was designed to look at the impact of relationship development in general, some of the most striking findings involved the couples who decreased their stage of involvement during the period between data collections.

The collection of contemporaneous longitudinal data made it possible for Milardo to get to the specifics of interaction, allowing assessment of some of the details of network changes. Changes due to the move toward relationship dissolution appear, interestingly enough, to be the reciprocal of the process of withdrawal from networks which has been observed, as couples become more romantically involved (Johnson and Leslie, in press; Milardo, 1980; Surra, 1980). Individuals whose relationships declined showed slight, but statistically non-significant increases in network size; the number of people with whom they interacted during the ten-day period increased from an average of 25.2 network members to 30.0. The more dramatic findings have to do with the frequency and duration of interaction with network members.

Briefly, deteriorating couples showed a significant increase in the number of interactions and the duration of interactions with network members. For the total network (not including the partner), number of interactions per day went from an average of 2.6 to 4.3; number of minutes per day spent in interaction went from 176 to 289. In interesting contrast with the Rands data, there were no significant changes in number of interactions or duration of contacts with kin. The clearest change was for intermediate friends (those not considered close or best friends), with the number of interactions per day increasing from 1.1 to 1.8 and duration increasing from 59 to 106 minutes.

These two studies are important for two reasons. First, they represent a reasonable introduction to some of the possible contributions of the network perspective to the analysis of social features of relationship dissolution. Second, the results certainly show the impact of relationship dissolution on other relationships. The changes in network structure which this approach allows us to identify clearly draw attention to issues of social process which need to be addressed more fully in the future.

Basic processes

The appearance and disappearance of links in networks actually take place through a complicated set of social events; networks are abstractions from the real interpersonal processes of relationship development and dissolution. The factors involved in these social processes may be somewhat arbitrarily placed into four categories.

First, some network changes flow from what might be called circumstantial consequences of the relationship dissolution (Boissevain, 1974). For example, suppose I used to play tennis with my spouse and she had some very close friends at the tennis club. After our divorce, I stop going to the club and no longer have the casual encounters with its members which might sustain my relationship with them, and the links disappear from my network. Second, some network changes are initiated by the former partners themselves. For example, I might self-consciously decide to avoid contact with those same close friends of my former spouse because I assume that they disapprove of my initiation of the divorce and the pain it caused their dear friend. Third, network changes may be initiated by the members of the network. Those close friends might make it clear to me that they no longer want to have anything to do with me after what I did to my wife. Finally, there may be changes in the character of the relationship between the former partner and a network member which lead to the atrophy of the link. I may continue to see my former wife's friends for a while, but when we find that the only thing we really had in common was our mutual association with her and that our encounters have therefore become painfully boring, the relationship atrophies through a "natural" process of disinterest. Through some combination of these very different processes, the various sectors of the network are gradually transformed following dissolution.

Network sectors

When is a network link no longer a network link? This question, which really needs to be addressed for every loss of a network link, will be dealt with here with regard to the dissolved relationship itself. What is a dissolution? The answer is to a large extent arbitrary. Six months after separation, one former spouse said to her ex-husband: "I've been working through a lot of things this week and I just want to say goodbye to you as a husband and hello to you as a friend". Is the relationship dissolved? They are certainly no longer married; since they still see each other every week and help each other out, the link would still be intact in any study utilizing either Milardo's or Rands' procedure for identifying a network. The answers to this question are as varied as are the ways of defining aspects of relationship. One seemingly straightforward approach is subjective and hinges on the label which is attached to the relationship. If the members of the couple are no longer married, then at least their marital relationship has dissolved. But whose application of the label is crucial? The members of a couple may consider themselves single long before the legal divorce is complete. Or one partner might consider the relationship ended, while the other still considers it intact. When the researcher reaches this sort of labeling impasse, the interactional criteria may seem to become more attractive. But relationships do not always dissolve to *no* interaction. Rather, there is some reduction of interaction or a transformation of its nature. So there is no simple answer other than the advice to keep in mind the incredible complexities of social relationships and to address them as fully as necessary for the immediate issues involved in one's research.

Changes in the kin network are likely to be of major importance only following the dissolution of a "kin" relationship. The use of quotes around kin above is necessary because there are some relationships which are clearly kin-like, but in which there are as yet no formal kin ties, probably the most familiar one being engagement. During the period of engagement the partners are integrated into each other's kin networks, frequently beginning to use kin terms for their prospective in-laws and beginning to perform kin-like duties (Slater, 1963). Thus, the dissolution of an engagement may reverberate through the kin network in much the same way as a dissolution of a "real" kin relation such as marriage. The loss of a friendship, however, is unlikely to affect interaction with one's own kin and relationships with friends' kin are likely to be minimal; but there will be those ambiguous cases where "he was like a son to me".

These ambiguous cases serve in part as a contrast to the dissolution of true kin relationships, which typically have an important impact on relationships with the wider kin network. One of the most direct kin network changes involved in a dissolution is the effect of divorce on relationships with children. The custodial parent, if he or she had not taken major responsibility for childrearing before the dissolution, will have a dramatic increase in involvement with children. If he or she had been the major child caretaker and must now go out to work, there will be a reduction in involvement. For the non-custodial parent, the relationship with children will attenuate dramatically. Here the subjective and interactional aspects of relationships may come to be at odds. One's child may subjectively be just as much one's child after as before the divorce, even though interaction has been eliminated entirely or reduced to a bare minimum.

Changes in relationships with other kin will vary as a function of a number of factors. One's own kin may rally around to provide support during the troubled times of dissolution and its aftermath, while one's partner's kin may become hostile and reduce contact or behave aggressively. The partner who has initiated the divorce may find it difficult to face the relatives of the ex-spouse, even when they may desire to maintain contact. Also parental relationships affect the attenuation of other kin relations, including the relationship with the former spouse (Weiss, 1975; Rands, 1980).

Both Milardo and Rands found an increase in interaction with friends following relationship dissolution, and Rands' identification of network changeover makes it clear, for marriage at least, that the population of the network changes dramatically. There are a number of general processes involved in such changes. First, the dissolution of a relationship may simply make time free for the development of new friendships, and in the case of marriage at least, the decrease in interaction with kin will provide additional time for friends. Second, the change of one's relationship status will alter what one has in common with other people. Common interests will also be affected by other network changes, as when a divorced non-custodial parent loses things in common with other parents. Third, relationships with those friends with whom one was linked primarily through one's former partner are bound to be affected by the dissolution. Fourth, the change in relationship status may sometimes place one in new contexts in which friendships may be formed: for instance, a formerly dependent spouse may now want to or have to go to work to support his or her new household unit. The new work context will put one into contact with a host of new people and probably with a variety of new types of relationships, e.g., relationships of formal power, or of shared subordination.

Summary remarks

Changes in the network occur in a strikingly cumulative fashion. If the dissolution of a particular type of relationship leads directly to the loss of four links in the partners' social networks, we must then look into the social features of each of *those* relationship dissolutions, and so on. We have dissolution raised to a power. Thus, differences in the social impact of the dissolution of different types of relationships are likely to be quantitatively striking. These quantitative effects have implications not only for the daily interaction process, but also for the structure of the former partners' subjective worlds.

Cognitive Aspects of Relationship Dissolution

Since the dissolution of a relationship involves changes in the daily lives of the former partners, some change in their routine thoughts is inevitable. At the very least, they will no longer have to interpret new events connected with the dissolved relationship or to assimilate new relationship memories into their biography. The breadth and depth of this cognitive impact will vary tremendously, in large part as a function of the centrality of the former relationship in the partners' lives and the extent of their personal and structural commitment to it. My discussion of this variability is organized into to two major sections. First, I will present a general discussion of three major processes which contribute to the reconstruction of thought following a relationship dissolution. Because these processes can potentially produce change in almost any aspect of the former partners' thinking, the second section will be more narrowly focused, attending to the transformation of one's biography.

Basic processes of cognitive reconstruction

The Impact of Network Changes. Any relationship involves, by definition, some regularity of social interaction, the elimination of which will produce changes in the development of one's memories, experiences, and anticipations. If the cognitive elements of such changes in one's life were mere one-to-one representations of them, the cognitive features of relationship dissolution would be no different from the cognitive features of any change in one's everyday life. But, as Alfred Schutz (1967, 1970) has forcefully demonstrated, drawing upon the work of Henri Bergson, Edmund Husserl, and Max Weber, human beings do not experience their environment in its infinitely differentiable, temporally flowing reality, but in its retrospective translation and interpretation into a world of typifications. It is a major tenet of the phenomenological perspective that this world is socially constructed, that we develop our understanding of the life which we live and the environment in which it is embedded largely through conversations with other people. Every relationship has an impact on the version of socially constructed reality through which participants make sense of the world, and some relationships are more important than others. As Berger and Kellner (1970) put it,

"The plausibility and stability of the world, as socially defined, is dependent upon the strength and continuity of significant relationships in which conversations about this world can be continually carried on." (p. 53)

Thus, the loss of the dissolved relationship produces cognitive change beyond the effects of the mere elimination of the concrete events which comprise it; relationship loss also involves the loss of a perspective. All of the other network changes which follow from the dissolution also involve the change of socially developed understandings.

There are a number of aspects of any relationship which can reasonably be expected to affect the cognitive impact of the elimination of its particular events and perspectives. As I discuss each of these in turn, it should be noted that one would expect relationships to which individuals are strongly personally and structurally committed to be "high" on every dimension which produces cognitive impact (Berger and Kellner, 1970, would point to the particular example of the marital relationship). On the other hand, this is not to say that the dissolution of relatively uncommitted relationships cannot have a tremendous cognitive impact, as some of the cited examples will suggest.

One of the major determinants of the cognitive impact of a relationship, and thus of its dissolution, is its *cognitive uniqueness*. If its events and perspectives are duplicated in other relationships or are easily replaced by newly developed relationships, the cognitive impact of dissolution is likely to be minimal. One may, for example, be involved in a friendship with a coworker which involves lunch every day. If her perspectives are similar to those of other coworkers then when she moves out of town another friend may essentially replace her in one's cognitive world. But if she was a fervent advocate of the violent overthrow of capitalism or a committed Christian missionary, the loss of the relationship would be likely to have considerable impact. Although uniqueness and commitment are probably far from perfectly correlated, as partners become more personally and structurally committed to the maintenance of their relationship, they tend to feel safer in allowing unique aspects of their thinking to be displayed in their encounters with each other. Thus, uniqueness and commitment are probably also related to a second important cognitive characteristic of the relationship: depth.

By *depth*, I mean the extent to which the relationship is tied to important aspects of the partners' identities. Altman and Taylor (1973) have devoted considerable attention to the processes by which mutual self-disclosures become deeper as relationships develop, and this process is reflected in the self-concept component of personal commitment discussed above. Many theorists consider the self-concept to be *the* most important aspect of one's cognitive system (e.g. Mead, 1934) and the social confirmation of self is one of the cornerstones of symbolic interaction theory in social psychology (e.g. Hewitt, 1976). Much of the information about ourselves comes from interaction with significant others (Kuhn, 1964), and much of our behavior is based on our notions of who and what we are. Thus, the loss of a relationship with a person who knows us well (and therefore provides confirmation of deeply important aspects of self) will have a more important cognitive impact than will the loss of a relationship which takes place primarily at a surface level.

The final cognitive feature of lost relationships to be discussed here is *breadth*. Relationships vary tremendously in what Parsons (1951) called diffuseness. Some relationships have a very narrow focus, involving interactions which never go beyond the confines of some particular task. For example, I may have an acquaintance with whom I play tennis once a week and with whom conversations are narrowly focused on our respective games. On the other hand, I have another acquaintance with whom conversations range widely from the quality of food at a local pub to abstract political ideology to the pleasures of Impressionist art. The loss of the former acquaintance will affect my perspectives on tennis only; the latter will affect my perspectives on a wide range of topics which are therefore more commonly relevant to my everyday life.

In summary, the breadth, depth and uniqueness of the dissolved relationship all have important implications for the extent of the cognitive impact of the dissolution. But in addition to the loss of the particular relationship in question, the dissolution will have an impact on the wider social context in which one's perspectives are developed, confirmed, and altered. These are the changes in network membership discussed in the previous section and the changes in the content in relationships which remain intact. It may now be helpful, therefore, to present a few examples which illustrate how changes in network membership and changes in the nature of continuing relationships contribute to cognitive change.

It is clear that the loss of a close daily relationship with children which often accompanies divorce for one of the former spouses could produce major cognitive transformations (Lerner and Spanier, 1978). Purrington (1980a,b) has identified a number of major ways in which children alter the thinking of their parents, including providing the parents with an opportunity to participate in the world of childhood and forcing the parents to face value issues which they could more easily avoid if they were not responsible for their children's moral development. If the custodial parent has not previously had major childrearing responsibilities, all of the effects of regular interaction with children will become part of his or her cognitive structure. Even parents who experience no major change in their responsibilities for their children may find that new avenues of communication have opened up between parent and child. The experience of dissolution will have made formerly private aspects of the parents' relationship more accessible to children, leading to conversations which will provide the parent with new access to the children's perspective on himself or herself and on the marital and parental relationships. The children may also be more able or willing to say things they never could have dealt with in the presence of the other parent.

To the extent that the dissolved relationship had provided a major source of intimate conversation, the former partners may open themselves up to new sets of others to find the solace and advice which cannot now be provided by one's former partner. Although loss of a mere acquaintance may generate very little need to develop new lines of communication with others, the loss of a significant other may prompt one to become a friend to one's children, to go home to mother, to seek new romantic attachments, to talk more with one's friends or to seek a professional listener. Each of these alternatives will offer the possibility of learning new perspectives.

Another major source of new conversation will be the effects of dissolution on other people's ideas regarding appropriate ways of interacting with the former partners. Changes in privacy norms following the dissolution may radically transform information flow even before the networks formally change. The reactions of others which were kept to themselves out of respect for the privacy of a hallowed relationship may now legitimately be voiced, as in "You know I really always thought he was a bum". Others may now define one as accessible to formerly forbidden types of discourse, as when friends of a formerly married couple see fit to make passes at the newly available partners.

Finally, dissolution may produce exposure to new meaning systems through interaction with the experts who now pervade private life. Lawyers teach us to view former spouses as adversaries, while divorce mediators teach us to listen to each other and negotiate. Both of these universes of discourse differ dramatically from the love system in which a marriage began or the conflict system in which it may have ended, and of course neither of them is generally involved in other kinds of relationships. The psychological counselors who help us address the personal difficulties of dissolution will introduce their particular version of reality in ways identified by Frank (1974) and welfare workers to whom we turn for financial aid embed our lives in a bureaucratic system of definitions (Weiss, 1973).

The dissolution process and the need to explain change

All in all, it is clear that the major cognitive impact of relationship dissolution will follow from the changes in social interaction which flow from it. To the extent that the dissolution produces a great many network changes and/or changes in particularly deep, broad or unique relationships, the cognitive impact will be extensive. To the extent that the dissolution is one that produces little change in one's network or produces changes which involve only shallow, narrow and common relationships, the cognitive impact will be less pervasive. But even if the social changes are minimal, there are still two other reasons why relationship dissolution can be expected to produce cognitive change.

First, to the extent that the partners are still personally or structurally committed to their relationship, the process of dissolution itself will require major cognitive work. On the one hand, a major aspect of the pain of dissolution is the suffering involved in the impact of structural commitments. One may have to face the loss of irretrievable investments, deal with the reactions of significant others, struggle with the legal system, and adapt to possibly unattractive changes in the structure of one's life. All of these processes will introduce one to new ways of thinking, and the events involved will each leave their sediment in the experience of the individual. The dissolution process will also require cognitive changes which serve to neutralize structural and personal commitments in order to facilitate dissolution. A committed relationship may never end if the partners do not change their views of the attractiveness of the alternatives available to them, their understanding of the termination procedures, or their beliefs about the morality of relationship change; but a relatively uncommitted relationship may be dissolved without this extensive cognitive restructuring.

Second, to the extent that the relationship was a central and/or committed aspect of one's life, its dissolution is an event which requires interpretation. Why did the relationship end? If the relationship was uncommitted, the answers to this question may be trivial and produce little cognitive change. When a coworker acquaintance is transferred to another city, the loss is easily interpreted and requires little thought. A divorce, on the other hand, cries out for a major consideration of important aspects of one's self and one's life. The fact of the dissolution forces itself upon the consciousness of the partners and requires more than mere acknowledgement; it requires interpretation. Why should this be particularly the case for committed relationships? The first answer is "hedonic relevance" (Jones and Davis, 1965), i.e., the rewards and costs involved in the event. The concept of commitment speaks directly to the extent to which dissolution will change the quality of one's life, either improving it or making it worse. For the individual who has a dissolution imposed upon a relationship to which he/she is still personally committed, the costs are psychologically immediate. But even for the person who is no longer personally committed to the relationship, and may have initiated the dissolution, the costs will vary considerably as a function of structural commitment. Changes which have important consequences for us need to be understood, so that our understanding of their causes can be utilized for the development of plans of action for the future (Johnson and Ewens, 1971).

Another answer regarding the relationship of commitment to the necessity of interpretation is the role of change in directing one's attention. The constant, the ongoing, the unchanging are all easily ignored. Of course, relationships are constantly changing even when they remain intact, but a dissolution is a change which has been labeled, and the labeling enhances the difference, silences the sameness:

"In the flux of life, it is the changes which get named that are dwelled upon, and the changes dwelled upon that get named."   (Travisano, 1970, p. 598).

Whether a dissolution gets named or not is in part a function of the extent to which the ending of the relationship involves an important violation of cultural expectation, a major aspect of structural commitment. In the American vernacular, we have no word for the ending of a friendship, but a romantic involvement which has gone beyond a certain stage "breaks up" and spouses get "divorced" or "separated" or "deserted" or "widowed". We name the endings of relationships which were supposed to last but did not, and our attention is then focused on the cause of the premature dissolution.

Thus, when a dissolution involves noticeable change, when it gets labeled, when it violates expectations or when it produces major costs or rewards, the individuals involved struggle to interpret. Their interpretive efforts will interact with the procedures of dissolution and the changes in their social networks to produce changes in a wide variety of aspects of their cognitive worlds. One central aspect of this cognitive world is biography.

Transformation of biography

The changes of perspective which go with major changes in the structure of one's social life—what Berger (1963) and Travisano (1970) call "alternations"—contain at their core transformations of biography, and relationships differ in the extent to which their dissolution will require or facilitate a "rewriting" of biography. The dissolution of some relationships will have little impact on the former partners' lives; other dissolutions will offer "the chance of a new lifetime" (Brown et al., 1976).

The process of reconstructing one's own biography involves three temporally distinguishable components. First, one alters one's view of the past, one's history. Second, the present tense of biography may change; former partners will develop new notions of who and what they are, and their identities and self concepts will be transformed. Third, the future will be expected to be different as one's plans of action are altered by the relationship dissolution and the social processes that accompany it.

History. As former partners struggle to reinterpret the end of their relationship, their view of the past will inevitably be altered. Our past is always changing as we gather new information on it, forget details or even major events and perceive things from the new perspective of our constantly changing experience. The formerly minor disagreement about housecleaning may loom large in the context of a divorce proceeding. The new knowledge concerning one's former spouse's daytime activities which the children let slip to their new custodial parent may completely alter that parent's view of the dissolved relationship.

Although these two examples are focused on redefinition of the dissolved relationship, the rewriting of one's history may encompass any aspect of the past. First, any of the events of the past can be reinterpreted in light of the new general perspectives which may have developed from the process and consequences of dissolution. For example, the formerly traditional housewife who is exposed to a feminist perspective on the job may now completely reinterpret her early childhood years in terms of their impact on her sex-role ideology. Second, neither the biographical conversations which took place in the dissolved relationship nor the new ones which take place in one's network are necessarily focused only on relationship-related events. I have personally experienced the amusing situation, to which Berger and Kellner (1970) refer, in which my wife has corrected my recounting of events which took place in my life long before she and I met. The nature of one's relationship with the persons to whom autobiographical stories are told will shape presentational form and content (Goffman, 1959), and storytelling is the great sedimenter of one's history.

Identity. The present tense of biography is identity, and relationship dissolution may affect all three major sources of information about self. The first major source of information is feedback from the environment regarding who and what one is. As Stone (1962, p. 93) put it, "One's identity is established when others *place* him as a social object by assigning him the same words of identity that he appropriates for himself or *assumes.* ..." Sometimes this information from others is relatively independent of the actions of the individual; for example, others may react directly to one's relationship status: "Treated as irresponsible financially, as 'fair game' sexually, often as psychologically disabled, she (the divorced woman) must fight these images in each negotiation between herself and those people and bureaucracies around her." (Brown *et al.*, 1976) More frequently, however, feedback from the environment regarding self is a response to the "announcements" of which Stone speaks. One's self concept works in concert with tactical considerations to produce presentations of self which are then confirmed or denied by their consequences. Sometimes these presentations are offered to other people (Goffman, 1959) who respond to them with verbal or non-verbal communications which confirm or deny one's sense of self, at other times the feedback may come from a non-social environment as one's success or failure at tasks provides information about self.

The second major source of information about self may, interestingly enough, be the announcements themselves. As Bem (1972) has pointed out, when people do not know for sure what they are, they may make inferences from their own behavior, as does one woman quoted in Weiss' (1975, p. 98) study of marital separation: "In separating from someone you discover in yourself things you had never felt before in your life ... now I discover, wow, I can hate!'' Thus, a dissolution may affect one's self concept by placing one in a position to behave in new ways. The impact of one's actions in this self-perception process will be enhanced if the relationship was one which was central enough to one's identity that its dissolution creates conditions of ambiguity which lead one to search for cues regarding one's self. Another condition which will contribute to the self-perception process is frequently described by the formerly married. Brown *et al.* (1976, p. 123) quote one woman as saying, ''The hard part is having to make important decisions alone—not having anyone to share these with, having the feeling of sole responsibility.'' Sole responsibility may be a hardship and it may provide an exhilarating sense of self-control, but it also provides fertile ground for inferences about self from behaviour.

The third major source of information regarding self is inferences which one makes from already clearly identified aspects of self. These inferences are based on the implicit theories of personality (stereotypes, if you will) which are a part of learned perspectives on social life. For example, the woman who is exposed to new feminist perspectives on the job following her divorce may develop new ideas regarding what women are like, and therefore, what *she* is like.

Plans of Action. The final component of biography is the future. To the extent that former partners were committed to the long-term maintenance of their relationship, they will have had a future which may in large part have been developed around the structure of that relationship. The dependent spouse, for example, will have had a future which centered around the assumption of full-time house- and child-care responsibilities and no work for wages. After divorce, the situation is likely to change dramatically and a new future will have to be constructed. Although commitment will usually be a major factor, there are interesting cases in which a fully expected dissolution is not really faced until it occurs. Rubin's (1979) recent discussion of the reconstruction of the future which is the core of the so-called ''empty nest'' problem faced by mothers upon dissolution of their custodial relationship with their children is an informative example. Whenever one's future was built around a relationship or had not been constructed beyond it, its dissolution will require the reconstruction of plans of action.

Concluding Remarks

By now it is clear that the discussion of commitment and the social and cognitive features of relationship dissolution can only arbitrarily be separated. While there are aspects of each which are to some extent independent of the others, the changes in thought which follow from a relationship dissolution are in large part a function of commitment to the relationship and the social features of dissolution which follow from that commitment.

It is all too easy to deal with relationship dissolution as an individual or dyadic phenomenon. This discussion of the social and cognitive features of dissolution has made it clear, however, that even the seemingly most individual and psychological aspects of relationship dissolution, such as changes in cognition, are supremely social in character. We cannot ignore the wider social context of networks and structural commitments in our quest for an understanding of the lives of dyads and the individuals embedded within them.

Acknowledgements

Thanks are due to Susan Shuman for the varieties of help without which this paper would never have been completed, and to Steve Duck for his good-natured tolerance of my shortcomings. My work was supported in part by the Central Fund for Research, College of Liberal Arts, The Pennsylvania State University.

CHAPTER 4

The Joining and the Parting of the Ways

William G. Graziano and Lynn Mather Musser

In an article written for a volume on consumer behavior, Alan Kerckhoff (1978) reviewed the literature on patterns of marriage formation and dissolution—as if wise consumers would do well to know the product they are buying, lest they invest in an inferior product. A few examples will provide a flavor of the kinds of data that have been collected. The rate of divorce in the United States has gone up considerably in the last 80 years, but increases have been irregular, and apparently respond to wars and economic depressions. A closer analysis reveals that certain persons are more vulnerable to divorce (e.g., persons in religiously mixed marriages) than are other persons, but that Catholic–Protestant marriages in which the wife was Catholic survived more often than those in which the husband was Catholic. Half of all people who obtain a divorce remarry within three years, but a female divorcee of 40 is twice as likely to remarry as a widow of the same age.

Yet wise consumers will have great difficulty in making a rational decision on the basis of such information alone since there are several limitations to this kind of data. The focus is generally on distal social-structural correlates of the established institution of marriage, so the data are only *suggestive* of causes for the dissolution of marriage. They tell us relatively little about the proximal processes that operate within a marriage to influence its maintenance or dissolution. Furthermore, generalization to future time periods, much less other kinds of relationships, is hazardous in the absence of information about specific underlying interpersonal processes. The elucidation of such interpersonal processes may help us not only to refine our predictions about dissolution, but also to uncover general principles underlying other kinds of relationships such as non-marital romantic relationships, friendships, and children's peer groups. It is also possible that many processes in relationships reflect a relationship's developmental components, complete with milestones and transformations.

It is the purpose of the present chapter to investigate relationship processes that influence the course of those relationships. The ultimate goal is a model or approach to relationships that will predict and explain why some relationships are maintained and others are dissolved. The focus will be psychological, in that the primary unit of analysis will be processes operating within individual persons. The context for these processes will be the particular relationship within which the individual acts or expects to act.

Three Basic Issues for an Approach to Relationship Dissolution

Before we can build such a model of relationship dissolution with reasonable predictive and explanatory power, it is first necessary to consider three basic issues. These are: the idea that relationships occur across time; the influence of affect; and the focus of present theoretical styles in this area.

Sequences

At the very least, relationships involve sequences of behavior. For example, a period of mutual excitement in a relationship may be followed by a period of relaxed tolerance, which is then followed by a "make-or-break" period. Some theorists have even argued that relationships, like individual persons, have stages of development and whatever position one takes on the issues of sequences, stages, and development, one must at least entertain the possibility that different variables may have different effects on relationships at different times in their course (e.g., Duck, 1973, 1977; Huesmann and Levinger, 1976). A fundamental issue, then, centers on how a relationship's course can be segmented. For heuristic purposes, and for reasons elaborated later in this chapter, we will consider relationships to occur in a sequence of three segments: an initiation period, the maintenance/channeling period, and the dissolution period. No strong assumptions are made about invariance or reversability of the sequence, or qualitative differences between periods in the proposed sequence. We claim no originality in proposing such a sequence: we merely hope to build on the work of others (e.g., Cairns, 1979; Duck, 1977; Hinde, 1979).

Affect

The second issue revolves around the role of feelings and affect in relationships. It is no small paradox that a great deal of the literature in the areas most relevant to relationships has paid lip service to affect but has emphasized "cold cognitions". Studies of causal attributions for relationship decline, for example, are more typical than studies of affective reactions to relationship decline. Clearly, cognitions and affect are mutually interdependent, and any dualistic bifurcation is likely to lead to a profitless trip across the trackless wastes of the mind–body problem (Isen and Hastorf, in press). There is evidence that one person's cognitions about another can have an impact on how the relationship proceeds (Snyder *et al.*, 1977; Snyder, 1979a). Still, close examination of many cognitively oriented relationship studies reveals that they are generally not intended to predict the course of relationships, but to provide the participant's retrospective phenomenological account of events (e.g., Harvey *et al.*, 1978; Orvis *et al.*, 1976). The importance of cognitions, relative to feelings, as determinants of behavior is now being challenged (Zajonc, 1980), and it may prove to be a costly strategic mistake to continue to emphasize cognitions and attributions, and to de-emphasize affect, if our goal is to predict and explain the course of relationships.

Although it would be difficult to find a "relationship" researcher who denies the importance of affect, it would be less difficult to find relationship researchers who will go to considerable lengths to avoid explicitly motivational constructs in their own work on relationships. Of course, the terms "affect" and "motivational" are not synonymous, but, at least historically, motivation was thought to have affective, hedonic qualities. The relationship researcher who avoids explicitly motivational constructs may be following the lead of the psychological learning theorists (e.g., Bolles, 1967), who have attempted to explain motivation largely in terms of external events. For these theorists, need-related affective and motivational processes were simply transferred to external "incentives" or "reinforcers", and potentially important processes—both within the organism and between the organism and the environment—were ignored.

For the relationship researcher, there are two serious problems with ignoring motivational constructs and de-emphasizing their affective components. First, if one defines motivation in P. T. Young's sense that "motivation is the process (a) of arousing or initiating behavior, (b) of sustaining an activity in progress, and (c) channeling activity into a given course" (Young, 1961, cited in Madsen, 1968), then it becomes clearer how motivational constructs may be useful for studying the course of relationships. That is, relationships are initiated, maintained, channeled, and dissolved; the factors that influence each of these processes, especially the affective factors, should be of interest to the relationship researcher.

Second, most relationship researchers rely on affective, motivational constructs, whether they are stated explicitly by the researcher or not. Even the very cognitively oriented attribution researchers assume that attributions are made because persons are motivated by needs to predict and explain their environment (Berscheid et al., 1976; Berscheid and Graziano, 1979; Kelley, 1972, especially p. 22). Presumably, when these needs are not met there are affective and behavioral consequences. By making explicit the motivational constructs assumed to be operative, we may make it easier to uncover processes important to relationships.

Theoretical focus

The third issue is related to the first two issues. For most researchers interested in personal relationships, the "parent discipline" has been the social psychology of interpersonal attraction (Duck, 1981). Consequently, most researchers have attempted to use established social psychological theories to explain relationships. While some of these theories have been useful (e.g., Kelley, 1979; Levinger, 1979; Walster et al., 1978), on the whole they tend to be cognitively oriented, and have tended to produce a narrow view of relationships. In recent years, a small group of researchers has recognized the potential of other disciplines' literature for understanding relationships. For example, we may learn a great deal about relationship dynamics from the comparative and developmental studies of attachment (e.g., Cairns, 1966, 1979; Hinde, 1979), or from studies of "addictive" behaviors (e.g., Solomon, 1980). It is interesting that these alternative approaches assign an important role to affect.

This is not to imply that social psychologists have not made important contributions to the understanding of relationships. In this chapter, we will draw heavily on many concepts proposed by social psychological theorists. For example, in a 1970 paper, Bernard Murstein drew a distinction between two types of social encounters: "open-field" and "closed-field" encounters. An open-field encounter involves the casual interaction of persons who are not yet well acquainted, and whose interactions are largely "voluntary". Examples are "mixers", presence in a large class at the beginning of a semester, and brief contacts at the office. A closed-field encounter, on the other hand, involves the interactions of persons who, by reason of some situational constraint, are "required" to deal with each other. Examples are students in a small seminar in a college, partners in a law-firm, a "boss" and his/her employee, and a doctor–nurse team working together in the same clinic. This distinction between open-field and closed-field encounters will be useful for examining the different processes operating in relationships.

In this chapter, we will consider relationships as having a course, roughly divided into a sequence consisting of an initiation period, a maintenance and channeling period, and a dissolution period. A primary focus within each period will be the affective and motivational components of the individual person's behavior. It will be argued that (a) both the initiation and dissolution periods of a relationship can be usefully conceptualized as open-field encounters, while the maintenance period can be conceptualized as a closed-field encounter, (b) different processes operating in the relationship periods may be related to different motivational systems activated by open-field and closed-field encounters, and (c) processes operating in the initiation period will cast a shadow over the processes operating in subsequent periods. For reasons to be elaborated later in this chapter, more attention will be devoted to processes within the initiation and maintenance/channeling periods than to the dissolution period. In brief, it will be argued that processes occurring within these two periods will have important implications for the dissolution period.

The Initiation of Relationships

When researchers investigate personal relationships from the social psychological perspective of interpersonal attraction, it is usually the case that the initiation period is their principal concern. The large number of studies on physical attractiveness, similarity and attraction, and proximity all testify to these researchers' interest in the processes that lead one person to choose another particular person from an array of many others for further interaction. This research has been criticized, however, on the grounds that these studies involve "superficial" and often trivial encounters between persons, that the outcomes are constrained by limited methodology, and that these results provide relatively little information about relationships generally (e.g., Rosenblatt, 1974). While we are sympathetic with many of these criticisms, and while we will add several other criticisms to the bill of particulars, these critics seem to have overlooked an important point: relationships do occur across time, and the factors that influence the initiation of relationships may well steer the relationship in its course (Berscheid and Graziano, 1979). Thus, from the perspective of the present paper, the most serious deficit in the attraction-based research is *not* the alleged superficiality of initial encounters nor limited methodology, but a more general theoretical failure to identify the needs that motivate relationship initiations and how these needs influence subsequent aspects of the relationship.

The role of needs in the initiation period

There are problems in proposing that the course of relationships should be investigated from the perspective of need-based motivational processes. As noted earlier, many psychological theorists have emphasized the external determinants of behavior, relocating motivational properties in stimuli rather than persons. Many behavioral scientists consider needs as unnecessary theoretical "waystations", and as non-observable, internal, quasi-mental events with questionable causal status (see, for example, Skinner's, 1975, recent discussion of the "steep and thorny path" to a science of behavior). As the operationist and behaviorist movements began to lose their revolutionary fervor, more theorists were willing to consider needs as hypothetical constructs (see, for example, Tesser, 1980). None the less, many behavioral scientists still retain an unreasonably hostile stance when "needs" (especially non-physiological needs) are proposed (cf. Atkinson, 1981). For present purposes, needs will be conceptualized as non-observable hypothetical constructs whose attributes and effects can be observed and measured through operational definitions. These needs will be generally conceptualized as having affective components.

Another problem in proposing a need-based system is the precise specification of the needs and the mechanism for satisfying the needs. We will postpone for the moment a discussion of the first part of this problem (specification of needs), so that we can address the second part (mechanism for satisfaction). Without offering a detailed rationale, we will take the position that the mechanisms for need satisfaction in relationships will be different for different periods in the relationship. For the initiation period, where the principal focus is the activation of behavior directed towards a particular object or person in an open field, we take the position that *expectations* about the need-satisfying properties of objects or persons will be related to behavior sequences directed towards that object or person. If

Jonathan feels a need to play his oboe with another person, and he expects that Lisa would be more willing to play with him than Tony, he is more likely to initiate interaction with Lisa than with Tony. For the initiation period, we would anticipate that expectations would be derived from stereotypes, personal reputations, observation, or limited social interaction. Furthermore, we will take the position that Lisa's abilities to meet Jonathan's expectations, her actual behavior, or the "reinforcement" that these partners actually provide each other are less important for the initiation period than are expectations. Finally, we will take the position that expectations about the need-satisfying potential of other persons in an open-field encounter will be systematically influenced by need levels. For example, as motivational levels increase, expectations about others' potential to satisfy that need may also increase (e.g., Stephan *et al.,* 1971).

Now let us turn our attention to the specification of needs associated with the initiation of relationships. First, it is important to recognize that the issue of needs and the initiation of relationships is of interest to a wide range of scientists, although the issues have been interpreted in diverse ways and given different labels. For example, biologists and comparative psychologists have been interested in the reasons for the fact that some species of animals are solitary (e.g., weasels, moose) and much less likely to initiate contact with conspecifics than are other species (e.g., sheep). Even within certain species there are differences in patterns of social initiation in different subgroups. While species differences probably reflect important genetic differences, subpopulation differences within species may be attributable to experience differences within groups. Relatively little is known about this important topic (see Rosenblum *et al.,* 1975), but within species noted for their "sociableness" (e.g. *Macaques*) inadequate ability to initiate social interaction is associated with pathology (Suomi and Harlow, 1975).

Second, workers interested primarily in human behavior have suggested a wide variety of needs that may induce persons to enter one or another kind of relationship. Rather than listing all possible candidates, we shall consider in detail how one need has been theoretically implicated in one kind of relationship, see how parts of this theoretical system have been investigated, and note the strengths and weaknesses of these investigative procedures.

An example: Reik's need/motivation system. The need/motivation system we shall consider in detail was proposed by the psychoanalyst Theodore Reik (1944, 1957) who suggested that "Everything is all right with the person who is in love, but all is not well with the person who is about to fall in love" (Reik, 1957, p. 32). In essence, Reik proposes that the person most likely to initiate a romantic relationship is a person who is filled with self-doubt and self-abnegation. These persons *need* someone or something that will help them evaluate themselves more positively ("The man lost his soul to a girl to save it").

But who will be the target of an initiation attempt? The target most likely to be selected from the open field is a person who seems to the perceiver as cool, self-confident, and self contained. Something in the target person's

> "very existence and indifference seems to make us more aware of the discord in ourselves. That she [the target] is so unperturbed and unperturbable seems to excite and bewilder us, makes us slightly resentful, almost offended, and this is an excellent mixture for the preparation of love." (Reik, 1957, p. 49)

Feelings of envy follow, and these feelings are a necessary condition for falling in love. Thus, the need to be satisfied with the self is the distal cause for the initiation of a romantic relationship. When this need is not met, affective reactions motivate the person to choose a target person for a relationship who possesses qualities that the perceiver desires for him/herself; perceivers select from the open field targets believed to be similar to their own "ideal self".

There is another aspect of Reik's work that makes it noteworthy: unlike virtually any other theorist, Reik suggests processes that underlie relationship dissolution. Love fades because reality cannot match our image of our love object. In Reik's words, "Thus, the falling out of love means really falling out of a dream, the daydream of a better self" (Reik, 1957, p. 88).

Recent attraction research and needs. Parts of Reik's conjectures about needs and romantic love have been investigated in the research of Karen and Kenneth Dion. In one study, Dion and Dion (1975) asked college students to complete paper-and-pencil self-report measures of self-esteem, defensiveness, and estimates of the intensity and frequency of romantic love experiences. Persons low in self-esteem reported more intense romantic experiences than did persons high in self-esteem. Furthermore, these experiences showed some stability within persons: there were significant correlation between persons' self-reported intensity of love and duration of the love experiences across successive experiences of love.

The Reikian interpretation of this study is complicated, however, by the finding that self-reports of love are an interactive function of self-esteem and defensiveness: individuals simultaneously high in self-esteem and low in defensiveness reported greater frequency of romantic love than did individuals simultaneously low in both self-esteem and defensiveness. A further complication is that high self-esteem persons, not the low self-esteem persons predicted by Reik, showed the greatest congruence in their descriptions of "ideal self" and romantic partners. Finally, there were sex differences in self-reports of love experiences: females reported greater love, more rewarding love experiences, and greater trust in their love partners, than did males.

In another study, Dion and Dion (1973) investigated the relationship between individual differences in locus of control and self-reports of romantic love in college students. According to Rotter (1966), individual differences in locus of control reflect two different types of generalized expectancies. "Internals" typically view events as being under their personal control, while "Externals" consider events affecting them as resulting from forces beyond their personal control. Since the cultural stereotype of romantic love is that it is a powerful external force, and since individuals' feelings of vulnerability and influenceability become more salient as intimacy increases, Dion and Dion hypothesized that Internals would report less frequent and less intense experiences of romantic love than would Externals.

Results indicated that proportionally fewer Internals than Externals reported having experienced romantic love, but Internals did not differ from Externals in total frequency of romantic love experiences. Internals rated their subjective experience of love as less mysterious and volatile, and tended to have less idealistic views of love than did Externals. Contrary to prediction, however, among males romantic love was reported to last longer for Internals than for Externals. As in the other study, there were sex differences in self-report of love experiences: proportionally more females reported having experienced romantic love, and agreed less with a cynical view of love (but agreed more with a pragmatic view), than did males.

Beyond their obvious substantive relevance there are several reasons why these two studies are discussed in detail here. In one sense, they are prototypes of current rigorous, methodologically sophisticated, attraction-oriented research on important relationships. They can also be used to highlight some of the strengths and weaknesses of this type of recent relationship research. In terms of strengths, these studies show how individual difference measures, derived from established psychological theory, can be used to probe needs and relationship processes. This is not the ideal way of dealing with needs, but it is at least a reasonable starting place (cf. Atkinson, 1981). In terms of weaknesses, they do not explicitly discuss needs or motivational processes systematically, although several motivational constructs are implicated (e.g., need to control the environment). If needs had been dealt with more explicitly and systematically, some general patterns might have been more apparent. For example, is there a common reason for the finding that both women and Internals report love as a more "rational", pragmatic phenomenon?

Another weakness in the prototypical study is the focus. From the perspective of the present paper, attraction-oriented researchers focus neither on the dyadic nor the sequential nature of relationships, but on the cognitive/attitudinal activities of one individual. Consequently, we know almost nothing about how need-motivated initiation attempts influence choices in open-field encounters, how these needs might steer relationships into closed-field encounters, nor even whether different needs might play different roles in different periods in a relationship (but see the treatment of unrequited love discussed in Dion and Dion, 1975, p. 51).

Whatever the validity of Reik's conjectures, or the limitations of the prototypical investigations of relationship phenomena, some promising leads emerge. First, it may be useful to consider relationship processes, particularly initiation processes, in terms of needs and motivational systems. Some likely candidates are needs associated with (a) retaining a positive evaluation of the self, and (b) feeling effective in dealing with the environment. Second, it may be useful, for the time being, to use individual difference measures to probe the impact of needs on relationship processes. Third, the needs that contribute to the initiation of a relationship may not only influence the maintenance of that relationship, but may also provide the framework for its potential dissolution. For example, a person seeking to retain a positive self-evaluation may initiate a relationship with an extraordinarily competent partner. As the relationship progresses and the initiator gains competence similar to the partner, rivalrous competition may occur. Such rivalrous competition could lead to breakdown and dissolution unless some other processes intervene. Thus, the same needs that lead to initiation may influence maintenance and dissolution.

Relationship initiation, needs, and attention

Although may theorists have attempted to forge links between needs, cognitive activities, and behavior (e.g., Atkinson, 1981; Atkinson and McClelland, 1948; Bruner and Goodman, 1947; Freud, 1900, Hebb, 1949; Mowrer, 1938), the potential relevance of these variables to relationships has not been developed. Part of the reason for this lack of development may have been the apparent dissimilarity between the different theorists' conceptualizations of motives. Despite the diversity of constructs and theoretical mechanisms proposed, however, there are some remarkable similarities in the predictions made by these different theories. Without doing great injustice to these theories, it is possible to extract at least one general prediction and, in keeping with the purpose of the present chapter, rephrase it in terms of needs. Stripped of excess theoretical appendages, several theories predict that when needs are activated there is a narrowing of attention, cognitive activities, and the behavioral repertoire. Activities instrumental to the satisfaction of the need are likely to occur.

Three of these processes have implications for relationship initiation and thus, we will argue, for liability to dissolution: (a) when needs are activated, the perception of the size of the open field will be reduced; (b) perceptual and cognitive processes will be focused on a small subset of persons in the narrowed, but still open, field who are expected to be potentially able to satisfy the need; and (c) attributes of persons relevant to the need will be emphasized relative to need-irrelevant attributes. In sum, relationship initiation may be conceptualized as a need-induced narrowing of an open field.

To proceed further into our discussion of needs and relationship processes, a brief digression on the nature of initiation will be necessary. Although relationships in progress involve more than one person, relationships in both the initiation and dissolution periods may be usefully conceptualized as activities involving one person. For example, Levinger and Snoek (1972) offer the reasonable suggestion that a relationship begins when one person becomes "aware" of another person. For present purposes, the individual activity in the initiation period that we shall emphasize is attention. Attention has been related to needs and motivational states (e.g., Bruner and Goodman, 1947; Erdelyi, 1974), several different social behaviors (e.g., Berscheid and Graziano, 1979; Tesser and Reardon, in press), and may be conceptualized as a kind of perceptual narrowing process (e.g., Berlyne, 1974; Neisser, 1967). Thus we shall argue that one person initiates a relationship with another person when the latter is the object of selective and sustained attention from the former (Berscheid and Graziano, 1979).

The need for effective control. A study by Ellen Berscheid and her colleagues provides an example of how these conceptualizations can be used. Berscheid et al. (1976) investigated the hypothesis that people have a need to feel effective in dealing with other persons. This need is activated when a person recognizes that another person has some control over the rewards or punishments that the former may receive from the latter. In the terminology of Thibaut and Kelley (1959), the need is activated when the former is "outcome dependent" on the latter. The degree of outcome dependency is determined by the intensity of an individual's needs for effective control, as well as by the magnitude of rewards and punishments that the other is expected to be able to bring to bear in the particular relationship. These hypotheses were investigated within the context of the initiation of heterosexual dating relationships.

College students volunteered to date only the person(s) assigned to them for five weeks. Half were led to believe they would be dating one person exclusively, while the other half thought they would be dating five different people over the five-week period. After receiving the name of their first (or only) date, volunteers saw a videotaped discussion involving three other "volunteers" (actually confederates) of the opposite sex. Half way through the videotape, the discussants mentioned their names, and the subject "discovered" one of the discussants was his/her assigned date.

Prior to the mentioning of names, volunteers divided their attention equally among the three discussants. After names were mentioned, however, significantly more attention was directed to the anticipated date than to the other two persons. This effect was intensified when an exclusive relationship was expected. Furthermore, volunteers remembered more details about their expected dates, were more extreme, confident, and positive in their trait attributions, and liked their expected dates more than they did non-dates.

In terms of the original hypotheses, it seems that when the volunteers' need for effective control was activated by the recognition of outcome dependency, attention was directed towards the object of the need and the open field was narrowed. Perceptual and cognitive activities (i.e., memory and attributions) were focused on that person expected to satisfy the need. Furthermore, there was a "facilitative distortion" of the attributes of the expected date (e.g., dates were seen as warmer and less sexually prohibitive) relative to the non-dates.

Berscheid *et al.* (1976) also considered the possibility that there are chronic individual differences in needs for effective control and perceptions of outcome dependency, and that these individual differences are related to relationship initiation processes. Mark Snyder (1974, 1979b) has developed an individual difference measure of "Self-Monitoring" which may tap needs for effective control in interpersonal contexts. This scale was designed to measure concerns about the situational appropriateness of behavior, and the ability and/or motivation to adjust behavior to appear "appropriate" in different social contexts. Since persons scoring high on the scale (i.e., high self-monitors) depend more on cues provided by others to adjust their behaviors than do persons scoring low on the scale (i.e., low self-monitors), high self-monitors were expected to show a pattern of behavior similar to persons in the high situational outcome dependency condition. In general, this was the case. High self-monitors remembered more about their expected dates (but not non-dates), were more extreme, confident, and positive in their trait attributions for the expected date (but not non-dates) and liked their expected date (but not non-dates) more than did low self-monitors. High self-monitors did not differ from low self-monitors, however, in attention awarded to either dates or non-dates.

In general, the Berscheid *et al.* (1976) study suggests that when needs are activated there is a narrowing of the open field and facilitative distortion of attributes of a small subset of persons within the field in the direction of need-fulfillment. Results from both situational manipulation and individual differences in motives converge on the same conclusion: namely, that persons generate need-motivated distortions as they enter relationships. Currently, there are no data on the long-term fate of such distortions; yet it is possible that, with repeated exposure to the partner, distortions may fade under the cruel assault of reality constraints (e.g., Tesser and Paulhus, 1976). Thus, two things may be lost: the charming person the initiator once knew; and the possibility that needs will be met. This may be an ideal breeding ground indeed for processes leading to dissolution.

Facilitative distortion and self-generated attitude change. For our analysis, the issue of facilitative distortion is very important. It may be the case, for example, that needs produce distortions which lead to the initiation of relationships; as needs are met distortions may decrease and some of the glue holding the relationship together dissolves. Consequently, specifying the precise mechanism underlying the distortion process is important, because it may predict how long the distortions, and relationships, will last. The motivational aspect of this phenomenon—*why* distortions occur at all— is not clear. Generally, we assume people are motivated to maximize their own outcomes and to be effective in dealing with the environment. Still, greater specification is needed. We offer three interrelated speculations. First, it may be that distortions are self-generated excitations that are instrumental in increasing the value of the goal and thus increasing the likelihood of a behavioral sequence directed towards a particular goal (cf. Stephen *et al.,* 1971). A second, related, possibility is that when some behavior *must* occur (i.e., is manded), there is a narrowing of alternatives which helps the perceiver avoid the problem of being, if we may paraphrase Edwin Guthrie, "lost in thought at a choice point". A third possibility is that distortions represent part of a general behavior strategy designed to influence others, as well as the self. In order to elicit positive response from a female partner B, person A may positively distort B's qualities and act very positively towards B. When person B discovers A likes her and sees her as having many positive attributes, there will be a tendency for B to generate a reciprocally positive evaluation of A (e.g., Backman and Secord, 1959).

A promising lead for the "how" of the distortion processes may be found in Abraham Tesser's theory of self-generated attitude change. (We cannot do justice to the theoretical richness of Tesser's system here. For more details, see Tesser, 1978b; Tesser and Reardon, in press.) Tesser hypothesizes that if a person has some initial attitude, then the more the person thinks about the attitudinal object, the more polarized attitudes and affective reactions become. Two empirical studies conducted by Tesser and his colleagues are relevant to our discussion of distortions within relationship processes.

Tesser and Paulhus (1976) investigated "love" as a specialized kind of attitude polarization. College students rated their dating partners twice over a two-week period and reported how frequently they actually interacted with their partners. Tesser and Paulhus found that feelings of love induced thought about the date, with amount of love and amount of thought positively correlated. These thoughts about the date further polarized love for the date. However, the more intense rating did not carry over to the second session. Actual contact with the date seemed to serve as a reality constraint on the polarization/distortion process, and decreased the amount of love.

In another study, Tesser and Danheiser (1978) specifically addressed the issue of persistence and changes in affective reactions to partners. In romantic relationships, for example, feelings for a partner can change quickly from positive to negative. Based on previous research, these researchers hypothesized that thought would polarize initial attitudes, but the direction of the polarization would depend on the particular "cognitive schema" being applied to the partner at any given point in time. A cognitive schema is a naive theory held by an individual that makes certain aspects of a stimulus situation salient. The cognitive schema for "cooperative partner", for example, makes certain aspects of a partner more salient than the cognitive schema for "unfaithful spouse". Subsequent thought would polarize attitudes, but the direction of the polarization would be determined by the schema employed.

Tesser and Danheiser had subjects listen to self-descriptions of a partner who was made to sound either likeable or unlikeable. Initial attitudes were assessed, and then subjects were told they would be either cooperating or competing with the partner. The purpose was to induce subjects to adopt a new cooperative or competitive schema after initially having a likeable or dislikeable schema. Then some subjects were encouraged to think about their partners, while other subjects were distracted from such thought. Although the initial likeability manipulation was highly successful, affective change was in the direction of the new schema. Given no new information, when subjects thought about the partner and learned they would be cooperating, their feelings became more positive; when subjects thought about their partner and learned they would be competing, their feelings became more negative, regardless of their initial impression of the partner. Thus, intensity of affective reactions to partners is influenced by thought, and direction of affective reaction is determined by the particular schema being applied.

Resistance to changing cognitive schemas. From the perspective of the current chapter, it is important to know what factors motivate persons to change a schema, and how resistant people are to changing a schema once it has been applied. We may speculate, for example, that the unexpected behavior of another person or a stressful life event for the perceiver may trigger schema-changing (e.g., St. Paul's apparent change of schema for Christians that occurred on the Damascus road). There are at least two reasons, however, for expecting persons to be generally resistant to schema-changing. First, it may be effortful to change a schema once it has been constructed and "successfully" applied. Even the worst schema may have some minimal explanatory power, and the perceiver may develop a partially reinforced illusion of understanding (e.g., Fischhoff, 1976; Greenwald, 1980). Distorting attributes of other persons to match an existing schema may require less effort. (Evidence for schema-biasing of memory can be found in a series of studies by Zadny and Gerard, 1974.) Using Piagetian terminology, accommodation may be more cognitively difficult than assimilation.

A second reason is that perceivers may behave in such a way as to elicit schema-congruent behavior from the other person through a kind of "self-fulfilling prophecy". Using Skinnerian terminology, the perceiver is selectively reinforcing and "shaping" the partner to meet prior expectations. Evidence for schema-based "shaping" can be found in a study by Snyder et al. (1977). These researchers reasoned that expectations, stereotypes and schemas not only bias information-processing about the target but also influence the behavior of the perceiver and the target. That is, schema-based expectations lead a perceiver to process information selectively and to behave in accordance with this "information". The target then responds to the perceiver's behavior and "confirms" the perceiver's expectations. The schema with which they chose to work involved physical attractiveness. Could it be the case that the physically attractive are "shaped" into socially skillful behavior by the expectations of those who seek to initiate relationships with them (e.g., Berscheid and Walster, 1974; Goldman and Lewis, 1977)?

In the Snyder et al. (1977) study, previously unacquainted pairs of male and female college students were scheduled to arrive at separate laboratory rooms for an "acquaintanceship process" study. Unbeknown to the female partner, the male partner was given a photograph of either an attractive or an unattractive female, and told that it was a picture of his partner. Prior to any actual interaction, the males completed questionnaires, and it was found that males who expected to interact with an attractive female attributed more socially desirable traits to their partner than did males who expected to interact with a physically unattractive partner. Next, the partners interacted over a telephone connecting the two separate rooms and the conversation of each partner was unobstrusively recorded on separate channels.

Judges, blind to the experimental hypotheses and conditions, rated segments of the females' conversation. As predicted, females who had male partners who believed they were attractive were rated more positively than women who had male partners who believed they were unattractive. Females whose partners believed they were attractive were rated as more self-confident, more animated, and as enjoying the conversation and their partner more than females whose partners believed them to be unattractive. When the males' conversation was rated by the judges, it was found that males who believed they had an attractive partner were more sociable, sexually warm, interesting, bold, humorous, outgoing, and generally more positive. Apparently, the behaviors that the males elicited from the females during the interaction were those behaviors which the males expected of them prior to the interaction.

Taken together, these studies suggest that when needs are activated there is a narrowing of attention and an increase in need-related cognitions. We may speculate further that there are several implications for relationship processes. First, once attention has been narrowed and a particular schema has been applied, not only will an initiator process incoming information in terms of that schema but the initiator will also "shape" the partner's behavior to be schema-consistent. Second, through their coordinated set of expectations, schemas may make the partner seem more predictable and hence controllable. Such perceptions may help the initiator set the stage for an ongoing exchange in which the initiator believes he/she can provide the partner with some commodities, with a predictable and controllable response in return from the partner (Walster et al., 1978). Presumably, the initiator seeks a predictable response from the partner that is need-satisfying. Third, to the extent that an initiator is successful in shaping the partner's behavior to be schema-consistent, the initiator sets the relationship in a trajectory that leads to stable exchanges and maintenance. If the initiator is unsuccessful, however, schema-inconsistent behavior may begin to accumulate and the relationship may begin to break down. Fourth, since needs may induce both need-related thoughts and the selection of a particular schema, we would anticipate that needs would lead to "distortions" (i.e., polarized attitudes and affects).

The function of distortions. At the present time it is unclear what functions distortions serve or how long they persist. It might be argued, for example, that distortions are more likely to characterize the initiation period than the maintenance period of a relationship because the primary function of distortion is to *begin* a behavioral sequence, and/or because distortions are transitory illusions that are vulnerable to the reality constraints of an ongoing relationship (e.g., Tesser and Paulhus, 1976). On the other hand, it might be argued that distortions will periodically reoccur in the maintenance period whenever needs are not met. That is, people may resist changing a schema due to the effort involved, the schema-biased observation of the other person's behavior, and the perceiver's own elicitation of schema-consistent behavior from the target (e.g., Snyder *et al.*, 1977). When needs are met neither need-related thoughts nor schemas are applied, but when needs are not met the entire system is re-examined. The issue is further complicated by the likelihood that in the maintenance period, to be discussed below, partners may occupy more roles, meet more needs, and may be cognized in terms of more schemas than may partners, or potential partners, in the initiation period. In any case, further theoretical and empirical work should be devoted to the interrelationship of needs and the persistence of distortions across the course of relationships. We shall examine the issue of distortions further when we consider the maintenance period.

The Maintenance of Relationships

At the beginning of this chapter we offered two general hypotheses. First, we hypothesized that factors that influence the initiation of relationships may also influence the course of the relationship. We also offered the seemingly contradictory hypothesis that a need that influences a relationship during one period need not influence the relationship in another period, or may influence it in a different way. Before we discuss more concretely how these processes might occur, it may be helpful to consider an analogy, drawn from developmental psychobiology, to resolve the apparent contradictions between the two hypotheses.

In 1966, C. H. Waddington presented a graphic presentation of a general model for describing the interaction of genes and the environment called the "epigenetic landscape" (see Fig. 1). In this system, development is the process of moving across an *n*-dimensional space along a "creode" (stabilized or buffered pathway). The contours of the landscape are determined by the genotype, while the position of the ball represents the value of the phenotype. Development is characterized by the ball rolling forward. Environmental forces may move the ball laterally across the landscape, but the amount of lateral movement is determined by the depth of the channel at a particular time. At certain critical moments, an environmental force may induce the ball to alter its trajectory. The strength of the environmental force necessary to alter a trajectory depends on both the contours of the landscape (e.g., depth of the channel in which the ball is currently moving) and the time at which the environmental event occurs.

In terms of relationships, the contour of the landscape may be seen as

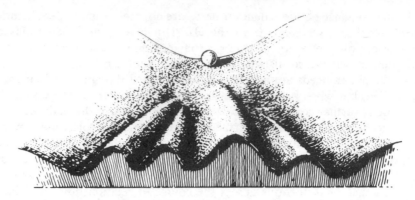

FIG. 1   The epigenetic landscape. The various regions of a developing embryo
have in front of them a number of possible pathways of development, and any
particular part will be switched into one or other of these potential paths. From
Waddington, C. H. "Principles of development and differentiation." The
Macmillan Company, 1966. New York: (p. 49) (copyright 1966 by C. H.
Waddington. Reproduced by permission).

determined by needs. Persons with strong needs travel in a narrow channel.
Once a need has induced a person to initiate a relationship and enter one
channel, a trajectory is set. The initiating need may no longer be operative,
but the course of the relationship, and its ultimate outcome, were
determined by the need. Of course, the trajectory of a relationship can be
altered by environmental forces, but the impact of such forces will be
determined by the time at which they occur and the depth of the channel
through which the person is traveling at that time. We will first attempt to
apply this analogy to maintenance processes and the focus on dissolution
processes.

Theories with implications for maintenance

Let us now re-examine some of the issues we considered earlier, but from
the perspective of a relationship in the maintenance period. That is, a need
or set of needs has induced a person to move from an open field to a closed
field. The person has expectations that the partner can satisfy some needs,
and the person has a prospect of continuing interaction with the partner.
There are several theories which may give some insight into the processes of
relationship maintenance.

   Opponent-process theory of acquired motivation. Richard Solomon and
his colleagues (Solomon, 1980; Solomon and Corbit, 1973, 1974) have
developed an opponent-process theory of acquired motivation that has

important implications for relationship processes. Solomon proposes that many kinds of emotional experiences, including emotional reactions associated with attachment, exhibit a "standard pattern". This standard pattern is presented in Fig. 2. When a relatively novel unconditioned stimulus (UCS) is first presented to an organism, there is a rapid departure from the organism's baseline emotional state, which quickly reaches a peak.

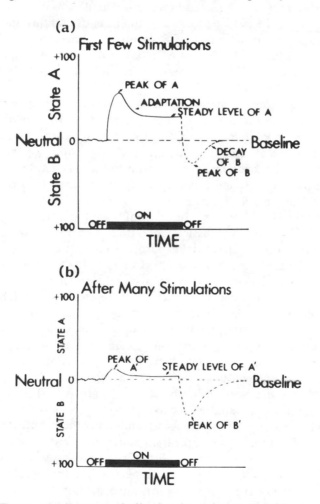

FIG. 2(a) The standard pattern of affective dynamics produced by a relatively novel unconditioned stimulus. (b) The standard pattern of affective dynamics produced by a familiar, frequently repeated unconditioned stimulus. From Solomon, R. L. The opponent-process theory of acquired motivation. *American Psychologist,* 1980, 35, 691–712. (p. 695) Copyright 1980 by the American Psychological Association. Reprinted by permission of the publisher and author.

Consider the case of an inexperienced dog which receives electric shock in a laboratory study. The dog's heart-rate rapidly accelerates from baseline and reaches a peak in seconds. As the dog continues to receive shocks, however, there is some habituation and although the heart-rate does not return to baseline it is somewhat lower than the peak. Let us call this State A. When the dog is removed from the shock apparatus, the dog's heart-rate does not immediately return to the base-rate but "undershoots" the baseline, remaining below the baseline for some time. Let us call this State B. After repeated exposure to the novel UCS, however, something very interesting happens: when the UCS is presented, State A decreases in amplitude from (i.e., above) the baseline, while State B increases in amplitude from (i.e., below) the baseline.

Acording to Solomon, emotional reactions occur in opponent pairs. Once an emotional reaction is elicited, a "slave process" of opposing hedonic tone is also recruited, but with some temporal delay. The initial State A may be either positive or negative, depending on the nature of the UCS, but State B will have a hedonic tone opposite to that elicited by the UCS for State A. Since States A and B occur as opponent pairs, the presentation of State A will automatically dispel State B, and vice versa. With repeated exposure to the UCS, however, the onset of State B occurs sooner, and with greater amplitude, due to classical conditioning. Consider the case of the use of addictive drugs. The initial exposures to the drug lead to a rapid rush to a euphoric state. The removal of the drug leads to some small withdrawal cravings. The unpleasant cravings can be eliminated by taking the drug again. The addictive cycle is now set. With repeated use of the drug, the euphoria lessens, but the withdrawal cravings increase in intensity. Soon, the addict takes the drug primarily to avoid cravings.

Relationships, especially in the maintenance period, may be conceptualized as a specialized kind of mutual addiction. The initial exposure of a perceiver to a target who satisfies some need operates as a novel UCS, eliciting a hedonically positive State A. When the target is removed, some small withdrawal cravings occur.

Since such cravings are unpleasant, and since the return of the target automatically eliminates the unpleasant state, the perceiver will attempt to regain contact with the target. With repeated exposure to the target, however, the euphoria of State A decreases, but the negative affective reaction at the loss of the target becomes much greater. Consider the case of the couple who have been married 30 years. The couple seem to show no special pleasure, much less euphoria, in each other's presence; the sudden death of one partner, however, may produce strong negative affect in the survivor.

Although Solomon's opponent process model is phrased in the language of classical conditioning, it may be interpreted in terms of the present chapter. First, needs give the UCS its power to elicit State A. If dogs were not motivated to avoid shock or to approach food, neither classical conditioning nor the opponent processes discussed above could occur. Second, reinforcing events have an initiation, maintenance, and post-termination period, within which different processes may be operating. Events in the initiation period, however, exert their influence throughout the entire sequence. A perceiver may initiate a relationship with a target to satisfy some needs, and at least initially, experience an occasional euphoric moment. The perceiver may work to maintain the relationship with the target, however, not for the decreased incentives of State A, but for the avoidance of the negative affect of State B associated with loss.

Cairns' theory of attachment. Another learning-oriented theory relevant to our discussion of relationship maintenance processes has been proposed by Robert Cairns (1966, 1979). In brief, Cairns proposes that the development and maintenance of attachments is a by-product of a continuing conditioning process. Since behavior occurs in sequential response chains, environmental cues can be associated with parts of the response chain and, eventually, become "maintaining stimuli" for the chain. Highly conspicuous or response-involving stimuli are more likely to be integrated into the response chain than are less conspicuous or less involving stimuli. The rewarding or punishing quality of the partner is important only because it increases salience and the likelihood that the partner's cues will be integrated into the response chain. When maintaining stimuli are removed, the response chain is disrupted and disorganized behavior occurs. Consider the case of the couple, married for 30 years, whose custom is to eat supper together every night. According to Cairns, if one of the partners were to die, one behavior likely to be disrupted in the survivor would be supper-eating. The more mutual behaviors the couple engaged in, the wider the range of behavioral disruption.

Cairns' elegant theory has general implications for relationship maintenance and dissolution. First, persons are likely to become attached to salient targets, but needs give the environmental stimuli their "salience". Rewarding or punishing targets would not be especially salient if organisms were not motivated to approach the reward or avoid the punishment. Second, relationships may be initiated for a variety of reasons, but repeated exposure to a target, even a punishing target, can lead to attachment and relationship-maintaining behavior because cues associated with the target have been integrated into the perceiver's own response chains. None the less, factors that influenced the initiation would influence the course of the entire relationship, because it would influence the targets to which the perceiver was exposed.

Exposure and affect. The theories of both Cairns and Solomon paint a somewhat bleak picture of relationship's maintenance. According to Cairns, people tend to form attachments to others and then find it disruptive if the behavior chains associated with the other person are broken. Solomon's work suggests that people remain in relationships because it becomes aversive to withdraw from them. Solomon's theory, in particular, suggests that positive affect disappears or becomes much diminished with repeated contacts.

Other theorists (e.g., Zajonc, 1968), however, suggest that there is increased positive affect with repeated exposure to stimuli. Zajonc proposes that the initial reaction to a strong stimulus is uncertainty. With time, however, this uncertainty and any accompanying anxiety and fear dissipate, and we grow to like the object. There is ample evidence that repeated exposure to non-social stimuli (words, patterns, colors, etc.) increases liking (for a complete review of the literature on mere exposure, see Harrison, 1977).

At this point in time, it is not clear how applicable Zajonc's theory is to maintenance activities in ongoing relationships. Most of the research on mere exposure has used non-social stimuli (but see Brockner and Swap, 1976; Mita *et al.*, 1977), which remain objectively constant from exposure to exposure. In ongoing relationships, the stimuli are people who change both objectively (e.g., new hair styles, moustaches, clothing) and subjectively from exposure to exposure. Another problem in applying the mere exposure theory to ongoing relationships is that social stimuli engage in impression management and differential self-disclosure. As persons become better acquainted, they disclose increasingly intimate details about themselves to their partners (Chaikin and Derlega, 1974; Cozby, 1973). These new details may induce a reorganized impression of the partner. Thus, it could be argued that perception of partners in ongoing relationships is less a problem of mere exposure than a problem of object constancy. It is still theoretically possible, however, that mere exposure to social stimuli does increase positive affect, and such repeated exposure might serve to help maintain a relationship once the emotional "highs" of the initiation period have dissipated.

Responsiveness and maintenance. While it is possible to look at the maintenance of a relationship as a whole, it is also possible to look at the maintenance of interactions within a relationship. Work by Deborah Davis and her colleagues suggest that responsiveness to one's partners is one mechanism which helps to maintain a relationship. Davis (in press) hypothesizes that there are four factors which affect responsiveness in interactions: (a) attention, (b) accuracy in understanding the other's communications, (c) a response repertoire that makes adequate response possible, and (d) the motivation to be responsive. That is, in order to be responsive to another, one must first attend to the other, accurately decode the communication along non-verbal as well as verbal channels, be able to respond in a relevant manner, and then actually make the appropriate response.

Davis proposes that responsiveness to one's partner affects both the process and the outcome of the couple's interaction; it has implications for both the initiator and the responder. In terms of process, responsiveness to the other helps to maintain an interaction. At the same time, it allows the initiator some control over the situation since he/she may expect and elicit relevant responses. In terms of outcome, responsiveness increases attraction of the initiator to the other and makes the other appear to be more attracted to the initiator. Thus the initiator likes the responder more when he/she is responsive, and also feels that the initiator is attracted in return.

Davis and Perkowitz (1979) investigated the way in which the probability and relevance of responses influenced interpersonal attraction. In the first study subjects believed they were taking part in a study on acquaintanceship processes. They exchanged messages about themselves with another "subject" (in actuality, tape-recorded messages were used). Subjects were told to answer one question each time it was their turn. Half of the subjects received responses on only one third of their turns, while the other half were responded to two thirds of the time. Subjects who experienced the higher rate of responsiveness liked their "partner" significantly more than those who were in the low responsiveness condition.

It may not be enough, however, to simply respond if the response does not indicate attention and interest. A second study examined the effect of relevant responses on liking. Again, under the guise of an acquaintanceship study, subjects were paired with confederates who responded in either a relevant or an irrelevant manner. As predicted, subjects were much more attracted to a confederate who made relevant responses.

In our earlier discussion of needs and attention, we noted that when needs are activated there is a narrowing of the perceptual field and a focusing of attention on the one who will hopefully fulfil those needs. As needs are met, attention need no longer be so intensely focused on the need-fulfiller. To the extent that one does not attend, opportunities for responsiveness decrease. Both non-responsiveness and irrelevant responding will negatively influence attraction towards the non-responder.

Equity theory

There are several other ways of conceptualizing the interrelationship among needs, expectations, the prospect of future interaction, and maintenance processes. One of the more promising of these other conceptualizations comes from equity theory (Walster *et al.,* 1973). From the perspective of equity theory, complex social behaviors have their origins in the needs of individuals. Individuals are motivated to meet their needs and maximize their outcomes at the lowest cost. Since no individual possesses all the resources that he/she needs, individuals must exchange resources. An exchange is considered equitable ("fair"?) when an individual perceives his/her outcomes (the positive and negative consequences received in the course of the relationship) to be proportional to his/her inputs (the positive and negative contributions to the exchange). When people perceive a relationship to be inequitable, they will experience distress and attempt to restore equity.

From the perspective of equity theory, individuals are motivated to satisfy their needs and maximize their outcomes through exchange in relationships, but when future interaction is anticipated, selfish behaviors are less likely to occur due to fear of the partner's potential retaliation. An equity theorist would argue that cooperative, unselfish behavior occurs in the maintenance period of a relationship because the partners each control some resources that the other partner needs. If the partner controlled no needed resource, or was unwilling or unable to retaliate for selfish behavior, exploitative selfish behavior would occur. The distress of the victim of inequity would lead to relationship dissatisfaction but not necessarily to relationship dissolution.

Equity theory, balance theory, and cognitive consistency. These theories imply that when people anticipate continuing interaction with another person, they are more generous and cooperative because these behaviors will maximize their own outcomes. The picture of ongoing relationships that emerges is one of affectless calculation involving, if we may paraphrase Dostoevsky, people with the souls of accountants. A somewhat different picture emerges if we focus on a different kind of need. Berscheid and her colleagues have suggested that the prospect of continuing interaction may be interpreted in terms of needs for cognitive consistency. Using Heider's (1958) balance theory, Darley and Berscheid (1967) argued that when people anticipate continuing interaction with another person they begin to see themselves and the partner as part of a common unit. Assuming persons think well of themselves, being part of a unit with another person should lead to thinking well of the other person too (cf. Deutsch and Solomon, 1959; Dutton, 1972).

Darley and Berscheid gave female college students two folders to examine. The folders contained the same amount of neutral information, supposedly describing two other female college students. The subjects were told that one of the two would be a future partner for discussion of personal sexual behavior. When the subjects rated the two persons, the "partner" received more positive ratings than did the non-partner.

Berscheid *et al.* (1968) used procedures similar to those of Darley and Berscheid to determine whether the prospect of continuing interaction would enhance the ratings of initially negative persons. Female college students read two folders containing information about two other students. Within each folder was a "clinical evaluation form" describing the person in either positive ("intelligent", "outgoing", "personable") or negative ("moody", "unclean", "unpopular") terms. Subjects were told they had been randomly assigned to either the positive or negative partner for an extended intimate discussion of marriage. Subjects in a control condition read the two folders and chose a partner. When subjects rated the two persons, the positive female was liked more than was the negative female, and more favorable traits were attributed to her. Once the ratings had taken place, the experimenter returned, explained that she had made a major procedural error, and told the subjects that they were to choose one of the two to be their partner. The negative partner was selected only 10% of the time in the control condition, 5% in the positive partner condition, but 35% of the time in the negative partner condition. Apparently, when forced to associate with an undesirable person, at least some people will attempt to "balance" the situation by increasing their liking for the undesirable person. In a closed field, this "paradoxical attraction" may be highly adaptive because it may help make the inevitable contact less aversive. On the other hand, such balancing acts may keep people in unpleasant relationships when escape might be a more appropriate response. In any case, the Berscheid *et al.* (1968) study suggests that once a relationship has been initiated, it may be buffered against dissolution, even when initial commitment is low and more pleasant options are available (cf. Cairns, 1966).

What are the characteristics of persons who would choose to remain in a relationship with an undesirable partner? Graziano *et al.* (1980) investigated the hypothesis that individual differences in coping reactions may be related to paradoxical attraction. That is, when people find themselves in a continuing closed-field relationship with a partner, they may attempt to "balance" the situation by increasing liking. But closed-field encounters with negative persons can be threatening and difficult to control. Persons who chronically cope with threat by exaggerating the threat (i.e., sensitizers) may amplify the negative aspects of the partner, and this may help the person dissolve the relationship. Persons who chronically cope with threat by denial or by directing attention away from unpleasant events (i.e., repressors) may de-emphasize the negative aspects of the partner and stay in the potentially aversive relationship.

Female college students wrote brief answers to questions and were told these answers would be evaluated by two peers. In fact, the evaluators were videotaped confederates who gave standardized positive or negative evaluations. A TV monitoring apparatus allowed subjects to watch only one evaluator at a time. Subjects were randomly assigned to either a prospect of continuing interaction or no prospect of continuing interaction condition, and were classified as either sensitizers or repressors, based on their scores on Byrne's (1961) repression-sensitization scale. After listening and watching the evaluations, subjects rated the two evaluators (see also Berscheid et al. 1976).

As predicted, reactions to criticisms were an interactive function of coping strategy and prospect of continuing contact. When there was no prospect of continuing interaction, sensitizers evaluated the critic more positively than did the repressors. Where there was a prospect of continuing interaction, however, this pattern was reversed: repressors evaluated the critic more positively than did sensitizers. These findings are even more interesting in the light of the findings that repressors and sensitizers did not differ in either condition in their attention to the critic or their liking for the positive evaluator. Apparently, criticism within the context of a continuing relationship is threatening and activates chronic coping strategies. When the coping strategy is sensitization, the criticism may introduce considerable turbulence to the relationship. When the coping strategy is repression, the threatening criticism increases attraction to the critic.

Several issues are important here. First, some persons' coping strategies may make it easier for them to weather the inevitable storms of ongoing relationships than other persons' strategies do. Whether such "weathering" is adaptive or maladaptive depends, among other things, on how long the "storms" last. It is adaptive if the threatening events are transitory; it is less adaptive when the threatening events are chronic. For the abused and battered wife who chooses to remain with her tormentor, repressive coping may even be fatal (e.g., Martin, 1976). Of course, it may be the case that a repressive coping strategy breaks down when threats are prolonged. That is, repression may be an ineffective coping strategy under the "reality constraints" of prolonged threat, and so new strategies are attempted. If repression-based distortions do persist, however, a partner's objectively negative inputs to an ongoing relationship may not have the effect predicted from equity theory because they are not subjectively perceived by the partner as negative.

Maintaining the self and maintaining relationships

We began our discussion with a proposition that an individual's needs induce him/her to initiate a relationship, and that these needs will cast a shadow over the entire course of the relationship. Although we have avoided precise specification of needs, we have hinted that needs for feeling effective and for retaining a positive evaluation of the self were important. In this section, we shall consider how an individual's need to maintain a positive sense of self may influence the initiation, maintenance, and dissolution of relations with others. Again, we shall draw heavily on some recent theoretical work by Abraham Tesser and his colleagues at the University of Georgia.

According to Tesser (1978a; 1980), people are motivated to maximize their self-evaluation (or minimize loss in self-evaluation). Self-evaluation is *not* conceptualized as a stable, enduring trait, but as a dynamic process, derived from relative performances on a variety of tasks. Persons can influence their level of self-evaluation not only through enhancing their own task performance but also through affiliation with others. When another person, or group of persons, is successful, we can associate with them and, through a kind of identification process, vicariously enjoy their success. College students chanting "We're Number One!" after a football victory is an example. Furthermore, people are more inclined to associate with successful others and "bask in reflected glory" after having a personal failure experience than after having a personal success experience (e.g., Cialdini *et al.* 1976).

There are dangers, however, in such associations. The successful person's performance could make our own performance pale by comparison, leading to a lowered self-evaluation. According to Tesser, the key to determining when a person will choose to associate with another is the *relevance* of the performance to the person's own defintion. When another's successful performance occurs on a dimension relevant to our own self-definition, we will avoid association; when another's successful performance is on some other dimension, we will seek association.

Thus, Tesser's theory has three major components: performance, closeness, and relevance. More formally, "performance" refers to the relative quality of task behaviors from one perceiver's perspective. The relative performance of another can be decreased by improving one's own performance or by decreasing or interfering with another's performance. "Closeness" refers to the psychological proximity between the other person and the perceiver, and is comparable to Heider's (1958) notion of a unit relationship (i.e., persons in a unit relationship are close). "Relevance" is the extent to which another's performance occurs on a dimension that is self-defining to the perceiver. If a perceiver aspires to be a good flute player, but does not aspire to be a good long-distance runner, then another's flute playing is relevant but his/her long-distance running is not. These three components form a system: a change in one component will lead the perceiver to change one or both of the other components. Tesser offers a simple example of how the system might work. Jim, who thinks of himself as a chemist, finds himself in a chemistry class with John. John outperforms Jim in chemistry. Jim could do the following to raise or restore his own self-evaluation: (a) he could decrease the relevance of chemistry, and convince himself chemistry is not really important, (b) he could decrease his closeness to John, and/or (c) he could act to change relative performance, either by working harder for chemistry exams or by interfering with John's performance in chemistry.

Tesser's theory is very new, but there is some solid corroborating research (Tesser, 1980; Tesser and Smith, 1980; Pleban and Tesser, 1980). Self-evaluation processes operated as predicted in college friendships, sibling pairs, and father–son relationships. Although no research has yet attempted to apply the self-evaluation model to relationship dissolution, the implications are clear. Persons may initiate relationships to enhance, or at least maintain, a positive self-evaluation. Like several other theorists, Tesser predicts that the most likely targets of initiation are persons perceived as competent in some regard. Unlike most other theorists, however, Tesser makes refined predictions about those dimensions of the target's competence that may contribute to maintenance and those dimensions that may contribute to dissolution of the relationship. The extraordinary competence of a colleague that leads us to initiate a relationship may become increasingly pleasurable or painful as the relationship progresses, depending on the relevance of the target's competence to our own self-definition. More specifically, since relationships occur across time, and since both the relevance of certain performance domains and competencies within these domains can change with repeated exposure, the competent performance of the partner that was initially attractive may become progressively more painful. The pain may be reduced by redefining the partner's performance as irrelevant, interfering with the partner's performance, or decreasing closeness to the partner.

Tesser does not precisely specify which of these three modes of resolution is most likely to occur, but we may speculate that the resolution mode depends on both the partners' chronic coping strategies and the perceived openess of the field at the time the conflict occurs. For example, redefining the relevance of the performance may be more likely to occur for repressors and for partners who perceive the conflict as occurring within a closed field. In this case, resolution leads to maintenance processes. Decreased closeness may be more likely to occur, however, when the conflict is amplified through sensitization and when the conflict is perceived as occurring within an open field. Estrangement and social distancing may be easier to bear when alternative relationships appear available. In this case, resolution may lead to dissatisfaction and possibly to dissolution. In both cases, resolution is motivated by self-evaluation processes.

The Dissolution of Relationships

Predicting when declines in closeness lead beyond breakdown to outright dissolution is an important task awaiting future research (Duck, 1981, and Chapter 1, this volume). From the perspective of the present chapter, however, some broad outlines are apparent. If persons initiate a relationship to satisfy needs for positive self-evaluation and these needs are not met, or if alternative sources of reward do not compensate for the needs not being met, people will be dissatisfied with the current relationship. From the perspective of the perceiver, the unsatisfied needs induce him/her to move from a closed-field to an open-field context, and the perceiver will seek to initiate alternative relationships. There will be a need-induced attentive search for potential sources of satisfaction, just as in the initiation period of the now unsatisfactory relationship. Since the dissatisfied partner is seeking alternatives, the prospect of continuing interaction with the current partner is reduced as are the associated facilitative distortions. The perceiver has come full cycle and returned to the starting point: initiation in an open field.

We could speculate further that dissatisfaction is more likely to lead to dissolution when the perceiver believes more rewarding alternative relationships are available than when no such alternative is perceived (cf. Thibaut and Kelley, 1959). When no alternative is perceived, the broken relationship may be "maintained" at some low level, but need-induced dissatisfaction leads to attentive searching for such alternatives. None the less, for some persons, freedom from the aversive states occurring in the broken relationship may be a sufficiently rewarding alternative to dissolve the relationship (Levinger, 1965).

Tesser's theory in particular has important implications, not only for the maintenance period but also for the dissolution period of relationships. The closeness component is especially important to the present discussion. First, relationship processes are directly tied to individuals' needs for self-maintenance (cf. Reik, 1957). Persons may initiate a relationship (i.e., increase closeness) when self-evaluations are at a low level and the target is likely to be someone who can raise the person's level of self-evaluation (e.g., Jacobs *et al.,* 1971; Walster, 1965). That is, we may initiate relationships with the physically attractive or the competent other not merely because of our schematized or distorted expectations about them, but because we have expectations about what they may be able to do for us (cf. Walster *et al.,* 1973). We may expect that having a relationship with an attractive or competent person will allow us to feel effective in dealing with the social environment, to bask in reflected glory, and ultimately to restore a positive self-evaluation.

Second, once a relationship has been initiated, the need to maintain a positive self-evaluation does not disappear. We may continue to bask in a partner's reflected glory, but only so long as the partner's glory is not based on performance along one of our own self-defining dimensions. If the partner's superior performance does occur along a self-defining dimension, there should be changes in relevance, closeness, or both. Consider the case of two persons, enrolled in the same graduate program in psychology, who choose to marry. Being a psychologist is relevant to each person's self-definition. Assuming both pursue careers as psychologists, a superior performance by either of the two should produce a change in the "inferior" partner's perception of the relevance of psychology or a change in closeness to the "superior" partner. Alternatively, the "inferior" partner could attempt to interfere with the "superior" partner's performance. To maintain the relationship, partners may redefine the relevant aspects of their field (e.g., "I am interested in the motivational basis for thirst, but she is interested in the functional neurology of the hypothalamus"). Thus, partners in a relationship may emphasize their difference in order to maintain the relationship, while "objective" observers, who have a less strong interest in maintaining the relationship, may be struck by the similarities in the partners. When such redefinitions of relevance are not possible, we would expect changes in closeness.

Third, even if there are changes in closeness during the maintenance period, we may speculate that such changes need not necessarily lead to relationship dissolution or even dissatisfaction. Rather than dissolving the relationship, the partner with the inferior performance may reduce closeness by interacting with the partner over fewer domains (e.g., never discuss certain topics) or by becoming less intimate or self-disclosing (Duck, 1981). Furthermore, since threat to self-evaluation is a critical proximal motivator, we might expect differences in chronic coping strategies to moderate the threat-closeness link. If, for example, one of the partners coped with the threat by repression, the partner's superior performance might even lead to greater closeness (cf. Graziano *et al.,* 1980). On the whole, however, we would expect changes in closeness to lead to dissatisfaction. Even if the "inferior" partner attempted to maintain the relationship by interacting over a more restricted domain or by decreasing intimacy, these behaviors would lead, at least from the "superior" partner's perspective, to a net decrease in the partner's responsiveness, and decreased responsiveness does not lead to attraction (Davis, in press).

Summary and Conclusions

Relationships occur across time and may be conceptualized as having an initiation, maintenance, and dissolution period. Persons in an open field select another person with whom to initiate relationship because the perceiver has expectations that the target can satisfy needs the perceiver cannot meet alone. The needs induce selective attention and biased processing of information about others, and consequently, the narrowing of the open field. Distortions, induced by needs and steered by schemas, may facilitate the initiation and maintenance of relationships. The needs that lead to initiation exert influence throughout the entire course of the relationship, if for no other reason than that they establish a relationship "trajectory". However, different need-related mechanisms may be operative at different periods in the relationship.

Once a person has been selected from the open field, the relationship moves to a closed field and into the maintenance period: in this situation, the prospect of continuing interaction leads the person to perceive him/herself and the partner as being part of a common unit. Such perceptions may lead to efforts at cognitive balancing, facilitative distortions, and increased attraction, even when the partner has negative attributes (e.g., Berscheid et al., 1968). In closed-field encounters, the inevitable negative aspects of partners become more salient and potentially more threatening. The partners' success at maintaining their relationship when a partner's negativity is salient may be determined by each partner's coping strategies. Sensitizers, who cope with threat by amplifying it may find relationship maintenance under such circumstances more difficult than repressors, who cope with threat by denial or by redirecting attention (e.g., Graziano et al., 1980).

In addition to such cognitive activity as balancing and coping, processes within the relationship itself may buffer it from dissolution. First, repeated exposure to a partner may induce cues associated with the partner to be integrated into the perceiver's response chain. The partner becomes a "maintaining stimulus" and removal of the partner produces aversive behavioral disorganization (Cairns, 1966; 1979). Second, repeated exposure may induce a kind of "addiction". Exposure decreases the positive affect that occurred early in the relationship, but increases negative affect when the partner is removed (Solomon, 1980). Third, repeated exposure may decrease uncertainty and fear, and increase attraction (Harrison, 1977; Zajonc, 1968).

Finally, we considered the possibility that a very general need, the need to maintain a positive self-evaluation, can be tied to processes that influence the initiation, maintenance, and dissolution of relationships (Tesser, 1980). A person's self-evaluation is influenced not only by his/her own accomplishments, but also by the accomplishments of his/her associates. When another person is relatively successful on a dimension that is not self-defining to a perceiver, the perceiver will associate him/herself with the other person, and "bask in reflected glory". When another person is relatively successful on a dimension that is self-defining to the perceiver, however, the perceiver's self-evaluation is threatened. The perceiver may attempt to change the performance difference (Tesser and Smith, 1980), and/or decrease closeness (Pleban and Tesser, 1980).

Decreased closness in a relationship does not necessarily lead to relationship dissolution. The threatened partner may decrease intimacy or the domains of interaction in an effort to maintain the relationship. However, such decreases in responsiveness may also decrease the partners' mutual attraction (Davis and Perkowitz, 1979) and decrease satisfaction with the relationship.

Decreased satisfaction may not necessarily lead to relationship dissolution, either. Dissatisfaction may lead persons to enlarge the closed field of their present relationship, selectively searching for more rewarding alternatives (Kelley, 1979; Thibaut and Kelley, 1959). Dissolution may finally occur as a joint function of dissatisfaction and the perception of an alternative relationship in which self-evaluation needs may be better met.

Taken together, the theory and research we have summarized suggest that research on relationship dissolution should focus on the relationship processes occurring across time. While different need-related processes may influence the relationship during different periods of the relationship, the needs that lead to initiation may steer the relationship through its entire course.

Acknowledgement

The authors would like to thank Arthur Aron, Thomas Berndt, Jennifer Campbell, Wyndol Furman, John Harvey, Robert Pollack, Sidney Rosen, Stevens Smith, and Abraham Tesser for their helpful comments on an earlier version of this chapter.

CHAPTER 5

An Attributional Approach to Relationship Breakdown and Dissolution

John H. Harvey, Ann L. Weber, Kerry L. Yarkin and
Bonnie E. Stewart.

It is paradoxical that at the present time the quality of life is determined for so many of us by quality of relationships instead of by income (Campbell, 1981), and yet the initiation and maintenance of close relationships are so often problematic. Campbell has commented:

> "What appears to have happened is that an increasing number of people have achieved a degree of economic security that has liberated them from an obsessive concern with income, with a consequent increase in the importance of nonmaterial needs—the need for a sensitive and responsive marital relationship.... "   (p. 25)

Accelerating divorce rates, consequent increases in one-parent families, and projected differences in the age of natural death for husbands and wives all signal massive social changes in the ways in which large percentages of people must meet interpersonal intimacy needs. Berscheid and Campbell (in press) concluded a recent analysis of these trends in the nature of modern close relationships by suggesting that the only conclusion that can be safely drawn is that, whether an individual welcomes or deplores the revolutionary changes that have occurred in our society within a very short period of time, no one can escape their consequences. Despite these momentous trends, psychologists and others have only recently begun to attempt to understand

107

the principles common to dissolution of different types of relationships (Duck, 1981). Other workers have begun the attempt to discover the particular features that are found in some instances of breakdown and dissolution but not in others.

We believe that attribution concepts and research have much to contribute to the success of this endeavour. The present discussion will therefore offer some perspective on the ways in which our interpretations of causality and imputations of personality characteristics to others, and to ourselves, represent central activities involved in all stages of close relationships. Just as such activities are inevitably entailed in relationship initiation and maintenance (Regan, 1978), we will maintain they are inextricably involved in relationship breakdown and dissolution.

We will provide first some discussion of definitional issues relevant to an attributional approach to relationship breakdown and dissolution, and then discuss evidence on attributional conflict in adult heterosexual relationships and children's friendships. In another major section we will treat the topic of attribution and getting over close relationships. This latter section, which is unique in writings in the attribution literature, is the main section that deals explicitly with therapeutic possibilities. Finally, we will draw some general conclusions about the merit of an attributional approach to relationship breakdown and dissolution.

We should emphasize at the outset that the focus of the chapter will be on the dyad, or the closely relating couple. In taking this focus, we give less attention both to intrapsychic or individualistic conceptions, on the one hand, and to sociological or demographic treatments of problems in relationships, on the other hand. An emphasis upon the interlocking nature of the *social* and the *psychological* facets of attributional processes is being increasingly recognized (e.g., Stryker and Gottlieb, 1981), and this emphasis provides a key background premise for the present analysis.

Some Definitional Issues

Understandably, close relationships yield a myriad of interpretations for a couple. These interpretations may concern significant events or one another's behavior over time and in a variety of circumstances. Attributions in relationships are causal inferences that are made both explicitly and implicitly and in both public and private ways. The inferences refer to the causes of events relevant to the relationship (e.g., "why we got married") and dispositional features of other or of self (e.g., "He is a gentle lover", "I'm the caretaker of this relationship"). These inferences may be part of the attributor's phenomenal experience, or they may be inferred to exist (as a hypothetical construct) based on some response pattern other than the verbal report of an attribution. As Heider (1976) suggested, attributions may be made spontaneously and without much deliberation (e.g., "I heard the door slam and knew instantly that my wife had returned"). Or attributions may be made after considerable deliberation, not unlike the logical analytic activity of a scientist (Kelley, 1967).

If there is any transcendental message in this chapter, it is that these interpretations have a major influence on the quality of a relationship throughout its life-span. As we will show in the following review, the evidence about the interplay between relational conflict and attributional divergencies is quite strong. The question of whether attributions cause conflict, or vice versa, should not be our sole area of concern in the present chapter. We know that attributions and conflict are strongly related and that, most likely, they are often related in intricate causal loops. However, it is clear that different aspects and components of these loops may be distinguished, for purposes of analysis.

One important early qualification is that we do not wish to suggest that all types of conflict are antagonistic to the maintenance of a relationship. Conflict may, in fact, be positive in stimulating partners to consider and explain their relationship more carefully and to define its possibilities more clearly. Attribution about conflict at this point may also be used as a vehicle for clarifying communication (see below, our later discussion of Orvis *et al.*, 1976), with the partners' full expectation of relationship maintenance and growth.

A related point is that attribution may take many forms at different stages of a relationship. While attributions may take the form of a simple ascription of attractiveness to other at the earliest initiation point, at a later point they may become quite elaborate in content and scope. A newly wed couple, for instance, may encounter conflict about how to handle offers of help from parents and relatives. This conflict may be resolved via agreed-upon attributions such as "We'll feel better and our relationship will be stronger if we refuse help from our parents and relatives — we have the resources to make it on our own". These conflict-attribution episodes may be recurrent over the first few years of a relationship, but in general their consequence may be that of conciliation.

But as time goes on, a couple may have less facility to resolve various types of conflict via attribution. Indeed, divergencies in attribution about important matters (e.g., how much time each person devotes to the need of the other) may become more pronounced; and these "understandings" may or may not be communicated to other—they may in fact be communicated to third parties who in turn may reinforce them. Thus, the progression of a relationship, as the participants understand it, may be towards distortion by each party with little attempt to work out attributional disagreements. Such a progression often leads to dissolution of the relationship. During this latter stage, attribution may take the form of justifications regarding one's own course of action or blaming of other. Or it may take the form of self-guilt and self-derogation. Weiss (1975) reveals these tendencies in his report of the seemingly endless reviews and recounts of relationship histories exhibited by persons newly separated or in the process of separating. Again, at the end of a relationship, attributions may or may not be communicated to one's partner. They probably will be communicated to someone, such as a comforting friend or relative. But it would be a most illuminating study to try to assess the extent to which a person's most poignant interpretations and imputations about self and other at this most distressing moment in human affairs were matters of *private reflection and hurt*.

We know too little about these long-term patterns (but see Duck and Gilmour, 1981b). Obviously, a host of critical attributions are made (sometimes communicated to the other person, sometimes not) at various critical points during the course of a relationship. An attributional approach to relationship breakdown suggests that there is much value, and unfulfilled potential, attendant on the formulation of theory and research about these patterns of attributions and related behavior over the life-span of a relationship. Presently, most of the evidence pertains to attributional conflict. In the next section, we will review this evidence.

Evidence on Attributional Conflict in Close Relationships

Research on attributional conflict (which refers to disagreement in ascriptions of the sources of conflict) has become the central focus of attribution investigators working in the area of close relationships. This focus has been on conflict in *heterosexual* relationships both implicitly (Weiss, 1975) and explicitly (Orvis et al., 1976; Hill et al., 1976; Harvey et al., 1978). As the quest to apply attributional ideas to real-world phenomena has increased, this area of work has concomitantly taken on greater stature in the attribution literature, as a recent review by Newman (1981) attests. Unfortunately, attribution researchers have paid little corresponding attention to conflict in other types of relationships, although the promise offered by an attributional perspective is just as rich there, too, as will be suggested in a later section on children's friendships.

Adult heterosexual relationships

Although the focus of Hill *et al.* (1976) was on dating relationships, their work has strong implication for research on conflict in long-term close relationships. They conducted a longitudinal survey of the perceptions of over 200 dating couples in the Boston area. Respondents were surveyed at intervals of six months, one year, and two years. Hill *et al.* found that eventual breakups were related to such factors as unequal involvement in the relationship, dissimilar age, educational aspirations, intelligence and physical attractiveness.

In the Hill *et al.* data, there is evidence of attributional conflict that may obtain persistently in later close relationships. After the fact of a breakup, former partners tended to agree on the conflictual influence of *external* factors in their discord (e.g., other lovers), but not on the weight of factors *internal* to the relationship (e.g., differing interests and backgrounds). Moreover, respondents indicated in retrospect that they themselves had made the first move to dissolve the relationship, regardless of the report of their former partners. In this case, the self-attribution may be a "better-late-than-never" way of retroactively taking control of the breakdown process. Women in the Hill *et al.* study appeared to engage in more causal analysis, to do so earlier than did men, and not surprisingly to terminate the relationship more readily than did men. Women appeared to probe the early signs of conflict in their relationships more than men did, and also took a pragmatic approach in responding to what they recognized as serious problems. Hill *et al.* noted that partners who felt they themselves had instigated the breakups reported less severe emotional after-effects than those who did not. Attributional queries and analyses seem to facilitate the address of conflict in relationships and gave the attributor an edge in preparing him/herself for a breakup. A central conclusion of Hill *et al.* is that in conflict-to-breakdown, partners are not likely to perceive or interpret the dynamics of their relationship in the same way. The response to the question, "Why did you break up?" depends on who is answering, and who made the first move to part.

A significant and perplexing issue for attribution researchers studying such divergency concerns whether or not attributions are accurate. As an illustration of this issue, Ross (1977) proposed that the very strong tendency for attributors to make attributions to the dispositions of others represents "the fundamental attribution error". As an illustration of this tendency, in a troubled close relationship each member may view the other's problematic behavior as a manifestation of the other's character. However, the idea that there is a fundamental attribution error was called into question by Harvey *et al.* (1981) who argued that this tendency may represent neither an error nor a fundamental tendency in social perception. They contended that a persuasive address of the accuracy of attribution necessitates much greater progress towards establishing criteria of accuracy than has occurred to date. The truth in relationships beset by conflict may perforce be difficult to discover on the part of both participants and scientists alike. Weiss *et al.* (1973) have suggested that in many cases of conflict, a considerable degree of mutual training in vagueness has occurred and that assertions and expectations about one's partner *overshadow* the data at hand.

One of the first studies to explicitly investigate divergency in attributions in ongoing relationships was conducted by Orvis *et al.* (1976). Orvis *et al.* asked individuals in romantic partnerships simply to list examples of behavior, for self and partner, for which each had a different explanation; this procedure was followed in order to minimize the possibility that the procedure would actually contribute to discord or conflict. Orvis *et al.* obtained data from 41 college-aged couples in a sample containing a mixture of dating, married and cohabiting partnerships. In the questionnaire, individuals not only listed examples of differently explained behaviors, but also provided their own explanations and what they felt would be their partners' explanations of these instances. Respondents' descriptions suggested several categories of behaviors that were explained differently by both partners. Examples of these categories included: Actor criticizes or places demands upon the partner; Actor is too involved in outside relationships and activities; and Actor inconveniences others. Again, these were not attributions about conflict, *per se,* by partners contemplating separation. In admitting their awareness of the discrepancies between own and other's accounts of the same actions, the respondents may have indicated a sort of "running attribution" through the course of a relationship from its outset. Awareness of discrepancy at one point may provide the seed for later major attributional conflict.

Orvis *et al.* suggested that partners in such close relationships may analyze causality in a manner *qualitatively* different from that of other Actor–Observer attributions. In their formulation of the divergent perspectives hypothesis, Jones and Nisbett (1971) emphasized that actors and observers have different information and thus infer different causes for the same behavior. In the romantic relationships surveyed by Orvis *et al.,* it was found that attributions were colored by intention and anticipation, as well as by different information. Orvis *et al.* theorize that when partners disagree about the causes of each other's actions, the threat of conflict precipitates an intense and searching causal analysis. The question, "Why did he/she do that?" is embedded among the questions "What can *I* do about this?" and "What *should* he/she do?". As Orvis *et al.* concluded, in continuing as well as initiating or dissolving close relationships, attribution represents a process of ongoing evaluation and re-structuring, whose quality must change as the relationship's basic premises are intensified or altered. The search for causes is undertaken at various times to smooth out the rough spots, identify central issues, and justify the behavior of self or other. A most important aspect of Orvis *et al.*'s argument is that people in close relationships use attributions to communicate feelings about the relationship. For example, when a person publicly attributes certain relationship problems to a partner's immaturity, the person may be expressing a personal feeling or a desire that the partner change various lines of conduct reflecting on maturity.

Evidence thus far suggests that the motivations, as well as the quality, of attribution change in the course of a close relationship. Family therapists counsel conflicted couples to "handle" the relationship first before they dissolve it or try to move on to another (Satir, 1972). Thus in terms of how attribution might be used to maintain a relationship, attributions about sources of conflict may be undertaken as a means of "keeping up with" relationship events so that they do not get out of hand. However, Altman and Taylor (1973) note that conflict, insofar as it threatens an intimate relationship, also threatens the *self*. People may be motivated to avoid even the perception of self-threat. Equity research tells us that a favored way of dealing with a perceived threat of inequity is a change in perception of the conflict (Walster *et al.*, 1973). Hence people may sometimes engage in misattributions—probably without much awareness—to dull the experience of self-threatening problems in the relationship. For example, reduction of affectionate contact from a partner can be translated, as, "He's been under a lot of pressure lately". We can choose to make the attribution situational ("outside pressures") rather than dispositional ("He has a less affectionate nature") or interpersonal ("He is less affectionate *towards me*"). The last example would be revealing but also devastating. Moreover, everything is happening at once: the emergence of conflict prompts these confused, mixed causal analyses. It is not surprising that communication becomes so difficult at such times in close relationships. The cognitions of either partner may themselves have confused motives and qualities. This line of reasoning is strongly suggested by laboratory work that reveals the interweaving of cognition and motivation in the attribution process (see Bradley, 1978; Weary, 1979).

The Orvis *et al.* (1976) methodology avoided unearthing attributional discrepancies that might prove sensitive or conflicting after the fact for the couples involved. In a study of longer term relationships, Harvey *et al.* (1978) examined the ways in which people account for the experience and sources of admitted conflict. Harvey *et al.* invited participation from couples who had been essentially living together for at least six months, and who acknowledged having experienced conflict in their relationship. Results indicated the "flip-side" of the Orvis et al. findings. The Orvis et al. study queried partners about discrepant attributions and found that these were possibly sensitive or conflictual foci in those relationships. Conversely, Harvey et al. asked individuals to judge their own and their partners' perceptions of sources of real conflict and found these attributions to be discrepant. Partners did not agree about the sources of conflict, yet they perceived themselves to be in agreement. In plain language, one partner assigned a certain weight to a conflict category (e.g., incompatibility in sexual relations) and indicated that the other would give it a similar weight. Although partners in fact did not agree on these issues, apparently they thought that they did agree. Harvey et al. speculate that it is not the agreement of partners that mediates relationships' endurance or breakdown, but rather the perception of agreement between partners. When encountering conflict in close relationships, people may focus their attributional efforts more on the illusion of agreement than on an incisive analysis of the conflict itself.

This evidence suggests that attribution is an ongoing, dynamic activity through the course of close relationships. The dynamism comes from the fact that the *quality* of the attributions must change as the relationship itself intensifies, falters, or terminates. A second study reported in Harvey et al. (1978) indicated that even once the relationship has been terminated, individuals continue to engage in causal analysis. At this stage, however, rather than contributing to relationship "maintenance" or "quality", the attributional queries are part of individuals' self-assessments and rationalizations for the dissolution. In a survey over a six-month period of separated individuals (mostly women), Harvey et al. found that respondents continued to rehash and ruminate on the whys and wherefores of relationship conflict, long after the relationship had ended. These post-separation attributions seemed to focus on fixing blame and adjusting (generally lowering) evaluations of the other and of other's significance to the attributing partner.

Harvey et al. (1978) suggested that attributional analysis may lag behind critical behavior as a relationship moves from conflict to separation. It is possible that partners are busy "being in conflict" and do not afford themselves the luxury of causal analysis. On the other hand, the findings of Hill et al. (1976) and the earlier study by Harvey et al. suggest that attribution about sources of conflict may indeed be continuous throughout the conflict period. As suggested earlier, it is possible that attributions at times of conflict are invested in protection or illusion rather than "analysis". People at the beginning of a relationship may ask and probe about the other's disposition across situations ("What is he/she like?").

Later, when the relationship has become to a degree committed, partners may begin to question behaviors and events as they influence the relationship rather than merely the self ("What kind of relationship is this?"). With the onset of conflict, partners may nurture certain misperceptions about each other's experience in the relationship. They may misattribute each other's awareness of the fact of conflict; so long as they do not see the divergence, they "do not diverge". So attribution about the sources of conflict is employed in the construction of a sort of illusion.

Should conflict progress (or deteriorate) to breakdown and dissolution, it appears that an individual checks this illusion process abruptly and rechannels the queries in the direction of the relationship's ashes: "What happened? What went wrong? Weren't we in agreement?" People are facile in seeking and constructing explanations. We are hoisted by our own attributional petard. If, as Jones and Nisbett (1971) conclude, we persist in seeing ourselves in situational terms and others, even partners, in dispositional terms, then we have no formulas for improvement of a conflicting situation. A shift must take place in the quality of attribution: "Why do I have such rotten luck, that I always end up with emotionally insecure men?" has to be restated as "Why do I select men who prove to be so emotionally insecure?".

Harvey *et al.* suggested that, after separation, particularly depressed individuals in their second study engaged in incessant causal analyses, especially at night, and instead of engaging in the type of "supplanting" activities and preoccupations that might make a healthier recuperation. It will be argued later in this chapter that the termination of a relationship marks only the beginning of heavy-duty attribution in "getting-over" close relationships. Thus the process is continuous, although in the course of a relationship attributional examinations shift in quality. We ask "Why?" in order to understand, but also in order to come up with better explanations, to be protected from painful acknowledgements. Harvey *et al.*'s data about the nature of attributions exhibited by separated people reinforce the earlier implicit treatment of this topic by Weiss (1975). Weiss conducted in-depth interviews with separated persons, who had been married for a number of years. Weiss suggested that people in this situation *adapt* by developing an account of what happened and why. He argued that the account settles the issue of who was responsible for what and imposes on the confused marital events that preceded the separation a plot structure with a beginning, middle, and an end. Weiss contended that this construction produces a conceptually manageable unity—something that can be dealt with—for the separated person. An excerpt of one such account is as follows:

"When my husband heard that I had a sexual relationship, he sort of congratulated me, he was so delighted about it. But then it turned out that when I wanted to see this man, my husband wasn't able to make a date with the person he was seeing. And he had to quickly find somebody else to fill the void. And it was just kind of unbelievable . . . [Woman, mid-thirties]." (Weiss, 1975, p. 22)

After the reasoning advanced by Orvis *et al.*, Newman (1981) has suggested that people engage in attribution as a way of communicating about the relationship. She contended that attribution—like non-verbal communications—have both a "literal" and "intentional" content. We engage in searches for explanations and justifications as a way of maintaining or qualifying the relationship. Newman's position is that attempts to understand a partner's behavior communicate both the question and the concern. Attribution-as-communication is a double-edged sword: We become angry when we attribute our conflict or distress to a partner's disdain or neglect. But it is not clear whether attribution preceded anger, or vice versa. It is not clear that we can distinguish our own upset from that of our partner. It is clear that attribution-making is far from affectless and can take on as many emotional flavors as we can experience in a close relationship.

Newman (1981) further argued that attribution is also multilevel. Most common is the dispositional (intrapersonal) level of attribution, in which an event or behavior is interpreted as a sign of a partner's nature. Situational attributions account for the influence of events and objects external to either partner. In addition, Newman argued, one exhibits an interpersonal attribution in explaining influences (especially in conflict) on the relationship itself. Thus a single behavior may implicate the other's disposition, the situation external to either party, and/or quality of the dyad. It may be that, in the course of a relationship's rise and fall, shifts in attributional quality become shifts between levels of analysis. In moving into or out of a close relationship, people may engage in more dispositional and situational attributions; in maintenance, and with the onset of conflict, people may increasingly interpret events in terms of how they affect the relationship as a whole.

Evidence from studies of adult heterosexual relationships is suggestive of the role of attributional processes in several stages of involvement. People may suspend such processes from time to time as they become involved in the emotions of conflict and/or resolution. Or it may be that the motivation of attributional activities changes with the acknowledgement of conflict. Attributions are not fail-safe, and we may sometimes use them to dull our awareness of threats to the relationship and to ourselves. We do ask the questions, however, and attribution clearly is associated with behavior in the waxing and waning of close relationships.

Attribution in children's friendships

A recent book by Rubin (1980) provides some of the meager data on children's dissolving friendships. His work indirectly speaks to the question of attribution in conflict and friendship termination experienced by children. The children in Rubin's analysis ranged in age from three-year-old toddlers to pre-adolescent children (11 through 13 years of age). We cannot assume that the following conclusions will be generally true since they do not concern older adolescents, and there is no other relevant work that does. It seems reasonable to assume that older adolescents will resemble adults more approximately than they will resemble young children.

As is true with adults, children appear to experience a variety of emotional difficulties when they separate from their friends. Rubin reports that difficulties include depression, loneliness, irritability, guilt, resentment, and anger. Separation usually occurs as a result of (1) a divergence of interests, especially as the period of childhood passes into the period of adolescence; (2) a change in proximity as children and their families make geographical moves for occupational or other reasons; (3) rejection by one or both members of the dyad.

The phenomenon of children's separation and its emotional effects has received very little attention by psychologists. But Rubin reports that the noted early developmentalist Harry Stack Sullivan declared that separation often proves to be "disastrous" in its influence on children's lives. Apparently, there may be a major attributional divergence between parents and children associated with the significance of separation. Rubin reports that parents often try to allay children's hurt by telling them "Don't worry, you'll find another friend". However, children may attribute great significance to the loss, often believing at the time of rejection that the loss indicates their unworthiness for friendship. And while parents may counsel their children that friends can be readily replaced, children may not think so, and indeed, as with separation in adult relationships, it is unlikely that clearly similar replacements can be found. Each friend plays a somewhat different role and makes a unique contribution to the child.

Rubin suggests that termination of children's friendships may not always have a negative impact on the child's emotional state. It may have a revitalization effect; often a more diverse and enlightening group of friends is established after termination. Also, the effect appears to vary greatly as a function of age level. Rubin notes that the impact of termination is striking as one moves towards adolescence with its inherent insecurities and uncertainties. Furthermore, Rubin suggests that children's reflection on an attributional analysis of their separations is much greater the older the child and is consistent with the development of the interpersonal skill of being able to take the perspective of other (see LaGaipa, 1981b). Presumably, perspective-taking provides the structural basis for the young person's knowledge of interpersonal relations. However, the extent to which friends often diverge in such analyses is not clear from research or theoretical work done to date. A critical question, however, for future work pertains to whether the *quality* and *quantity* of reflection and attribution differ for children and adults in various separation circumstances and within different age levels.

In summary, there are numerous significant friendships. In addition to the questions suggested above, Rubin suggests that sex differences may be prominent particularly with teenaged females, reflecting considerable uncertainty and interpretive activity relative to younger females and adolescent males.

Attribution and Getting Over Close Relationships

> " Lost in day-to-day,
> Turned another way,
> With a laugh, a kind hello,
> Some small talk with friends I know—
> I forget that I'm not over you
> For a while."
>
> (From "Watertown", composed by
> Bob Gaudio and Jake Holmes)

The bittersweet sentiments of the lyrics sung by Frank Sinatra reflect all too well people's feelings about how they go about "getting over" close relationships after those relationships are dissolved. Discussions of close relationships often stop at the point of dissolution, as though the formal parting of the ways between people was the end of the story. As most of us know, the dissolution or its acknowledgement is really only the beginning of a complex process of self- and other- examination, values-reassessment and behavior modification. How do people get over close relationships? What is the attribution process involved in "getting over" a relationship? The folk-remedy in the above and similar lyrics prescribes activity, alternatives, moment-to-moment loss of oneself among other people and things. We say that time heals all wounds, but we know we are impatient to have more involvement in the process of getting over a close relationship than simply marking time on a calendar. Do social psychologists have any more to say on the subject than the wisdom of "Get busy and you will forget"?

In this discussion, we will consider three stages in the process of "getting over" close relationships; (1) understanding the general characteristics of getting over close relationships: (2) a discussion of strategies of getting over relationships; and (3) applying attributions, derived from such strategies, that appear to be necessary in successfully getting over close relationships. The fact is that, regardless of how inadequately we have understood the sources of conflict in relationship breakdown, generations of people have found ways of accepting and overcoming the pain of relationship dissolution. Thus, it behoves us to examine the lessons of these practical strategies if we are to explain the general phenomenon of relationship breakdown. In this analysis we will speculate with some abandon in the light of the paucity of previous theory and research on this topic.

General characteristics

At various times and places it may be easier to get over a given relationship than in other circumstances. Although this facility may be associated with specific personality types, we suspect that situational context has much to do with one's ability to deal with the pain of separation. It is more acceptable to break up when everyone else is doing the same: it is more painful when yours is the only break-up on the block! We take our cues about the appropriateness of our feelings—before, during and after the break-up—from our total social context. What is the social context of close relationships now, and how is it different from other times?

One important and paradoxical aspect of our experiences and perceptions associated with "getting over" relationships is that *close relationships do not end—they merely change.* Insofar as the relationship exists in the mind(s) of the participant(s), it continues to exist cognitively although practical circumstances have reduced or eliminated contact. Relationships are as much symbolic events and images to the involved parties as they are interactional episodes or histories. We may put space or time or other people between ourselves and formerly significant others, but we maintain the relationships in our minds, sometimes in an increasing string of ex-partners. In fact, as we move through our life-space and add relationships to our personal histories, the dyads in our minds may pile up, and we may experience a sort of social-cognitive "overload". One way to cope with the stress of overload is to reduce the priority of attention awarded various inputs (Milgram, 1970). Thus a relationship on the wane is, in effect, a file that must be less and less often "accessed". We never erase it—we do not know how. We simply find a way to push the non-operative file to the bottom of the stack. This is cold computer language, but not new to the study of close relationships. For example, Walster and Walster (1978) have noted that women tend to be LIFO (last in, first out) of relationships, and men tend to be FILO (first in, last out)—both contrary to social stereotypes of clinging women and timorous, untrappable men. But the computer metaphor probably has some major limitations in explaining how people get over relationships. As Weiss' (1975) and Harvey et al.'s (1978) data show, separated people often engage in incessant attributional reviews of what went wrong—as if the print button were stuck with solace found only in the sleep brought about by tranquilizers.

There may be interesting side-effects to this close relationship "pileup". One therapist recommends dealing with a glut of relationships by mentally storing them in "freezer bags", to be removed and "thawed" as the client feels prepared to deal with them!

Another characteristic of the "getting over" experience is the fact that *the relationship has taken on an identity separate from either partner*. In a close, romantic relationship, people often feel as if there is a three-party negotiation under way: Oneself, the Other, and Our Relationship. Couples speak of having "O.R. talks", serious discussions about the course of the relationship, as if it were a cohabiting but separate being from either identity. Again, consistent with Weiss' findings, these "O.R. talks" often symbolize the death knell of the liaison, just as contract talks between labor and management portend conflict and strike. Is this "third party" experience the same for friendships as it is for romantic or cross-sex relationships? Given the vastly different messages of our media and social context, probably not. We speak more often about our "friends" than about our "friend*ships*". Yet we reserve a special language for the abstract merger of two people in a romantic partnership. Here the social context, the Big Picture, conveys a message of what is expected in a particular kind of close relationship. The media blitz focuses on heterosexual relationships as qualifying for that "-shipness" (see Levinger, 1977). We form expectations, perceptions, and words to match those images.

In friendships, it seems as if it is possible to maintain separate individuality, with closeness born of contact and interaction. In a romantic closeness this contact conceives of—and then becomes contingent upon—perceiving Our Relationship as a new creation, a third party. It is as if Our Relationship were a hollow mannequin to be filled by both parties thereto. When the relationship breaks down, the mannequin, once alive, sickens; with dissolution it dies. In retrospect it can even seem like murder! In any event, the death of Our Relationship highlights the myth of mutuality. There always were two separate people participating in the partnership, coexisting with an idea or symbol that was shaped by expectations all round. Neither party could or did subsume the other, and with breakdown and dissolution there comes a sense of loss and bereavement for something that never could support itself. Reactions to separation may involve the same stages as to a death: anger and denial, bargaining, acceptance and resolution (Weiss, 1975; and see McCall's chapter in the present volume). But this is more like the death of a child than one's own death.

We can summarize these general considerations before looking at specific strategies for getting over relationships. First, relationships do not end, they change. We maintain information about the relationships and their status in ever-increasing mental files, and then try to cope with the stress of information overload and turnover. Moreover, the relationship may have taken on a separate identity, which leaves an unsettling vacuum after dissolution. We learn our coping strategies from our social context, and try to maintain our cognitive files according to the rules of that environment.

Strategies for getting over close relationships

There is a dearth of scholarly work on this topic. Nonetheless, people appear to confront the problems of dissolution and somehow bumble and blunder their way to resolution. The experience of relationship dissolution is like those Robert Frost said you cannot go around—you must go through them. Duck (1981) notes that there must be "mechanisms of repair" which have yet to be studied and taxonomized (see also *Personal Relationships 5: Repairing Personal Relationships,* Duck, in preparation). We agree. But in the case of getting over close relationships, we are talking about self-repair, rather than repair of the relationship or resumption of the partnership.

The process of self-repair in getting over close relationships begins with a search for the "rules" of (socially) proper relationship change. It was social context and expectation that drew us into the close relationship, and on that we must rely for getting out. The search for the rules involves a myriad of causal analyses: Why did our relationship end? What do I do now? Where can I go from here? How do I get there? Here the general principles of relationship breakdown manifest themselves in information and role confusion. The relationship remains a cognitive schema, often filled with haunting memories and images but a real-world impracticality. We can think about it, but we cannot have it. Moreover, something feels lost, which was an investment of ego and emotion. The first experience of getting over a close relationship is usually anxiety, a search for rules, an undefinable sense of loss and bereavement (cf. McCall's chapter, this volume).

When in doubt (and anxiety), we look to other people. From social immersion and reference, we cull cognitive clarity, social comparison cues, and anxiety reduction (Harvey *et al.,* 1978). Misery loves company, and we have little trouble finding others to share in our confusion and offer friendly advice. We can observe definite social rituals connected with getting over close relationships. From these we often extrapolate to social psychological formulas for coping with dissolution.

Rubin (1973) notes that social institutions promote activities to facilitate dyadic commitment. For example, in a college sorority, "pinning" is — or used to be—a formality requiring the fellowship of one's friends in witnessing and creating a pre-engagement. Likewise, when a couple has broken up, they often seek out their respective gender-mates for consolation and analysis of what went wrong and what to do next. Frequently, the pin that was a love-token represents a trap or shackle to the griever. It is cathartic symbolically to sunder the relationship by throwing out the pin or ring, burning love letters, and destroying photographs. These rituals can even become social celebrations. Songs are written and sung about the tragedy of it all. For example, the opening lines of a popular country ballad warn that "Cigarettes and whiskey and wild, wild, women — they'll drive you crazy, they'll drive you insane". Jokes are recited with members of the opposite sex as their brunt. In some cities, friends throw "divorce showers" for new singles. Women and men flock to one of their own kind after a break-up and reinforce the dissolution with a list of the Other's shortcomings that becomes an obloquy. Weiss' (1975) data suggest that there is comfort and consensual validation in declarations like, "She wasn't good enough for you" and "I never liked him anyway". This activity reaffirms a new status. It can of course create severe cognitive discomfort as well: "If all my friends hated him, how could I ever have fallen in love with him?" or "How could I have spent all those years with such a loser?" Sometimes this scalping therapy backfires, the guest-of-honor defending the departed: "No, you're all wrong, he was wonderful. No one knew him like I did. I'll never get over him!"

These "blood sessions" are a chance to express emotions such as anger and grief in the wake of the relationship's death, and allow the participants to wallow in a camaraderie of pain. Beneath all this celebration, however, the individual continues his/her attributional quest. We try to understand how we defined ourselves, so that we can explain our original push towards commitment. And we try to understand and explain our ex-partner's motives, so that we can understand how we were pulled into a role and relationship that satisfied other expectations. In addition to interpreting our own and others' actions, we often use a communal relationship "*Putsch*" as a first step in changing others' perceptions of our "coupleness". If we can change their expectations of us and our social commitments, we will reduce the "pull" into any new close relationship (It should be noted here, too, that these relationship-weaning rituals can be initiated *before* dissolution, during early conflict or signs of breakdown. In a way, one tries to "get over" a relationship in advance, to soften the coming blow. Of course, it is just this sort of withdrawal and rationalization that can precipitate and finalize relationship breakdown. In such a case the third party Our Relationship never quite materializes, and is not as intensely mourned).

We can develop formulas for getting over relationships. These are formal applications of the principles in play in the blood sessions and social rituals described above. One need only read popular magazine headlines to ascertain the availability of "getting over" formulas: How to Find Someone New; What to Do When the Romance is Over; Feeling Good About Yourself After a Break-Up; Life After Divorce; and so forth. Men's magazines offer advice on coping with sudden singlehood by "categorizing" the types of women available and how to deal with them (Schickel, 1980). Single career women are counseled to try alternatives such as younger men, lesbianism, or celibacy (Doudna, 1981). "Seeing other people" becomes a strategy, not simply an extension of affiliation, and extramarital affairs are an ongoing means of insulation in moving from one close relationship to another (Hunt, 1973).

"Getting over" a close relationship is no longer viewed as a passive, natural habituation, but rather as an active self-improvement program. This activity is a real source of conflict, as romantic love still denotes in our society a willingness to *lose* control, to relinquish responsibility for one's emotions. How can we in good conscience *take* control of a process that was supposed to be pleasant because it was out of control (Rubin, 1973)? Even today, many people trace their first acknowledgement of "love" in a close relationship to the realization that they were *jealous* in some situation(s) ("If you've never been jealous, then you've never *really* been in love").

"Getting over" a close relationship is a learnable skill. A popular but academically sound book on the subject applies the principles of behavior therapy to a deliberate self-help program (Phillips, 1978). This approach recommends acknowledging the pain of break-up, wallowing in it briefly, before moving on to such techniques as thought-stopping, silent ridicule, and even repulsion, to eliminate the pain of the break-up. Book sales, counseling intake rates, and workshop attendance all testify to the interest and lack of information on "getting over" a relationship the "right way".

Other formulas for getting over close relationships emphasize self-assessment and education. We must determine our past behavioral patterns in relationships, assess their value and success, and program changes as necessary (Parker, 1978). We must learn to "handle" the first relationship, from our lone perspective, before we seek to establish another (Satir, 1972). Effective communication requires self-awareness and assertiveness, and there are formulas for learning those (Alberti and Emmons, 1970). After we have eliminated the departed Other from our thoughts and behavior patterns, and no longer wince or whine at the memory or glimpse of him/her, then we must embark on a course of positive self-image building (Phillips, 1978). We may now methodically undertake the "getting over" of a close relationship by consulting a range of therapies and self-help volumes as well as the "natural" healing effects of friends, purgative rituals, and time.

Attributional activites in getting over close relationships

At the foundation of our initiating and developing close relationships, our attributions about our experiences and others' are of great significance to us. Likewise, in the breakdown and dissolution of close relationships, we search for explanations of the sources of interpersonal conflict. Given the foregoing discussion of the rituals and formulas available, how do our attributional processes facilitate "getting over" close relationships? Weiss' (1975) analysis helps answer this question. Attribution is our dynamic response to the itching question "Why?": Why did we break up? Why did she/he leave me? Why could it not work? In the "getting over" phase of close relationship dissolution, a shift is necessary in these interpretive searches. The rituals and formulas for getting over close relationships prescribe that we move from asking "Why has this happened?" to the more self-attributive question, "Why am I in pain? Why do I care?" Successfully getting over a broken close relationship does not necessarily require an understanding of the relationship's inputs and dynamics, but most probably requires a *perceived* understanding of one's own feelings, their stimuli, their significance (e.g., their value in contributing to a sense of control in the wake of the relationship's end) and the nature of the departed Other.

   The social rituals discussed above—the communication and criticism that facilitate post-break-up recuperation—focus more on the immediate problems of reconciling the fact of breakdown and the prognosis for close relationships in the future. The individual survivor is often left alone to analyze and assess the personal impact of the break-up later, over a period of time, in a lingering confusion after the purging process has set the wheels of withdrawal into motion. The formulas of the self-help articles, books, and programs put more emphasis on personal control of the "getting over" experience. These formulas suggest that we have to focus on feelings, not motives, in order to make a success of getting over a close relationship. They say that we must concentrate finally on ourselves, not on the Other or on Our Relationship. Obviously, the empirical stature of such suggestions is open to question.

   If attribution is an ongoing process of questioning and interpretation in relationships, and dissolution and resolution require a shift in the source of one's attachment and caring, then moving *out* of a close relationship requires such a shift in the *quality* of the attributional analysis. The folk wisdom that recommends replacing love-time with activity time, work-time, or new-love-time is based on the principle that we have incorporated our relationships into our life and social context. The broken relationship does not end, remember, but changes, and also changes the cognitive structure in which it resides. In answering our self-query, "Why do I care?", we may assemble evidence that we do not, and the close relationship assumes a lower and lower priority in our cognitive files (Harvey *et al.,* 1978). We may burn letters and return rings and move to distant cities, but we do not end the relationship. We save it, and reinterpret our feelings and cognitions about it and the other. Thus, we may conclude this section by arguing that "getting over" a close relationship does not mean losing or relinquishing it, but rather accepting and understanding its altered significance in our experience.

Conclusions Regarding the Merit of an Attributional Approach

As the reader might guess, we would suggest that in general an attributional approach to studying close relationships—and conflict in particular—may be quite fruitful for the field. It cannot be conceived as an all-encompassing approach. There is a paucity of evidence on numerous important questions using this approach, and attributional conceptions in this area are still embryonic and only "suggestive" in character. Nonetheless, we believe that focus upon attributions (coupled with a focus on other key social perceptions and social behavior) is essential to our understanding of close relationships. It is thus an emphasis, rather than a theory, that we are endorsing in this paper. That emphasis is upon the dynamics and complexities of how people interpret important aspects of their relationships such as conflict.

As we have argued in this chapter, attributions are integral to all phases of the conflict experience and after the relationship has ended. They appear to be made incessantly when people encounter major problems in their relationships with significant others. They explain, justify, and communicate. They sometimes come out in verbal statements, at other times are made at subvocal levels, and at still other times must be inferred on the basis of statements and behavior that are not attributional in nature. In making these assertions, we do not wish to define attribution in a narrow sense. For example, the type of social explanation analysis focusing on "real world" excuse-making revealed in the writings of Harré (1981) is congenial to the breadth we espouse.

In his treatment of attribution and interdependence as they relate to the structures and processes of relationships, Kelley (1979) offers the following remarks about the meaning of close personal relationships:

> "The unavoidable consequence of human social life is a realization of the essentially private and subjective nature of our experience of the world, coupled with a strong wish to break out of that privacy and establish contact with another mind. Personal relationships hold out to their members the possibility, though perhaps rarely realized in full, of establishing such contact." (p.169)

Indeed, it is a recognition of the centrality of our private and subjective world that forms a core precept in an attributional approach. But, just as important, the type of attributional approach that we have depicted in this chapter epitomizes the significance of the act of seeking to establish social contact. Attribution is as much a social as it is an individual psychological phenomenon.

CHAPTER 6

Communication in Dissolving Relationships

Gerald R. Miller and Malcolm R. Parks

Studies of how people actually communicate as their relationships come apart comprise a null set. Only a few studies focus on the dissolution process and most of these rely on *post hoc* analyses of terminated relationships (Duck and Allison, 1978; Levinger, 1976). Participant accounts or retrospective self-reports are the most common form of data (e.g., Burgess and Wallin, 1953; Hill *et al.*, 1976; Weiss, 1975). Although such data are both very useful and readily obtained, they cannot offer an adequate description of the dissolution process itself. Individuals may have difficulty recalling anything beyond the most general emotional outlines of what was said and done during termination (Bradford, 1977). Members of the same relationship often give strikingly different accounts for its demise (Weiss, 1975). Moreover, accounts can change as time passes and prior attachments erode. Accounts and retrospective self-reports probably say as much about people's current circumstances as about their previous actions. Research on dissolution has consequently proceeded with an incomplete description of one of its major phenomena. This chapter seeks to remedy this deficit by first outlining a series of communicative markers for the dissolution process and by then discussing a preliminary typology of communication strategies which can be used to derive hypotheses about how people actually dissolve their relationships.

Although the challenges of conducting and interpreting behavioral research have been widely noted (Duck and Allison, 1978; Keiser and Altman, 1976; Knapp, 1978; Levinger, 1976), few of the ambiguities and controversies currently holding back dissolution research can be resolved without studies of communication behavior. These difficulties include (1) ambiguity in defining what the dissolution process is and specifying where it begins; (2) confusion regarding the role of affective–cognitive variables in describing the dissolution process; (3) controversy concerning the application of relationship growth concepts to the dissolution process; and (4) differences of opinion about whether dissolution processes are general or relationship-specific.

Failure to explicate the exact nature of dissolution has been a persistent source of ambiguity. Several investigators (e.g., Albert and Kessler, 1978; Knapp, 1978; Knapp *et al.*, 1973) view encounter endings as a model for relationship endings. Yet little attention has been devoted to exploring the validity of this common analogy. Previous attempts to identify parts or stages of the dissolution process have usually lacked either firm empirical support (e.g., Knapp, 1978) or generality across relationship types (e.g., Bradford, 1977; Burgess and Wallin, 1953; Weiss, 1975). Most researchers have simply avoided the problem of explicating dissolution by treating it as a more or less discrete act. This tendency is readily apparent in studies that merely compare ongoing and terminated relationships.

The incomplete explication of dissolution also contributes to ambiguity in the distinction between temporary relationship breakdowns and permanent dissolution (cf. Duck, 1981). There have been few empirical attempts to resolve the current debate regarding the relationship between breakdowns and dissolution. When the extended dissolution process has been more fully explicated, researchers will possess better grounds for discriminating between breakdowns which are part of a larger dissolution process and those which are relatively independent markers of passing turbulence. Studies describing the communication behaviors which mark the course of relationships and studies identifying the communication strategies which actively alter that course will inevitably make comparisons between breakdowns and dissolution more explicit by providing data about the contexts that surround them, their consequences, and their accompanying description by the parties involved. By gathering a detailed descriptive base of the relevant temporal sequences of observable behaviors, researchers will help to clarify the nature of relationship dissolution.

The uncertain status of affective–cognitive variables in theories of relationship change is another major source of ambiguity. Although most studies of relationship change have focused on such variables as attraction, similarity, intimacy, and commitment; it is doubtful that these variables alone provide an adequate framework for understanding either the growth or decline of relationships (Duck, 1981; Parks, 1981). For one thing, many relationships dissolve before variables such as intimacy and commitment come into play (Rodin, Chapter 2, this volume), and many social "Barrier Forces" can continue to bind a relationship that has affectively dissolved (Levinger, 1976). Furthermore, many other processes take over from the influence of purely affective–cognitive states once the relationship begins to develop, and the social management of the relationship becomes as much a communication issue as does the participants' communication of their own attraction to each other. Finally, since individuals can influence each other only through symbolic exchanges, investigations of communication provide the crucial link between participants and thus the means of transcending a purely individual level of analysis. Therefore, studies of communication are essential even when dissolution is conceptualized in terms of affective–cognitive variables. There is a great deal of research on variables which influence affective–cognitive states such as attraction and similarity, yet there is comparatively little research showing how changes in these states influence actual communication behavior (Siegman, 1979).

A third source of controversy centers on *the relationship between development and dissolution processes*. Altman and Taylor claimed that dissolution was "... analogous to a film shown in reverse" (1973, p. 174). The assumption that dissolution is the reverse of development has been widely adopted (Davis, 1973; Knapp, 1978; Schutz, 1958). Obviously, however, there are a number of asymmetries between development and dissolution. For instance, while development can be viewed in terms of progressive information acquisition and uncertainty reduction (Berger and Calabrese, 1975; Berger *et al.*, 1976; Miller and Steinberg, 1975), dissolution need not be characterized by progressive information loss. In fact participants in dissolving relationships often step up the search for new and damaging information. Development and dissolution may bring differing behaviors into play; and even when similar behaviors are present in development and dissolution, their mix and sequence may be quite different (Duck, 1981). Perhaps the most obvious asymmetry is that relationships require joint action to develop, but can be ended by unilateral action (Simmel, 1950).

While these asymmetries should not be ignored, a complete bifurcation in theories of development and dissolution would be premature, since there is little empirical basis for either accepting or rejecting the reversal assumption. The next section of this chapter attempts to stimulate an empirical resolution by defining a set of communicative markers which should describe both the development and the dissolution process if the reversal assumption is valid. After that, we will go on to view communicative attempts to terminate a relationship within the broader framework of compliance-gaining strategies. Gaining compliance is a central activity on both sides of the developmental cycle. Although it is true that relationships develop through joint action, it is also true that the desire to develop is not always shared at a given moment, causing participants to employ commmunication to nudge each other along. Thus, it is possible to consider both development and dissolution as aspects of the more general social influence process.

Much the same point can be made about the debate regarding *whether dissolution processes are relationship-specific*. Writers frequently accentuate differences between friendship, dating relationships, and marriage (e.g., Duck, 1981; Hill *et al.*, 1976). Research on divorce has often focused on relationship-specific variables. Although differences between relationships certainly exist, most relationships are mixtures of common and unique elements. The relative impact of each type of element must be examined before the question of generality can be resolved. The following sections identify sets of behavioral markers and communication strategies which can be observed across a wide variety of relationships. We believe that they are particularly useful empirical tools for sorting out the common and unique elements of the dissolution process across relationships.

Communicative Markers in Dissolving Relationships

There is no shortage of speculation about what happens when relationships disintegrate. Feelings of attraction, warmth, and intimacy diminish; similarity decreases along with the participants' ability to coordinate their interactions; dissolving relationships are ridden with anxiety and conflict; distance, in some metaphoric sense, increases between participants. Unfortunately none of these very general descriptions isolates observable features of the dissolution process. This section attempts to develop a behavioral description by linking specific characteristics of communication with assumptions about reversal and the role of the affective–cognitive variables. Four types of variables, each of which can be observed over time and across a broad variety of relationships, are discussed: (1) global interaction characteristics; (2) communication network characteristics; (3) non-verbal communication characteristics; and (4) verbal communication characteristics. Specific behaviors and their hypothesized relationships to dissolution are summarized in Tables 1 and 2.

Global interaction characteristics

Dissolution is frequently equated with a decrease in the overall amount of communication between participants (e.g., Altman and Taylor, 1973; Davis, 1973; Knapp, 1978). More specifically, we would expect dissolution to be characterized by both a decrease in the duration of encounters and an increase in the time between encounters. However, dissolution does not necessarily imply a total cessation of communication. Former partners may maintain contact as a matter of choice, continuing obligation, or by virtue of their similar location in the physical and social environment. Divorced persons, for example, often maintain contact not only with their former spouse, but also with the former spouse's family and kin (Spicer and Hampe, 1975; Weiss, 1975). Individuals may maintain indirect contact through third parties even when direct communication ceases.

Communication network characteristics

Most research has ignored the dissolving pair's relationship to the larger communication network in which it is embedded. Yet a number of network characteristics ought to change systematically as a given dyad dissolves. Members of a dyad may interact with outsiders less frequently as a couple because of increased uncertainty and difficulty in planning joint activities (Weiss, 1975). Their social circles should contain fewer mutual members as participants pursue increasingly independent goals (Knapp, 1978; Scanzoni, 1968). Also, communication with outsiders may contain more frequent negative statements about the partner and the overall relationship (Waller and Hill, 1951). Finally, in addition to these relatively specific changes in communication, it is possible that the stress accompanying dissolution may fan out to affect a person's general behavior in all of his or her other relationships (Bloom *et al.*, 1978).

Non-verbal communication characteristics

Changes in most non-verbal communication codes accompany the dissolution process. These changes have been grouped around four types of codes: proxemic codes, kinesic codes, codes involving paralanguage and the temporal features of speech, and codes involving the use of objects.

Proxemic codes. A large number of studies have linked spatial behavior with such affective states as attraction, affiliation, intimacy, and commitment (Argyle, 1975; Davis, 1973; Hall, 1966; Harper *et al.*, 1978; Kendon, 1967; Mehrabian, 1971a, 1972). Although there are some

TABLE 1   General and non-verbal communication characteristics of
dissolution

Global Interaction Characteristics
1. Decreases in the duration of encounters
2. Increases in the time between encounters

Communication Network Characteristics
1. Decreases in the frequency of mutual interaction with those outside the
   relationship
2. Decreases in the number of mutual members in participants' communication
   networks
3. Increases in the frequency of negative comments about the partner and the
   overall relationship to those outside the relationship.

Non-verbal Communication Characteristics
Proxemic Codes
1. Decreases in physical proximity
2. Decreases in the rate and duration of touch
3. Decreases in the ratio of forward to backward body leans
4. Decreases in the rate and duration of direct body orientation
Kinesic Codes
1. Decreases in the rate of head, hand, and arm movements
2. Increases in the rate of leg, foot, and self-touch movements
3. Decreases in the rate and duration of smiling
4. Decreases in the rate and duration of mutual looks to the face

Paralanguage and the Temporal Features of Speech
1. Decreases in pitch variation
2. Increases in the discrepancy between participants' mean vocal intensities
3. Increases in the frequency and duration of simultaneous speech
4. Increases in the "non-ah" speech disfluency ratio
5. Increases in the discrepancy between participants' mean speech durations
6. Decreases in the rate of speech
7. Increases in the frequency and duration of within-utterance pauses
8. Increases in the duration of switching pauses

Codes Involving the Use of Objects
1. Decreases in the similarity of dress and object preferences
2. Decreases in access to the other person's possessions
3. Decreases in the acquisition of joint possessions
4. Decreases in the frequency of "intimacy trophy" display
5. Increases in the rate of object manipulation during interaction

exceptions and qualifications (e.g., Argyle, 1975; Bartels, 1977; Mehrabian,
1972), most studies report positive associations between these affective
states and: (1) physical proximity; (2) the rate and duration of touch; (3) the
ratio of forward to backward body leans; and (4) the rate and duration of
direct body orientation. These patterns should reverse during dissolution if
the more general assumptions about reversing affective states are correct.

Kinesic codes. Assumptions about affective states also form the basis for hypotheses regarding bodily motions in dissolving relationships. The overall rate of head, hand, and arm movements has been positively related to affiliation variables (Argyle, 1975; Bayes, 1972; Mehrabian, 1971b; Mehrabian and Ksionzky, 1972, 1974). However, excessive motor unrest may signal disaffiliation (Wolff, 1945). Specific motions such as leg and foot movements, including walking around and touching one's own body, increase when individuals feel tense (Freedman *et al.*, 1972; Mehrabian, 1971b; Mehrabian and Ksionzky, 1972, 1974). Imminent dissolution would presumably be characterized by decreasing rates of head, hand, and arm movements; and by increasing rates of leg, foot, and self-touch movements.

Facial expressions and gaze behavior have long figured in discussions of development and dissolution. Smiling, as one would expect, is a relatively clear indicator of affiliation (Argyle, 1975; Bayes, 1972; Rosenfeld, 1966). Predictions about gaze are not so simple. The functions of gaze range from expressing liking to monitoring threatening opponents (Kendon, 1967). Researchers have developed a large and frequently confusing set of gaze variables (Cappella, 1981; Cranach, 1971; Harper *et al.*, 1978). Findings consequently do not form a consistent pattern. Comparisons of friend and stranger dyads show few differences in gaze behaviors (Bartels, 1977; Breck, 1978). On the other hand, studies have generally reported positive relationships between the frequency or duration of mutual looks to the face and a series of affective variables (e.g., Argyle, 1975; Exline and Winters, 1965; Harper *et al.*, 1978; Mehrabian, 1971a, 1972; Rubin, 1970). Although support is far from unanimous, most studies suggest that the frequency and duration of mutual looks increase during development of relationships and decrease during dissolution.

Interactional synchrony and congruent body positioning are widely mentioned indicators of closeness and involvement (Condon, 1975; Davis, 1973; Kendon, 1970; Knapp, 1978; Scheflen, 1964, 1973). Unfortunately, the actual evidence of synchrony in body movements is scant. Cappella (1981) could find only five studies which were directly relevant. Four of the five could offer only anecdotal support and the most thorough investigation (McDowall, 1978) disconfirmed the synchrony hypothesis. Failure to support such a frequently repeated hypothesis testifies to the need for more rigorous behavioral research.

Paralanguage and the temporal features of speech. Most discussions of relationship change have treated paralanguage as a psychological variable. Thus, tonal qualities are often said to become "warm" or "soft" as relationships develop and "cold" as they dissolve (e.g., Argyle, 1975; Davis, 1973; Knapp, 1978). These terms lack physical referents and therefore represent perceiver evaluations rather than behavioral variables.

Few studies have examined objective features of the voice in relationship to dissolution and development. Scherer's (1974) tightly controlled experiments using a Moog synthesizer are an exception. He found that lower levels of pitch variation were associated with negative judgments of emotion (e.g., anger, boredom, disgust, fear). Natale (1975) found that the discrepancy between participants' vocal intensities decreased over the course of several meetings. Dissolution should be characterized by decreased levels of pitch variation and increasing discrepancies in vocal intensity (loudness) if assumptions about reversal and the role of affective variables are valid.

Several characteristics of vocalization may be viewed as behavioral referents for more general images of synchrony. For example, conversations in intimate relationships are perceived as smooth, coordinated, and efficient (Knapp et al., 1980). Altman and Taylor concluded that "the well-developed relationship functions in a meshed fashion without verbal or physical stumbling" (1973, p. 133). Conversely, as relationships dissolve, participants should have greater difficulty managing their interactions. The frequency of simultaneous speech might increase as turn-taking patterns break down. So, too, might the frequency of speech disfluencies. A number of studies (cf. Harper et al., 1978) show that behavioral measures of disfluency, such as Mahl's (1959) "non-ah" ratio, are positively related to anxiety. Moreover, opportunities to participate in conversation may become imbalanced when individuals lack shared expectations about how to structure their encounter. In dyads composed of strangers, for example, the duration of one person's speech is negatively related to the duration of the other person's speech (Kendon, 1967); whereas in more established dyads, durations of speech are positively correlated (Chapple, 1940; Kendon, 1967; Matarazzo et al., 1964).

Several studies imply that the rate of speech and the amount of pausing ought to be related to the process of development and dissolution. Speech rate generally increases when individuals are more affiliated (Mehrabian, 1971b; Mehrabian and Ksionzky, 1972). Higher speech rates are positively related to perceptions of warmth (Bayes, 1972). Although the relationship between speech rate and anxiety is ambiguous (Mehrabian, 1971b; Murray, 1971), the amount of silence is positively related to situational anxiety (Harper et al., 1978). For instance, families with a history of emotional or social problems tend to spend more time in silence than normal families (Ferreira and Winter, 1968). Previous studies (Allen et al., 1965; Siegman, 1979) have also shown that perceptions of warmth are negatively related to pauses within utterances and pauses between speakers' turns (switching pauses). Taken as a group, these studies suggest that dissolution will be accompanied by decreasing speech rate, increasing frequency and duration of within-utterance pauses, and increasing duration of switching pauses.

Codes involving the use of objects. Behavior towards objects can provide powerful clues about the overall nature of a relationship. Knapp (1978), for example, notes that similarities of dress and object preferences often decrease in dissolving relationships. Access to the other person's possessions may decrease as well (Altman and Taylor, 1973). Furthermore, individuals in dissolving relationships will probably acquire fewer joint possessions. Rings, jewelry, photographs, and other "intimacy trophies" which symbolize better days will be displayed less frequently (Knapp, 1978). Finally, the increased discomfort thought to characterize dissolving relationships may be reflected by increased rates of object manipulation during interaction (Mehrabian and Ksionzky, 1972, 1974).

Verbal communication characteristics

Few studies actually focus on patterns of verbal communication in dissolving relationships, although verbal code use is widely presumed to change as relationships come apart. Self-disclosure figures prominently in discussions of development (e.g., Altman and Taylor, 1973), but it is beset with a host of measurement problems (Chelune, 1979) and often cannot be clearly applied to the dissolution process. Our discussion deals with the relatively observable features of verbal code use across two admittedly crude categories: (1) word choice and the construction of statements, and (2) statement choice and the construction of encounters. The specific behavioral changes outlined below are summarized in Table 2.

Word choice and the construction of statements. Wiener and Mehrabian (1968) have probably contributed the most to our speculation concerning very specific aspects of language change in dissolving relationships. Their exploration into the linguistic correlates of non-immediacy yields a wealth of variables. Some are not relevant to our purposes, while others are modified in order to apply more directly to the dissolution process. None the less, we have followed Wiener and Mehrabian in hypothesizing that dissolution should be accompanied by changes in three aspects of word choice and sentence construction: spatio-temporal designations, denotative specificity, and agent–action–object relationships.

Verb tenses, adverbs, and demonstrative pronouns reflect the spatio-temporal relationships between the speaker, listener, and the topic of conversation. Participants should have little difficulty focusing on the "here and now" in well-developed, smoothly functioning relationships (Wiener and Mehrabian, 1968). As relationships dissolve, however, word choice and statement construction might show progressive spatio-temporal

TABLE 2 Verbal communication characteristics of dissolution

Word Choice and the Construction of Statements
Spatio-Temporal Designation
1. Decreases in the use of the present tense
2. Decreases in the use of future-tense references to the relationship
3. Increases in the use of adverbial clauses
4. Increases in the use of temporal modifiers
5. Increases in the ratio of non-immediate to immediate demonstrative pronouns
Denotative Specificity
1. Increases in the frequency of over-inclusive statements
2. Increases in the frequency of under-inclusive statements
Agent-Action-Object Relationships
1. Decreases in the ratio of pronouns implying mutuality to pronouns implying individuality
2. Increases in the frequency with which negative superlatives and absolute statements are used to describe the other person
3. Increases in the use of the passive tense
4. Increases in the frequency of qualifying words and phrases
5. Increases in the frequency of explicit causal references to the other person, people outside the relationship, and events or forces outside the relationship

Statement Choice and the Construction of Encounters
1. Decreases in the frequency of evaluative statements
2. Increases in the ratio of reconciling and appealing acts to rejecting and coercive acts
3. Increases in the number of exchanges in conflict encounters
4. Decreases in topic dwell-time

---

distancing. We could expect a decreased use of the present tense to describe events actually occurring within the current encounter (Mehrabian, 1971a; Wiener and Mehrabian, 1968). Participants ought to make fewer future tense references to their relationship (Knapp, 1978). Spatio-temporal distancing may also be displayed in greater use of clauses beginning with terms like "when", "where", "during", and "while". Temporal modifiers such as "before", "after", "at first", and "later" should be used more frequently in dissolving relationships. Finally, spatial displacements might be reflected by a changing ratio among demonstratives. The frequency of the words "that" and "those" should increase relative to the frequency of the words "this" and "these". Although these are exceedingly specific variables, past research (Wiener and Mehrabian, 1968) has shown that each can distinguish between different levels of affiliation.

Mehrabian (1971a) assumed that ambiguity-producing behaviors were a sign of non-immediacy or disaffiliation. He further asserted that ambiguity resulted from statements which were either too specific or not specific enough. Inappropriate denotative specificity can be indicated by several features of word choice and statement construction (Wiener and Mehrabian, 1968). Statements become over-inclusive when the implied subject or object is placed in a more general class rather than standing alone. Responding to a question regarding how one liked dinner at a particular restaurant by saying, "The whole evening was nice", would count as an instance of over-inclusiveness. Conversely, under-inclusiveness occurs when the subject or object refers to just a part or attribute of an implied whole (e.g., "I liked the salad"). Negations of positive comments when affirmations are possible also reflect under-inclusiveness (e.g., "It wasn't bad"). Each type of inappropriate specificity implies a discrepancy in the way communicators categorize and respond to each other and the content of their discourse. Such discrepancies should become more frequent as relationships dissolve.

Individuals linguistically separate themselves from one another as their relationship dissolves. This process is exemplified by changes in agent–action–object relationships (Wiener and Mehrabian, 1968). Knapp (1978) hypothesized that pronouns which portray the participants as a couple (e.g., "we", "us", "our", "ours") will be used less frequently than pronouns which reinforce the separateness of the individual (e.g., "I", "me", "my", "mine", "you", "your", "yours"). Tangential support for this hypothesis can be gleaned from Premo's (1979) finding that strangers used fewer statements of "joint situation" than married couples. Speakers also distance themselves from the relationship by using negative superlatives and absolutistic statements to describe the other, his or her actions, or the overall relationship (Knapp, 1978). Finally, dissolution should be characterized by changes in the expressed responsibility for actions and evaluations. Individuals who wish to distance themselves from their partners or the overall relationship are more likely to place responsibility for their actions and evaluations in the other person or the external environment (see Harvey et al., Chapter 5, this volume). They are correspondingly less likely to express personal or shared responsibility. The redistribution of responsibility in dissolving relationships is indicated by increased use of the passive voice, more frequent qualification (e.g., "perhaps", "maybe", "somehow"), and more frequent explicit causal references to the other person or events and persons outside the relationship (Mehrabian, 1971a; Waller and Hill, 1951; Wiener and Mehrabian, 1968).

Statement choice and the construction of encounters. Researchers are presented with a vast array of theoretical possibilities for describing language use at the level of the overall encounter. Since our concern is limited to variables that have been linked to the dissolution process and whose measurement requires relatively low levels of observer inference, the paragraphs below only hint at the variety of ways in which linguistic changes could be described.

Altman and Taylor (1973) hypothesized that evaluative statements would occur more frequently as relationships developed and less frequently as they dissolved. Although we know of no complete tests of this hypothesis, three studies provide indirect support. Ayres (1981) found that persons make more evaluative comments as their relationship develops. Premo (1979) showed that married couples use more statements of agreement and disagreement than strangers. Ferreira and Winter (1968) reported that families experiencing emotional or social problems used fewer statements of agreement and disagreement than normal families. If our now well-worn assumptions are still valid, dissolution should be characterized by decreases in the overall frequency of explicit agreements and disagreements with the other person's views and actions.

An investigation of communication and marital conflict by Raush *et al.* (1974) offers a useful framework for exploring changes in the content of verbal communication. Couples enacted roles which either increased closeness or maintained distance. Spouses' communication was then coded into six categories, four of which occurred more often in one role than the other. Acts of emotional reconciliation were almost twice as frequent in closeness roles as distance roles, and acts appealing for the other's support or assistance were over seven times more frequent in closeness roles. Inversely, acts rejecting the other's views or selfhood were over four times more frequent in distance roles, and acts of coercion—e.g., power plays, personal attacks, threats, guilt inductions—were about twice as frequent in distance roles as closeness roles. These findings suggest that a useful measure of relationship change might be the ratio between reconciling and appealing acts on the one side and rejecting and coercive acts on the other. Such a measure reflects larger dialectical perspectives on closeness and distance in interpersonal relationships (Altman, 1975; Goffman, 1961, 1967; Parks, 1981; Schwartz, 1968; Simmel, 1950, 1971).

This closeness/distance ratio also encompasses several other findings and hypotheses about relationship dissolution. Davis (1973) and Knapp (1978), for example, concluded that the number of favors requested and given declines as relationships come apart. The ratio of disagreements to agreements is higher for distressed married couples than for non-distressed couples (Gottman *et al.*, 1977; Riskin and Faunce, 1972). Raush *et al.* (1974) found that coercive acts were more frequent in "discordant" than in "harmonious" couples. Threats to terminate the relationship are especially coercive and play an important role in the divorce process (Waller and Hill, 1951). The overall implication is that the frequency of reconciling and appealing acts ought to decrease relative to the frequency of rejecting and coercive acts as relationships dissolve.

Conflicts in dissolving relationships are swept along by the growing wave of rejection, coercion, and general emotional disaffiliation. Once a conflict begins, participants may have difficulty controlling it (Altman and Taylor, 1973; Knapp, 1978). Conflict episodes are consequently protracted in dissolving relationships. This view is indirectly supported by Raush and his associates (1974) who found that the number of conflict exchanges was almost twice as great among "discordant" couples as "harmonious" couples.

The amount of time participants devote to a given conversational topic generally increases as their relationship develops (Ayres, 1980, 1981). Conversely, "topic dwell-time" should decrease as the relationship dissolves. People may simply run out of things to say because they are less willing to disclose their personal feelings (Altman and Taylor, 1973; Baxter, 1979a; Davis, 1973; Knapp, 1978). In addition, participants may have greater difficulty holding conversation on a given topic as their ability to coordinate speech sequences decreases.

In this section we have described the communicative bits and pieces of the dissolution process. Our discussion stands in distinct contrast to perspectives which portray dissolution as a unitary act. Yet articulating the elements is only the first step towards constructing a more general description. The elements combine to form complex patterns characterized by compensation and matching, substitution, distinct sequences, and widely varying rates of change (Altman and Taylor, 1973; Cappella, 1981; Keiser and Altman, 1976). Moreover, patterns of verbal and non-verbal codes may reflect the uncertainty and confusion so often experienced as relationships come apart. Although research on patterns of multiple behaviors over time is certainly more difficult than research on single behaviors in single encounters, it is this more demanding research that yields some of the best opportunities to resolve empirically the ambiguities and controversies now hampering descriptions of relationship dissolution.

Selection and Use of Communicative Strategies in Dissolving Relationships

Having examined some possible behaviors that serve as communicative markers of dissolution, we now present a preliminary conceptualization of the role of communication in dissolving relationships. In developing our perspective, we shall identify specific types of communicative strategies that can be used in relational dissolution. When identifying such strategies, at least two alternative courses of action are possible: first, to explain dissolution as a particularistic behavior; second, to view it as a special instance of a general type of behavior. Some writers (e.g., Baxter, 1979b, 1980) have opted to treat communication during relational disengagement as a relatively particularistic, unique behavioral process. This approach has the advantage of producing a set of strategies whose labels are clearly linked to the act of disengagement—e.g., *withdrawal* and *avoidance* strategies, *positive tone* strategies, and *open confrontation* strategies—but at the possible expense of sacrificing conceptual and theoretical generality. Stated differently, if one assumes that communicative strategies aimed at accomplishing relational dissolution do not differ in kind from strategies invoked for a variety of other ends, a potentially useful conceptual web can be spun at a higher level of abstraction.

As implied earlier, we have chosen to accept the previous assumption; i.e., the generalist assumption that dissolution is a special instance of a general type of behavior, namely, compliance gaining or social influence. In other words, messages seeking to terminate relationships inevitably embody a *persuasive* intent. As we shall shortly demonstrate, acceptance of the assumption that communicative attempts to end relationships do not differ in kind from attempts to sell automobiles, to elect political candidates, or to marshall support for social policies permits application of a somewhat modified general set of compliance-gaining strategies, initially developed by Marwell and Schmitt (1967), to the process of relational dissolution. This is not to say, of course, that there are no relevant differences between the acts of ending a 20-year marriage or friendship and selling a used Ford, but rather that the same strategic options for achieving compliance apply to both situations.

Any preliminary conceptualization of the role of communication in dissolving relationships must also take into account differences in the relational dynamics of the involved dyad. Parties to a relationship may disagree about the desirability of termination or may differ in the intensity of their motivation to terminate. Since variation in either or both of these factors is likely to influence the particular disengagement strategies employed, the range of strategies used, and the probable response to specific strategies; a useful initial step lies in specifying some of the relevant alternatives available to relational partners. We next provide such a specification, utilizing a social exchange perspective that draws heavily on the seminal work of Thibaut and Kelley (1959; Kelley and Thibaut, 1978).

Some relational alternatives relevant to the dissolution process

Figure 1 contains examples of six possible dyadic alternatives in ongoing relationships, using two hypothetical participants, *A* and *B*. The six situations are but a small subset of possible alternatives; they have been singled out as useful cases for developing our conceptualization. Furthermore, an understanding of the six illustrative cases should allow the interested reader to extend our reasoning to other relational alternatives.

Three relational variables utilized by Thibaut and Kelley: Outcomes, Comparison Level (CL), and Comparison Level for Alternatives (CLalt) are central to our formulation. In common with most social exchange theories, the magnitude of relational Outcomes is determined by the ratio of perceived rewards to perceived costs (1959, pp.12–13). Comparison Level is the "standard by which the person evaluates the rewards and costs of a given relationship in terms of what he [she] feels he [she] deserves" (p. 21). In essence, Comparison Level represents a subjective yardstick based on all previous relationships that the individual has experienced. Thus, individuals with histories of highly favorable relational experiences will impose demanding standards on any particular relationship, while persons of more modest relational success will manifest less stringent standards of evaluation. Finally, Comparison Level for Alternatives is defined as "the lowest level of outcomes a [relational] member will accept in the light of available alternative opportunities" (p. 21). Consequently, if someone perceives that a number of attractive alternatives exist, he or she will demand reasonably high outcomes from a given relationship; if available alternatives are relatively unattractive, expectations concerning relational outcomes will be considerably more modest.

Application of these three variables to the situation diagrammed in Fig. 1a reveals that the relationship is quite attractive for both participants. Both are realizing Outcomes that exceed their Comparison Levels, and the perceived alternatives (CLalt) do not exceed their CLs. No contemplating of dissolution would be expected in this situation save for possible allusions to the ensuing hardship that would result if termination were somehow imposed—e.g., "I'd be lost without you!" or "I don't know what I'd do without you!". Popular literature, cinema, and television typically portray the intense initial stages of a romance in this way.

Perusal of Fig. 1b reveals a marked change in mutual relational alternatives. Although dissolution is not currently a viable option, relational attractiveness has declined for both participants, with Outcomes falling below CL but remaining above CLalt. The partners are mutually dependent but are relatively unenthusiastic about their relational lots.

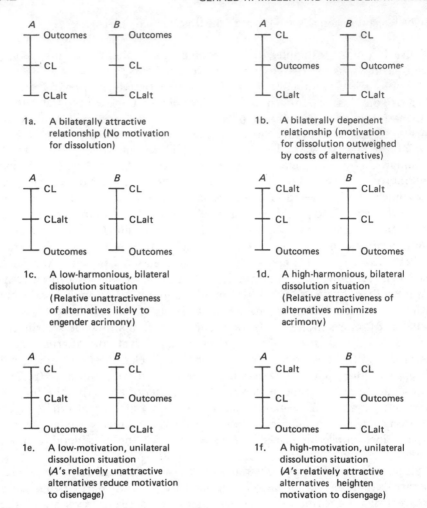

FIG. 1   Some relevant social exchange alternatives in *A*'s and *B*'s relationship.

References to dissolution may be introduced to try to bring the partner's behaviors more into line with desired Outcomes—e.g., "I don't know how much longer I can tolerate your selfishness and lack of concern without splitting". Indeed, continued displays of punishing behaviors coupled with threatening counter-messages could well produce the situation depicted in 1c. Here both parties agree that the relationship is beyond redemption and that dissolution is necessary. Unfortunately, their consensus takes the form of the "lesser of evils", since all perceived alternatives fall below CL. Parting is therefore likely to be accompanied by acrimonious, hostile message exchanges—e.g., "This is all your fault!" or "If you weren't so damned stubborn and self-centered, we could have worked things out!"

By contrast, Fig. 1d captures the conditions for a maximally harmonious, friendly termination. Not only do the participants agree on the necessity of relational dissolution, they also perceive the existence of alternatives whose Outcomes lie above their CLs. These alternatives may include the presence of another attractive relational partner, internalization of the belief that autonomy is highly preferable to psychologically debilitating relational dependence, or a variety of other factors. Regardless of the precise nature of the alternatives, they cushion the trauma of termination; and while it would be naive to anticipate absolutely no verbal conflict, the participants should be able to separate with minimal recrimination.

The four preceding situations share the important characteristic of symmetrical perceptions, i.e., both parties define the social exchange dynamics identically. Figure 1e represents the first instance of asymmetry: whereas A wishes to dissolve the relationship; B wants to maintain it, a circumstance that frequently characterizes troubled relationships (Burgess and Wallin, 1953; Davis, 1973; Hill et al., 1976; Waller and Hill, 1951). This situation, along with the one depicted in Figure 1f, most clearly underscores the persuasive nature of the dissolution process. Short of abrupt withdrawal, A can realize the goal of relational termination only by gaining B's compliance, by communicating with B in ways calculated to raise B's CLalt above his or her relational Outcomes. To be sure, A can decide to exit suddenly from the relational field, but this decision may itself pose additional costs for A; especially in highly developed, heavy commitment relationships or in relationships where B has the means for punishing A's withdrawal. Such sudden flight may be branded as socially irresponsible by some of A's significant others; or in certain instances, it may even open the door for legal action against A as when charges of desertion or failure to provide child support are lodged against an errant husband. For that matter, B may simply persist in pursuing A and in hectoring A to resume intensive contact. Thus, notwithstanding the dramatic appeal of instant dissolution and despite the fact that some relationships do end abruptly (Baxter and Philpott, 1980; Burgess and Wallin, 1953; Davis, 1973), A will often follow the more conservative path of using symbolic means in order to manipulate B's assessment of the relationship.

Obviously, A's motivation to disengage will vary, depending upon his or her evaluation of available relational alternatives. In the situation described in Figure 1e, motivation to dissolve the relationship is relatively low because *A*'s CLalt, while falling above Outcomes, is below CL. Since *A* perceives no exceedingly attractive alternatives, he or she is likely to proceed about the task of gaining compliance cautiously. Indeed, *A* may be unwilling to use certain disengagement strategies because of the potential costs associated with them. Punishment strategies, for example, are likely to result in greater relational stress and conflict, a price *A* may be reluctant to pay given the relatively low value assigned to CLalt.

On turning to the situation depicted in Figure 1f, circumstances are altered radically. Here *A* is strongly impelled towards dissolution by the availability of highly attractive alternatives. Compliance gaining can thus be expected to become a no-holds-barred activity, with *A* using every strategic weapon in his or her symbolic arsenal, if necessary, to persuade *B* to accept the desirability, or at least the inevitability, of dissolution. In fact, should all else fail, *A* may follow the course of unilateral withdrawal regardless of the potential costs associated with this decision.

Where bilateral agreement exists on the desirability of dissolution, as in Figs 1c and 1d, communication will typically concern *means* rather than *ends*; i.e., compliance-gaining attempts will center on the details of dissolution. If real property or other financial assets are at stake, which is usually true when the parties are living together, considerable negotiation and bartering can be expected. Negotiation is also the rule when custody and/or support for dependent others is involved, as in the case of divorces involving children. Sometimes the demands of one party may so sharply alter the social exchange perspective of the other that agreement about the desirability of dissolution ceases to exist. For example, when faced with the prospect of extremely expensive alimony or child-support payments, a husband's perceived costs may increase sharply, with the result that CLalt falls below Outcomes causing the husband to change his mind about dissolving the marital relationship. Exchanges regarding dissolutional details would typically be more stressful and conflictful under the circumstances described in 1c, since both parties' lack of highly attractive alternatives will motivate them to maximize the rewards and minimize the costs of dissolution. When attractive alternatives exist, as in 1d, both parties are more likely to compromise or to surrender certain means objectives to hasten the process of dissolution.

For those cases of unilateral disengagement described above (Figures 1e and 1f), our analysis has centered on the objectives of the relational partner who is motivated to dissolve the relationship. This is clearly an over-simplification, for the Outcomes of the two parties are interdependent. *B* is likely to resist *A*'s compliance-gaining strategies and to counter with strategies of his or her own. As Davis puts it, *B* may even *"filibuster* to delay the adjournment of the terminal talk for as long as possible, eventually forcing the other to call for *cloture* and thus twist the sinew-severing knife he [she] wields still deeper" (1973, p. 272, italics in original). A complete conceptualization of the role of communication in dissolving relationships must eventually take account of this transactional nature of the process. Though our preliminary conceptualization falls short of a comprehensive transactional analysis, it permits generation of some hypotheses about message exchanges which are based on a reciprocal view of the dyad.

Thus far, we have alluded to compliance-gaining strategies in generic terms. It remains for us to offer a more specific typology of strategies and to generate some sample hypotheses concerning the selection and the effects of compliance-gaining strategies during the process of dissolving relationships. Hopefully, these two steps will illustrate the heuristic merit of our conceptualization.

A typology of compliance-gaining strategies used in relational dissolution

An initial attempt to develop a comprehensive taxonomy of compliance-gaining message strategies was made by Marwell and Schmitt (1967). Drawing upon various sources (Etzioni, 1961; French and Raven, 1960; Jones, 1964; Kelman, 1961; Parsons, 1963; Schmitt, 1964; Skinner, 1953; Thibaut and Kelley, 1959), these researchers generated a list of 16 strategies. These strategies are summarized in Table 3, using examples related to the process of relational dissolution.

To determine the dimensionality of their strategies, Marwell and Schmitt asked 608 undergraduate students to indicate how likely they would be to use each of the 16 appeals in four different compliance-gaining situations. The resultant factor analysis yielded a five-factor solution, summarized in Table 4 along with the labels assigned to each of the factors.

Miller *et al.* (1977) extended the taxonomical work of Marwell and Schmitt by performing a modified replication of the latter researchers' original study. There was one substantive and two procedural differences in Miller *et al.*'s approach. Substantively, while Marwell and Schmitt's four situations were devised with no guiding criteria save the desire to devise situations that would encourage use of most strategies, Miller *et al.*, relying on a conceptualization developed by Miller and Steinberg (1975), sought to devise two non-interpersonal and two interpersonal situations. The non-interpersonal situations involved relationships that had developed only to the point where participants were assumed to have based most of their predictions about message outcomes on cultural and sociological

TABLE 3 Marwell and Schmitt's typology of 16 compliance-gaining strategies (from Marwell and Schmitt, 1967, 357–358. Reproduced by permission.)

1. Promise	(If you comply, I will reward you.) You offer to release community property if your relational partner will agree to dissolution.
2. Threat	(If you do not comply, I will punish you.) You threaten to take all community property if your relational partner will not agree to dissolution.
3. Positive Expertise	(If you comply, you will be rewarded because of "the nature of things".) You tell your relational partner that it will be a lot easier on both of you if he/she agrees to the dissolution.
4. Negative Expertise	(If you do not comply, you will be punished because of "the nature of things".) You tell your relational partner that if he/she does not agree to the dissolution, it will be an extremely difficult emotional experience for both of you.
5. Pre-giving	(Actor rewards target before requesting compliance.) You finance a vacation for your relational partner to visit friends before telling him/her you wish to dissolve the relationship.
6. Aversive Stimulation	(Actor continuously punishes target making cessation contingent on compliance.) You refuse to communicate with your relational partner until he/she agrees to discuss the possibility of dissolution.
7. Debt	(You owe me compliance because of past favors.) You point out to your relational partner that you have sacrificed to put him/her through college and that he/she owes it to you to let you live your life as you desire.
8. Liking	(Actor is friendly and helpful to get target in a "good frame of mind" so that he/she will comply with the request.) You try to be as friendly and pleasant as possible with your relational partner before bringing up the fact that you want to dissolve the relationship.
9. Moral Appeal	(A moral person would comply.) You tell your relational partner that a moral person would let someone out of a relationship in which he/she no longer wished to participate.
10. Positive Self-feeling	(You will feel better about yourself if you comply.) You tell your relational partner that he/she will feel better about him/herself if he/she lets you go.
11. Negative Self-feeling	(You will feel worse about yourself if you do not comply.) You tell your relational partner that denying you your freedom will make him/her feel like a terrible person.
12. Positive Altercasting	(A person with "good" qualities would comply.) You tell your relational partner that because he/she is a mature, intelligent person, he/she will want you to do what is best for you.

13. Negative Altercasting	(Only a person with "bad" qualities would not comply.) You tell your relational partner that only someone who is cruel and childish would keep another in a relationship which the other desired to leave.
14. Altruism	(I need your compliance very badly, so do it for me.) You tell your relational partner that he/she must free you from the relationship to preserve your sanity.
15. Positive Esteem	(People you value will think highly of you if you comply.) You tell your relational partner that his/her friends and relatives will think highly of him/her for letting you go.
16. Negative Esteem	(People you value will think worse of you if you do not comply.) You tell your relational partner that his/her friends and relatives will be ashamed of him/her if he/she tries to prevent you from leaving.

information, whereas the interpersonal situations involved more fully developed relationships where participants were assumed to have based at least some of their predictions on psychological information they had gained about the relational partner. Procedurally, Marwell and Schmitt sampled exclusively from a population of college students, while Miller *et al.* sampled from a broader population; and Marwell and Schmitt employed factor analysis to examine strategy dimensionality, while Miller *et al.* used a clustering procedure.

Results indicated a great deal of inter-situational variance in the clusters, suggesting that the 16 strategies are highly situation-bound. Only one of the strategies, *liking*, was likely to be used in all four situations, with respondents reporting a high likelihood of use for *altruism* in three of the four situations. Respondents also reported a high likelihood of use for more of the strategies in the non-interpersonal situations, with the interpersonal situations characterized by a tendency to report use of fewer strategies and to avoid the use of Punishing Activity strategies to a greater extent. Generally, then, the findings did not bode well for the possibility of reducing the 16 strategies to a smaller set which would hold together across communicative situations.

Later studies have further underscored the problem of imposing a heuristic, economical factor structure on Marwell and Schmitt's taxonomy. Hunter and Boster (1978) report that the strongest determinant of strategy use lies in whether the communicator perceives his or her goal to be self-benefit or benefit of the recipient of the communication. If the communicator believes that the message recommendation primarily benefits the recipient—e.g., "You should refrain from over-eating"—any strategy is fair game, but if the communicator believes that the recommendation

TABLE 4   Oblique factor loadings for the 16 compliance-gaining
          strategies.**

Technique	Factor I	Factor II	Factor III	Factor IV	Factor V
Promise	0.507*	0.210	0.023	0.035	0.010
Threat	0.056	0.566*	0.034	0.024	0.219
Expertise (positive)	0.010	0.002	0.521	0.259	−0.002
Expertise (negative)	0.101	0.118	0.488*	0.070	0.195
Liking	0.563*	−0.030	0.150	0.142	−0.017
Pre-Giving	0.663*	0.041	0.021	0.111	0.074
Aversive Stimulation	0.126	0.560*	0.062	0.071	0.095
Debt	0.023	0.210	0.070	0.037	0.486*
Moral Appeal	−0.111	0.150	0.103	0.363*	0.286
Self-Feeling (positive)	0.121	0.011	0.047	0.732*	0.042
Self-Feeling (negative)	−0.031	0.149	−0.012	0.556*	0.289
Altercasting (positive)	0.117	0.009	0.175	0.599*	−0.090
Altercasting (negative)	−0.010	0.209	−0.059	0.371*	0.343*
Altruism	0.217	0.013	0.116	−0.018	0.530*
Esteem (positive)	0.135	−0.066	0.118	0.557*	0.182
Esteem (negative)	0.010	0.099	−0.008	0.345*	0.526*

*Items used to define the five factors.
**From Marwell and Schmitt, p. 360 (reproduced by permission). They name the five
factors as follows: Factor I, Rewarding Activity; Factor II, Punishing Activity; Factor III,
Expertise; Factor IV, Activation of Impersonal Commitments; Factor V, Activation of
Personal Commitments.

involves self-benefit—e.g., "You should wash my car tomorrow"—certain
strategies are typically deemed inappropriate. Although provocative, this
finding suffers from two limitations when applied to the process of
relational dissolution: first, interpretation of self- versus other- versus *joint*-
benefit is likely to suffer from distortion and rationalization in highly
charged dissolution settings; second, the question of how to classify the
total set of compliance-gaining message strategies remains unanswered.

Most recently, Burgoon *et al.* (1980) have reported that the Marwell and
Schmitt typology fails to yield an interpretable factor solution. They argue
that the 16 appeals suffer from a good deal of conceptual redundancy while

at the same time failing to constitute an exhaustive inventory of strategies, the latter point having been granted by Marwell and Schmitt in their original study. Burgoon *et al.* conclude with the pessimistic prognosis that the typology has limited utility and needs revamping.

Several features of the Marwell and Schmitt typology point to the need to approach strategy classification for the relational dissolution process from a somewhat different stance. One of their strategies, *liking*, does not refer to a specific symbolic assertion but rather to a cluster of possible preparatory behaviors calculated to get the relational partner "in a good frame of mind" before presenting the compliance-gaining appeal. Though such an approach may sometimes be used in dissolving relationships—e.g., the party seeking dissolution may treat the reluctant partner in a friendly, empathic way immediately prior to confronting him or her with some specific proposal for termination—it may often be counterproductive because it actually enhances the perceived relational Outcomes for the party who is unwilling to end the relationship. Furthermore, as noted above, *liking* is not, strictly speaking, a specific message strategy, but rather a set of antecedent behaviors used to "prepare" the relational partner for the actual compliance-gaining message. The typology we will propose focuses entirely on specific message strategies.

In addition, preliminary research by the first author using college respondents attests to the complexity and potential redundancy of the 16 strategies proposed by Marwell and Schmitt. Not only do respondents typically require a great deal of time to respond, they frequently have difficulty distinguishing among and identifying the various strategies, even when these strategies are orally explained and written examples are provided. Indeed, when respondents were asked to write specific examples of the various strategies for the particular situations involved, many of their examples did not conform with strategy definitions. Such comprehension problems would undoubtedly be aggravated when studying the general process of relational dissolution, since many relational partners do not have the benefit of a college education.

A beginning step towards a simplified typology of strategies can be found in a list of control strategies posited by Miller and Steinberg (1975). These authors identify three, more metaphorically labeled, types of strategies: Dangling Carrot, Hanging Sword, and Catalyst strategies. The Dangling Carrot and Hanging Sword categories are analogous to Marwell and Schmitt's Rewarding Activity and Punishing Activity factors. The Catalyst strategies are represented by some of the items in both the Activation of Impersonal Commitments and Activation of Personal Commitments factors of the Marwell and Schmitt analysis. Miller and Steinberg characterize catalyst strategies in the following way:

A communicator tries to elicit a desirable response, but rather than offer a reward or threaten a punishment, he [she] reminds his [her] listener of a course of action that the listener would probably find desirable. This method relies for its effectiveness on getting the individual to behave in a self-reinforcing way without directly rewarding or punishing him [her]. The controller must supply the stimulus message to trigger this process, but the listener is largely acting as his [her] own change agent. (1975, p. 125)

In other words, Catalyst strategies place the onus for action on the recipient, with compliance occurring because the recipient perceives he or she is behaving in a self-reinforcing, ego-enhancing manner and not because of the communicator's active manipulation of rewards and punishments. Examples from the Marwell and Schmitt typology include *moral appeal*, *altruism*, and *positive/negative self-feeling*.

Obviously, as illustrated by the strategies of *positive/negative self-feeling*, a Catalyst strategy can be either reward- or punishment-oriented. This fact suggests that compliance-gaining message strategies can be classified on at least two general dimensions: a reward/punishment dimension and a communicator-onus/recipient-onus dimension. Such a classification yields the following four types of strategies:

1. *Communicator-onus/Reward-oriented strategies*: the communicator specifies the rewards that will be forthcoming to the recipient if the latter complies with the persuasive request.
2. *Communicator-onus/Punishment-oriented strategies*: the communicator specifies the punishments that will be forthcoming to the recipient if the latter fails to comply with the persuasive request.
3. *Recipient-onus/Reward-oriented strategies*: the communicator specifies the positive self-reinforcing contingencies that will accrue for the recipient if the latter complies with the persuasive request.
4. *Recipient-onus/Punishment-oriented strategies*: the communicator specifies the negative self-reinforcing contingencies that will accrue for the recipient if the latter fails to comply with the persuasive request.

This four-part typology is illustrated more fully in Fig. 2, which depicts the scheme as a four-cell grid with a modified list of the Marwell and Schmitt strategies grouped in the appropriate cells. For reasons noted above, the list does not include *liking*. In addition, Marwell and Schmitt's original *moral appeal* has been extended to include both *positive* and *negative moral appeal*, an extension that makes the *moral appeal* strategies consistent with the *self-feeling* and *altercasting* strategies. In any event, the precise strategies are relatively unimportant, since the purpose is not to support the exhaustiveness or the exclusivity of Marwell and Schmitt's

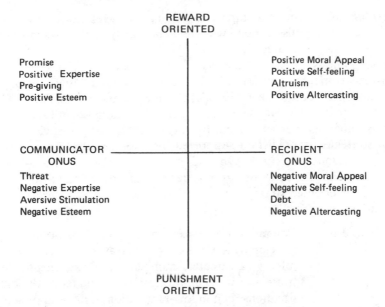

FIG. 2   Four category typology of compliance-gaining message strategies.

strategies but rather to demonstrate that a wide variety of particular compliance-gaining message strategies fit nicely into one of the four more general types of strategy.

We propose that these four general categories of compliance-gaining message strategies, when combined with the social exchange perspective of relational alternatives discussed earlier, can be used to generate numerous hypotheses concerning the role of communication in relational dissolution. The following section demonstrates the potential utility of our conceptualization by providing a sample of these hypotheses. The offered hypotheses do not exhaust the predictions that could be generated in the six illustrative relational situations, nor do they take into account the many additional dyadic situations that could be diagrammed. Clearly, an extensive programmatic research effort could be undertaken using this conceptualization, a program dealing with the details of relational dissolution as a compliance-gaining phenomenon.

Some sample hypothesis derived from the conceptualization

The following general hypothesis concerning serial selection of compliance-gaining strategies is expected to hold regardless of the relational exchange alternatives:

Hypothesis: Initial compliance-gaining messages aimed at relational dissolution will rely primarily on Reward-oriented strategies.

This hypothesis rests on the assumption that exchanges employing Punishment-oriented strategies increase relational costs for the communicator because such strategies heighten stress and conflict. Thus, a communicator seeking to achieve the goal of relational dissolution should initially construct messages using Reward-oriented, or pro-social (Roloff, 1976) strategies, a prediction supported by prior research on negotiating strategies (Donohue, 1978). In the event that these Reward-oriented strategies fail, the communicator's decision as to whether to shift to Punishment-oriented strategies will depend upon his or her perceptions of alternatives; specifically:

Hypothesis: Communicators seeking relational dissolution will: (a) employ a wider range of strategies *if necessary*, and (b) use a greater number of Punishment-oriented strategies in high-motivation, unilateral dissolution situations than in low-motivation, unilateral dissolution situations.

The rationale for this hypothesis has been outlined earlier. In low-motivation, unilateral situations, the relative unattractiveness of alternatives may deter the communicator from using strategies that are likely to increase further his or her own relational costs. When alternatives are attractive, however, as is true of high-motivation, unilateral dissolution situations; the communicator will often be willing to pay the relational costs associated with Punishment-oriented strategies, particularly since such strategies may be seen as also markedly increasing the relational costs for the reluctant partner.

Though we have suggested two hypotheses dealing with the selection of particular types of strategies, it should be emphasized that it would also be possible to posit a hierarchy of relational motivations and to link specific strategies with differing motivational goals. For instance, certain strategies—e.g., *debt* or *positive* or *negative moral appeal*—may be particularly effective for restoring or repairing relational Outcomes, while others may work better for such purposes as reformulating the relationship, reducing the level of relational intimacy, or withdrawing psychologically from the relationship. Future theorizing and research should seek to cast light on this possibility.

Predictions can also be generated concerning differences in strategy selection for low-harmonious, versus high-harmonious bilateral dissolution situations. It was suggested above that compliance-gaining exchanges in such situations typically center on the details of dissolution. When alternatives are perceived as relationally unattractive, relational partners are more apt to approach the dissolution process in a hostile frame of mind, a circumstance leading to the following hypothesis:

Hypothesis: Communicators negotiating the dissolution of their relationship will use a greater number of Punishment-oriented strategies in low-harmonious, bilateral dissolution situations than in high-harmonious, bilateral dissolution situations.

The three preceding sample hypotheses are but a subset of those that could be generated regarding strategy selection. At times our discussion of strategy selection and sequencing may have taken on an inexorably deterministic tone not in keeping with our actual view of the process. Strategies are not like missiles which, once fired, cannot be aborted. As a result of the counter-strategies employed by relational partners, the intrusion of changes in relationally extrinsic circumstances, or a variety of other factors, the party initially motivated to seek dissolution may change his or her mind, either in terms of electing to remain in the relationship or selecting a radically different strategy, or strategies, to bring about dissolution. Obviously, the analysis presented in this chapter has not taken into account the situational, communicative, and personal factors that may produce marked changes in strategic decision-making, and the issue remains open to future conceptual and empirical spadework.

A number of hypotheses concerning the effectiveness of various strategic alternatives can also be posited. For example, it can be argued that Recipient-onus strategies will generally be perceived more positively by message targets than will Communicator-onus strategies, thereby establishing a more favorable climate for dissolution negotiations. Similarly, some pro-social strategies may actually alter perceptions of relational Outcomes and of CLalt in ways calculated to reduce the probability of assenting to dissolution; as a consequence, these strategies are actually counterproductive *if* the desired goal is to achieve dissolution. All of these areas, as well as others, provide potentially fertile grounds for investigation, and each is suggested by the preliminary conceptualization that we have sketched in this chapter.

Conclusion

In this chapter we have identified some of the possible communicative markers of dissolving relationships, developed a preliminary conceptualization of the role of communication in relational dissolution—including a typology of compliance-gaining strategies that can be used to accomplish termination—and provided some research hypotheses derived from the conceptualization. Throughout we have focused on possible message exchanges that occur as relationships are coming apart. As a consequence we have largely ignored the act of physically leaving the relational field, even though we realize that some relationships are dissolved in this way, because we do not view such a course of action as a communicative strategy.

Although we believe that our conceptualization is relevant to relationships at all stages of development, we acknowledge that most of our discussion has centered on highly developed relationships entailing considerable commitment by the participants. Clearly, the calculus of CLalt and relational Outcomes often differs markedly for casual, less developed relationships; indeed, as Hill *et al.* (1976) have noted, casual college romances sometimes terminate solely because of a separation imposed by the summer vacation—popular song lyrics notwithstanding, many couples do not see each other "in September". Yet even if the primary value of our conceptualization lies in analyzing the dissolution of highly developed relationships—a concession we are not presently prepared to make—it will still be useful, since it is precisely these relationships which assume greatest significance in the lives of most people and, for that matter, in the eyes of many researchers interested in the process of dissolving relationships. Hopefully, future research will produce an empirical yardstick for assessing whether our approach advances understanding of the complex phenomenon of relational dissolution.

CHAPTER 7

Dissolving Long-Term Relationships: Patterns of Divorcing in Middle Age

Gunhild O. Hagestad and Michael A. Smyer

Social and behavioral scientists have recently begun to analyze processes of role transitions and the impact of life events on development in adulthood (e.g., Brim, 1980; Hultsch and Plemons, 1979). This chapter focuses on the social and psychological changes which accompany divorce, a critical life change likely to be faced by more than one third of the individuals who married during the 1970s.

In this chapter we argue that much of the recent work on divorce has failed to grasp the complexity of marital dissolution as a process. Social psychological work on marital break-up has tended to treat divorce as a discrete, unified event whose antecedents and consequences are examined empirically. We suggest that such an approach neglects two important factors. First, it does not reflect the complexity of marriage as a social and psychological reality. Second, it does not take into account *dimensions of time,* which are critical to life changes in general, of which divorce is a specific example.

Our discussion first outlines theoretical perspectives on transitions. Second, we examine transitions into and out of marriage, applying concepts outlined in the first section. Finally, we illustrate the need for a multidimensional, process-oriented view of marital dissolution through findings from a pilot study of divorce in middle age.

The Nature of Transitions

Ceasings and becomings

In a classic book which continues to inspire work on turning points in human lives, Van Gennep (1908/1960) wrote: "to live is to act and cease, to wait and to rest, and then to begin acting again, but in a different way" (p. 189). The same scholar encouraged social scientists to examine human ceasings and becomings as they occur in status passages, i.e., role exits and entries. He sensitized us to the fact that in most societies significant transitions are marked by rites of passage. Such public rituals help reorganize social matrices and make new identities public. Van Gennep pointed to several key characteristics of passages and of the ceremonies which accompany them. All of these characteristics involve *the social structuring of time*. First, passages are scheduled and help mark seasons of life—what Neugarten (1969) has called "the normal, predictable life cycle". Second, each transition has, within itself, a predictable sequences of events. Van Gennep saw rites of passage as having three subphases: separation, transition, and incorporation. Third, they provide some "lee-time", or time when the normal course of activities is interrupted, allowing all the actors to realign their patterns of interactions, perceptions, and expectations.

Since Van Gennep's seminal work, many scholars have examined transitions in modern societies (Neugarten and Hagestad, 1976). Rapoport and Rapoport (1965) offered direction for such research: "...it is useful to concentrate on 'critical' points of major role transitions, when the structural elements of both personality and social systems are in a somewhat 'fluid' state and new structures are in the process of being established" (p. 387). Writers from a number of theoretical approaches have agreed that roles and identity are intimately connected: "Identity evolves to some degree with each role change; self-integrity is jeopardized at every role exit and at every role entrance" (Blau, 1973, p. 212).

Temporal ordering

The extent to which life transitions are *scheduled* has been given much emphasis in recent work on adulthood. Culturally shared views of the scheduling of passages may involve cultural norms defining the *optimal timing* of transitions, through what Roth (1963) called social "timetables". However, they may also be based on what is statistically normal. That is, as part of a society, we come to share predictions about when certain transitions normally happen. An example of such predictions would be the timing of widowhood: we do not expect it to occur in the 30s and 40s, but come to think of it as something which one will quite likely have to deal with after the age of 65.

Starting with the assumption that human beings strive for predictability, authors who discuss life events argue that scheduled events which occur "on time" are less likely to represent crises than unscheduled or off-time events (Glaser and Strauss, 1971; Neugarten, 1979). Discussion of why timing is crucial has emphasized two factors. First, scheduled transitions allow the individual to prepare, through anticipatory socialization and necessary reordering of existing role involvements. Secondly, when a scheduled, expected transition is a common experience, individuals will have the comfort of peers who are "in the same boat" and can offer support.

Culturally shared expectations regarding passages not only define normal, expectable timing, but they also define normal, expected sequences of change. Across transitions there are careers—progressions of statuses which unfold in an orderly sequence (Hughes, 1971). Within transitions there are normal, expectable phases which follow in a set order. Both create "orderliness" for the individual.

> "When paths are institutionalized, a candidate can easily mark his progress, note how far he has come and how far he has yet to go. If there are the usual institutionalized acknowledgements of partial steps toward the goal, then these may constitute turning points in self-conception also."   (Straus, 1959, p. 94)

The orderly sequencing of transitions not only helps to make the future predictable and the present understandable, but it also helps individuals to create a sense of coherence in their autobiographies—their personal narratives of past life experience (Cohler, 1981; Ricoeur, 1979).

Role change and personal control

In the type of society described by Van Gennep, status passages typically involve ascribed status and roles. Thus, ceasings and becomings are role losses and role assignments, not controlled through individual choice. A number of authors have argued that when passages through ascribed statuses are highly structured and scheduled it gives *one* kind of personal control: predictability of what will happen and when.

In our society, in contrast to those described by Van Gennep, most key adult roles are achieved. Role entries and exits are voluntary and transitions are role exits and role assumptions. A sense of personal control is maintained through choice, planning, and preparation. Cultural norms, such as timetables, often serve as guidelines for individual choices.

Several authors have pointed out, however, that our society has incomplete passages, i.e., ceasings without readily available becomings. It has been argued that this is a common problem in the second half of life, given the structure of industrial society (Blau, 1973; Rosow, 1974). Blau suggests that if the ceasing is a voluntary one, the individual will seek to arrange for new becomings: "Voluntary role exit, in short, implies that the process of reintegration of the self began before the exit and that restitution for the relinquished role is at hand" (p. 212). She further argues that an involuntary role loss, on the other hand, leaves the individual in a situation where "the old pattern of his existence has been disrupted and he has no immediate plans or prospects around which to reform his self-concept" (Blau, 1973, p. 212).

In all cases of involuntary role change, *time* becomes critical. First, as we discussed above, timing determines the extent to which the individual will be prepared for the change. For example, forced retirement at age 55 may leave the retiree less prepared than forced retirement at the traditional age of 65. Secondly, the amount of warning time allowed will greatly influence the person's ability to *create* some sense of personal control and predictability. For example, in a case of unexpected "off-time" retirement at age 55, having two years compared to two month's notice allows retirees the opportunity to structure the role change to some extent, increasing their sense of personal control over the atypical role loss.

Finally, there is the issue of social markers and supports in making the transitions. For example, even when widowhood occurs off-time (early) and with no previous warning, the individual is allowed some transitional lee-time through rites of passage, such as wakes, funerals and, traditionally, a period of mourning marked by special dress. Many European societies have maintained the custom of announcing mourning. Often a small black button is the social signal that the person is in a moratorium period, a time when normal social functioning is not expected.

Transitions as crises

It follows from our discussion so far that the more role changes have the following characteristics, the more likely they are to constitute *crises* for individuals going through them:

1. They are unscheduled or off-time.

2. They are not controlled by individual choice.
3. They allow the individual little or no warning.
4. They entail status loss, not status gain.
5. They have no rite of passage associated with them.

We now turn to a discussion of marriage and divorce, using the conceptual framework outlined above.

Transitions into Marriage

Any standard family textbook will most likely point out that, in our kind of society, marriage is a complex phenomenon which can be discussed from many theoretical perspectives and on different levels of analysis. Shaped by "the romantic love complex", it is an expressive relationship which, according to cultural ideals, is based on mutual affection and attraction (Berscheid, in preparation; Huston *et al.*, 1981). It is also a social institution, which regulates key adult roles for men and women (Turner, 1970). Thus marital bonds are welded by a complex set of psychological and social forces and take many forms. Nevertheless, as members of our culture we share key definitions of marital relationships and careers.

Cultural scripts for first marriage: orderliness and support

In spite of the fact that our culture emphasizes individual choice as shaping the entry into marriage, this transition may be one of the most orderly passages for adults in our society, and one normally providing the social support of a rite of passage.

It has been found that there is strong consensus on the ideal *timing* for the passage (Neugarten and Peterson, 1957; Neugarten *et al.*, 1965). The entry into the legal status and role of being married also carries shared cultural expectations about *sequence*. The main phases in the sequence are outlined in Fig. 1. Our cultural ideals define it as normal for partners to have known each other for a reasonable amount of time prior to marriage, and for them to have strong bonds of attraction and affection. Thus, it is assumed that there is *an emotional relationship prior to a legal one* (Huston *et al.*, 1981).

The announcement of an engagement signals that the couple is ready to assume marital roles in the future. They have declared what Goffman (1961) calls *attachment* to the role. The duration, formal recognition, and quality of the engagement phase vary across western societies and from one social stratum to another. In some societies, the engagement period gives

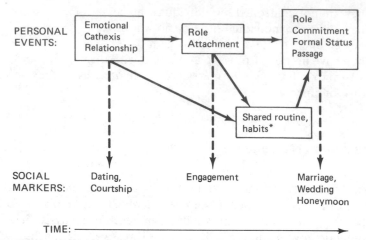

FIG. 1 Sequences of Transitions into Marriage. This may start early in the transition sequence, or following marriage.

ample practice in being socially defined as a *couple*. This is likely to start a process of what Berger and Kellner (1964) call a marital construction of reality: shared perceptions and expectations and a set of shared habits and routines.

The time of the wedding provides social arrangements to take care of the three phases that Van Gennep outlined as typical of rites of passage: separation, transition and incorporation. We speak of "giving the bride away" as a concrete expression of a separation from past family ties. Bachelor parties often take the form of mock funerals. The wedding and the honeymoon spell out "transitional time" set apart by special dress, food, and festivities. During wedding dinners and receptions those offering toasts often reminisce about past ties and relationships and welcome new ones. An overriding theme, however, is that while there may be a "loosening of ties binding the individual to premarital groups" (Rapoport and Rapoport, 1964), the change represents a *gain* of status and relationships, as expressed in the statement of folk wisdom: "You haven't lost a daughter...." The Rapoports have provided a thoughtful analysis of the honeymoon as a part of a transitional state. They describe this period as a

> "moratorium on regular participation with the expectation that the couple will use this time partly to prepare themselves for later entering and participating in society in their new social role. The honeymoon also has a function for society in that it gives others in the couple's social network time to prepare for the new relationship."   (Rapoport and Rapoport, 1964)

Even in cases where the couple choose not to have a formal rite of passage, the transition is marked by social recognition and, most likely, social support. Witnesses are required, no matter what form of ceremony marks the legal transition into marriage. Often, following a quiet, "private" wedding, friends and relatives organize social events later, almost as if they are saying, "we do not want to be cheated".

The sequence that we have outlined is typical of first marriages more than of remarriages. We would agree with Cherlin (1978) that remarriage is an incomplete institution, but we would nevertheless argue that even the process of becoming remarried has more structure than that of becoming divorced. Furthermore, remarriage means re-entering a culturally valued status. Divorcing involves giving up a valued status for one which is generally devalued and one with few, if any, norms to define the role (Goode, 1956).

The sequence that we have outlined above is a cultural ideal, a "script" provided by our social context. Reality does not always conform to the script. For example, there may be attachment to the spouse role before there is an actual person to make it viable (Huston et al., 1981). People often offer this as an explanation for marriage: "It seemed liked the right time to get married" or "What else was there to do?" In these cases, there may be considerable re-writing of personal narrative to make it closer to the script: "Of course, I was also in love". Regardless of motivation, there would be general agreement on an overall sequence, involving a period when a variety of psychological bonds are formed prior to the legal commitment of entering the marital status and role.

Evolving marital bonds

So far we have discussed three kinds of "cement" which operate in marital dyads: mutual attraction, attachment to the role, and a formal legal commitment through the institution of marriage. We further suggested that a fourth kind of bond — the creation of a shared routine of everyday living—is likely to start prior to the formal status passage. The couple develops sets of actions which are accepted as normal, typical, and associated with a certain comfort. Cherlin (1978) quotes Berger and Luckmann's notion of *habitualization*, which "carries with it the important psychological gain that choices are narrowed" (Berger and Luckman, 1966, p. 53). Throughout the transition into marriage the individual is provided with cultural guidance and social support. As we discuss below, this is not the case in the transition out of marriage.

In a previous publication, Berger (Berger and Kellner, 1964) built on Durkheim's analysis of marriage as protection against anomic and described the marital relationship as *nomos-building*: "Marriage in our society is a dramatic act in which two strangers come together and redefine themselves" (Berger and Kellner, 1964, p. 1). The longer the marital relationship, the more expectations, perceptions, and routines are likely to be taken for granted as part of an emergent "we-ness".

Turner (1970) has provided one of the most insightful recent discussions of family bonds. He argues that "the greater the number and diversity of bonds holding a relationship together, the greater its invulnerability" (p. 88). He furthermore suggests that some bonds, which he calls "crescive", emerge over the duration of a relationship. Such bonds, which were not involved in bringing people together in the first place, include (1) incomplete action, (2) shared experience, (3) interlocking roles, and (4) the reduction of reserve.

(1) Turner states that, at any moment, "family life is a tangled skein of unfinished actions that all tend to bring the members back together again" (p. 81). Remodeling the home, vacation plans, even debts, may be examples of his point.

(2) Turner's discussion of shared experience as a crescive bond is clearly inspired by Berger's work:

> "As two or more persons have a succession of shared experiences, they develop a wider and more firmly rooted common conception of reality, a conception that sets them apart from others who have not been part of the same experience circle. As the shared reality becomes more firmly differentiated from the realities of outsiders, the members need each other more and more for the confirmation of their views of events."   (Turner, 1970, p. 82)

(3) In the process of developing a routine for getting essential everyday business done, as discussed above, a division of labor emerges. Although this process is in part shaped by cultural definitions of male and female roles and prior socialization patterns reflecting them, couples also have their own idiosyncratic task allocations. Turner points out that as a result, partners relinquish tasks and skills they once mastered, and new interdependencies emerge.

(4) Finally, Turner discusses families as an arena of what Goffman (1959) calls "backstage behavior", a place where "elimination of the necessity to maintain the ceremonial image establishes a bond between those involved" (Turner, 1970, p. 87). The longer people know one another, Turner argues, the more personal idiosyncrasies become known and predictable.

Implied in Turner's discussion is the suggestion that while there may indeed be a weakening of the initial bonds of attraction as marriages endure —through what Pineo (1961) has labeled "disenchantment"—a variety of other bonds create new kinds of relationship "cement" (Spanier and Lewis, 1980). Thus, the longer a marriage exists, the greater the number of bonds which need to be severed in the process of divorce.

Marital Dissolution

Much recent work on divorce has treated it as a life *event,* for which causes and consequences are examined. We agree with authors who have argued that researchers need to focus on divorcing[1] as a complex, multidimensional process (Bohannon, 1970a; Edwards and Saunders, 1981; Krantzler, 1973; Salts, 1979; Weiss, 1975). We cannot treat the divorce decree as a direct parallel to the marriage certificate. While it is reasonable to assume that the legal document in the case of marriage falls in a sequence of bond-building, we cannot assume that the divorce decree similarly culminates a lengthy break-up of dyadic bonds. Indeed, for some individuals, being confronted with the formal document which takes away one of their key adult roles may mark the beginning of a long and painful period of mourning a variety of psychological bonds (cf. McCall, this volume). In the complex process of *divorcing,* the individual encounters a transition which is drastically different from the process of becoming married. Based on our previous discussion, we would argue that it is an incomplete passage, unscheduled, often out of the person's control, and with no ready social support in the form of a rite of passage.

Marital exits

Few newlyweds expect to be divorced, although the recent marital dissolution rate of close to 40% may have reduced some of the stigma previously associated with divorce and may provide some peer support. The divorce experience, however, still typically entails a sense of personal failure and a feeling that "this is not the way it's supposed to be". Normal, expectable life-course progress has been disrupted. There is no right time to get divorced.

This life change is also unscheduled in a second sense. There is no culturally defined sequence for exiting from marriage. We tend to assume that the final decree follows a prolonged period of disenchantment, growing apart, unhappiness with the spouse role, and breakdown of marital routines. However, the culture does not provide any scripts for dissolving marital bonds. Furthermore, while the creation of such bonds is a joint effort, the break-up of them is typically initiated by one partner only. For the other partner, this sets in motion a set of changes which are involuntary. To make it even more difficult for the person who is facing role loss because

---

[1]Reese and Smyer (1981) argue that gerunds should be used in all life-event research to reflect this process orientation.

of the other's decision to exit, there is often little opportunity to create transitional time.

Finally, while the acquisition of legal marital status is surrounded by social arrangements which facilitate identity changes and the reorganization of social interaction patterns, the legal termination of marital roles and relationships may be the most isolated and lonely transition faced by adults in our society. While engagement rings and wedding bands are put on amidst a supportive group who are marking and celebrating progress in a relationship career, they tend to be taken off in unplanned, private moments of relationship breakdown. The issuance of the final divorce decree is often handled through the mail. There are no witnesses, no ceremonies. The lack of ceremony and lee-time presents a problem not only for the individual going through the status change, but also for others who experience *countertransitions* (Riley and Waring, 1976) and face disruptions of established relationships and the prospect of becoming an "ex-". This is partly because divorce could be called an "incomplete" passage, since it entails the entry into a new status with few norms to create a role (Goode, 1956) — what Rosow (1976) calls "a tenuous role".

Marital dissolution and time: orderly versus disorderly divorcing

As we have outlined above, divorce is an *unscheduled* and socially unstructured transition. Some writers have referred to it as a "non-institution" (Price-Bonham and Balswick, 1980). Generally, the passage is incomplete, i.e., it involves status exit or loss without socially defined becomings. For many individuals going through marital dissolution, the experience is a highly *anomic* one. Because of the lack of cultural structuring and social supports, two factors become critical to their adjustment: *personal control* and *time*.

Although Durkheim's (1951) concept of anomie described characteristics of social systems, subsequent work has discussed the personal, psychological consequences of social anomie. An example would be the work by Srole, and his associates (1962). Recent work has discussed the personal sense of powerlessness resulting from lacking structure and predictability (e.g., Danish *et al.,* 1980; Rodin, 1980; Schulz, 1981; Seligman, 1975; Seligman and Garber, 1981). When cultural structures are lacking, as in the case of divorce, the individual's sense of control becomes more salient.

In most cases of divorce, the ceasing is one person's role *exit*; the other partner's role *loss*. The former is likely to have had more time to prepare for the ceasing than has the latter, and to create an orderly sequence of bond dissolution. Thus, people who first initiate movement towards marital dissolution will normally have time to go through a sequence of changes which reverses the transition into marriage. Such changes involve emotional withdrawal from the relationship, giving up the attachment to the marital role, disrupting the routines of everyday living, and severing bonds of shared experience and interdependencies. Individuals who have some control over the dissolution process can attempt to create 'lee-time", a time to grieve the relationship, establish new routines, seek new becomings, and build necessary social supports for making the transition.

In sharp contrast stand individuals who have little or no warning and who, therefore, are not allowed any lee-time in which to negotiate ceasing, build supports, and seek out possible becomings (Spanier and Casto, 1979; Weiss, 1975). We would expect a sense of personal powerlessnes, failure, and chaos to result from these divorces, particularly since divorce in our society is a transition which challenges the individual to create some order, control, and predictability because the culture has left it unstructured. These challenges will be felt in relation to three kinds of bonds which are dissolved:

1. *Emotional Cathexis*. We have chosen to use a term most commonly found in psychoanalytic writing. People are cathected to another when they have *emotional energy* invested in their relationship.
2. *Attachment to the Spouse Role*. Independently of feelings towards the role partner, people may want to keep "husband" or "wife" in their role portfolio and regard it as a key part of their identity.
3. *The Routines of Everyday Living*. As we discussed above, there is comfort in established habits and routines which make life predictable and ensure that the tasks of everyday living are taken care of. Related to such routines are bonds of shared experience and familiar, shared objects. Blau speaks of widowhood and says that part of bereavement is caused by "the termination of any enduring pattern of activity between one person and a significant other" (Blau, 1973, p. 210).

In the process of divorcing, people are asked to dissolve all three types of bonds (Bohannon, 1970b; Krantzler, 1973; Weiss, 1975). In what we refer to as *orderly* divorce, this has been resolved prior to the legal status change. We suggest that in an "orderly" process the marital dissolution follows the sequence found in the process of becoming married. That is, the individual decathects from the partner and the role of spouse and leaves the routines of shared living prior to the legal status change. Said differently, the person has experienced a *psychological and interpersonal divorce prior to the legal one*.

A *disorderly* divorce process is one in which some or all of the relationship ceasings are left undone at the time of the divorce. We shall discuss seven types of disorderly divorce, using case material, in a later section.

Managing Multiple Ceasings: The Case of Midlife Divorce

So far we have discussed one aspect of time: the duration of the period available for individuals to create their own sense of orderliness in a set of ceasings for which our society provides no or few cultural guidelines or support. However, temporal dimensions also create a wider *context* for the processes of marital dissolution. Three kinds of time contexts shape the significance and challenges of marital exits: individual life time, marital time, and historical time. Furthermore, a focus on divorces after lengthy marriages (i.e., midlife divorces) allows us to examine how time available to make a transition shapes the individual's passage through it.

Time as a context

The life context. In past work on divorce, there is a young-adult bias. Most research has focused on individuals in their 20s or 30s the most "divorce prone" years (e.g., Bloom *et al.*, 1978; Bohannan, 1970b; Goode, 1956; Hetherington *et al.*, 1978; Levinger and Moles, 1979; Wallerstein and Kelly, 1980). Divorce has, for the most part, been neglected in work on middle age and old age (Smyer and Hofland, 1982). In the Riley *et al.* (1968) comprehensive review of research on aging, divorce did not appear in the index. Ten years later, a 1978 issue of *The Family Coordinator* devoted entirely to the topic of family and aging did not include a discussion of divorce. Thus, it seems that Troll *et al.* (1979) are entirely correct when they state that divorce in the second half of adulthood is "one of the most neglected areas of research in social gerontology" (p. 80). In our recent literature search, we found only two pieces of published research on divorce in the middle years. A recent Canadian investigation (Deckert and Langelier, 1978) studied couples who divorced after 20 or more years of marriage, but focused more on the quality of the marital relationship than on how the process of divorce was related to developmental issues in later adulthood. Chiriboga (1979) appears to be the only investigator who, up to now, has approached midlife divorce from a life-course perspective. We would, with him, argue that the middle years present a very different life context for marital break-up than that of early adulthood.

Middle age has been discussed as a phase of life when many people encounter an emotional cross-roads — a period of change. People do not sense this transition because they reach a certain chronological age. Rather, a reassessment and reorientation are likely to stem from two main sources: a new sense of "the weakness of the body" and a re-evaluation of social investments. A sense of vulnerability stems in part from confronting death as a personal reality, through the loss of parents and friends. For many people this experience leads to a new time perspective. Rather than thinking in terms of *years lived*, they think of *years left* (Neugarten, 1967).

Women face a distinct physical change not experienced by men, namely menopause. However, men are more likely to become preoccupied with bodily change and what some people call "body monitoring". There are good reasons for this. Middle-aged men have higher death rates than do women, mainly due to heart disease and certain types of cancer. For women, the physical changes of aging hold a different set of social meanings. Our society has a "double standard of aging": wrinkles and grey hair make a man look "distinguished"; they make a woman look "over the hill".

A sense that "time is running out", combined with changes in social roles, leads to a reassessment of personal investments of time and energy. For the woman, such re-evaluation is likely to come from seeing the children leave the nest after many years as the major focus of her life.

For the man, work is likely to present a midlife feeling of being at a crossroads. He has a sense of having gone about as far as he will go in his job or career. Opportunities to explore new options are getting fewer, and he might be bored (Levinson *et al.*, 1978).

For some middle-aged individuals, a decision to seek divorce is closely tied to issues of their life stage: a reordering of priorities; a new sense of freedom from social constraints; a realization of unfulfilled potentials. For others, divorce becomes a shattering of their whole life matrix at a time when they already feel vulnerable. Thus, their experiences of marital ceasings are likely to vary dramatically. Common to all individuals going through divorce in midlife, however, is less available peer support than is the case for persons experiencing marital break-up in early adulthood. Since divorce rates are much lower after 40 than in the 20s and 30s, it is likely to be a more lonely transition among the older divorcees. Furthermore, long-term friendships may crumble as a result of the divorce (Raschke, 1977).

Once the marital exits have been made, there is a search for becomings. The prospects of new marital roles and relationships are drastically different for men and women, due to the combined effects of sex differences in death rates and the double standard of aging. Men have a much larger pool of possible partners to choose from. Not only are there more women than men in this age group, but men can "recruit" women much younger than themselves.

Marital time. Closely related to age at divorce is the duration of marriages which are being terminated. The majority of divorces end marriages which have lasted less than ten years (National Center for Health Statistics, 1979, 1980). Clearly, the bonds which are severed in the typical divorce are qualitatively different from those found in marriages which have passed the marker of the silver anniversary. Daily routines have become ingrained and taken for granted, and there are decades worth of shared memories, photo albums, home movies, and material possessions symbolizing shared lives and meanings. Many couples have lived in the same house for the duration of their marriage and have come to see it as an anchor of their existence.

Historical time. Finally, the personal and social significance of divorce is shaped by historical context. For historians, sociologists, and psychologists, "cohort" has recently become a household word. "Cohort" refers to a group or generation of people born in a certain period, who share the "imprint" of historical events which may affect their values, lifestyle, outlook, and opportunities (Bengtson and Cutler, 1976). Recent marriage cohorts will have a dissolution rate of nearly 40%. Couples married earlier in this century have had much lower divorce rates (National Center for Health Statistics, 1979, 1980). Thus, individuals who are currently experiencing marital break-up between the ages of 40 and 60 belong to a generation who are more likely to regard divorce as a personal failure. Furthermore, expectations regarding what constitutes a "good" marriage have changed over recent cohorts.

Time and process. As we have discussed above, divorce after the age of 40 has been greatly neglected in past research. We would argue, however, that there are compelling reasons to pursue research in this area beyond the dearth of factual information. If our theoretical interest centers on a multidimensional process of change, the study of divorce which ends marriages of long duration allows us a better perspective than does divorce which has a time frame of less than five years (the more common divorce). An analogy might be depth of field in photography. The greater spectrum of time may enable us to distinguish phenomena which in a shorter time-frame may appear indistinguishable or blurred.

We do not, given the present state of scholarship, know how midlife divorce differs from divorce in early adulthood. As we briefly discussed above, we would expect contrasts in life context and marital duration to make a difference in the personal experience of divorce. At the present time, however, our central argument is that with a marital time frame of twenty years or more, we may discover nuances in divorce experience which would be difficult, if not impossible, to detect if we focused on dissolution of marriages of short duration. We therefore feel that the study of midlife divorce is critical if we seek to develop conceptualizations of divorce processes. Once we have developed a conceptual framework, we can ask if it is applicable to divorce at all ages or if it is age-specific.

We now turn to a brief discussion of the exploratory research which prompted our attempts to conceptualize divorcing as a process.

Details of our study[2]

Sampling. Names were drawn from the public records of divorce decrees in a major metropolitan area. People who met the following criteria were included in the original study population: (1) they were between the ages of 40 and 59 at the time of the divorce; (2) they had been married to the last spouse for 16 years or more; and (3) they had at least one child aged 16 or older. From the resulting pool of 350 we contacted 133, and our final sample consisted of 43 men and 50 women. They were interviewed between October 1979 and May 1980.

Data collection. Social workers with extensive clinical experience were used as interviewers. The interview (averaging 2½ hours) included both open-ended and fixed-format items. In addition, the protocol had several standard measures (e.g., the well-being index developed by Campbell *et al.* (1976), and the Beck Depression Inventory (Beck *et al.,* 1969) as well as several measures developed for this study (e.g., a check-list of physical symptoms).

The interview was organized around several points of information: (a) current life situation and functioning (e.g., work situation, economic status, etc.); (b) availability of living relatives; (c) marital history; (d) events leading up to the divorce; (e) the respondent's reaction to the divorce as well as reactions from kin; (f) perceptions of present, past, and future events; (g) current life satisfaction and adjustment.

Characteristics of the respondents. The men and women we interviewed ranged in age from 41 to 61, with a mean of 50 for men and 48.6 for women. Prior to the divorce, they had been married from 16 to 37 years, with an average length of marriage of about 25 years. The oldest among them had their childhood years affected by the Depression (Elder, 1974). Many of our respondents were young adults during World War II, some of the men being veterans of that war. Most of our respondents were married

---

[2]The report of some details of this study has been reduced because of consideration of space. The full details can be obtained from the authors.

in the 1950s, and are the parents of the post-war "baby boom". On the average, they had three children.

Our respondents came from all walks of life, with a wide range of income and educational backgrounds. The majority had not remarried since they were divorced in the early part of 1978. One third of the men were remarried; 10% of the women.

The issue of retrospective data. Our reader may feel some uneasiness over reliance on respondents' retrospective accounts of the divorcing process. We are aware that such procedures raise complex problems of validity, and that we have no way of knowing "what really happened". However, we feel that the extent to which the individuals were able to weave together an orderly, cohesive account of what happened is important to explore. *All* of our respondents had been legally divorced for 12 to 18 months at the time of the interview. The similarities stop there. For some of them, all of the mourning of the relationship and the psychological exit from a marital role had been done 10–15 years ago. Their stories reflected a perspective gained from plenty of time to create a clear and meaningful story. These people were also the most likely to speak of new beginnings. Their past was in order, and they were focused on the future. For others, it was as if it all hit yesterday. They looked at us in bewilderment and said "I know I am divorced, but I can't really tell you what happened". For them, a long process of creating some order and sense had barely begun ... they had a lot of ceasing to do before beginnings could be contemplated.

Such observations shaped our thinking about orderly and disorderly divorcing, discussed above and further illustrated below.

Time, control and multiple ceasings: measuring key concepts

As the study progressed, we became increasingly struck with the complexity and diversity of divorce experiences which emerged from the interviews. The concepts of orderly and disorderly divorce were developed after a long and frustrating process of data analysis which eventually made it clear that we had assumed considerably more "orderliness" than was to be found in the personal narratives we were examining. The concepts of time, control and patterns of attachment emerged later in perusals of our complex data.

For some of our concepts we had interview questions which provided adequate measures. For others we relied on comprehensive reading of the entire transcript by two raters. Below is a discussion of how we operationalized the concepts which we presented earlier. We start with time and control, the main dimensions which differentiate among orderly divorces, i.e., cases in which psychological divorce preceded the legal status passage. Next, we discuss the disruption of daily routines, and the giving up of attachment to the former spouse and the husband or wife role. These three factors differentiate among disorderly divorces—cases in which some or all of the psychological ceasings had not taken place at the time of the legal status change.

Time frame for marital break-up. We now turn to *transitional time,* i.e., the question of how much time the individual had to anticipate and go through a process of marital dissolution.

All of our respondents shared one time-marker. They all had final divorce decrees isued in the first half of 1978, approximately a year and a half prior to the interview. Practically all of them had petitions filed in 1977. Those are the final, legal markers. Beyond these, our respondents gave strikingly different time frames in their stories of marital break-up.

Several questions in the interview aimed at defining time frames for the process of marital dissolution. In this section, we asked our respondents to give approximate dates when they

(1) First knew that their marriage might not work out;

(2) Openly thought or talked about the possibility of divorce.

For most of our respondents, the answer to the first question gave the longest time frame. It is important to note, however, that we cannot automatically interpret these answers as indicating the start of the divorce process. Indeed, when asked when she first knew that her marriage might not work out, one respondent smiled and said: "Before the wedding!" One man, at the opposite extreme, replied: "To tell you the truth—I *never* thought it wouldn't work out!" Nevertheless, most of the answers to this question reflected a process of marital *disenchantment.* As one woman put it: "It wasn't like in the books". For some, this process was long and gradual; for others, it was sudden and dramatic.

Because of the considerations discussed above, much of our subsequent discussion will be based on answers to the second question: the time when the respondent openly recognized the possibility of divorce. We consider this a good marker for the beginning of a period of leave-taking—a time of transition, of multiple changes. Again, respondents gave strikingly different time frames. Some of them said they did not expect a divorce until the decree arrived. Others had carefully planned the divorce over a period of two decades.

Many of our respondents spoke powerfully about the need for time. Some of their statements also reflected a felt need for what Van Gennep called *separation.* Several of the women, most of whom were severely limited by financial constraints, said "If I only had been able to get away for a while...."

In our subsequent discussion, we concentrate on the amount of time that the respondent reported between the first thinking about divorce and the issuance of the decree. For simplicity's sake, we have dichotomized this variable into long (nine or more years) and short (eight years or less).

Control of the divorcing process. As indicated earlier in the chapter, several authors have suggested that personal control over stressful transitions, such as divorce, is an essential element in the adjustment to the transition. Similarly, control is an important determinant of the sense of order or disorder of the divorcing process. The divorcees with little or no control over the divorcing process may find it difficult to complete the ceasing process as well as begin the process of starting over (Spanier and Casto, 1979; Weiss, 1975).

In previous research on divorce, a common marker variable for control of the divorce has been who *filed* for the divorce, i.e., who actually sought the final legal status change. However, the person who filed may not be the person who wanted the divorce. As our interviews progressed, it became increasingly apparent that the issue of control over the process of marital break-up is very complex. For example, among our respondents there were often different motivations for seeking a separation and for seeking a final divorce. Frequently, the spouse who wanted the separation was not the same person who sought the final divorce decree. Furthermore, we would concur with those who have argued that separation and divorce often constitute qualitatively different experiences even within a single couple (Bloom and Caldwell, 1981; Chiriboga *et al.,* 1978; Kraus, 1979; Pearlin and Johnson, 1977).

In the discussion which follows, we have focused on both elements of the divorcing process—the separation and the final divorce. Both steps in the dissolution of a marriage are important, and both should be considered. As we reviewed each interview, we rated several pieces of information: who wanted the separation; who filed for the divorce; who wanted the divorce. Based upon this information, we assigned each respondent to one of three categories: Total Control, Partial Control, or No Control. In Table 1, the distribution of the respondents into these categories is displayed by sex.

We categorized 41 respondents (46% of the sample) as having had total

TABLE 1   Perceived control over divorce process by sex of respondent

	Men	Women	Total
Total control	44% (18)	47% (23)	46% (41)
Partial control	34% (14)	47% (23)	41% (37)
No control	22% (9)	6% (3)	13% (12)
	100% (41)	100% (49)	100% (90)

control. These individuals said they were in charge from the beginning and throughout the divorce process, and saw themselves as controlling both the separation and the divorce itself.

We categorized 37 respondents (41% of the sample) as having had partial control. Their control, however, was instrumental in only part of the process—either the separation or the final divorce. For example, some respondents, when faced with infidelity by their spouse, decided that "If that's the way it is, I will seek a divorce". These respondents did not totally control the dissolution of the marital relationship, but once the dissolution had progressed past a subjectively defined limit, these respondents exerted personal control over the process. Other respondents who reported partial control over the divorcing process were in charge of the initial separation phase. Many said that they assumed that separation was as far as things would go—divorce was not what they had in mind. Most of them had decathected from their spouses and their relationship, but they maintained an attachment to the role of husband and wife. Their spouses, however, sought the final decree—either because they had met someone else during the separation or because the spouse found the separation difficult to endure.

Finally, the 12 respondents (13% of the sample) who were categorized as having no control over the divorcing process reported that the entire process —both separation and legal status change—was pursued and controlled by their ex-spouse. These respondents were those most likely to feel "dumped" or abandoned, the victims of both role and relationship losses.

Interruption of shared routines—living apart. For most couples, the final separation represents a clear and difficult break with established routines and joint experiences (Hetherington *et al.*, 1978; Krantzler, 1973; Weiss, 1975). We used this as the marker for the interruption of shared routines of daily living. Only three of our respondents were not separated from their spouses at the time of the final divorce decree.

When asked about problems in setting up separate households, men and women tended to mention different things, reflecting long-standing scripts and interdependencies. A number of the women mentioned the awesome responsibility of dealing with adolescents alone, while others focused on finances. Men typically complained of lacking housekeeping skills.

However, there were more complex problems involved in leaving 25 years of shared existence. The symbolic significance of objects came through in many of the interviews. Women spoke of putting family pictures in "a safe place". One man, said: "Even the goddam furniture is alien to me!" A woman who had been caught unprepared for the divorce proceedings talked tearfully of how her former husband *did not* want any of their former belongings: "I can't understand it! Those things that had so many memories.... Now they don't seem to mean a thing to him...."

Three of our respondents and their "former" spouses were still living together at the time of the divorce decree and at the time of the interview, a year later. For these couples, the shared routines had been disrupted very little and may indeed have provided the main bond which kept the "former" spouses together.

Relationship cathexis. A major step in the divorcing process involves the withdrawal of emotional energy from the relationship with the spouse. The semi-structured interview format allowed our respondents many opportunities to reflect upon and to express their current feelings and involvement with their former spouses. One section was especially valuable for this purpose: we asked all respondents how they felt about their ex-spouses at the time of the interview. Much of the information concerning current cathexis to the former spouses came from this section of the interview where two independent readers rated each respondent as cathected or decathected. It is important to note that cathexis is not only positive, but may also consist of strong negative affect.

Some respondents likened the process of withdrawing emotional attachment to the process of mourning (cf. the chapter by McCall in this volume). Those respondents who said that they had their former spouses "out of their systems" described their current feelings as those you would feel for an acquaintance. Some expressed indifference; some pity. As has been found in previous work (e.g., Cleveland, 1979; Hetherington *et al.,* 1978; Hunt and Hunt, 1977), a number of the men and women we interviewed were still emotionally involved with their former spouse. Nearly a quarter of our respondents (14 men and 8 women) expressed what Weiss (1975) calls "persistence of attachment", i.e., continued strong emotional investment in their former spouses (see Table 2). Some of them reflected totally negative feelings about their former mates.

One respondent said: "You never really get over it.... I'm not going to go out and hurt her, but I want to see her hurt.... I've become not hateful towards marriage but resentful towards the woman I was married to...." What he was expressing was that he is ready to reinvest in the marital role, but he still feels that he has "unfinished business" with his former wife.

TABLE 2　Cathexis to ex-spouse by sex of respondent

	Men	Women	Total
Still cathected	34% (14)	16% (8)	24% (22)
Decathected	66% (27)	84% (41)	76% (68)
Total	100% (41)	100% (49)	100% (90)

Role attachment. As with their emotional investment in their ex-spouses, our respondents reflected their views of attachment to the roles of husband and wife at many points throughout our interviews. However, there were a few questions which frequently elicited comments on the role and its meaning, e.g., when we asked about changes in the respondent's life since the divorce, what advice they would give to others contemplating divorce in middle age, and what would be the best thing which could possibly happen for themselves in the future. As in the case of the relationship cathexis, two readers rated respondents regarding their attachment to the spouse role, based on interview transcripts.

As can be seen in Table 3, the majority of our respondents had given up their investment in the spouse role. One woman spoke of the few benefits of the role and the ease of letting it go: "I had to do everything alone. I felt like a married widow".

TABLE 3   Role attachment by sex of respondent

	Men	Women	Total
Still attached	37% (15)	27% (13)	31% (28)
Not attached	63% (26)	73% (36)	69% (62)
Total	100% (41)	100% (49)	100% (90)

Other respondents (31% of the sample) were still mourning the loss of the role and security of married life: as one man put it, "I don't like being a bachelor".

As we show in our discussion of disorderly divorce, 18 of the 28 individuals who were still attached to the spouse role also had continued emotional investment in their ex-spouses. Most of these were men (15). For women, it was quite common to have attachment to the role without any relationship cathexis. Ten women showed this pattern.

Marital ceasings: men and women

Sex differences are of interest in our study, both by their *absence* and their *presence.* Stereotypes suggest that men control divorces more than women, particularly in this age-cohort group. When we rated divorce accounts on personal control over the process, however, men and women were surprisingly similar in some respects. Between 40 and 50% of *both* men and women indicated *total* control of the process. If we look at the reports on who made the final decision about divorce, men have a slight edge over women (65% versus 58%). On the other hand, a greater proportion of the men (22%) than of the women (6%) related stories of divorce over which they perceived themselves as having *no* control.

We are more likely to find accounts of partial control among women than among men. Many women's stories involve cases of "if that's the way it's going to be...." That is, their husbands started actions which set the divorce process in motion, but the women took some control over the process, such as determining the timing of the divorce and the shape of the settlement. Thus, while these women may not have had any say over *whether* to divorce, they did exert influence on decisions regarding *when* and *how* the divorce were to take place. In general, what these women managed to do was to create some "lee-time", in which they could work through some of their ceasings. The men seemed less able to create such time. Thus, for more men than women in our sample, the process of psychological divorce had barely started at the time of the legal ending of the marriage. One way of interpreting this difference is that our culture, somehow, prepares women in middle age more for the possibility of divorce than it does in the case of men. There may be two kinds of such preparation. The first reflects cultural stereotypes and age-related perceptions of men and women. The second involves male and female role patterns, particularly concerning informal, expressive roles.

The double standard of aging may, on some level, prepare women for the possibility of midlife divorce. Television commercials present us with women who take vitamin pills and use night creams so that *they* will keep their youthfulness and their husbands will keep *them*. Furthermore, popular imagery has created a caricature-like prototype of the man seeking the ending of a lengthy marriage: he goes through a midlife crises, lets his hair cover his ears, wears jeans, trades the stationwagon in for a sports car ... and trades his wife in for a younger model. Because of such cultural stereotypes, it may be easier for women than for men facing the experience of a midlife divorce to "understand" and feel "understood" by a social environment. In the extreme, what such stereotypes may do is to provide some sympathy for a woman who is a "victim" of late-life divorce, while it makes a man in the same situation a laughable figure—a double loser.

The second cultural explanation for the differences that we observed points to long-standing differences in the way men and women structure their lives and their social investments. Much past work on adult role patterns and the early socialization for them has stressed that emotional-expressive aspects of relationships are more salient to women than to men. Furthermore, women *monitor* interpersonal relationships more closely than do men. Thus, previous work on changes, including break-ups, in relationships has suggested that women register trouble earlier than do men (e.g., Harvey *et al.* 1978; Hill *et al.,* 1979); such generalizations seem to be supported by our data on *time frames*. When our respondents were asked when they first realized that their marriages might not "work out", 68% of the women said nine years or more before the divorce decree, compared to 54% of the men. At the other extreme, 30% of the men said five years or less — 20% of the women. Very similar contrasts emerged when we asked about the time when they first openly considered the possibility of divorce. Nearly 40% of the men said less than three years before the final decree, compared to 28% of the women.

We see a difference in time frames in response to another question: what constituted the most difficult point in the process of marital dissolution? Nearly one third (30%) of the men said *after* a final decision had been made, with 15% saying after the issuance of the decree. Only 10% of the women saw the latter part of the process as the most difficult. For 70% of them, the period *before* a final decision had been made was the most traumatic. Thus, it appears that more women than men recognized for some time that the marriage might dissolve, and started a process of mourning and ceasing as well as attempts to create some order and control. These results are consistent with earlier investigations (Albrecht, 1980; Bloom and Caldwell, 1981; Brown *et al.,* 1976; Chiriboga, 1979).

Our data indicate that not only are women more likely to be aware of marital troubles at an earlier date than men, they also seek out more social support in their work on marital ceasings (Raschke, 1977). For example, two-thirds of the women, compared to a quarter of the men, discussed marital problems with their children. When we asked our respondents if there was a particular person who was especially helpful during the worst part of the divorce process, men were more than twice as likely as women (35% versus 14%) to say "nobody".

Some of our initial impressions of differences between men and women were strengthened when we invited our respondents to an informal gathering with members of the research team half a year after the interviews took place (needless to say, we had separate meetings for men and women). It soon became clear that men and women had quite different reasons for coming to these sessions. The men who showed up tended to be men who had been left. They came because they wanted to share feelings of anger, frustration, and pain. We found that some looked around the room in relief and said, "I thought I was the only one who needed so much time... I can't seem to get over it...."

The women who came were typically ready to work on new beginnings, on becomings ... saying, "I have done my kicking and screaming.... I have cried my eyes out ... that's behind me ... It's time to start over". It became clear that what they wanted from the workshop, both from the research team and the other women, was practical advice: How do you meet new people? How do you handle sex? Where do you find a job? How can you learn about financial management?

Currently, research on divorce adjustment provides no clear answers as to who is "better off"—men or women. It is pretty clear that when it comes to financial security, women are significantly more likely to be at risk than are men. Furthermore, becomings may be harder to accomplish for women than for men, particularly in middle age. However, from our data, it would seem reasonable to conclude that women may be more able to work themselves through marital ceasings than are men, especially when the process of marital dissolution is not one which they themselves initiated.

A Typology of Divorce Experiences

Above, we described dimensions which we use to differentiate among divorce patterns. In the case of orderly divorce, the emotional investment in the former spouse, the attachment to the role of wife or husband, and the routines of shared living had all been given up prior to the legal ending of marital role commitment (see Fig. 2). What differentiates among such divorces, in our scheme, are two factors: the amount of control the individuals had over the divorcing process, and the time they had available for managing marital ceasings.

In disorderly divorces, on the other hand, some or all of the psychological ties to married life had not been severed at the time of the legal exit from married status. The different patterns of disorderly divorces, seven in all, will be discussed in detail below. In the following sections, we present case material to illustrate the types delineated by our framework.

Patterns of orderly divorce

Sixty-one of our respondents gave accounts of orderly divorces. Two-thirds of them appeared to have controlled the process of marital dissolution from the very beginning. Among these "total control" individuals, the majority (61%) reported a long time frame (nine or more years) between the time when they first openly recognized the possibility of a divorce and the issuance of a final decree. Among those who described themselves as having had partial control over the divorcing process ($N = 22$) the majority (64%) gave accounts of relatively short time frames. Given these contrasts, we feel that difference in amount of control is the critical differentiation among orderly divorces. Typically, partial control is found in cases where individuals realized that a process of dissolution had been set in motion by their partners. Rather than remaining passive "victims", they assumed some control in shaping the subsequent phases of the process.

In the following section we present case material to illustrate contrasts between total and partial control in cases where the individual accomplished psychological and interpersonal divorce prior to the legal ending of the marriage.

Total control. The interviews with people who reported total control of the divorcing process had many similarities. Overall, they related stories of longstanding dissatisfactions and problems. Their common element was a long struggle to keep the marriage together, followed by a final realization that it was not possible. There was a final resolution that "enough is enough!". For some it was expressed as a matter of psychological survival, after years of physical and verbal abuse or repeated infidelity. For others, leaving the marriage became a matter of physical survival because abusive, alcoholic husbands made them fear for their lives. Often they had stuck with the wife role for financial reasons or "to keep the family together".

A 51-year-old mother of six reported recurrent periods of separation and family violence. Twelve years before the divorce, her husband had left for another woman. He returned soon after, although he continued to see other women. At times, his temper outbursts became violent. Through it all, she continued to take him back. As she put it, "I was 50 years old and I didn't want to lose my marriage". Finally, after her husband again moved in with another woman, the respondent's children convinced her that enough was enough—"My son told me, you don't need him and if he got sick you'd be responsible.... This helped me decide...." In the interview she gave her own account of a sudden realization that she had let go: "One night around 1 a.m. I laughed and thought to myself: who would have thought that my husband could be replaced by an electric blanket!"

For women like this, the last hurdle before taking legal divorce action was giving up their attachment to the wife *role,* not to the husband. Often there had been recurrent disruptions of shared living prior to the final separation and, as the interviewer summed up her impression of one woman: "She mourned this relationship a long time ago".

For the majority of respondents who ended up saying "enough is enough", the process was less dramatic than the case described above. Most related a steady accumulation of irritations and disappointments—a slow, steady process of disenchantment. Fundamental incompatibility, lack of communication and financial irresponsibility were frequently mentioned. However, a common pattern found in a number of these interviews was the delaying of the final marital exit because of children or other factors. About one fifth of the divorces in which the respondents saw themselves as having controlled the process involved such *delayed exits,* long after they had said "enough is enough". Some waited for the children to grow up; others waited until their own financial situation allowed for independence. Two delayed because their own parents opposed divorce.

Typical of this group of delayed exits was a 44-year-old woman who had one daughter. Soon after her daughter's birth, her marriage started to decay, since her husband did not want children: "[The child] didn't cement my marriage. It just tore it apart". Soon after the baby was born, she began to tell her husband, "One of these days you're going to wake up and I won't be here". The husband discounted these warnings. Meanwhile, she made plans to leave him when her daughter graduated from high school. In the interim, she returned to school, developed a career, and finally bought a caravan for her daughter and herself to move into. She left six months ahead of schedule. Her exit was as planned as the rest of the process. The movers came one day while her husband was at work and moved half of the furniture to her caravan. She left her husband a note telling him that they had moved out in order to avoid his "vindictive hassle". When asked why she left ahead of schedule, the respondent indicated that her husband's drinking was getting worse: "And when I've had enough, I've had enough. That's it!"

A final group of respondents who reported total control of their divorce process represent what we would call "goodbye inertia". These two women and two men described a long period of marital disenchantment and increasing distance. There were no big, loud confrontations—"It just wasn't very good". Then something happened to move them towards marital exit: another person or perhaps a sense of unexplored potential. A 51-year-old professional man recalled both a sense of midlife reassessment and the discovery of another person. After his wife accused him of infidelity, there followed a period of six years of increasing tension and distance within their marriage. As his wife withdrew, he found himself seeking companionship elsewhere: "She was quiet and reserved and I sought the company of other people. I'd find more reasons to be out of the house". After this six-year period of a deteriorating relationship, things changed when he met someone else. "I met a girl that I liked in 1972, but she wasn't my girlfriend or anything like that. But she was nice ... My wife and I hardly spoke at all.... I can remember one night I was sitting and I thought to myself, 'I'm 45 years of age and this is what I have to look forward to for the rest of my life'. It was a difficult situation. I decided to leave, but I might not have left if I had nobody to leave to".

For all the people who gave accounts of orderly divorces which they controlled from the start, we find accounts of long processes of decathecting from the relationship. For most of them, the detachment from the spouse role and the giving up of shared living came after a realization that the costs of staying far outweighed the benefits.

Partial control. Some of the orderly divorce processes were typically not set in motion by the respondent. Rather, the former spouse first expressed the wish for separation or divorce and the persons we interviewed said, "If that's the way it's going to be" — and decided to create some order and control for themselves. Eight of them had nine or more years of "warning"; 14 had less than that.

Most commonly, cases of "if that's the way it's going to be" involved spouses who separated because of other romantic involvements. The respondents reported trying to salvage the marriage until one final indignity. For example, one 56-year-old woman described her ex-husband's long history of alcohol abuse. For nine years, she put up with recurrent drinking binges and separations: "I really loved him, that's why I kept going back. I wanted it to work". The final indignity came when her husband moved and took in an alcoholic woman and her five children. Soon afterwards, one of the children stabbed him. Within six months, he was back with the woman and her children. "Before that, he had no other women. Probably deep down I hoped that things would work out before that." After her husband returned to the other woman, our respondent filed for divorce, despite his protestations.

The most extreme cases of "taking charge" of a process initiated by the spouse are what we have called the "hold-outs". These three women were confronted with husbands who wanted divorces and decided to take charge of the process. They postponed the final legal status change until it was the right time, according to their terms.

An example is a 48-year-old woman who long ago was confronted with her husband's desire to leave. According to her account, the husband delayed the exit and then wanted a "goodbye inertia" divorce: "Our little boy said to him, 'Who's going to play ball with me?' He said, 'Well, maybe I won't leave then'. It took him 10 years to get the courage to leave me. Sounded like for those ten years he wanted to leave me, but then upon meeting this person that he liked . . . that's what really gave him a strong reason for leaving." After the final separation in 1973, the husband pushed for a divorce, but his wife took her time. She had a very good reason for postponing the legal status change: "The social security laws were that you could collect on your husband's social security if you're married 20 years. I wanted to make sure that 20 years had passed, so it took four years before I filed".

Other women in the "hold-out group" postponed the divorce until their ex-spouses were involved with someone else and therefore were more willing to agree to a favorable financial settlement in order to win legal "freedom". The common theme for these three women, regardless of the circumstances, was clear ending of the psychological relationship in all ways before the legal status change of divorce.

In a way, these respondents were saying that the other person's actions killed the cathexis through repeated efforts, and this enabled our respondents to take control over the rest of the ceasings, as they refused to be "victims".

Patterns of disorderly divorce

One third of our respondents reported divorces which were disorderly, i.e., divorces in which the ending of the relationship and attachment to either the person, role, or shared routines of marriage was not complete. These 15 men and 14 women had not totally finished the process of ceasing, much less had they started the process of becoming. Despite this commonality, there was a wide range of diversity within the disorderly divorces. Some were still very much attached to their ex-spouses, some so much so that they were still living with their former husband or wife—all that had changed was the legal status. Others were no longer attracted to the role of husband or wife, and had left the routine of shared living, but they had so much emotional energy invested in the former spouse that they had been unable to begin to invest in another close relationship. As can be seen in Fig. 2, there were seven types of disorderly divorcing. Each will be discussed below, using case material.

Apart from differences in marital involvement, the disorderly divorces

	Orderly Divorce	Disorderly Divorce						
		A	B	C	D	E	F	G
Emotional Cathexis	−	+	+	+	+	−	−	−
Role Attachment	−	+	+	−	−	+	+	−
Shared Routine	−	+	−	−	+	+	−	+
Legal Role Commitment	−	−	−	−	−	−	−	−

FIG. 2   Patterns of Divorcing.

also showed contrasts in time and the experience of personal control. Unlike the orderly divorces, which were nearly evenly divided between long and short time frames, the disorderly divorces were overwhelmingly within the short time frame (22 of 29 were in the short category). While almost two-thirds of the orderly divorces reported total control of the divorcing process, only two of the disorderly divorces (7%) were within the total control cell. Twelve respondents related stories which reflected *no* control of the process of marital dissolution (see Table 4).

TABLE 4 Types of disorderly divorces as they are distributed by dimensions of time and control[a]

	Total control	Partial control	No control	Total
Long time-frame[b]	$N = 0$	Type B = 6 Type C = 1 Type F = 5 ($N = 12$)	Type B = 9 Type F = 1 ($N = 10$)	22
Short time-frame[c]	Type A = 2 ($N = 2$)	Type B = 2 Type F = 1 ($N = 3$)	Type A = 1 Type B = 1 ($N = 2$)	7
Total	2	15	12	29

[a] Type A ($N = 3$) = "Divorced in name only"   Type F ($N = 7$) = "Married status
Type B ($N = 18$) = "I wish it hadn't happened"   has its advantages"
Type C ($N = 1$) = "I've got you under my skin"
[b] Short = less than nine years between open recognition of the possibility of the divorce and the final decree
[c] Long = nine years or more between open recognition of the possibility of divorce and the final decree

Type A: Divorced in name only. Three of the disorderly divorces presented a pattern which appears paradoxical. The only change which had occurred was the legal status change from married to divorced. These two women and one man were still living with their "former" spouses, still attached to the person and the relationship and still invested in the spouse role. In other words, there was never any interruption of "life as usual".

The two women had total control of the divorce process, the man reported having none. For the women, the divorce was a way to protect themselves. Their divorces were obtained in order to have legal leverage in dealing with abusive husbands. However, one of them commented: "I feel that I'm still married in the eyes of God and the Church".

Type B: "I wish it hadn't happened". The most common pattern of disorderly divorce was Type B, those divorces where the individual still had emotional energy invested in the former spouse and was still attached to the spouse role, but had lost the routine of shared living and the legal status of being married. Eighteen of our respondents related stories of being in such a situation, 13 men and 5 women. Some of them reported partial control of the divorce process; some felt totally without control.

Five men gave their wives ultimatums at some point in the process of relationship break-down. All indicated that they gave the choice of "Come back home where you belong, or there will be a divorce", with the confident belief that their wives would see the error in their ways, and things would work out. In all cases, the opposite happened. For example, a 52-year-old man recounted 18 years of marital difficulties. His wife had recurrent bouts of depression and they had financial difficulties. Finally, after a brief separation and some financial reversals he gave her an ultimatum: "I said, 'Okay, you've been talking about divorce or separation or something. I've decided it's one way or the other. If we're married, then we're married and there's no in-between. So what's it going to be?' .... So she said, 'Well then I want to get a divorce'". Despite the fact that he had pushed the decision, this respondent was really unprepared for his wife's eager readiness to divorce.

Ten respondents reported Type B divorces which reflected no control at all and lingering attachments to both the spouse and the role. The common theme of this group was "What happened?" For the most part, they were still reeling from the shock of an abrupt end to their relationship. Many of their stories were not coherent narratives, since the respondents themselves did not fully understand why their marriages ended. Contrary to popular stereotype, however, there were only two women in this group of "cast-offs"; 8 of the 10 respondents in this group were men.

Only one of them reported a long period of recognition that there might be a divorce. In spite of the warning, however, he was caught unprepared. After nine years of marriage, he discovered that his wife was having an affair. There followed a period of twelve years in which they alternately lived together and were separated, while she continued to see other men. The future was fairly clear to see, but this 49-year-old man was still shocked when the actual divorce occurred: "I just couldn't believe that we were divorced. I would come home and go to bed and I just couldn't believe it. I was used to having her next to me at night. In the last month or so (a year after the divorce) I'm just trying real hard to accept it's just over." Despite the ample warning, this man was not ready for the end of the relationship: "My wife and I should be enjoying life now. It should be the best time of our lives."

A 47-year-old man reported that his wife told him she would leave when the children were through school. Despite the warning, he did not think their relationship was in trouble. When asked when he first realized the relationship might not work out, he replied: "I don't think I *ever* came to that conclusion".

Two elements were consistent throughout the experience of the men and women who were left, with no control and little warning: there was little time for preparatory mourning and there was little monitoring of the state of the relationship prior to the divorce process.

Type C: "I've got you under my skin". In this type of disorderly divorce, there was no sharing of daily life and no attachment to the spouse role but continued emotional investment in the spouse. One woman exemplified such cathexis — a very strongly negative one. Despite a long and difficult process of marital dissolution, this 48-year-old professional woman still had a lot of emotional energy tied up in her ex-spouse: "[We] run into each other: it used to just kill me. Sometimes I used to go the long way home just so I wouldn't see him. . . ." Her strong emotions about the man came out in explosive statements: "I wish I could go to the other end of the world. . . . He went away, but not far enough. Like a bad cold he keeps popping up. I could just pick his eyes out." With this amount of concern, albeit negative, directed at her ex-spouse, it was not surprising that this woman had not turned to the task of establishing new relationships: "I'm not ready to get involved with men. . . . I'm not ready for a close attachment."

Type D. "The common-law arrangement". This column in Fig. 2 represents a pattern which was not present in our sample. It is essentially a "common-law marriage". Individuals who have relationship cathexis and want to share the routines of everyday living but do not have attachment to the role of spouse are not likely to get married in the first place. Given the cohort background of our sample, we were not surprised that this pattern was not represented. However, we know of couples from younger cohorts who became legally divorced because they found marriage to be "a hassle", but continued to live together and described themselves as "in love". Sometimes tax laws prompted the legal status change.

Type E. "Why not be room-mates?" Based on their life situation and responses at the time of the interview, no respondents fitted this pattern exactly: a case of shared living and continued attachment to the marital role, with no emotional attachment to the former spouse. However, a man who would fit this pattern was one of the respondents who expressed a desire to move back with his former wife out of desperation. If he moved back, he would be a Type E. Currently, we have him classified under Type F, as having continued attachment to the husband role but with no shared living and no attachment to his former wife. His feelings towards her had not changed, but they had both found single life to be a hardship.

Type F: Married status has its advantages. In Type F disorderly divorces, there was no longer an investment in the former spouse, but the individual was still attached to and invested in the marital role, for a variety of reasons. Not surprisingly, this pattern was more common for women than for men (6 women, 1 man). Many of these repondents initiated marital separation to escape from a situation of emotional distance or conflict. However, they were not prepared for a legal divorce, which their spouse then decided was the next logical step.

A 42-year-old woman described the change in her marital relationship following the unexpected deaths of both of her parents. She became more dependent upon her husband and he could not handle these new demands. Subsequently, he developed a series of psychosomatic complaints. She sought a separation, deciding that the relationship was not helping either one of them, but did not want a divorce. During the separation, her husband met another woman and filed for divorce without giving the respondent any warning. Although she had mourned the loss of her relationship, it was clear that she was still very much attached to the role of wife. As she put it, when commenting on the most difficult part of the divorce: "[It's] letting go of all those dreams . . . the sailboat that I will never have, the later part of life walking off into the sunset together".

Type G: Business as usual. Our sample did not include anyone who reported no attachment to the former spouse or the spouse role, but with continued shared living. However, the story related by a man who reported a Type A pattern (divorce in name only) suggests that had we been able to interview his former wife, she may have fitted in the G category. According to him, she wanted to leave the legal status of being married and did not love him, but they continued to share everyday work and activities as they did prior to the divorce.

Summary and Discussion

This chapter reflects lessons learned from an exploratory study of divorce after two decades or more of marriage. The respondents showed striking but systematic contrasts in their divorce experiences. Some of them had twenty years in which to prepare marital exits, others had little more than two months. Some of them carefully planned and controlled the marital dissolution, taking one thing at a time. Others had a whole complex of changes thrown at them with no warning: the interruptions of long-standing routines, the severing of emotional bonds, and the legal status change. The baffling complexity and diversity in the experiences reported by the 43 men and 50 women who were interviewed made us strongly aware of the severe limitations of existing conceptual orientations. In particular, we realized the error of conceptualizing divorce as a unified *event*. The data from our study convinced us of the necessity of viewing divorcing as a multifaceted process of multiple social and psychological ceasings. This process may be made up of an orderly sequence of changes, culminating in the legal exit from marriage, or it may be disorderly, presenting a sequence in which the legal divorce represents the signal for other marital exits. For men and women with disorderly divorces, work remains to be done on ceasings before they can turn their energies to becoming.

In developing our conceptualization of divorcing as a process, we contrasted the exit from marital roles and relationship with the entry into them — the transition into marriage. Unlike becoming married, becoming divorced is a culturally unscheduled event. There is no "right" time to get divorced. Moreover, as a transition, it is unstructured. It does not have a culturally defined sequence of ceasings. There is no ritual marking, no ready-made social support. Finally, divorce, in our culture, marks the loss of a socially valued status and role and the entry into a status which still carries some stigma and which has few clear role definitions.

All of these factors put a considerable burden on the individual experiencing the process. If there is order and predictability in the transition, it is created only by the person going through it. If social support is available, it has been actively sought out. Therefore, the availability of *transitional time* becomes critical, especially in cases where the initial movement towards marital dissolution was *not* started by the individual. It appears from our sample that women, more than men, are able to take charge of such a process, to create lee-time, and to seek out transitional support, particularly in cases when the dissolution was not originally sought by them.

We feel that our preliminary findings have both theoretical and practical implications. For the study of divorce, it suggests the importance of a multidimensional process approach to this transition, with strong emphasis on time as a critical dimension. For intervention, it suggests that it is important to gain an understanding of where individuals are in a process of multiple ceasings, since this will greatly determine the type of help they need and will help us discover the best ways to offer help.

Acknowledgements

We would like to thank several colleagues and students who commented on earlier drafts of this chapter: Margaret Cohn, Anthony D'Augelli, James Garbarino, Karen Hooker, David Hultsch, Ted Huston, Helen Kivnick, Pat Piper, Ray Horn, Gwen Sorell, and Graham Spanier.

This research was supported, in part, by a Research Initiation Grant from The Pennsylvania State University, a grant from the Society for the Psychological Study of Social Issues, and a grant from the College of Human Development of The Pennsylvania State University.

CHAPTER 8

Rules and Rituals in Disengaging from Relationships

John J. La Gaipa

Disengaging from personal relationships is seldom simply an individual or dyadic process: indeed, it can rarely occur without the partners paying heed to the social context, the network, and the culture in which it is conducted. Not only does the surrounding culture provide guiding rules for disengagement but the immediate network responds actively to the repercussions of the relationship dissolution. Whilst cultural ideals about friendship influence the individuals and place them under social pressure to maintain the relationship, it is the members of the immediate network ("outsiders") who act directly to intervene and take a part in the management of disengagement processes. A full understanding of dissolving personal relationships thus requires attention not only to the two parties directly involved but also to the actions of the other persons in the network.

Accordingly, the present chapter is based on a systems approach to personal relationships (La Gaipa, 1981a) and seeks to relate the individual psychological level of analysis to broader cultural and social levels of analysis. In so doing it imports a wider range of factors than those considered by a purely individual level of analysis, since it presupposes that an individual's freedom of choice or freedom of action is constrained by the form of the dissolving relationship and the properties of the network in which the dyad is located. Such properties include the interconnectedness of the network and the multiplexity of the relationship. For instance, if the network is highly interconnected, it becomes difficult for an individual to stop seeing an antagonist without also cutting him/herself off from the other persons in the network. This thought may itself make the parties more inclined to keep open the option for repairing the relationship and to avoid extreme forms of action like excessive verbal abuse. Thus the form and course of disengagement is modified by the anticipation of future interaction—itself a function of the network, not merely of the dyad members themselves.

The present chapter explores the notion that the different levels of analysis in the systems approach are best illustrated by consideration of the rule-governed behaviour which follows from the interrelation of psychosocial, social and cultural influences on relationship dissolution. In exploring this view I have been influenced by the ethogenic approach, with its focus on the kinds of accounts that persons give to explain and justify their actions, and on the rules or rituals employed (Harré and Secord, 1972). If dissolution episodes are ritualistic, then we would expect performances to occur in accordance with the rules laid down in the script of the rule book. This script does not determine the actual course of the interaction, but serves as a guideline to action. This chapter attempts to come up with parts of such a rule book derived not just from what the antagonists do but, more importantly from the perspective of this chapter, on what is done by the observers and outside participants in the disengagement. In this chapter, then, an attempt is made to identify rules and rituals that provide structure to dissolution episodes, as described in protocols and interviews that I have collected for this purpose, and in some of the insights and findings available in various anthropological studies.

In these discussions, a ritual is a rule-governed activity of a symbolic character which draws the attention of its participants to objects of thought and feeling which they hold to be of special significance (Lukes, 1975). By "rule governed" is meant that rituals are usually patterned, repetitious behaviours which carry a "normative pressure" on their adherents. The concept of rituals, of particular significance to social anthropologists, cuts across different disciplines, though with some variation in meaning and significance. The classic work on religious rituals was done by Durkheim (1915) but more recent work has been done by Lane (1979) on the use of political rituals by the Soviet government, by Glaser and Strauss (1975) on the use of a ritual drama of mutual pretense for terminal patients; and by O'Day (1974) on intimidation rituals of control used by middle management to blackmail would-be reformers in the organization.

In the area of personal relationships suggestions have also been made on the potential value of research on social rituals. For instance, McCall (1970) has noted the importance of studying rules and rituals governing entry and exit from social relationships. Certainly, ritualized ways of forming and maintaining a relationship are well known; for instance, gift giving. Yet less attention has been given to enmity rituals and rituals governing the breakdown of relationships (Denzin, 1970) although Harré (1977a) has made the distinction between *Brüderschaft* and *Feindschaft* for expressions of rituals involved in "making friends" and "making enemies" respectively. The analysis of status degradation ceremonies by Garfinkel (1956) comes closest to the interpretation of social rituals used in this chapter. A status-degradation ceremony involves the total identity degradation of a person, and moral indignation serves to effect the ritual destruction of the person denounced. In addition to the psychological impact of the ritual, the denunication serves the extra purpose of reinforcing group solidarity and calling attention to the cultural values. Yet for such a degradation ceremony to be successful, the denouncer has to be perceived as acting as a public figure rather than as a unique person; the dignity of the supra-personal values of the community must be made salient, and the denouncer must be viewed as speaking in the name of the ultimate values and defined by the witnesses as a supporter of their values.

The argument of the present chapter, then, is that rituals are an effective means of dealing with the multilevel aspects of personal relationships undergoing change. The experiences of the individual in a termination episode are related by disengagement rituals (D-Rituals) to a higher system level, to membership in the local social network, and to the more global cultural system. Since the ending of a relationship is a shared kind of experience with which others can identify, D-Rituals also provide a mechanism for translating private experiences into something of broader social import and experience. Rituals, in general, thus serve to integrate individual and social experiences (Durkheim, 1915) and D-Rituals are particularly useful for dealing with the tensions, anxieties and ambiguities that exist regarding the proper course of action to follow when a relationship breaks down. D-Rituals serve an adaptive function in the reaffirmation of order and predictability of existing social interactions (see Turner, 1977). They also help to ease the tension and clarify status changes in much the same way as the more traditional "rites of passage" (Van Gennep, 1908/1960).

The kind of ritualized action generated by a relationship breakdown can be understood in part in terms of the specific problems faced by most dyads. In many instances, dyads involved in breakdown are able to negotiate the conflict and re-establish the relationship. But an essential condition for successful negotiation is the existence of trust, without which negotiation becomes difficult as distortion of communication occurs. The loss of trust, then, creates a barrier to reconciliation and repair: accordingly, the network's job is to provide mechanisms for restitution of trust.

Against such a background I will now consider in detail the social mechanisms and rituals that govern the management of relationship dissolution. Prominent amongst these are the use of "gossip" and of socially recognized intervention teams who take on the embodiment of the supra-personal network values and help to manage the disengagement process. Gossip is an important primary social mechanism activated by the breakdown of a relationship and it alerts outsiders that there is a problem that may require attention. However, it merely introduces the dyadic problem to the network and it is incapable of solving it. The situation, then, is ripe for bringing in a "third party" which, in the present analysis, is a secondary social mechanism for coping with relationship dissolution. Yet third-party support, e.g. in the form of an intervention team, is not likely to be effective unless certain conditions are met (see below). For instance, the intervention team in its problem-solving stance cannot really operate until it does something about the loss of trust. Trust-binding rituals enacted by persons in the intervention team communicate such messages as "You can count on us", and " ... but what are friends for". Such protestations serve to build trust in the new support system. It is necessary, then, to lay the groundwork for a problem-solving group that will provide the essential intervention. A compensatory support system is needed that is perceived as reliable and trustworthy—characteristics found wanting in the dyad.

These ideas (D-Rituals, rules, third-party interventions) are derived from the single observation, then, that the dissolution of a relationship cannot be fully understood apart from its location in the wider social system that surrounds the disrupted dyad. It now remains for the rest of the present chapter to evaluate the contribution of such notions to the understanding of dissolution processes. I will start with a general consideration of rules and rituals, proceed to consider the functions of gossip in highlighting these rules, and end with a discussion of the activities of the intervention team that is the network's agency of last resort.

Rules, Beliefs and Rituals

Much of social life rests upon a set of agreed rules that govern our patterns of actions. Meaningful human behaviour is rule-governed (Winch, 1971), and the system of rules is built around such notions as roles and institutions (Harré, 1977b). A role is a subset of rules. For instance, the role of adult daughter obliges the person to provide various services to an aged mother. Collett (1977) suggests that there is more to rules than just expectations. Rules serve as subjective yardsticks to evaluate behaviour and they encapsulate cultural notions about correct and incorrect ways of doing things. A characteristic of such rules is that they are normative: that is, the language of "ought" and "should" is appropriate when one makes an appeal to normative rules. As a consequence their violation is not only regarded as foolish but leaves one open to the notion that one is wicked. In the present context moral rules are viewed (after Wright, 1971) as foundational in that they are concerned with the maintenance of trust, mutual help and justice in human relationships. Unless such moral rules exist in some degree, it becomes almost impossible to continue any social activity, so that the significant category of moral rules is the one that affects social relationships.

Rules, myths and the tactics of dissolution

Moral rules governing personal relationships have a touch of the sacred that has significant implications for dissolution tactics and strategies. For instance, "helping and support" make up some of the moral rules governing intimate relationships (La Gaipa, 1977a). When a relationship break is imminent, the validity of such notions is seldom if ever an issue; they are axioms, not open to debate. It is assumed that without such guidelines, there would be chaos and disorder in close personal relationships and that persons should adhere to such ideals even when a relationship starts to break down. Moral rules, then, form the subjective yardstick against which the social network evaluates specific activity (Wright, 1971). Moral rules and sacred norms are the criteria and, like law, are not open to challenge, but instead, provide bases for social evaluation of individuals.

In severing a relationship, the individual thus has the peculiar problem of reducing the level of commitment to another person, whilst maintaining a commitment to the abstract ideals of "a relationship". There is a constraint to affirm the truth-value of the relevant sacred norms while actually engaging in dissolution. The person cannot simply leave a close relationship without some dramatization of adherence to the social values. Otherwise he or she would be viewed as a social deviant and be considered to be a poor credit risk for future close relationships (cf. Denzin, 1970). Separation rituals permit the individual to be articulate and dramatic in expressing adherence to the relevant social norms. They thus serve to relate the personal experiences of dissolution to the wider social context in a way that is essential to the proper completion or execution of a *recognized* and *accepted* termination of a relationship.

As an essential part of this process, the individual and the embedding social network must attend to the cultural ideas and ideals about relationships. For whilst a ritual is essentially a form of action or behaviour, it is the cultural beliefs that are themselves the guiding principles for such actions. These may have an idealized or "mythical" element, although a myth is not always identical with a specific set of ideals. Myths reflect shared or common needs rather than any abstract evaluation system.

There are varieties of social myths underlying different kinds of close personal relationships, some of which are evident from an examination of the mass media. For instance, the myth of friendship in the mass media is of a person with almost super-human qualities that comes to one's aid in time of need. Ideals of friendship such as of equality or reciprocity are given less attention by the mass media. Instrumentality and charismatic qualities are emphasized rather than the ideals of authenticity and spontaneity in a "best friend" (cf. La Gaipa, 1979).

Relationship myths have considerable impact on the growth and dissolution of personal relationships since they guide and influence not only the network's ritual actions, but also the type of accounting for a break-up that is socially acceptable. Thus, the accounts given to "make sense" of a break-up are often reconstituted and restructured in terms of the value system underlying friendship. Separations are accounted for in terms of violation of cultural values such as unending trust and loyalty. Reasons such as boredom would be inconsistent with the prevailing myths and little social support would be obtained by someone offering such explanations. Such a reason would not receive much social approval in that there is an implication that the relationship had been entered into for instrumental rather than for expressive reasons.

We can expect, then, that accounts resulting from a dispute are often not simply a result of individual "cool" analysis of what actually occurred. On the contrary, we would predict that they will be fictionalized to make them consistent with the prevailing myth (a cultural phenomenon). The relationship between the myth and the psychological is evident in such defense mechanisms as fantasy, which is used to narrow the gap between fact and fiction. Such a gap is evident also in the frequent distortions in the evaluations that people make of their friends and other loved ones (cf. Sullivan, 1953, Newcomb, 1961). Qualities are attributed to Other on the basis of the myth-like qualities associated with the role. For instance: one of the things we most fantasize about our friends is how trustworthy they are. This provides an imagined safety factor (Gillies, 1976). Relationship myths, then, contribute to the distortion in the perception of others in close relationships and are essential to our understanding of what is going on in the termination of relationships.

Upholding sacred norms and core values

As a symbolic mechanism ritual abstracts certain aspects of reality by calling attention to them and making certain aspects of social life more obvious than others. Da Matta (1977) notes that "The ritual world is . . . a world of oppositions and conjunctions, of abstractions and integrations, of the emphasis and inhibition of elements" (p. 259). This world of ritual, then, is quite arbitrary: rituals can hide and reveal, or can both delude and clarify. What is important is the specific problem that ritual tries to solve and the mechanisms that are used in the make-up of events where meaning is either hidden or not clearly revealed.

Some of the ambiguities and contradictions inherent in close personal relationships are likely to come to the fore during disengagement. It is important to note that D-Rituals do not always reduce ambiguities; instead they sometimes operate merely to gloss over them (Lane, 1979). Various "masking" techniques operate to reduce awareness of contractions in order to lessen some of their negative consequences. Conflicting issues can be clouded, for instance, by bringing in irrelevancies, particularly those that are entertaining. Masking, then, is essential for protecting sacred values and ideals. One of the effects, for instance, of disparity between "real" and "ideal" is that of cynicism. Carried to extremes cynicisms about cultural values will eventually weaken normative sanctions when adherence to the ideals in behaviour is found to have lapsed.

Axiomatic treatment is one ritualistic tactic used to prevent the empirical testing of principles of close personal realtionships. There is some kind of unwritten agreement to treat certain aspects of close relationships as being above and beyond discussion. For instance, debate on such topics as the role of loyalty in friendship, thus, remains outside of the arena surrounding disputes. Freedom of discussion as to whether "true friendship" really exists could be damaging to the continuity of prescriptions and expectations related to such role relationships. Axiomatic treatment, then serves to protect the sanctity of certain ideals and values (cf. Rappaport, 1971).

There are also "rules of irrelevance" that specify what should and should not be paid attention to during focused interaction (Goffman, 1961). Such rules are essential for maintaining the non-verifiability of sacred principles and norms. For instance, the notion of reciprocity would be regarded as irrelevant in discussions involving help to an aged parent: to argue that such a person had not really been a "good mother" would be viewed as irrelevant to the task of meeting one's own role expectations. In defining certain topics as irrelevant to the dispute in question, the basic assumptions underlying important sacred principles are made safe.

Other ritualistic acts operate to control the kind of abstractions or inferences made from specific experiences during the disengagement process. Various conclusions are possible from direct experiences with specific acts of disloyalty in a close friend. The inferences to be discouraged are those bearing on the general principle of disloyalty in friendship. In its simplest form, friends and acquaintances may question the relevance of such experiences.

D-Rituals can protect the culture core-values by concentrating on the psychological aspects of the disengagement. One technique is to focus on the more dramatic aspects of the break, including any lurid details, speculation on the "real" motives, etc. This focus on the more mundane, concrete and "down-to-earth" matters can thwart inquiry away from the more sacred prescriptions, such as the respect and honour due kin.

A common technique for avoiding inquiry into the validity of social ideals is that of denial: for instance, denial that a true friendship ever existed. If two persons were not really friends, then acts of disloyalty have little relevance to the sacred prescriptions regarding friendship and such values are not threatened. As part of such denial rituals, there is a documentation of long lists of past behaviours inconsistent with the definition of true friendship.

Maintaining social identity and integrity

Two focal problems faced by each member of a disrupted dyad consist of maintaining and protecting their own social and psychological identity, irrespective of the social norms and ideals. A common procedure for *protecting social identity* during the break-up of a relationship is for the person starting the action to initiate engagement with a third person. Adolescent girls, in particular, in describing the termination of a relationship, will often say that the friendship was quite stable until the "other girl" came along. Such comments were frequently identified in examining protocols of terminations (see Bigelow and La Gaipa, 1980; La Gaipa, 1979). The third person is interpreted by these girls as a causal factor, when in many instances it appears that the "other girl" served mainly as a medium of change.

This third-person rite is an identity-management technique designed to foster a positive self-image, and a positive other-image of oneself in the observers. What is involved is the nearly simultaneous playing of an initiation rite with one person and a termination rite with another. This engagement–disengagement cycle involves counterbalancing positive acts with negative acts, and hopefully buffering the intensity of any negative evaluations associated with the break. As such, it is a protective device to offset the possibility of being labeled as a social deviant.

Not all efforts to start a new friendship while breaking another can be called rites. What makes such behaviours ritualistic is that they are exaggerated, dramatic, and have symbolic significance. Particularly important regarding the ritualistic definition of such actions is that such behaviour has shared meaning to both the antagonists and to the network audience. The "new" friendship is viewed in these instances as instrumental to the termination of the "old" friendship. Accordingly, the initiation rites are interpreted as symbolic instead of as defining the growth of a new relationship. The third-person rite, then, is a transitional medium—a vehicle of change.

The second concern (*the protection of the psychological identities* of the parties to a dispute) is an essential task for "outsiders" when mutual self-protection of the dyad becomes an ideal. The confidentialities exchanged during the growth of a relationship often "haunt" the members of a dyad during its dissolution. Sometimes rules were established earlier within the dyad on how to handle confidentialities in case of a breakdown. In many instances, however, the events leading up to the break tend to nullify such earlier agreements. Of course, negotiations can be established during the course of the breakdown on the handling of confidentialities. This is likely to occur, however, when some semblance of trust continues in spite of the dispute. On the other hand, if trust has been reduced, the strong possibility exists that neutralization or discreditation tactics will be used to reduce the opponent's credibilty regarding sensitive information about onself. Third-party intervenors or "outsiders" are likely to emphasize the impropriety of taking advantage of or exploiting the other's vulnerability. Rules may be imposed on the use of defamation rituals to minimize such vulnerability and to protect each of the individuals from accusations of wrong-doings. Such D-Rituals and rules are likely to be most effective when they are part of a larger group effort to protect each party from the other.

These latter considerations of the problems of social and psychological identity maintenance begin to highlight the important influences of the direct and indirect action of other persons during a relationship disengagement. Whereas the members of the dyad are guided by cultural ideals, it is the members of the network who must ultimately police the norms. In the following two sections I will discuss the means by which they do this, first through the informal channel of gossip and secondly through the direct activities of intervention teams.

The Uses of Gossip

Other people start "talking" when a personal relationship starts to break down, particularly if it has some effect on them. This section considers the function and social relevance of such gossip about dissolving personal relationships. But what is gossip? The common definition is that of "idle talk" though Rosnow (1977) adds that it is really idle talk with a purpose. Rosnow defines gossip as an instrumental interaction in which A and B trade small talk about C for something in return. This could be more gossip, status, social control or anything else capable of satisfying a person's needs. It is important, then, to note that gossip is much more than slander and malice. Gossip often does have overtones of evaluation and moral judgment, but the intention is not necessarily to hurt the person being talked about. A much broader definition of gossip, then, would see it as an essential mode of communication among people who are familiar with one another involving topics of common concern. Gossip is a vastly neglected area of research considering that this communication vehicle accounts for a significant portion of real-life sociable interaction.

Functions of gossip

It should be apparent that problems of dissolving personal relationships are very likely to be the objects of gossip, but not simply in terms of slander and malice. The above broader framework, essential for examining the multiple functions of gossip, allows us to group the functions of gossip in terms of several systems: the impression management system; the evaluative system, the social system; and the information/cognitive system. Gossip has an input into each of these subsystems. Observations made by several scholars regarding each system will be made here and then applied to the present dissolution context.

Impression Management System. Persons involved in the breakdown of a relationship are sensitive about the identities that they are projecting and the kinds of analyses that other people are making of these projections. Gossip is often used to try to change or manipulate the impressions which another actor seeks to foster (Gluckman, 1968). Much of gossip is concerned, then, with impressing, influencing and persuading others regarding a particular image or impression that is preferred.

Evaluative System. Gossip is an important mechanism of social control. It is a vehicle whereby moral rules and sacred norms underlying personal relationships are stated and reaffirmed. When gossip is information about norm-breaking, it deals with under-achievement with regard to accepted standards (Hannerz, 1967). When gossip is measuring the performance of others against the norms, it ensures that the norms will be underlined again and again.

Flexibility is essential in the application of the evaluative systems. The viability of such systems cannot be maintained if they become too rigid. Such flexibility can be safeguarded in several ways; for instance, by emphasizing the frailties of man, human limitations, and the inevitability of deviation from the ideals. Flexibility, then is maintained, even while condemnation goes on (Abraham, 1970).

Social System. The social boundaries of the group or network are sharpened and highlighted by talk about dissolution. Such reinforcement occurs when gossip is used by insiders to underline the differences between themselves and outsiders (Hannerz, 1967). It is important, then, to note that gossip is a hallmark of membership. The right to gossip about certain people is a privilege which is extended only to a person when he or she is accepted as a member of the group (Gluckman, 1963). The very process of communication about the possible damage to the group resulting from disengagement, then, serves an integrative function, both in general and specifically in that it encourages the other members of the network to look to their own relationships.

Gossip is essential for updating one's knowledge of existing and future interaction patterns in the social network. Any dispute has the potential of restructuring ongoing patterns, since the dissolution of a dyad may lead to new coalitions within the network and one needs information to locate such regroupings. There is a search for information on expected changes in the structural patterning of interactions (Roberts, 1964). Examination of the flow and content of communication as a function of status differences provides some clues as to the possibly emerging configurations.

Information/Cognitive System. Gossip is employed to illuminate those ambiguous areas of behaviour about which group members have little consensus (Suls, 1977). One key area of such behaviour would seem to be that of relationship dissolution since individuals often lack the knowledge and skill for breaking a relationship without doing some damage to themselves or to others. There are, indeed, few formal rules laid down, so gossip can provide the necessary "slow scanning" of the information resource of the group (Roberts, 1964). It helps one to set up a more satisfactory map of the social environment as well as serving to pattern dissolution issues that are but vaguely perceived.

Gossip, then serves different information functions in dissolution transactions. These go far beyond the process of merely informing the public that a dispute exists. Gossip provides an information base for the later phases of the dissolution process, particularly the intervention of outside parties to help the pair in reconciliation or the transformation of the relationship. Gossip, then, provides a preliminary establishment of a negotiated account of the relationship dissolution, its "causes", it effects, and the nature of the causative dispute between the two parties.

Assumption underlying gossip. The sequence of events during information/gossip sessions is guided by a set of assumptions held by the participants. The major reason for making these assumptions explicit is that they also help us to understand the rationale underlying some of the rules and rituals that are used within the communication framework of gossip. These assumptions are quite easily identifiable by simply interviewing people about their gossip experiences. I have translated the "everyday" language to fit the psychological jargon used here.

There are some serious sampling problems in interpreting the information received by means of gossip (this is translated from: "You never get the full story in gossip"). One reason for the incomplete information is that there are constraints on the flow of information in the communication channels carrying gossip. The negative evaluations received are also quite premature. Information is transmitted on moral judgments before sufficient information is available. Information is also unreliable because of the questionable motives underlying negative evaluations. It is to be expected that individuals will engage in face-saving efforts to present the most positive image and this is reflected in biased information.

The level of reliability essentially depends upon the specific purpose of obtaining information. If the exchange of information is motivated by a desire to maintain the integrity of the self-concept of the participants, the accuracy of the information is of little relevance, especially if there is agreement regarding the reciprocity of face-saving. Information of relatively low validity, then, may have utility. Fictitious information that strengthens social bonds is more useful than accurate information that disrupts the social network.

Rules of gossiping

Gossip is a highly controlled mode of communication. Forms of gossip and its rules constrain the individual. "Rules constrain him by determining what he may say, and to whom he may say what, and how he can say anything"

(Gluckman, 1968, p. 29). I have identified some of the rules regulating the flow of communications using a gossip format.

Target. Do not gossip with persons about whom you have limited knowledge. Make sure you can predict the kind of response that will be made to your information. Otherwise, if the participant is uncomfortable or disagrees with what you say, there may be some negative consequences.

Do not gossip, then, with persons that are not fully fledged members of the group. Do not reveal confidences to persons with peripheral status in the group. Do not gossip about kin with non-kin. Do not gossip about close friends unless there is a desire for you to terminate the relationship. Do not gossip with a person who is likely to gossip about who gossips with him (cf. Yerkovich, 1977).

Information Management. Be selective in the amount of information presented and the timing of the presentation, depending on your own motives, and the listener's characteristics. Use gossip to reduce the credibility and power of an opponent, but do so with extreme care. Disguise the motive underlying your gossip to maintain high credibility. Question the motives of your opponents to reduce their credibility.

Limiting Accountability. Do not become too extreme in your moral evaluations of others. Be careful to avoid being labeled as a slanderer. Do not criticize another directly. Provide information in such a way that listeners will make the inference that you desire.

Take any preventative actions to reduce accountability and to avoid being a target of negative evaluations. Create an appearance of spontaneity in your gossip; otherwise, your motives may be suspect. Create the appearance of articulating and supporting ideals rather than of one overly concerned with the negative performance itself.

Maintain flexibility in moral evaluations to modify your position if subsequent information exonerates the object of the gossip. Keep open a way of retreat if later information does not support any early negative moral evaluations.

Ritualistic gossip

Ordinary gossip takes on a ritualistic colouring when it becomes more transcendental. This occurs when its focus or latent function increasingly emphasizes the maintenance of the sacred values, norms and ideals regarding the sanctity of the relationship in its more abstract form. Gossip, then, becomes more ritualistic as it cuts across the psychological, social, and cultural levels. The shift is from the concrete to the abstract; from the mundane to the sacred; from signs to symbols. Different ritualistic actions can be identified regarding the contribution of gossip to dissolution.

Affirmation by way of contrast. It is difficult to call attention to a deviation from a norm or ideal without specifying the prevailing standard being transgressed (cf. earlier section in this chapter). Evaluative criteria are made explicit by the attention given to the deviations. In the very act of defaming another, one reaffirms the ideals and cultural values underlying the relationship. In being a critic, one implies that he/she is a "true believer" and defender of the "faith", or why else the fuss?

Sequencing of sacred and profane. In ritualistic gossip systems "bits of information" are moved up and down the levels—from the psychological, to the social and the cultural. Details are placed, for example, first within an ideological context with allusions to the common core values, followed by a shift to the more secular or profane context with attention given to such possibilities as human frailties, functional overloads, interpersonal strains, and then with references to the social consequences of the break. This juxtapositioning of the dispute within these various levels attaches ritualistic significance to the break.

Innocent victim theme. Admission of primary responsibility for the break-up of a relationship appears to be quite uncommon. I have examined hundreds of protocols of broken relationships and have rarely identified admissions of responsibility. The theme of being an "innocent victim" is, instead, quite prevalent. Self-deception regarding one's responsibility is often supported by one's friends, acquaintances or even kin as face-saving devices (cf. Goffman, 1955), and hesitation to provide some face-saving support is interpreted as lack of commitment to a person rather than as evidence of honesty.

Benevolent deception. This involves semi-fictionalized accounts of the break that are knowingly accepted as false or exaggerated but are accepted with little, if any, challenge. To question the validity of statements opens one up to group sanctions and accusations of being cruel and heartless. There is often a kernel of truth in the content but points are exaggerated and pertinent data is omitted to present a more credible and coherent account. Benevolent deception is negotiated deception in that the initiator, the target, and audiences are aware of the elements of fiction. Strategic self-deception receives group support in that it is perceived as less divisive and destructive both to the individuals concerned and to the larger network. The criteria employed are generally psychological instead of social-cultural, e.g., stresses and strains that a person is under, psychoanalytic rationalizations in terms of early childhood experiences.

Gossip thus represents an indirect and informal means through which the social network can police the norms of personal relationships and is a primary social mechanism with considerable social force. When such indirect means fail to work, however, the network begins to take more direct action and calls in an intervention team, to which we now turn.

The Intervention Team

An important agency in the conduct of the dissolution of relationship in a social network is the intervention team. This is a group of individuals whose function it is to manage for the network the implications of the relationship break-up within the network. Its aims and objectives can be loosely specified in terms of different levels of analysis regarding the consequences. It is the *social consequences* that are of paramount importance and any intervention strategy is designed to minimize unfavourable social consequences for the network as a whole. The task is to maintain and protect the structural integrity of the network. A secondary task is to maintain the respect and reputation of the group as a socially defined unit.

Nevertheless, the *psychological consequences* for the two partners in the dissolving relationship are also important. The intervention team seeks to minimize unfavourable consequences to the integrity and identity of the antagonists and this includes protecting them from each other. Conflict resolution is also important. The intervention team seeks to repair damage and to help the dyad get through dissolution with minimum tension. At the *cultural-normative level,* an important task is to reaffirm and uphold the social norms and moral rules. It is this task that provides the flavour of ritual to intervention. Though not always made explicit, the intervention team also seeks to avoid the ritual destruction of the individual such as can happen in a degradation ceremony (cf. Garfinkel, 1956).

The intervention team as a problem-solving group

The intervention team takes over from gossip as a potentially more effective tool for dealing with dissolution problems. Certainly gossip is useful in providing a background against which disputes can be handled; but a point is reached where there is awareness that the "minor" problems addressed by gossip are getting out of control. There is a recognition that the self-corrective devices in a relationship are not working properly, and that more direct and outside remedial action is necessary for the good of all concerned. By the time, then, that an intervention team is called in there is a firmer recognition of a dispute. Once a dispute is socially recognized and brought out into the open, it needs to be handled by a more generalized social system such as the intervention team with the implication of its greater legitimacy and its more formalized and structured system of communication.

There are some important differences between the activities of the intervention team and what happens during gossip. Intervention is more instrumental, rational and network-oriented, whereas gossip is more dramatic, expressive, and concerned with judging or face-saving. Intervention focuses on information-processing, whereas gossip deals with information retrieval—who did what to whom and why. The intervention team is more systematic and organized in its problem-solving approach, whereas gossip is more flexible in scanning the information resources, Gossip shifts from one level of abstraction to another—from the psychological, to the social and the cultural, though in no particular order, often sporadically, and ineffectually, but in so doing, gossip does provide a data bank for the intervention team that follows. The intervention team's communication system is relatively well planned and deliberate, whereas informed gossip is much more spontaneous. Finally, the intervention team is under some pressure to establish some consensus, to make a recommendation, take a decision, or perform some kind of action, whereas the gossip-mongers are not under such pressures.

There is the suggestion of a forensic model in the way in which intervention teams operate. The analogy with a law court is evident in the similarity of the problems faced by these judicious agencies, such as the collection of evidence, the interpretation problems, and the application of rules to specific cases. In the collection of evidence, the intervention team, unlike gossip, is more systematic in the sequence of questioning and in the placing of information within an appropriate evaluative scheme. The problems of applying cultural rules are, however, quite complex and include the following: What degree of precision is implicit in a rule statement; for instance, what is the nature of a son's obligation to an aged parent? Under what conditions can a rule be applied? What is the range or threshold beyond which sanctions must be enforced? Are there quantitative or qualitative differences in the violation of a moral rule; for instance, is a friend either loyal or disloyal—or are there degrees of disloyalty? Which evaluative categories are most relevant in a particular case—moral, psychological, etc.? How much weight should be given to a person's intentions when one is assessing the seriousness of the moral transgression? It should be apparent that intervention teams cannot mechanically apply sacred principles to a dispute. The absence of explicit laws and statutes makes this form of jurisprudence much more complicated than what occurs in a traditional law court. A level of wisdom is required of the participants that is not readily found.

Properties of intervention teams

The successful operation of an intervention team depends on its ability to meet certain conditions. First of all, the team has to be perceived by all concerned as a reliable resource for satisfying a variety of needs—psychological, social, and in some instances, as in an agricultural community, economic. Trust and confidence in the team is essential: the legitimacy of the team for intervention into different areas of the dissolution problem has to be accepted by all. Secondly, it is necessary that the members of the team possess qualities that enhance its cohesiveness. The interdependency or common fate of its members is important here. Members of the team should be perceived by outsiders as belonging to a clearly identifiable group—perceived as a viable unit such as, for instance, a family clan, clique or gang. Sometimes a dispute within the network itself becomes the object of ridicule and one motivation for group work is to avoid situations whereby the extended family, for example, is open to ridicule and seen as a laughing stock. Kinship respect can be a motive for maintaining the stability of the larger group. Thirdly, the success of the team depends on how well the members perform their roles. The critical roles to be filled include that of the arbitrator, the defender, the jury or evaluators, and the witnesses. It is essential also that such roles are enacted with sufficient detachment for effective problem-solving, but with enough emotional response to communicate the message of concern for the parties involved. Fourthly, the intervention team needs to assign priority to its interpretative function, playing down enforcement. The team needs to act much like an interpretative court in defining the situation in terms of the normative order for the participants. It is necessary to increase their knowledge about other rights and duties and the consequences of alternative actions both for themselves and others. Fifth, the team needs to maintain flexibility in the application of the moral rules, taking into account the circumstances surrounding the transgressions. Sensitivity to human fallibility is important here. The intervention team also needs to ensure that the participants have flexibility of action. The team cannot seek to establish binding contracts regarding the internal relations of the antagonists. This would hamper the element of flexibility that the antagonists need for making adjustments to new situations. Finally, in the long-term, the intervention team needs to serve as an effective model of social reality. Much of its reason for being is the loss of trust within the dyad. The intervention group, then, should be perceived as operating under principles of justice, fairness and equity. In so doing, the intervention group re-enacts the important social myth of trusting one's fellow man—a cornerstone of any system of intimate relationships.

Intervention rules

The basic assumptions or necessary conditions that I have specified are implemented in practice by the team members in the form of rules serving to guide the behaviour of the team. These rules, then, help to provide structure in different areas of the intervention arena.

Timing. Do not intervene unless the consequences of not intervening are serious for the group. Avoid premature intervention, do not intervene unless there is some evidence of support by one or both of the antagonists.

Role-playing. Experiment with different roles to identify the one that is most appropriate and in which you are most comfortable. Select the role that best "fits in" with the nature of the existing relationship between the antagonists, and that is most consistent with the group's expectations. Do not get overly involved or under-involved in your role. Maintain the necessary detachment essential for implementing the role. Avoid roles where there is such an obvious conflict of interest that it could reduce your credibility.

Information retrieval. Examine the previous history of the relationship: assume that any current dispute reflects a host of prior disputes. Look for circumstantial or hearsay evidence: bring out facts that are relevant, and classify evidence as relevant or irrelevant to the grievances.

Upholding social norms. Defend the sanctity of "friends" and "family". Avoid inquiry that is too analytic. Give examples of similar disputes where violators of sacred norms experienced negative consequences. Use humour techniques to facilitate conformity, such as teasing, ridicule and sarcasm. Use moral reproaches only if you have the proper standing with the individual, i.e., the appropriate role relationship with the violator of the norm (Sabini and Silver, 1978).

Monitoring role performance. Monitor role-playing in order to improve the quality of performance and to make it intelligible when seen as a consequence of the dramaturgical standpoint. Enhance dramatic aspects of performance so as to achieve idealized impression of self. Accentuate certain facts and conceal others. Enhance dramatic aspects also so as to mask intentions regarding self-interests and to conceal real motives of self and others that might, in particular, endanger essential illusions for meeting objectives.

Interpretation of moral rules. Be fair and objective in your interpretation in the light of the circumstances of the case. Do not be too harsh or severe in the application of rules. Maintain flexibility in applying rules. Give higher priority to those interpretations that are congruent with the best interests of the group.

Resolution. Try to get antagonists to reconcile their differences. Put pressure on any antagonist unwilling to accept an apology from the other. Try to get litigants to admit where they have erred. Try to reconcile while at the same time stating the code by which each party has to deal with the other.

Role of accounts

The successful resolution of a conflict or the successful management of a dissolution, whether by gossip or by intervention team, yields one important product: it creates a negotiated and socially accepted account of the dispute. Some of the steps in the development of the account will now be made explicit. Scholars differ in the focus given to various aspects of an account and regarding its key function. Scott and Lyman (1968) suggest that an account is a linguistic device used whenever action is subjected to evaluative inquiry. Accounts provide a critical element in a social order in that they help prevent conflicts from arising by bridging the gap between action and expectations—disparities between the real and ideal, between actual performance and role expectations.

The most common feature of accounts cited by scholars include those of excuses and justification of one's actions (cf. Goffman, 1959; Harré, 1979). I would suggest a broader definition. By dissolution accounts I mean a comprehensive description of the antecedents and consequences of the breakdown of a relationship, either real or fictionalized which as such are transmitted by means of conversation *vis-à-vis* gossip or more formally through the communication channels of an intervention team. A systematic description might include some of the stages of the dissolution process: for instance, as described by La Gaipa (1980). These would include the critical event instigating the dissolution; the coping devices used in adapting to changes in role relationships; the labeling of Other's behaviour; and the tactics used for reconciliation or termination.

A key assumption here that is consistent with the point of view of the social constructionists is that accounts are not "givens" but undergo change as a result of social interactions. Harré (1979) notes two stages in the formation of accounts. The first-stage accounts are essentially dramatic accounts and include interpretations and justifications of actions by an individual. The second stage involves problem-solving accounts which are negotiated accounts in which the larger group theorizes about the actions and develops hypotheses in folk sociology and folk psychology.

I would suggest that the distinctions made here between gossip and the intervention team can be carried over into the types of accounts. The medium of gossip relies on dramatic accounts whilst the intervention teams work best with problem-solving accounts. The more dramatic presentations via gossip include descriptions of rule-violations, some of the circumstances involved in the transgression, attempts at justifications, and trial and error with different evaluation systems in the search for the causal variables to structure the account. The intervention team, however, cannot operate effectively with this kind of data—the goals of the intervention team go far beyond the individuals' needs to justify behaviour. Instead, the team needs to obtain a more varied input of information to deal with the more complex task of negotiation, as well as system maintenance and repair. With the higher priority assigned to social stability, the intervention team attempts to rationalize the break in terms of its social and ideological implications instead of the integrity concerns of the members of the dyad.

Problems of justification and responsibility cannot be resolved until there is some agreement on the appropriate evaluative system. It is often quite difficult to obtain consensus as to the most relevant judgemental system. The choice of an evaluative scheme appears to differ as a function of role relationships with each of the antagonists. The members of an intervention team are usually divided into those supporting one faction or the other. For instance, in the break-up of a marriage the split will occur usually along blood lines. It has been noted that differential attributions are sometimes made on the basis of such role relationships. Different interpretations, for instance, are likely regarding the "in-laws" as compared to one's own kin.

Different psychological theories also may be employed by opposing parties. Those supporting a particular person are likely to draw on psychodynamic theory and focus attention on early childhood history and rationalizations for the aberrant behaviour. Those opposing are more likely to use a personality-trait theory approach and seek to explain the negative behaviour as a sign of weakness of character. Other approaches, of course, are used, including situational factors focusing on contextual data. But again, even here the more "charitable" explanations are given for that antagonist with whom identification exists.

A vital task, then, of the intervention team is to integrate and negotiate the separate accounts being circulated by each of the parties to the dispute. Making the necessary changes in the separate accounts is not always easy. Some reinterpretation of the data is often required and agreement of the antagonists must be obtained regarding the validity of these interpretations. Resolution often requires that each party accepts or recognizes the incompleteness of the account and/or the fictitious elements in them and seeks instead of face-saving, to cooperate so as to establish and construct a relatively coherent pattern that provides each party with some semblance of justice and equity, and, most importantly, promotes the stability and the continuity of the larger group or network.

There are a number of consequences following unsuccessful resolution of conflict by the intervention group. The social bonds within the network are likely to be weakened. Coalition formation contributes to this problem as a restructuring occurs in interaction patterns. The antagonists are likely to continue in their struggles for identity and engender "scenes" that are a source of embarrassment to all concerned. Cynicism regarding the sacred norms is likely to increase. Disenchantment with the sacredness of social bonds is likely. The antagonists are also likely to continue mutual shunning or physical avoidance and to engage in negative evaluations of one another or various forms of restrictive communications. Finally, excessive time and energy continue to be spent by both the antagonists and the participant observers. The importance of success in the activities of the intervention team is thus obvious and goes some way to explaining its central final role in the social conduct of a dissolving personal relationship.

Summary and Conclusions

The present analysis of the rules and rituals in relationship breakdown has been shaped by a systems-orientation described elsewhere (La Gaipa, 1981a)[1]. Some of the key systems notions include hierarchy of levels, interdependency, and coping mechanisms to maintain subsystems. In this chapter I have called attention to some of the rules and rituals involved in implementing cultural notions since much of the impact of culture on termination processes is visible in the rules and rituals used.

At the social level of analysis, Duck (1981) has called for a " ... shift of emphasis away from the study of the dyad in isolation from network systems ... " (Duck, 1981, p. 27). I have suggested that there is an interdependency between social networks and culture. Without the cultural norms and ideals much of the social interaction within the network would be rather chaotic and meaningless. The culture, then, places some constraints on network actions. The importance of the activity *outside* the dyad is equally important and Duck (1981) has observed with regret that practically nothing has been discovered about the influence of outsiders in the preservation or destruction of relationships. At attempt was therefore made here to identify some of the activities of such "outsiders" as they participate in gossip and intervention teams, noting the assumptions upon

---

[1]Further extensive research by the present writer in a similar vein addresses problems of friendship in childhood (Bigelow and La Gaipa, 1980; La Gaipa, 1981b); adolescence (La Gaipa, 1979; La Gaipa and Wood, 1981), and old age (La Gaipa, 1980, 1981c)—*Editor.*

which they act, the rules they follow and the kind of rituals that might be used.

At the level of psychological problems, Duck (1981) has further noted the systematic distortions that occur in the person's own justification of the causes of a break. I have tried to show how this is manifested in the construction of accounts used to explain and justify one's actions. Of particular importance is that systematic distortions are also generated outside of the dyad via the intervention group in its attempts to maintain group stability. Distortion can be a group phenomenon.

The role of gossip in breakdown has been interpreted here as a means of directing individuals' attention to the cultural ideals. Gossip is also used by outsiders to reorient themselves to possible network changes, to prepare for later intervention, and to reaffirm cultural norms and values. Some of the rules of gossip were made explicit in the present chapter. Such rules, again, show the influence of culture in a breakdown. The specific ritualistic types of gossip were also described. Such rituals seek to preserve the "yardsticks" and "guidelines" provided by the culture.

The focus of the present chapter has been on rituals as system-type mechanisms for dealing with breakdown as examined from a multilevel perspective. I have stressed the role of rituals in preserving the ideological bases of intimate personal relationships although this sometimes involves the use of fiction. Rituals, then, safeguard some of the "necessary myths" associated with close relationships.

The role of third-party conflict intervenors is a recognized technique for the repair and reconciliation of relationships. I have tried to conceptualize the intervention team in a somewhat different way, noting that such groups are likely to have a vested interest in the dispute affecting their actions, and more important, serve as a social model in supporting some of the sacred norms. The intervention team is not simply a repair mechanism for coping with either a dyadic or network problem, but is truly an instrument of the culture, though, admittedly, it serves a latent function about which the group is seldom aware.

Acknowledgement

I am grateful to Steve Duck for his editorial work on this chapter.

CHAPTER 9

Becoming Unrelated: The Management of Bond Dissolution

George J. McCall

Dyadic relationships are at once a peculiarly fragile and a highly durable species of social organization: fragile in that the loss of only a single member spells the death of the organization, durable in that they are much harder to dismantle than to create (Simmel, 1950). Even when both members of a personal relationship act upon a mutual decision to terminate it, they may find the task of dismantling beyond their capabilities. Still more frequently, a member's wish to terminate the relationship does not even eventuate in a personal decision to do so.

Yet, as Freud often said, the wish is father to the deed. Although a member's wish to terminate a relationship need not lead either to a decision to terminate or to an actual termination, such a wish typically does *spoil* a personal relationship. At core, a personal relationship (more than other sorts of dyadic social relationships) is distinctively a moral order, a matter of honor and respect. The central features of a personal relationship are loyalty, commitment, genuineness, and intimacy (Bigelow and La Gaipa, 1980; Suttles, 1970; Allan, 1979). A member's wish to terminate is itself disloyal and directly impugns the honor and self-respect of both partners, spoiling the nature of their relationship.

Although not all spoiled relationships subsequently dissolve, spoiling is

211

the most critical step in the process of relationship dissolution. Indeed, spoiling is to dissolution of a relationship as critical illness is to death of an individual. The social-loss consequences of spoiling are largely tantamount to those of dissolution, with the result that a relationship need not actually "die" to set in motion the social coping process of "mourning". The personal network approach outlined in the following section of this chapter clarifies what a relationship is that it may be spoiled, its personal and social significance, and its precarious dependence on the waxing and waning of interpersonal bonds. The second section examines why the spoiling of a relationship precipitates mourning and how the collective evolution of "accounts" of its spoiling is the key feature of the mourning process. The third section explores how differing modes of management of a wish to terminate lead to different degrees of spoiling and, hence, to variations in mourning and account evolution that directly affect outcomes of the dissolution process. Maintaining that accounts of spoiled relationships are the principal devices for management of relationship dissolution, the fourth section analyzes different forms and contents of such accounts and links these variations to stages of the mourning process.

Personal Network, Relationships and the Individual

Every individual maintains and depends upon a personal network—a set of persons with whom one is knowingly involved and cross-linked through a web of direct and indirect relationships. This personal network constitutes the effective interpersonal environment, the resources from which are derived the necessities and amenities of elementary social life (Homans, 1974). Chief among these are (Weiss, 1968):

(1) social integration (sharing of interests and concerns; companionship and fun; exchange of information and ideas; development of shared interpretations of experience);
(2) reassurance of identity and worth;
(3) assistance in dealing with problems;
(4) emotional integration;
(5) opportunity to care for and take responsibility for another human being.

How spare or rich the individual's elementary social life is depends upon the number and characteristics of the persons included, the relationships among these others, and their relationships with the focal individual. But all these in turn depend upon one's skills and efforts in *cultivating* this network. Passive exploitation of the fruits of the interpersonal environment rapidly depletes resources, while active cultivation—the skillful and caring investment of self in managing the demands and opportunities of the various relationships—may conserve, maintain, or even enrich these resources. One's network, then, represents a "personal economy" of relationships to be managed more or less effectively (Marks, 1977).

One facet of the individual's dependence upon the personal network— namely, one's identity, or self-conception—merits special attention for the light it sheds on personal relationships themselves. As Simmel noted, the focal individual appears differently to—indeed, *is* different with—each of the persons in the network; the individual presents a somewhat different *persona* to each of these others (McCall and Simmons, 1978; Harré and Secord, 1972). A personal relationship holds not between two persons but between two personas, and its nature (flowing from the fit between these personas) will therefore never be fully comprehended by any of the other persons in the network. Each of these persons serves as a differently distorted looking-glass, reflecting a somewhat different image of the focal individual (Cooley, 1902; Kuhn, 1964). As William James (1890, p. 179) put it, "a man has as many social selves as there are individuals who recognize him and carry an image of him in their mind". A person's self-conception then depends not only upon the character of each of his or her relationships but also upon the *social organization* of the personal network; that is, the organization of his or her various personas into an integrated self-conception mirrors the organization of the personal network.

The stability of both a person's elementary social life and one's sense of self thus hinge upon the stability of one's own personal network. Yet persons enter and depart this network fairly regularly throughout the flow of one's life trajectory. What holds another within the personal network are generally referred to as *interpersonal bonds*.

The one bond almost universally recognized among students of relationships is the subjective bond of *attachment*. Attachments to others are formed as the individual's identities evolve and change. One's dreams of oneself, the idealized pictures one has of oneself in certain social positions, are seldom constant over long periods of time. As a person faces new tasks and new others, these tasks and others become incorporated into one's daydreaming about oneself in these social roles. Consequently, specific persons and their behaviors get built into the contents of role-identities and become crucial to the legitimation and enactment of those identities. To so build a specific other into the very contents of one's self-conception is to become "attached" to that person.

At the opposite extreme, sociologists emphasize the importance of *social structural bonds* in maintaining interpersonal contact. That is to say, by virtue simply of the positions two persons occupy within some social structure (family, community, business firm, or the like), a significant linkage exists enhancing the probability of their interaction. In some cases these positions may have been entered into in the light of their personal relationship, as when lovers enter into marriage or two friends decide to join a tennis club together. More often, of course, the linked positions are entered prior to and independent of the personal relationship. In either case, however, occupancy of these positions similarly serves to link the individuals.

Intermediate between these subjective and objective extremes lies the key interpersonal bond of *commitment*, an avowed intention to honor some kind of exclusive or restrictive covenant within the relationship, such as to pursue sex only within the dyad or to trust the other with personal secrets. A central commitment in all personal relationships is to honor the paired personas. Such commitments may be either explicit or tacit, and either official (such as a marriage vow) or unofficial (such as an understanding between friends). Even if a commitment is not made on moral grounds, the person is under some moral obligation to fulfill it. To have made a commitment is to have bound oneself, and it requires a very good excuse to withdraw without losing face and perhaps receiving other negative sanctions. Even personal relationships are thus at least partly public affairs.

Two further types of interpersonal bond are distinctively associated with the personal economy of a network of relationships. *Benefit-dependability* is, of course, a major reason for the existence and continuation of many relationships. As a consequence of a person's recurring needs for joint activities, role-support, and the mundane resources of elementary social life, one is disposed to seek dependable sources of such benefits. Whenever one locates another who for whatever reason is able, willing, and ready to provide scarce benefits, a certain dependence arises. And finally, *investment* is a ubiquitous and powerful bond between persons. When one has expended such scarce resources as money, time, and life-chances in establishing and maintaining a relationship, one cannot afford to throw them away without realizing substantial "returns" on those investments.

Several features of the interpersonal bonding between two persons affect the stability of their relationship (i.e., the probability that either party will remain within the other's personal network) as well as the closeness of their relationship (i.e., the degree of centrality of Partner within Person's network).

One such feature is the stability of the component bonds. The various bond types themselves differ in degree of stability: the "carrots" of attachment and benefit-dependability rest solely on personal tastes and opportunities, whereas the "sticks" of commitment, investment, and social structure are more broadly based and socially enforced. Since forms of relationships differ characteristically in the relative prominence of each of these bond types, differences in stability of relationships are to be expected. Both romance and friendship, for example, rest primarily on bonds of attachment, benefit-dependability, and rather tentative commitments; and these forms are well known to be easily and frequently broken off. Marriage, in contrast, involves strong structural bonds, very serious commitments, and major investments, even if entered into largely on grounds of attachment and benefit-dependability; marital relationships are less often and less readily terminated. Sibling (Sutton-Smith and Rosenberg, 1970), in-law, and other kinship relations—as well as collegial and neighborly relationships—are essentially defined by structural bonds and not preceded by bonds of benefit-dependability or attachment, although these may develop and give rise to more specific commitments (Allan, 1979).

Similarly, the relative prominence of the various bond types varies with the age and sex composition of the dyad, affecting the stability of a relationship. Children's friendships, for example, are notoriously volatile. The incomplete socialization of young children entails major reliance on bonds of benefit-dependability and attachment in both friendship and kinship relations; it is not until adolescence that commitments and investments become serious factors in children's friendships (Rubin, 1980; Foot *et al.*, 1980). But even in such adult relationships as marriage, the ages of the members influence the character of bonding and the stability of the relationship. Investment, for example, assumes greater weight for aging couples than for young marrieds, and older pairs are more stable than younger pairs. Sex composition is also influential. Females appear to give greater weight than males to bonds of commitment at virtually all ages in all personal relationships (Bigelow and La Gaipa, 1980; Hill *et al.*, 1979), which is perhaps a factor in the tendency of same-sex relationships to prove more stable than cross-sex relationships.

A second influential feature of bonding is the degree of alignment of the various bond types. A person's commitments, for example, may differ from those ascribed on the basis of structural bonds; individuals frequently forgo the potential benefits of joint ventures and exchanges because of "prior commitments", or fret over interpersonal investments that have not yet yielded dependable benefits; a person seeks to secure attachments through mutual commitments and formation of structural bonds, and, conversely, may resignedly fulfill commitments that no longer reflect attachments. Such malalignment of bond types for either member significantly diminishes the closeness of their relationship and affords the most vital point of leverage for disruptive forces.

Other key features of bonding include the number of bonds between the two parties, the strength of each bond, and the symmetry of those bonds. The more numerous and diverse the commitments (or attachments, investments, etc.) with which Partner is bound to Person, the more central will Partner be to Person's network. On the other hand, a relationship featuring fewer but very strong bonds may also be a very close relationship; an intense attachment to Partner may, for example, place Partner at the very heart of Person's network. These effects of the numbers and the strengths of bonds are, of course, significantly qualified by the symmetry of each bond; if many such bonds are essentially unreciprocated, the relationship is only one-sided in its closeness and thus quite unstable.

Yet the character of bonding of any relationship is but one static factor in an individual's personal economy of relationships. While stable and close relationships are less likely to dissolve outright, neither the stability nor the closeness of a relationship confers much protection against the possibility of its spoiling. A personal relationship is, after all, a precarious affair beset by numerous dynamic threats to the fit between its constituent personas. Change is the true enemy of the personal relationship, a fact which dictates attention to dynamic strategies of management, of cultivation of one's personal network.

One major category of dynamic threats is *personal change,* in either Person or Partner. To begin with, a persona is, after all, a partial and somewhat misleading representation of self; as Partner gradually learns more about Person, he or she is likely to find Person to be a rather different individual than had been thought (or hoped). Furthermore, selves evolve rather steadily; Person may eventually become uncomfortable with the persona to which Partner has become attached. Children's friendships (Rubin, 1980) and marriages of young adults are especially likely to be severely stressed by differential rates of maturation and personal change; collegial relationships are often strained by differential rates of job advancement. Of course, personal change is not always progressive but may be retrograde; Partner's loss of wealth, beauty, health, or social position may alter not only persona but also benefit-dependability to Person.

The second major category of dynamic threats to the fit between personas is *network change.* An attractive new individual may enter Person's network as a rival to Partner, possibly replacing Partner (in the same type of relationship) or displacing Partner (through establishing with Person some other type of relationship which takes away from Partner Person's customary time and attention). Or an established member of Person's network may depart, causing Person to make widespread adjustments in the personal economy of relationships. Partner may then be asked to assume a greater burden of Person's personal economy, or alternatively may find that Person's forced adjustments leave little time for Partner.

Such consequences of personal and network changes do, of course, alter the number, strength, symmetry, and (especially) the alignment of various interpersonal bonds—thus diminishing the closeness and/or stability of the relationship. More directly and more centrally, however, personal and network changes affect the judged desirability of continuing to fulfill the core commitment to honor the fitted pair of personas that constitutes the relationship.

Spoiling and Mourning Relationships

The ubiquity of both personal change and network change dictates constant appraisal of the place of each relationship within one's personal economy of relationships. Such personal evaluation of a relationship is normal and necessary (Thibaut and Kelley, 1959) and is not itself a disloyal act. Yet through such personal evaluation of the relationship either member may find it desirable in their own personal economy to cease fulfilling the commitment to honor the fitted pair of personas. That is, some personal and/or network changes have caused in the individual a wish either to escape the relationship or to redefine it. In so wishing, one's own loyalty to those personas lapses and the fiction of solidarity is broken. The relationship is, to some extent, spoiled. Like a food, the relationship may only have an "off-taste" to one member, may smell definitely suspicious to both, or may be virulently toxic in the opinion of all observers. The degree of spoiling depends on how public and how enduring the member's dishonoring of the fitted personas is.

The spoiling of a relationship is important not just for its two members alone but for many others in their respective networks (cf. La Gaipa's chapter, this volume) and for the social management of spoiling among all these affected persons.

Consequences of spoiled relationships

Every member of an individual's personal network has some stake in the stability of that individual's many relationships—stability not in the sense of dead permanence but in the sense of evolutionary continuity and gradualism. First of all, every member has a stake in the personal economy of the individual's relationships; if that economy is altered, a member's standing "bargain" with Person is likely to be renegotiated. Member may be displaced and asked to forgo customary levels of benefits from Person, or Member may be expected to take up the slack and make greater contributions, at least temporarily. Further, every member has a stake in the stability of each of Person's personas; if one member finds Person to be someone different from what has been imagined, every other member cannot help but wonder whether their own image of Person may be misleading.

The spoiling of a personal relationship necessarily spoils its constituent personas; the partners, together with their significant others, are effectively bereaved and mourn the spoiling of these personas. Willard Waller (1938) first called attention to this collective mourning process as a key element in the process of marital alienation and divorce: "one mourns the object that never was what one thought it was". Misleading though any persona may have been, its passing is experienced as a disruptive (and often a disturbing) loss to all concerned and thus engenders mourning—a collective process of coping with that loss. Although analysis of this social process of mourning a spoiled relationship is the principal task of this chapter, an understanding of the nature of that process first requires a more detailed examination of the bereavement.

In the years since Waller's analyses, a considerable literature has accumulated regarding the generic phenomena of bereavement and mourning that casts further light on the more particular case of spoiled personas. For example, Colin Murray Parkes (1972) notes that there are to be healed in any mourning process three wounds of bereavement— deprivation, grief, and stigma—the severity of which reflect the closeness of the relationship.

The wound of *deprivation,* in the context of a spoiled relationship, displays several facets. First of all, the individual suffers some loss of benefits previously received from the now-spoiled relationship—social integration, reassurance of identity and worth, assistance, emotional integration, opportunity for nurturance. Second, one's personal network is disrupted; one is effectively cut off from others with whom one had been connected primarily *through* the now-spoiled partner, such as "friends of friends" (Boissevain, 1974) or in-laws. Third, one's daily routine is disrupted; one is cut off from familiar habits and surroundings—from routine sources of information, access, help, and material resources—which loss may lead to a sense of disorientation. In the face of such deprivations, the individual is forced to reassess "What does partner really mean to me and to my life?"

Grief commonly involves a wide range of individual feelings and emotions beyond worry, fear, and loneliness resulting from the wound of deprivation. On one side, the individual often feels some anger, bitterness, hurt, sadness, and self-pity from the spoiling of the relationship, and asks "Why me?". On the other side, the person often feels some guilt, shame, self-doubts, and diminished self-esteem, and asks "What's wrong with me that this should have happened?". The spoiler and partner typically experience both sets of feelings, although in differing proportions (Helmlinger, 1977).

Because personal relationships are almost universally viewed in success/failure terms, any party to a terminated or even a spoiled relationship is tarred by failure and — even more than the widowed or the orphaned—regarded as somehow odd, deficient, or deviant. Thus, the *stigma* of failure is a third wound, feeding the embarrassment, shame, and guilt which are such a salient part of the wound of grief. First of all, the other persons in the individual's network have had only outsiders' views of the now-spoiled relationship and are therefore themselves confused and ambivalent about the spoiling; such others often communicate stigma through shunning the individual, passing judgment, or taking sides. The two members are effectively forced to begin to disentangle their respective personal networks and to realign their remaining relationships. To do so requires both individuals and all members of their personal networks to reassess these questions: "What is Person really like?" "What is Partner really like?" "What happened (i.e., issues of responsibility, blame, guilt, credit)?"

Coping with spoiled relationships

Bowlby (1961) distinguishes three main stages in any mourning process. First there is a stage of *protest,* characterized by "protestations" of every sort expressing the whole variety of grief feelings, ranging from protestations of relief and even joy, on the one hand, to protestations of anger and outrage on the other. Following this period of initial shock, the individual's early attempts to adjust constitute a stage of *disorganization,* characterized by disorientation, indecision, loss of ambition, and depression. Eventually, however, life resumes some stable direction in a stage of *reorganization.*

In negotiating such a passage, the individual mourning a spoiled relationship must endeavour to heal the wounds of deprivation, grief, and stigma. In resolving deprivation, one must somehow repair the personal network and revise one's personal economy of relationships, forming and/or revising alternative relationships providing new routines through which one can make up for—or get by without—the lost resources. In resolving grief, one must "work through" one's emotions to "come to grips" with oneself and with one's situation; social support and being able to talk to others are vital factors in this resolution (Walker *et al.*, 1977). Typically, however, these factors are themselves significantly blocked by the effects of social stigma. Therefore, resolving stigma is the key for unlocking the highly social process required in the resolution of deprivation and of grief.

That is to say, reintegration of self depends on reintegration of self with others; self, network, and its constituent relationships may all need to be altered or redefined. To do so requires *social construction of shared answers* to the series of questions set forth in the preceding section: What does Partner really mean to me and to my life? Why me? What's wrong with me? What's Partner really like? What am I really like? What really happened? As shared answers to these questions are worked out, stigma and grief are gradually resolved and the personal network is reorganized, resolving deprivation.

The central social process in coping with a spoiled relationship thus would seem to be the negotiation of shared answers, that is, the collective evolution of *accounts* (Scott and Lyman, 1968; Harré and Secord, 1972)— stories about the relationship which give or imply some kind of answers to these six key questions.

The degree to which this account-evolving process becomes widely and openly collective varies significantly, depending on how thoroughly the relationship is spoiled. As we shall see, individuals and relationships vary considerably in their management of a member's wish to terminate.

Managing the Wish to Terminate

One factor influencing the management of such a wish is the extent to which the wish has been made known to others. The wish to terminate a relationship may be *secret* (known only by the wisher—and perhaps his or her closest confidants outside the relationship), *private* (known only by the two partners and perhaps their closest confidants), or *public* (known by both partners and by at least some concerned others).

Secret wish to terminate

In the case of a secret wish to terminate, it is to be presumed that the wish spoils the relationship—destroys its idealization—only for the wisher. Even for that person, the wounds of deprivation and of stigma are then entirely anticipatory in nature; only feelings of grief are immediate, and even these are yet secret. Consequently, the process of evolving accounts for its spoiling is minimally collective. The process is largely a tacit and vicarious consultation with others, through the mental mechanism of role-playing (i.e., of "taking the role of other toward the self" [Mead, 1934] and imagining their responses to one's views and actions). The more direct involvement of others tends to be covert, as the wisher sends up subtle "trial balloons" regarding his or her own character (or that of Partner or their relationship) as deceptive attempts to elicit unwitting social validation for some of the wisher's own evolving interpretations. In some cases, of course, the secret wisher may be able to speak openly with a trusted confidant, who may critically shape Person's interpretations of the spoiled relationship.

But in the main the process of account-evolution here amounts to Person's silent *thinking about* the relationship—contemplating its place in the network of relationships, and deliberating as to how one feels and what one should do. Although this important process has scarcely been studied (Duck, 1980a), we may suppose that two factors inevitably entering into such a deliberation are one's beliefs as to (1) whether Partner also secretly wishes to terminate and (2) whether one could oneself successfully resolve the deprivation and stigma of actual termination.

Often enough, such deliberation leads to a decision *not* to terminate; contemplation often brings the secret wisher to a new appreciation of the strengths of the existing interpersonal bonds and a receding of the felt wish to terminate. Not infrequently, Person's less than conscious withdrawal of involvement from the secretly spoiled relationship also confers a power advantage, through Waller's (1938) "principle of least interest", with the result that he or she comes to find the relationship more satisfying through obtaining more rewarding terms.

On the other hand, deliberation may indeed end in a decision to terminate. Most often, implementation of this decision takes the form of an unexplicated withdrawal—a backing off from the relationship through a deliberate lowering of any further investments in it, in the hope that it will simply wither away painlessly (Rubin, 1980). Whether it does so depends largely upon Partner's response. In the face of Person's withdrawal of involvement, whether deliberate or merely an unwitting reaction in the course of one's deliberation, Partner may respond in either of two directions: by matching this withdrawal with a corresponding decrease in his or her own involvement, thus establishing a cycle of progressive attenuation of the relationship, or by offsetting Person's withdrawal through increasing his or her own involvement in an effort to shore up the relationship. Attenuation is thus not an automatic consequence of Person's withdrawal. Curiously, Person's withdrawal (1) may cause Partner to believe that Person does secretly wish to terminate, (2) may cause Partner also to wish to terminate, or (3) both. In this way the secret wisher may thus cause Partner to move to terminate, a result Person often finds distressing.

Of course, not all relationships are even permitted to attenuate beyond certain limits; husbands and wives, parents and small children, debtors and creditors are not allowed to simply stop seeing each other. In all relationships featuring strong structural bonds and serious public commitments, society forbids unchecked attenuation. These relationships can terminate only with a bang, not a whimper. An open break, societally policed, is required.

A personal decision to terminate such a relationship necessarily requires not simply a secret wish to do so but a public announcement of the wish and of the decision. Such an announcement embroils the two partners in some type of negotiation with pertinent social institutions—family, court, community, and the like—as to whether, and on what terms, their relationship shall be terminated and their mutual commitments revised.

Therefore, to terminate a relationship featuring strong structural bonds and public commitments, a secret wish must give rise to a public wish. Typically, however, it first either becomes or engenders a *private* wish—one known to both partners and perhaps to their closest confidants.

Private wish to terminate

A secret wish to terminate may *become* a private wish in one of three basic ways. First, Person may directly inform Partner of the wish to terminate their relationship. Second, Person's actions may lead Partner to suspect that Person wants out; at some point Partner may confront Person with this suspicion and obtain confirmation. Third, Partner may learn from someone else (perhaps Person's confidant) that Person has expressed the wish to terminate. This third means of the secret wish becoming private is the most devastating to the relationship, since Person's loyalty is twice-broken—by the wish itself and by its having been revealed to an outsider sooner than to Partner. Typically, too, Partner is embarrassed (if not humiliated) by having been shown ignorant of the state of a personal, private relationship.

A secret wish to terminate may *engender* a private wish, in that Person's deliberate or unwitting withdrawal of involvement causes Partner to wish for and openly propose termination (Davis, 1973).

For both partners, the wounds of grief and of some deprivation are direct and immediate, though seldom equal in type or magnitude. Stigma is yet largely anticipatory in nature, except for the shame and embarrassment felt within the dyad itself. Account evolution is therefore mainly dyadic, supplemented perhaps by the contributions made by close confidants.

Where a secret wish has become (rather than engendered) the private wish, the character of account-evolution is importantly shaped by Partner's own wishes regarding the relationship. Perhaps most frequently, Partner is dismayed (if not always shocked) to learn of the other's wish to terminate but refuses to capitulate, even though this revelation has significantly spoiled the relationship for Partner as well. Partner's bonds may be so strong, and the alternatives so bleak, that he or she strives to preserve and repair the relationship, offsetting Person's reduced involvements. Person may then exploit this situation, capitalizing on the principle of least interest to obtain substantial benefits from the spoiled relationship—perhaps even causing the wish to recede. While the accounting process here is a truly dyadic one it is heavily skewed toward explaining why Person—but not also Partner—has come to find their relationship unsatisfactory. Typically, this dyadic accounting emphasizes Partner's failings and principal responsibility for the spoiling. This joint interpretation may lead to a metamorphosis of the relationship and its continued endurance, with neither partner any longer wishing its termination, but often it does not. Person remains dissatisfied and immediately or eventually moves on the expressed wish to terminate.

Often enough, however, Partner too has secretly wanted out — either independently or in response to Person's conduct during the secretive contemplation of the secret wish. In such a case, both partners find the relationship spoiled and often agree to terminate; together they work out an account of why their relationship went wrong. This is not to say that the accounts held by the two partners are identical but only that they agree on certain key elements and themes.

Finally, Partner may not previously have held any wish to terminate but the insult of learning of Person's wish so completely spoils the relationship that it causes in Partner a corresponding wish and precipitous decision. Accounting then is minimally dyadic, as Partner is enabled to fix on the spoiling effects of Person's wish to terminate.

Where a secret wish has engendered (rather than become) the private wish to terminate, account-evolution is most heavily influenced by Person's response to Partner's expression of that wish. Person may be relieved (if not actually pleased) by Partner's wish, in which case accounting is truly joint, as in the consensual case above. On the other hand, even though one had oneself previously entertained a secret wish to terminate, one may be surprised to find oneself hurt and shocked by Partner's expressed wish, perhaps to the extent of abandoning one's secret wish and resisting termination. In such cases, Partner may obtain the advantage through the principle of least interest and dyadic accounting is skewed in a reciprocal of the first scenario above.

Thus, a private wish to terminate may or may not become a *public* wish. But if so, it occurs by means of some more widely social announcement by Person, by Partner, or both (even though others may have been long aware of the private wish).

Public wish to terminate

The wounds of grief, deprivation, and especially of stigma become fully immediate only when the wish to terminate becomes public knowledge. At that point the fiction of solidarity is undeniably broken and the relationship is thoroughly spoiled. Even a resisting Partner, striving to hold on to a troubled relationship, generally finds public disclosure of Person's wish too gravely damaging and dishonoring to continue these efforts. At that point, too, the evolution of accounts becomes fully and overtly collective as others in the networks begin to participate quite directly (cf. La Gaipa's chapter, this volume).

> "The couple then begin to [learn] how their relationship appears to others, and from that time on the process of emancipation from marriage goes on at an accelerating rate. It is likely that each mate has been somewhat blinded to certain aspects of the relationship; he now begins to see those clearly through the eyes of others. It does not matter whether the others really see anything at all ...; the process of alienation through the intrusion of an alien estimate of the marriage goes on anyhow."   (Waller, 1938, p. 551)

Both partners find themselves called upon by others in their personal networks to provide an account of the relationship's spoiling—some story of the relationship that in some way answers the six key questions discussed above [viz. What does Partner really mean to me and my life? Why me? What's wrong with me? What's Partner really like? What am I really like? What really happened?]. Almost certainly the stories told by the two partners will prove substantially different, even if preceded by a period of truly joint account-evolution, owing to the divergent social forces stemming from their progressively distinct respective personal networks.

> "At this time the former friends of the couple frequently become wholly or in part attached to the one or the other of the former mates. These two groups then sympathize mainly with the persons about whom they are organized. ... The wife's friends see her in near perspective but see the husband only dimly—there are few of us who photograph well; few who can stand merely objective interpretation—they see the effects which the husband's actions have had upon her; they see the extenuating circumstances for any acts of hers of which they do not approve, but they do not see the effects of her acts upon the ... husband; they must more or less depend on her for an account of the nature of the

difficulties leading up to the break, and even though in telling the story she tries to tell the husband's side too she can never really tell more than her version of the husband's story; even the telling of a story which casts discredit on her really draws her friends closer to her, for they think that if she is so fair now she has always been that way—all these things work together to build up in the eyes of her friends the notion that she could not have been at fault in this matter, and the result is that sympathy for her runs quick and deep while enmity for the husband grows.''   (Waller, 1930)

For either partner, the account is seldom once and for all. Accounting is usually both multiple (i.e., separately to numerous others) and repeated (i.e., on several occasions to the same other). The numerous accounts provided by either partner tend to vary considerably in both form and content. Since all parties to the accounting—both partners but especially those persons who have had only an outsider's view of the relationship—are disoriented, confused, and ambivalent regarding the spoiling and probable termination of the relationship, either partner's accounts may oscillate wildly from one extreme to another.

In part this phenomenon is due to audience factors; the form and content of the account offered will vary according to the other's intimacy, stake in the relationship, and anticipated reaction. For example, one tells rather differing stories of one's impending divorce to one's parents, children, confidants, coworkers, and friends (Adam and Adam, 1979). In part this diversity of offered accounts can be attributed to stages of the mourning process itself. During the stage of protest, the accounts of a given partner vary substantially for the reason that these accounts are colored by current feelings which themselves vary widely and unpredictably—from protestations of relief, to cries of anguish or of self-blame, to angry protests and bitter recriminations, and back again. During the stage of disorganization, the diversity of accounts flows naturally from the instability of the person's new directions and self-images.

Over the course of time, however, the diverse accounts offered by a given partner gradually evolve and converge through a mechanism of *collective selection* by (and with) his or her reforming personal network—quite like the collective selection involved in the development of scientific theories (Campbell, 1974) or other fashions (Blumer, 1969). Indeed, arrival at some stable basic account is necessary to attain the stage of reorganization of the self and of one's life (a reorganization which, it must be noted, may sometimes involve a reconstruction—rather than a termination—of the spoiled relationship).

The Forms and Contents of Accounts of Spoiling and Dissolution

As noted in the preceding paragraphs, the forms and contents of accounts of a single spoiled relationship often vary rather widely, depending on "side", audience, and—especially—stage of mourning. Moreover, an examination of the content of such accounts should reveal a good deal about cultural or "folk" categories of relationships and interpersonal bonds, as La Gaipa (Chapter 8, this volume) contends.

Forms

Let us consider how the stories that are told about a spoiled relationship vary in length, detail, tone, and literary form across the three stages of the mourning process.

Some accounts, for example, resemble various "journalistic formats", the most elementary of which is the simple *announcement* (e.g., "Bill and I haven't been able to work out our differences and we've decided to stop seeing each other"). Similarly "objective" accounts of greater length and detail may resemble the classical *newspaper story* in their structure, reporting the who, what, when, where, why, and how, beginning with a headline and a lead paragraph containing the essential facts, followed by a series of progressively less essential paragraphs facilitating a shortening or lengthening of the same report according to level of audience interest. More partisan accounts may resemble *editorials,* in which essential facts are adumbrated as a prolegomenon to expression of a position regarding those facts, or even—less disciplined—*letters to the editor* which may be more impassioned, imprudent, and perhaps rambling expressions of opinion.

Other accounts are more literally stories, employing "dramatic narrative forms" such as the *short story*. Such narratives are governed by dramatic logic—a plot—in which a sequence of events is made sensible by being shown to flow from the characters of the participants. Accounts of this type tend to be moderately lengthy, are generally understood as interpretive reconstructions, and embody a personal viewpoint.

Public accounts during the stage of protest are predominantly journalistic in form; editorials and letters to the editor are forms well suited to protestations and the expression of grief feelings, and the apparent objectivity of announcements and news stories afford relatively safe means of initial public accounting in the face of labile personal emotions. But the short story remains the quintessential account, owing to the explanatory power of its dramatic logic. Much of a given partner's account evolution during the stage of disorganization amounts to formulating, trying out, and revising a variety of different short stories about the spoiled relationship, trying to make sense to self and to others of how that spoling came to pass and what lies in store for the characters. Indeed, it may be argued that stabilization and perfection of a basic short story is a fundamental prerequisite for passage to the stage of reorganization.

But the need for public accounting does not cease with attainment of that final stage. Even years later, new others enter the personal network and exchange biographies; and as the children of divorce mature, they may ask anew what happened between their parents. As reorganization consolidates, more distant and tranquil—perhaps even somewhat nostalgic—reflection on the spoiled relationship tends to sublimate the essential dramatic logic of the eventual basic short story into a *poetic image*. The person's own accounting gradually becomes more poetic, resembling the extended forms of epics, ballads, and even lyrics, but drifting towards the briefest form of *aphorism* crisply expressing that poetic image. When the spoiled relationship has been thoroughly mourned—that is, when the wounds have truly healed and the self has been reintegrated with others; when the spoiling has been properly buried — its account will have become an aphorism, an epitaph to be trotted out as a socially acceptable memorial.

Contents

Such poetic images of spoiled relationships represent the core content of accounts and themselves reveal much about folk categories of relationships and interpersonal bonds. Figure 1 displays a rough typology of root images.

Monadic images liken the now-spoiled relationship to some type of unitary phenomenon predestined by the natural course of its inner dynamics to terminate. For example, the relationship may be likened to a bubble

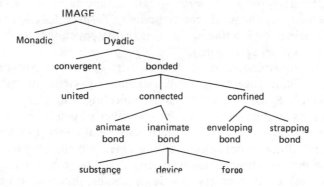

FIG. 1 A typology of relationship images.

(which grows until it bursts), a flower (which buds, blossoms, and dies), a fruit (which ripens until it rots), an organism (which is born, matures, and eventually dies), a fire (which warms and grows until it burns out), a switch (turning on and then off), a natural event (beginning, happening, and finally over), a photograph (developing, fixing, and eventually fading), sunlight (inevitably fading and turning to darkness), or a volatile compound (unstable and perhaps explosive). Such imagery emphasizes the unity of the now-spoiled relationship and connotes that "it was great while it lasted but it naturally had to end", owing to its own inner nature.

The family of *dyadic* images, on the other hand, emphasize the existence of two distinct elements which were somehow related. Most pronounced in this respect are images of *convergent* relationships: those holding between two things which had been in some way "going together" but are not together any longer—are now diverging. Dyadic images of this convergent type liken the now-spoiled relationship to, for example, fellow-travellers ("going together" down life's highway, until there is a parting of the ways, perhaps at a fork in the road), flotsam and jetsam (drifting or thrown together until carried off by the tide of events and drifting apart), passers-by ("seeing each other" until their relative motion brings it about that they no longer see each other), trees (growing together, perhaps interpenetrating, until growing apart), or timbers (leaning on one another for support until a collapse or a falling away). Such images emphasize that what had appeared to be interpersonal bonds were merely external relations; there were really no bonds to be overcome in the eventual divergence of the two elements of the relationship.

A much more diverse set of dyadic images portray *bonded* relationships. The central dictionary meaning of a bond is anything that binds, fastens, or confines—a substance, device, or force which holds things together or unites them. The most forceful imagery of bondedness implies that the two parties to the relationship had *united*—had become as one—through some process likened to chemical compounding, fusing, forging, weaving, knitting, braiding, or interlacing; two elements so united could only be divided (e.g., broken up or torn).

By contrast, other images of bondedness portray *connected* relationships, implying a holding together of two elements by virtue of "something between them". Some images of such connecting bonds are animate in nature, such as enchantment ("under the other's spell") or an embrace ("holding on to each other"). Inanimate imagery of connecting bonds may liken them to adhesive substances (such as glue, cement, mortar, or solder which cause the two elements to "stick together" or to be "stuck on each other"), to linking devices (ties, strings, chains, hitches, knots; bolts, carpentered joints such as dovetails; mechanical couplings; stitches;

bridges), or to physical forces (magnetic or electrostatic attraction, adhesion, cohesion). Glue does not always hold, may dissolve or wash out, may turn brittle and crack, with the two elements then coming apart. Ties may come undone, snap, or sever; carpentered joinings—however nailed down, shored up, or braced—may collapse and fall apart; coupled railway carriages may uncouple and even derail. Attractive forces may weaken, be overcome by stronger counter-attractions, or be offset by the addition of forces of repulsion. All such images imply that, once connected, two elements may yet become separated (i.e., disconnected).

A final group of images of bondedness emphasize a holding of things together by means of external constraints—a *confined* relationship. In such imagery a relationship is something one gets into and perhaps gets out of, through departure or escape. Confining bonds may be imaged as wholly enveloping (e.g., wrappings, as on a package or parcel; a bag, box, cage, or coop; or a vessel, in the sense of either a container or a ship) or as more narrowly strapping two elements together (through such circumferential bindings as rope, twine, bands, tape, wire, or a fence). Such confinement imagery envisions the possibility that one or both partners may break out, fall out, drop out, bail out, or jump ship.

These root images poetically convey a viewpoint on several important features of a relationship. First, its degree of closeness and solidarity: monadic images connote greater solidarity than do dyadic images, bonded images than convergent, united images more than connected or confined. Second, a root image connotes something of the nature of the principal interpersonal bonds: for example, confinement imagery suggests that social structural bonds and commitments were predominant, connection imagery implies the predominance of the bonds of commitment, investment, and benefit-dependence, while united images emphasize unusually strong bonds of attachment. Third, a root image suggests something about the degree of alignment of bonds: woven fabric images, for example, connote greater parity among the various types of bonds than do the various images of single threads, cords, or the like. Fourth, such images imply something of the causation of the relationship's spoiling: monadic images suggest that inevitable inner dynamics were responsible, united images imply that a strong external stress would have been necessary, and convergent images suggest that the relationship was not only fortuitous but more apparent than real.

As revealing and suggestive as such root images may be, they do not themselves constitute an account—even an aphoristic account. Images are only kernels of accounts, which generate accounts through acquiring modifying features, much as sentence kernels are supposed to in generative linguistic theory. These successive transformations are depicted in Fig. 2.

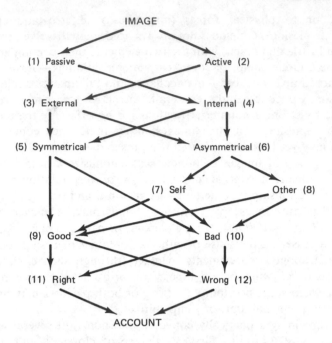

FIG. 2   The Structure of Image-Transformations in the Generation of Accounts.

The first acquired feature is some marker regarding the active/passive dimension of causation of the spoiling: "passive" implies that the spoiling was something that merely happened to the relationship, whereas "active" implies that the spoiling was something that was done to the relationship. For example, the root image may liken the relationship to a fire, which may either burn out (passive) or be put out (active).

The second acquired feature is a marker regarding the locus of responsibility: external to the relationship or internal to it. Cold water may have been thrown on the fire, for example, by one or both of its members or by a third party or by an external event.

The third acquired feature marks the degree of symmetry of the partner's responsibility for the spoiling. If asymmetrical, a fourth acquired feature is a marker for which partner was primarily responsible.

In any case, an image acquires further markers indicating whether the spoiling was a good thing or a bad thing, and whether it was "right" (i.e., fair, just, etc.) or "wrong". The good/bad dimension refers centrally to benefit/cost balances, whereas the right/wrong dimension represents a moral judgment. A spoiling that is "wrong" need not be "bad", nor need a "good" outcome be "right". Compare, for example, two transformations of the enchantment image: "she finally came to her senses" (right and good) and "she had a rude awakening" (good but wrong).

The accretion of all these modifying features to a root image goes a long way towards characterizing what happened to the relationship and explaining how it came to be spoiled. Issues of responsibility, blame, and the like are addressed, and answers to the other key questions in accounting are at least implied even in the sparsest aphoristic formulation and more directly developed in many of the extended forms (particularly in the short-story form).

Summary and Conclusion

A personal relationship—as a fitted pair of personas—is necessarily spoiled by a member's wish to terminate, since that wish shatters the fiction of pair solidarity, dishonors the constituent personas, and destroys their idealization. The two members and affected others in their personal networks are effectively bereaved of these valued personas and collectively mourn that loss—healing the wounds of bereavement through the evolution of socially validated accounts of the relationship and its spoiling — even though not all spoiled relationships actually terminate. Whether a spoiled relationship does terminate depends on the character of its bonding and on interpersonal modes of management of the wish to terminate. The central variables differentiating these management modes are how widely and how openly collective the account-evolution process becomes. Three stages of mourning, or account evolution, were distinguished in the present chapter and the diversity, forms, and contents of accounts were shown to vary across stages.

Spoiling is the most critical step in relationship dissolution, and mourning is the principal means for managing the dissolution process. The keystone bond in dissolving a relationship is the core commitment to honor the constituent pair of fitted personas; once that bond fails, all remaining interpersonal bonds are susceptible of rapid dissolution. Whether and how they do dissolve depends heavily on the contours of the mourning process.

Greater attention, therefore, must be given to the study of account evolution—most particularly in its less public forms of individual accounting (members' secret thinking and covert trial balloons concerning the spoiled nature of the relationship) and dyadic accounting (the private discussions, arguments, and confrontation between members that shape their respective views on the spoiling of their relationship).

CHAPTER 10

Towards a Model for the Prediction and Primary Prevention of Marital and Family Distress and Dissolution

Howard J. Markman, Frank Floyd and Fran Dickson-Markman

Interest in predicting and preventing marital and family distress and dissolution is not new. Yet relative to what is known about the treatment of marital and family problems, little is known about the factors that predict distress and help to prevent it. We argue that a major reason for our limited knowledge is the lack of a conceptual framework to guide research and intervention programs. The prediction of marital and family problems is addressed primarily by sociological studies (e.g., Burgess *et al.*, 1971) while preventive interventions for couples and families are usually designed by mental health professionals (e.g., Rutledge, 1968a). The areas have long and parallel histories. Towards the end of integrating these diverse areas within a common conceptual framework we present a model which outlines a method for interfacing prediction and prevention research efforts. Our objective here is to provide a conceptualization of the enterprises of both prediction and prevention as they relate to marital and family relationships across the lifespan. We then review approaches to prediction research and summarize major findings which have emerged as they relate to the etiology and prevention of marital and family problems. Finally, we review the strengths and weaknesses of approaches to prevention and highlight some of the more promising primary prevention programs. It is not our intent to provide a comprehensive review of prediction and prevention research and programs. Rather, we strive to provide a way of thinking about the enterprises of prediction and prevention, to focus attention on some important issues, and to highlight major trends and future directions in these fields. The chapter highlights results from our research program at the University of Denver on the prediction and prevention of marital and family distress.

Prediction and Prevention of Marital Distress: Conceptual Issues

Marital and family distress and dissolution are no longer rare occurrences. Indeed, U.S. Government figures indicate that approximately four out of ten first marriages will end in divorce (U.S. Government, 1981); with consequent effects on the children of the marriage who now have a high chance of living in a single-parent family for at least a few months (Glick and Norton, 1979). In addition to the issues thus created for policymakers, there are consequent personal costs also, such as increased risk of psychopathology in family members (Bloom et al., 1978), suicide (Stack, 1980) and loss of social support buffers against mental and physical disorders (Heller, 1979).

Several intervention strategies have been directed towards provision of relief for these people—but after distress develops (see, e.g., Gurman and Kniskern, 1978a, Olson et al., 1980). We believe that prevention is better than cure and will, in the present chapter, attend to research programs on relationship development which help us to predict and understand the problems that we hope to prevent.

Prediction and Prevention

Prediction involves the longitudinal relationship between variables measured early in development and criteria of interest measured later in development. The predictive validity of a variable is usually indexed by a correlation coefficient reflecting the degree of relationship between that variable (the predictor variable) and some other variable measured at a future time (the criterion variable). In order to be useful, predictor variables must possess validity coefficients which allow statements to be made about performance on the criterion variable which are more accurate that those made on the basis of base-rate expectations alone. Although a predictive relationship does not necessarily provide information about causation, factors associated with future problems can be identified and modified in primary prevention programs.

Classically, prevention is divided into three types: primary, secondary, and tertiary (Heller and Monahan, 1977). *Primary prevention* involves interventions aimed at populations who are not experiencing current problems, and provides social resources to help prevent problems from developing. These interventions are usually focused at transition or milestone periods (e.g., entering school, planning marriage) when stress is high and coping skills are needed to deal with the demands of the period. When discussing primary prevention our language alternates from a "deficit" to a "competency" orientation (Heller and Monahan, 1977). Deficit language uses phrases such as "preventing family distress", whereas competency language uses phrases such as "helping the family acquire skills". *Secondary prevention* involves interventions aimed at populations which are at risk for problems as indicated by early identification or screening. The goals are to decrease the length or severity of problems through such early detection. *Tertiary prevention* involves interventions aimed at populations who have already experienced problems and are designed to reduce the chances of recurrence of similar problems.

Although the majority of psychological interventions—including those directed at married couples and families—have only tertiary preventive or treatment effects, secondary preventive interventions (aimed at "high risk" populations) are gaining popularity in psychology. In relation to marital and family issues, secondary prevention requires using prediction research to identify what Chiland (1974) terms "conditions of risk" for developing marital and family distress. Two intervention strategies follow: "at risk" couples can be identified and (1) be discouraged from marrying (e.g., Ellis, 1948), or (2) be offered interventions. While at first glance these seem to be viable strategies, they are problematic because of both statistical and ethical limitations. Prediction research can provide only probability estimates of the development of relationship distress, estimates which are accurate only for groups of couples or families rather than for an individual couple or family. For example, evidence from child studies (e.g., Anthony, 1974) indicates that some high-risk children are invulnerable to disorders while some low-risk children are vulnerable. Further, without the data to accurately classify couples and families as high and low risk, ethical considerations preclude making this designation known to them. As we will see below, primary prevention avoids the problems associated with secondary prevention interventions based on risk factors.

A conceptual framework for prediction and primary prevention

The rationale for primary prevention with couples and families is based on the assumption that changing behavior patterns early in a couple's or family's development, at a point when their behavior patterns are not well established, decreases the probability of maladaptive behaviors developing later on. In contrast to secondary preventive approaches which view "risk" as a quality of specific couples and families, our approach to primary prevention views risk as a function of an interaction between transition periods and skills-related coping strategies. Primary prevention uses prediction research to identify coping strategies which are important to *all* couples and families as they progress through the normal stages or transitions of family development. Different transition periods require different coping skills, and different roles (e.g., parent v. lover) require different competencies. Thus it is important to understand the role of transition periods as stressors as well as the coping skills used by couples and families (Markman and Furman, 1981). Each of these issues is discussed below.

Family transition periods. The basic primary prevention strategy proposed here rests upon the premise that family members progress through identifiable transition periods which are associated with increased stress. From a sociological perspective (e.g., Nock, 1981) these are periods which call for one or more family members to discard old roles and assume new ones. During such times the individual encounters new situations and role demands which he or she may be unprepared to master. Similarly, from an interpersonal/systems (exchange) perspective (e.g., Thibaut and Kelley, 1959; Burgess and Huston, 1979) these periods call for the couple or family system to modify its interaction patterns in a way which maximizes rewards and minimizes costs. Interactional change is needed because sources of rewards and costs are changing and those which were available in an earlier period are no longer operative. Examples of family developmental transition periods include planning marriage (transition to marriage), early stages of marriage, birth of first child (transition to parenthood), and children leaving home (transition to empty nest).

The importance of transition periods for research and prevention has been highlighted before (e.g., Bloom, 1968; Duvall, 1971). Perhaps the earliest contributor was Goodrich (1961) who wrote, "These developmental transitions . . . are all subject to some type of preventative action as well as formal study" (p. 250). Goodrich recommended that research focus on how families attempt to master (i.e., cope with) social tasks (e.g., role changes) inherent in transition periods. Bloom (1968), from a crisis-theory framework, considers these situations as having a great potential for psychological risk and recommends that primary prevention programs be developed to help people cope with them. These periods offer ideal opportunities for treatments or interventions because the patterns of communication are not yet firmly established. However, with few exceptions (e.g., Raush *et al.*, 1974; Vincent *et al.*, 1980) there has been little systematic research on how people cope with the demands of the transition periods. The majority of research on transition periods has focused on whether or not the transitions have a negative effect on the participant (e.g., Lemasters, 1957; Nock, 1981) rather than on how people are coping with the demands of the transitions. Similarly, despite the fact the theorists have long recognized that intervention during transition periods is likely to have preventive effects, there have been few efforts to develop and evaluate such programs. One reason for this state of the field may be the need for a paradigm to guide research and preventive intervention in various transition periods.

In the next section we present a model which has been useful in guiding our research on the prediction and prevention of marital and family distress during the transition period of planning marriage. The model (1) is applicable to relationships in general, (2) elucidates the relationship between prediction and prevention research, (3) provides a useful framework for understanding research and conceptualizations concerning relationship dissolution presented in earlier chapters in this volume, and (4) is designed to foster the development and evaluation of prevention/enhancement programs.

A lifespan social competency model for identifying coping strategies

Goldfried and D'Zurilla (1969) present a behavior-competency approach to assessment which we have applied to the problem of identifying coping strategies which enable couples and families to master developmental tasks in transitional periods (Markman and Floyd, 1980; Markman and Furman, 1981). The model, outlined in Fig. 1, basically involves assessing the behavior of groups independently identified as either competent or incompetent in specific transition periods. Comparison of behavioral characteristics of population members who have developed disordered behaviors with those who have not, in situations relevant to the tasks of the transition periods under study, generates variables which may discriminate between the coping skills of the two groups. As recommended by Olson (1978), a comprehensive assessment of coping skills requires that data be collected from both an outsider's point of view (e.g., behavioral observations) and the couple's/family's own perspective (e.g., self-reports).

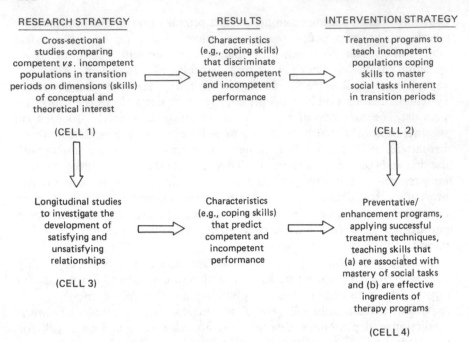

FIG. 1 Lifespan Social Competency Model for Prediction and Prevention Research Programs (After Markman and Floyd, 1980; Markman and Furman, 1981).

Once variables which have discriminative validity are identified using cross-sectional studies (Cell 1), longitudinal studies can assess questions relevant to predictive validity such as, "Do coping skills predict positive outcomes later in development?" (Cell 3).

To the extent that longitudinal studies identify variables which have predictive power, the variables can then be used as behaviors to be modified in preventive intervention programs (Cell 4). Thus, ideally, prediction research has direct implications for prevention. The methods of preventive intervention are derived from those found to be successful in treatment programs (Cell 2). Note that the model emphasizes examining how couples and families *behave* in situations common to the transition periods. Thus we study *behavioral* indices of future dysfunction, which can be modified in subsequent interventions. Behavioral indices are used rather than personality or demographic indices which may be good predictors but are not easily modifiable in interventions.

To summarize, essentially our model asserts that in order to prevent marital and family distress we need to know something about its etiology. Thus, prevention programs should be based on the results of research on factors associated with (Cell 1) and predictive of (Cell 3) marital and family distress and dissolution.

Research on the Prediction of Marital Distress

Empirical attempts to identify factors predictive of and associated with marital distress represent four distinct research traditions: sociological, mate-selection, communication, and behavioral psychology. Below, representative examples of studies from these research traditions are reviewed and critiqued in relation to the two goals of prediction research: (1) to address theoretically relevant etiological questions; and (2) to identify areas for preventive interventions.

Sociological tradition

Longitudinal studies in the sociological tradition, investigating the degree to which individual factors are predictive of marital distress and/or dissolution, are based on a large number of cross-sectional studies examining individual characteristics (e.g., demographic, personality) which discriminate between members of distressed and non-distressed marriages (Cell 1). The reader is referred to chapters in earlier volumes in this series (Burgess, 1981; Huston et al., 1981; Newcomb and Bentler, 1981) for a review of these cross-sectional studies. Longitudinal studies attempt to establish the predictive validity of variables identified in the cross-sectional studies when they are assessed either prior to marriage, or in the early stages of marriage (Cell 3).

One of the earliest longitudinal studies on the prediction of marital distress from individual factors was conducted by Burgess and Wallin (1953). These investigators reported the results of a longitudinal study of 1000 engaged couples, 666 of whom were followed up 3–5 years after marriage. They also integrated the findings of their study, begun in 1937, with those of earlier studies (e.g., Burgess and Cottrell, 1939; Terman, 1938; Terman and Oden, 1947). Since the purpose of this study was to predict the marital adjustment of couples who remained married, divorced couples were not included in the collection of follow-up data. Predictor variables were self-report responses to questionnaires, and included background items (e.g., family history), engagement history, personality characteristics, and anticipated contingency factors (e.g., expectations regarding marriage). The correlations between predictor variables and marital adjustment ranged from $r = 0.18$ to $r = 0.39$. Multiple regression procedures, now standard, were not conducted on these data and no single statistical index of the predictability of the entire set of items was presented. Despite the relatively low predictive validity this classic study highlighted the need for longitudinal research and paved the way for future studies.

A more recent longitudinal study, examining the roles of background and personality factors as predictors of marital adjustment scores, was conducted by Bentler and Newcomb (1978). The predictor variables were background and personality characteristics from 162 newly married couples. The major criterion variable was the marital adjustment of at least one member of 60 couples four years later. All predictor variables were entered into a series of stepwise regression analyses with marital adjustment scores as the criterion variable. In contrast to Burgess and Wallin's (1953) study, information obtained from divorced couples, including adjustment scores, was included in these analyses.[1] The correlations between individual items and the composite adjustment scores were, again, fairly low, ranging from -0.29 to 0.33. However, the multiple correlations for the prediction equations obtained from the regression analyses were in the range of $R = 0.75$. These multiple correlation coefficients should shrink upon cross-validation; nevertheless the findings suggest that future marital adjustment can be reliably predicted from background and personality information obtained from newly married couples. Interestingly, consistent with several other classic (e.g., Burgess and Wallin, 1953) and recent (e.g., Floyd and Markman, 1981) studies, the wives' characteristics were more predictive than the husbands'. While a discussion of the theoretical implications of sex differences is beyond the scope of the present chapter, this area deserves more attention and we recommend that all marital/family studies examine potential sex differences.

Although the results of these studies are encouraging in suggesting that marital distress and stability can be predicted from measures taken before or in the early stages of marriage, these lines of research are limited in the extent to which they fulfill the goals of prediction investigations. First, studies fail to examine a comprehensive theory of the development of relationship distress and dissolution. In some cases the studies address isolated hypotheses about factors associated with marital problems (e.g., Bentler and Newcomb, 1978). In the other cases, however, these studies represent blind empiricism, demonstrating correlated relationship between variables which have no theoretical relevance. As a result, the findings of these studies fail to provide a clear picture of the etiology of marital distress

---

[1]Bentler and Newcomb's marital adjustment measure is problematic since data from divorced couples were included. This may have introduced a "negative halo" effect. In any event, it does not make sense to measure retrospective marital adjustment of divorced couples.

and dissolution.

Second, little information is provided about possible areas for preventive intervention. The variables investigated in these studies are not easily amenable to change in preventative interventions. Specifically, demographic background characteristics are impossible to modify, while personality characteristics and perceptual variables can usually be modified only in relatively in-depth, individual interventions.

Mate-selection studies

In contrast to the previous studies which attempt to predict satisfaction, mate-selection studies try to answer the question: "What factors influence the development of a *stable* marital and family relationship?". There have been three general types of mate-selection studies: (1) those using cross-sectional designs (Cell 1) to test hypotheses about the factors presumed to be important in mate selection (e.g., Winch, 1954); (2) those using longitudinal designs (Cell 3) to assess how well these factors identified in cross-sectional studies predict the extent to which seriously attached or engaged couples make progress towards marriage (e.g., Lewis, 1973); and (3) those using retrospective designs to identify the different paths toward permanency that couples follow (e.g., Huston et al., 1981).

Since the results of these studies have been summarized in an earlier volume in this series (Huston et al., 1981) we will only highlight the major findings. Briefly, three major variables have emerged which predict future relationship permanence: (1) perceived similarity (e.g., Kerckhoff and Davis, 1962; Lewis, 1972): (2) the woman's perception of partner (e.g., Murstein, 1970, 1971), and (3) the couple's own prediction of future stability (Levinger et al., 1970; Markman, 1977). It is noteworthy that all these variables reflect *cognitive* dimensions of relationships, and again underline the importance of understanding sex differences in marital and family relationships.

The research designs used by the three mate-selection traditions have provided important information on the evaluation of premarital relationships. However, implicit in most mate-selection theories is the assumption that good communication is a prerequisite for a stable relationship. Despite the fact that many mate-selection studies conclude with a statement that future research should investigate communication (e.g., Murstein and Beck, 1972; Levinger et al., 1970), there are few mate-selection studies that directly observe the couple's communication or interaction. Rather, these studies rely on individual level measures which are combined in order to describe qualities of the couple's relationship.

Communication research

Unlike the first two traditions which essentially conceptualize the couple's relationship as the sum of their individual characteristics, communication researchers have gone a step further by viewing the couple's relationship as the unit of analysis and examining the perceptual role of communication in the development of marital and family relationships.

The research in the field of communication reflects two traditions: the individual tradition and the transactional tradition (Berger, 1975). The individual tradition in the study of communication focuses on the effects that an actor may produce in another person and on the characteristics of the actor involved in the communication process. Examples of such research include studies examining communicator style (Norton and Miller, 1975), communication apprehension (McCroskey, 1970), and communicative competence (Weimann, 1977). Unfortunately, there have been no studies, to our knowledge, examining these important constructs in the context of marital and family relationships. Further, these studies still focus on the individual characteristics of dyad members, although these characteristics are likely to reflect communication skills which are modifiable.

In contrast, the transactional tradition is more concerned with the reciprocal nature of the communication process between couples. The unit of analysis is the relationship as a whole, not the characteristics of each separate dyad member. There are two major types of studies conducted within the transactional tradition: (1) studies that examine self-perceptions of communication within the marital relationship and (2) studies that examine interaction patterns of the marital dyad. The typical design of the self-perception studies involves couples completing self-report measures on the perceptions of their own communication, the communication of their spouse, and how that affects the marital relationship. For example, Boyd and Roach (1977) found that sending direct, clear messages, active listening, and respect and esteem for one's spouse were related to marital satisfaction.

Another approach to studying self-perception of communication is provided by Fitzpatrick and associates who have attempted to capture the complexities of communication through the development of marital typologies. Fitzpatrick (1977) empirically developed a typology of marriages based on couples' perception of communication behaviors. The three types of marital relationships which emerged were classified as: *independent couples,* characterized by high degrees of autonomy, little conflict avoidance, and commitment to an ideology of uncertainty and change; *separate couples,* characterized by little sharing and high degrees of conflict avoidance; and *traditional couples,* characterized by low autonomy, high degrees of sharing and corresponding tendencies to engage rather than avoid conflict. This typology has been utilized to discriminate (Cell 1) among a number of self-report dimensions including instrumental and expressive communication (Fitzpatrick, 1977) and dyadic adjustment (Fitzpatrick and Best, 1979). This promising approach highlights the complexity of marital and family relationships. However, longitudinal studies (Cell 3) are necessary to examine the predictive validity of the typologies.

Stephen (1980) used a combination cross-sectional/longitudinal design to research the development of dating couples' perceptions of a shared view of reality. The theoretical framework guiding this research consists of a synthesis of social exchange theory and symbolic interactionism which Stephen labeled "symbolic exchange theory". The initial study established the reliability and validity of a measure of symbolic interdependence (The Relationship World Index) which used a Q-sort methodology (Stephen and Markman, 1981). Then a cross-sectional study (Cell 1) found that high levels of symbolic interdependence were positively associated with high levels of commitment and relationship satisfaction. Finally, a longitudinal study (Cell 3) indicated that symbolic interdependence increased over time (Stephen, 1980). This study is important because it represents a systematic attempt to research the role of perceptual factors in relationship development. However, one major problem with Stephen's study, and the perception of communication studies in general, is that communication processes are not directly observed.

Studies examining interaction patterns of marital couples attempt to measure behaviors, not self-reports of behavior. These studies have in common the goal of identifying specific communication behaviors associated with types of intimate relationships. For example, Krain (1975) investigated how the sequence of utterances of dating couples influenced progression to a committed relationship, using different cohorts of couples to approximate longitudinal effects. He found that negative communication was most characteristic in the early stages, and facilitative communication was most characteristic in later stages, of relational development. Krain (1975) interpreted these findings as suggesting that later stage couples manage conflict through use of facilitative communication.

While Krain was interested in the role of communication in the commitment process, Rogers and Farace (1975) were concerned with control patterns in marital relationships and changes in these patterns over time. Using a coding system to measure control patterns in marriage, they found that role conflict was positively associated with struggles for control (Rogers, 1972), that rigid control patterns were related to agreement and understanding about relational issues (Millar, 1973), and high levels of wife control were associated with lower marital and communication satisfaction for both partners (Rogers-Millar and Millar, 1979).

To summarize, the communication tradition is concerned with describing patterns of communication and characteristics of marital relations. These studies have identified communication behaviors associated with distressed and non-distressed couples (Cell 1) and provide the foundation for longitudinal studies that would examine communication behaviors that predict marital distress and dissolution. However, the main problem with these studies is that they are measuring abstract constructs instead of actual communication behaviors.

The behavioral psychology tradition

One of the major contributions of behavioral psychology to the study of marital and family relationships is the application of behavioral observation techniques which attempt to describe behaviors rather than to measure constructs (Markman et al., 1981a). Although behavioral psychologists have been relative latecomers to the study of marital and family relationships, they have made important conceptual and methodological contributions to understanding and preventing marital and family distress and dissolution.

The theoretical basis for most behavioral marriage research comes from the behavioral model of marriage (Stuart, 1969; Weiss, 1978; Weiss et al., 1973) which states that marital satisfaction results from the exchange of positive, rewarding behaviors between spouses, while distress results from the reliance on coercion to produce desired changes. Recent theoretical developments include the synthesis of cognitive (e.g., Weiss, 1980) and family systems (e.g., Birchler and Spinks, 1980) perspectives within a broadly defined cognitive-behavioral framework. This perspective asserts that the quality of the couples' and families' interaction is the key determinant of relationship satisfaction. Numerous cross-sectional studies (Cell 1) have tested this hypothesis by examining the behaviors of distressed (dissatisfied) and non-distressed (satisfied) couples while engaged in dyadic interactions.

There are three types of investigation: studies using objective observers; studies using couples as observers in lab settings; and studies using couples as observers in home settings. Investigations examining objective observers' (i.e., trained coders) evaluations of couples' problem solving interactions in laboratory settings (e.g., Billings, 1979; Birchler et al., 1975) consistently demonstrate that distressed couples engage in more negative verbal exchanges than do non-distressed couples. Similarly, distressed spouses emit more negative non-verbal behaviors, and tend to become engaged in unproductive negative interactional cycles when attempting to reach problem solutions (Gottman, 1979; Gottman et al., 1977; Markman et al., 1981a). Studies with couples as observers in lab settings demonstrate that when spouses themselves evaluate the pleasingness of each others' interactional behaviors, distressed couples report less satisfaction with their interactions (Floyd and Markman, 1981) and evaluate their partner's behaviors more negatively (Gottman et al., 1976a) than do non-distressed couples. Similarly, studies examining couples' behaviors in the home demonstrate that both daily relationship satisfaction (Wills et al., 1974) and overall marital satisfaction (Barnett and Neitzel, 1979) are positively correlated with more frequent displays of pleasing behaviors and less frequent displays of displeasing behaviors.

Based, in part, on these results several behavioral marital therapy programs have been developed to help distressed couples (Cell 3) (e.g., Gottman et al., 1976b; Jacobson and Margolin, 1979). Evaluations of the effectiveness of these interventions indicate that increases in relationship satisfaction following intervention are associated with increases in the positivity of couples' problem-solving interactions in lab settings (e.g., Jacobson, 1977) and increases in the pleasingness of their behaviors emitted in the home (e.g., Margolin and Weiss, 1978).

Taken together, these findings provide strong support for the behavior model's assertion that unrewarding marital interaction is associated with marital distress. Nevertheless, longitudinal studies (Cell 3) must demonstrate that couples' negative interactions and poor problem-solving skills before marriage are predictive of the development of marital distress or dissolution.

The first longitudinal study of couples' interactional behaviors (Raush et al., 1974) provided only indirect evidence that marital satisfaction can be predicted from interactional behaviors before marriage. This study assessed the interactional styles of married couples at three points in time, before, during and after the transition period of the birth of the first child. Comparison of couples' behaviors at these three points in time revealed that, although there were minor changes during pregnancy, spouses behaved consistently from early in marriage until after childbirth. Raush et al. (1974) concluded from these findings that interactional styles which are present within the first few months of marriage remain consistent throughout, at least, the early years of marriage. Although this study fails to demonstrate that marital distress can be predicted from premarital interactions, it does suggest that the interactional behaviors of married couples, including those associated with marital distress, can be predicted from their interactions early in marriage.

Only one study (Markman, 1979) has examined the interactions of couples before marriage (i.e., couples in the transitional period of planning marriage) as predictors of future relationship satisfaction. The results indicated that couples' evaluations of the positivity of their interactions were unrelated to their relationship satisfaction scores at a one-year follow-up point but were predictive of their satisfaction at a 2½-year and a 5½-year follow-up (Markman, 1981). These findings provide evidence that the ability to develop rewarding interactions patterns is an important skill for couples, in order to master the stresses inherent in the transitional periods of planning marriage and the early stages of marriage. Although these findings need to be interpreted with caution pending replication which is currently in progress (Markman et al., in press), the results provide preliminary evidence that communication deficits may precede the development of marital distress. Premarital couples might therefore benefit from prevention programs designed to teach premarital couples communication and problem-solving skills that are predictive of future marital satisfaction. Thus, data is provided which helps clarify our understanding of the etiology of marital distress, and, in examining the *behavior* of couples, direct suggestions are provided about possible preventive interventions.

Programs Designed to Prevent Marital and Family Distress and Dissolution

There are a number of available approaches to preventing marital and family distress (Cell 4). These programs vary in terms of service provider, service receiver, setting, point of time in lifespan, and format of service. Thus, paraphrasing Kiesler (1971) we can ask the question: Who provides what services to whom at what point in time and in what setting? The answer is summarized in Table 1 which presents a lifespan framework for conceptualizing programs already available and also highlights areas in which there has been little or no work. Table 1 lists either general approaches to prevention which are available or references to specific programs which have been developed.[2] The large number of empty cells demonstrates that there is a tremendous amount of work to be done in this area. We should also note that many writers express the view that preparation for effective family functioning begins at birth. In this sense,

---

[2]There may be developed programs of which we are unaware; we hope that authors of such programs will contact us to make us aware of their efforts.

TABLE 1 Approaches to primary prevention of marital and family distress

Approach to prevention	Representative Stages of Lifespan							
	Dating couples	Couples planning marriage	Married couples	Couples having first child	Families	Families in launching stage	Divorcing couples and families	Couples and families getting remarried
Educational/ counseling programs	Marriage preparation courses	Premarital counseling by clergy Rutledge (1966)			Family Life Education. Church/synagogue-sponsored workshops, programs.		Bloom et al. (1978)	Premarital counseling by clergy
Enrichment programs		Mace (1972)	Marital enrichment programs. Sexual enrichment programs.		Family enrichment			
Non-specific communication-enhancement programs	Ginsberg and Vogelsong (1977, PRIMES) Ridley and associates (e.g., Ridley et al., 1978)	Miller et al. (1975, 1979, Minnesota Couples Communication Program)	Haynes (1978) marital effectiveness training					
Specific skill-acquisition programs		Markman and Floyd (1980, Premarital Relationship Enhancement Program, PREP)		Lamaze training	Alexander and associates (e.g., Alexander and Parsons, 1973)			PREP for remarital couples (Markman, in press)

healthy psychological development can be viewed as serving preventive goals. While we basically agree with this position (who wouldn't?) we do believe that there are specific skills for marital and family relationships that are needed, that are not generally provided, and that can be acquired in prevention programs.

We will discuss three general approaches to preventing marital and family distress and dissolution which focus on relationships as targets of the interventions: (1) premarital intervention programs, (2) marital and family enrichment programs, and (3) family skill training programs. These approaches are the most widespread and have an impact on thousands of couples and families each year. Although the focus of most of these programs is on couples, according to systems theory the enhancement of the couple's relationship will radiate to improving the family's functioning (Satir, 1967).

Premarital intervention

Until recently, most of the literature on premarital intervention was to be found in *The Journal of Pastoral Counseling* which reflects the facts that (1) certain religions require premarital counseling, (2) people tend to seek out help from the clergy rather than mental health professionals (Gurin *et al.,* 1960) and (3) the clergy as a group are committed to enhancing marital and family relationships. Although the contribution of the clergy and other community resources to the primary prevention of marital and family distress and dissolution deserves attention, we will focus on contributions from the social sciences.

The goal of premarital intervention (PMI) is to intervene in couples' relationships before marriage in order to prevent the development of marital and family distress and dissolution. We prefer the term PMI instead of the terms premarital counseling or marriage preparation since PMI implies a focused, non-judgmental approach to providing services to healthy couples. Since the focus of these interventions is on couples who are functioning well, there is a clear overlap between the premarital intervention program literature and marital enrichment literature. One of the major differences between premarital intervention and marital enrichment is that the interaction patterns of premarital couples are not yet solidified and hence the potential for change may be greater. The premarital couples may be "trying on" different interaction patterns and may be more willing to experiment with interactional styles. From a sociological perspective the basic tasks for the couple are to change from the roles of either a family member in the family of origin or a single person to that of a partner in a marriage and then to that of a parent. From an exchange perspective, the basic task is to develop a mutually rewarding interaction pattern.

Brief review of the state of the art. Since Rutledge has already provided an interesting account of the early history of PMI, we will focus on summarizing approaches to PMI using the prevention framework described earlier (Table 1). As seen in Table 1, we can identify four types of PMI programs: educational/counseling (e.g., Rutledge, 1966), enrichment (e.g., Mace, 1972), non-specific communication enhancement (e.g., Miller *et al.,* 1975), and specific skill acquisition and cognitive restructuring (e.g., Markman and Floyd, 1980). A more detailed review of PMI programs is provided elsewhere (Markman, in press). We will now describe four major approaches to premarital intervention which have in common a focus on modifying couples' interaction and are easily adaptable to other types of relationships (e.g., friends, families).

The Rutledge program. Rutledge (1966, 1968b), who has been the foremost champion of the need for what he calls premarital counseling, developed the first systematic framework for PMI. He claims that if

> "all clinicians would devote one quarter of their time to premarital counseling, they could make a greater impact upon the health of this country, than through all their remaining activities combined."   (Rutledge, 1966, p. 77)

The objective of the program is to help couples to master developmental tasks inherent in the transition period of planning marriage in order to prevent future problems. Although Rutledge acknowledges the importance of communication and problem-solving skills training, he provides few techniques to achieve these goals and no empirical bases for intervention. Essentially his program is much like therapy in that it involves discussing with couples their personality, expectations, and current and potential problem areas. Nevertheless, Rutledge's pioneering program paved the way for future premarital intervention programs.

The only evaluation of Rutledge's program, to our knowledge, is a small *N* single-group study (Meadows and Taplin, 1970). These authors developed a premarital intervention program based upon Rutledge's approach and met with six couples in several joint and individual sessions. All participants reported that they responded positively to the sessions. However, the potentially most interesting finding was that three couples subsequently broke their engagement, and two partially attributed their relationship dissolution to the intervention program sessions. We will return to the issue of potential negative effects of PMI below. This study is essentially a series of case reports and therefore does not provide an adequate test of the effects of the program. However, it is unfortunately representative of many "evaluations" of prevention and enhancement programs with couples and families.

Minnesota Couples Communication Program. One of the most popular premarital intervention programs is a short-term, structured, educational program, the Minnesota Couples Communication Program (Miller *et al.,* 1975, 1979). The Minnesota Couples Communication Program is theoretically based on Reubin Hill's family development theory and systems theory emphasizing the role-governed nature of relationships. The major objective of the program is to teach couples to increase self-awareness and communication skills. Although initially focused on the transition period of engagement, the program has been widely used with couples at other stages of the lifespan and for marital enrichment. The implicit preventive theory underlying the Minnesota Program is that good communication is predictive of later marital and family satisfaction.

There are several evaluations of the Minnesota Program. However, the majority of these are unpublished doctoral dissertations, the results of which have not been adequately disseminated and evaluated. Miller (1971) and Nunnally (1971), in the first evaluations of the program, provided evidence that intervention couples increased awareness of dyadic interaction and increased usage of positive communication styles compared to controls. Similarly, Campbell (1974) found that married intervention couples (as compared with controls) increased self-disclosure as measured by interaction samples, but not levels of awareness. In a more recent report, Miller *et al.* (1976) found that intervention as compared with control couples increased in ability to observe interaction and in ability to "work" on problems in their relationships. Although these results are promising, these studies evaluated only the short-term (pre–post) effect of the program. Recently, Wampler and Sprenkle (1980) conducted the first published follow-up study of the effects of the Minnesota Program by comparing an intervention to a placebo control group.[3] Unfortunately, they mixed married, engaged, and dating couples and did not clarify whether groups were matched on these and other important dimensions. The immediate (pre–post) results indicated that intervention couples used more open communication in an interaction sample and had more positive perceptions about the relationship. The four-month follow-up indicated that changes in communication skills were not maintained whereas the perceptual changes were. These studies, taken together, indicate that the program may achieve its purposes of teaching couples skills and of

---

[3]According to Wampler and Sprenkle (1980) two unpublished studies (Dillon, 1975; Zimmerman and Bailey, 1977) reported preliminary positive long-term effects on self-report measures ranging from 10 weeks to 5 years.

increasing awareness about relationship issues. However, the question arises as to the extent to which the changes are maintained. The use of both self-report and behavioral observation of interaction samples in these studies is clearly a strength as is the creative use of an attention-placebo control in the Wampler and Sprenkle study. Hopefully, these authors plan to follow up their couples over time to assess the preventive effects of their program.

Rogerian skill training programs. Although most enrichment and premarital intervention programs train couples to use what are typically considered "Rogerian skills", two programs specifically are derived from Guerney's (1977) Conjugal Relationship Enhancement program which is based on Rogers' principles of direct expression of feeling (self-disclosure) and empathic listening. Ginsburg and Vogelsong (1977) developed a program called PRIMES (Premarital Relationship Improvement by Maximizing Empathy and Self Disclosure) which applies the Guerney approach to enhancing the self-awareness and communication skills of premarital couples. Two studies have evaluated the short-term (pre–post) effectiveness of this program (Schlein, 1971; D'Augelli et al., 1974). The Schlein study analyzed self-report and behavioral data and the D'Augelli et al. study reanalyzed behavioral data from the original Schlein study. The results indicated that for intervention couples, as compared to controls, empathy skills increased but self-reports of communication and relationship satisfaction generally did not change.

Ridley and his associates at the University of Arizona (Ridley et al., 1978; Avery et al., 1980) have expanded the Guerney program using an interpersonal competence approach that involves teaching premarital couples skills which are associated with marital success. These skills are designed to help the couples increase what Ridley (1980) calls "lines of action" or flexibility, which help the couple achieve their relationship goals. Basically three major groups of skills are taught: (1) reciprocal self-disclosure skills, (2) empathy skills, and (3) problem-solving skills. Results of studies evaluating Ridley's work have indicated that intervention, as compared with control couples, increased in both empathy and self-disclosure (Avery et al., 1980) and problem-solving skill levels (Ridley et al., 1978) at both posttest and six-month follow-up. These findings are impressive and the random assignment of couples to groups and the short-term follow-up increases our confidence in the validity of the results. Further, the use of both behavioral and self-report assessment perspectives is to be commended. Ridley and associates exemplify the type of systematic research needed to advance the field of PMI. Once again, we hope that the authors are planning to assess the long-term effects of their program.

Denver Family Development and Intervention Program. The rationale for our premarital intervention program is based on four established empirical findings which have been described earlier in the chapter. First, comparisons of the problem-solving skills of distressed and non-distressed married couples (e.g., Gottman et al., 1977; Floyd and Markman, 1981) have indicated that distressed couples are characterized by deficits in communication skill (Cell 1). Second, treatment programs have been developed based on the results of the cross-sectional studies (e.g., Gottman et al., 1976b) indicating that these skills can be successfully taught to distressed marital couples (Cell 2). Third, skill improvement positively affects current and future relationship satisfaction (Jacobson and Margolin, 1979; Gottman, 1979). Fourth, longitudinal studies of premarital couples (Markman, 1979, 1981) have provided preliminary results that communication deficits precede the development of marital distress (Cell 3). Based on these results, a prevention program (PREP, Premarital Relationship Enhancement Program) was developed aimed at teaching premarital couples communication skills that are predictive of developing successful marriages and family relationships (Markman and Floyd, 1980) (Cell 4). In other words, PREP provides training for premarital couples on the very skills (i.e., communication and problem-solving) in which distressed marital couples are deficient. The goal of PREP is to teach premarital couples skills important for effective marital and family functioning *before* problems develop.

The program is best described as an anticipatory guidance program with cognitive restructuring and skill-acquisition components (Markman and Floyd, 1980). Since the program is presented in more detail elsewhere (Markman and Floyd, 1980; Markman, in press) we will only briefly describe our approach. There are seven components of cognitive restructuring in the program: learning a language system, learning the behavioral model, examining expectations, the concept of "engaging the skills", information about couples planning marriage, information about marital discord, and information about sexual functioning and dysfunction. There are also seven specific skills taught in the program: listener skills, speaker skills, behavior-monitoring skills, learning which behaviors are pleasing or displeasing to their partner, making specific requests for behavior change, contracting skills, and pleasuring skills. Consistent with our model the program is aimed at the transition period of planning marriage.

We have completed two studies evaluating the effects of our program. In a preliminary small N study, Markman et al. (1981b) compared the relationship satisfaction and stability of PREP and control couples at posttest and one year later. The results indicated little difference between PREP and controls at posttest; however, one year later, PREP couples were more likely to maintain a stable relationship and less likely to experience a decline in relationship satisfaction from posttest to follow-up. The time-lagged preventive effect highlights the importance of conducting long-term follow-up to adequately evaluate prevention programs. However, given the lack of a behavioral measure of communication, the small sample size, and the short-term (i.e., one year) follow-up period, the results must be interpreted with caution.

In our next study (Markman *et al.,* in preparation) we asked the question, are the PREP couples learning the skills we are teaching them and does this improve their relationship satisfaction in the short run? Couples planning marriage recruited for basic research purposes were matched on several predictor variables and randomly assigned to PREP ($N = 14$) or no-treatment control ($N = 14$) conditions. The results indicated that PREP as compared to control couples improved their level of communication and problem-solving skills and increased their level of global relationship satisfaction. Control couples, in fact, demonstrated some evidence of a decrease on these dimensions.

Taken together, these results suggest an interesting possibility about effects of premarital intervention programs in particular and prevention programs in general. The pattern of results raises the hypothesis that the positive effects of the intervention program were due to the *prevention of a decline* in couples' relationship satisfaction which normally occurs over the lifespan (Rollins and Galligan, 1978). This hypothesis is consistent with a "bank account model" which suggests that all couples start their relationship with a sizeable "relationship bank account" and couples who become distressed slowly "withdraw" from their "account" through unrewarding interactions (Gottman *et al.,* 1976a; Markman, 1979). This type of finding has also been reported in other areas of prevention, including programs designed to enhance intellectual functioning of preschool children (Heber and Garber, 1975) and programs designed to improve adjustment of children entering school (Cowen *et al.,* 1973).

To summarize, these studies provided preliminary evidence for the possibilities of preventing marital distress through a cognitive-behavioral intervention program. Future research with longer term follow-up is clearly needed as well as replications of these preliminary findings. We are currently conducting a large N longitudinal study to replicate and extend our prediction and intervention studies (see Markman *et al.,* in press, for a more detailed description of this project).

Enrichment strategies

Marital and family enrichment programs. Since the early 1960s an increasing amount of attention has been paid to the development and implementation of marital and family "enrichment" programs. Prior to this time, the only type of service available to couples who were involved in relatively happy marriages, but who wished to make their relationships more satisfying, had been didactic courses in marital and family living offered by colleges and universities as part of their regular curriculum (e.g., Womble, 1961). More recently, both mental health professionals and church-related agencies have begun to recognize the necessity of dealing with the prevention of marital and family distress through marital/family enrichment programs. The popularity of these programs has greatly increased in the last decade, and Otto's (1976) estimate that about 180 000 couples and families have participated is certainly an underestimate.

The goal of marital and family enrichment is to help "healthy" couples and families realize their full potential by increasing the quality of their interactions and awareness of their own, their partner's, and children's needs (Mace, 1979; Otto, 1975, 1976). Although the content of each program differs, almost all programs emphasize enhancement of communication skills (Otto, 1976). These programs clearly have primary preventative implications since the targets are healthy couples and families. The program is designed to "inoculate" the couples and their families against future distress and dissolution. Although not documented, our experience indicates that a lot of couples participate in these programs in anticipation of family transition periods (e.g., children leaving home). Although the formats of programs differ, most utilize a combination of group and individual sessions carried out over a period of several weeks (e.g., Haynes, 1978; Rapaport, 1976) or in weekend retreats (e.g., Travis and Travis, 1975).

Although Otto (1976) reports that there are at least 71 marital and family enrichment programs across the United States, few of these programs have been systematically evaluated as to their short- and long-term effectiveness. In a comprehensive review of the outcome research in the area of marital enrichment, Gurman and Kniskern (1977) report only 22 marital enrichment studies. To our knowledge, two major marital enrichment programs, i.e., Methodist Marriage Communication Lab (Smith and Smith, 1976) and Marriage Encounter (Bosco, 1973), remain unevaluated, although hundreds of thousands of couples have participated in these programs.

Among the programs which have been systematically evaluated, the empirical evidence of the effectiveness of marital and family enrichment programs is promising. Significant positive change is consistently demonstrated on 60% of the outcome measures from each of three categories, i.e., overall marital satisfaction, relationship skills (including communication skills), and individual personality variables (Gurman and Kniskern, 1977). However, as Gurman and Kniskern point out, most of these studies suffer from serious methodological flaws which preclude the clear interpretation of these data. In particular, the majority of these studies (58%) utilize self-report data as the only criterion for change. Additionally, only 16% of all outcome measures involve evaluation by non-participant observers. Other methodological shortcomings include the lack of sufficient follow-up data, the failure to obtain measures from non-treatment control groups of couples, and the failure to evaluate the effectiveness of various components of the treatment package (e.g., communication skills training, program format, facilitator factors, etc.)

Sexual enrichment programs. The need for enhancing sexual relationships is evidenced by Masters and Johnson's (1970) estimate that about 50% of all marriages need help in the area of sexual relations. Further, many "normal" married couples lack information and skill in both sexual technique and interpersonal communication (Mace, 1972). The goals of sexual and sensual enhancement are fostering open and honest sexual communication, and deeper interpersonal affection, thereby helping to prevent the occurrence of many marital and family problems (Travis and Travis, 1975; LoPiccolo and Miller, 1975; Rosenthal *et al.*, 1981).

Few programs which place an emphasis on sexual enrichment have evaluated the effectiveness of this procedure. For example, Travis and Travis (1975) conducted an overall evaluation of their enrichment program, but failed to examine the extent to which the sessions devoted to sexual enrichment conributed to the overall increase in marital satisfaction for their couples. One controlled study which did evaluate the effectiveness of a sexual enhancement program (LoPiccolo and Miller, 1975) demonstrated significant positive changes in the couples' satisfaction with the range and frequency of their sexual activity, and their acceptance of their own and their partners' sexual preferences. However, these investigators failed to evaluate the effect of this sexual enhancement training on the couples' overall marital satisfaction. Rosenthal *et al.*, (1981) found an increase in sexual knowledge and decrease in acceptance of myths, but not in relationship or sexual satisfaction using a matched-pair posttest only design.

In summary, there is a general consensus of opinion that sexual skills training and promotion of open and honest sexual communication between partners leads to increases in overall marital satisfaction. However, although there exists evidence which shows that sexual enhancement training leads to increased sexual knowledge and satisfaction, it must also be *empirically* demonstrated that training in sexual skills and communication leads to short-term and long-term increases in overall marital and then family satisfaction.

Family-life education. A third major force in the enrichment area is one that has a long and illustrious history: family-life education. This field has been responsible for teaching marriage and family courses and disseminating family-research findings to the public. It provided early advocates of marriage preparation, the precursors of what we term "premarital intervention". However, a review of the current status of family-life education is beyond the scope of this chapter. Research and intervention is focused upon normal couples and families across the lifespan and therefore is consistent with our model. An example of one of the topics under investigation is leisure across the lifespan (Rapoport and Rapoport, 1975). The primary preventive implications of the efforts of family life educators deserve attention. Interested readers are referred to journals such as *The Family Coordinator* and recent books (Stinnett *et al.*, 1979, 1980, 1981) on education approaches to enhancing family development.

Family skills training

The work of Alexander and his associates with families of delinquents represents a program of research which approximates our model of identifying coping skills, establishing predictive validity, and developing and evaluating preventive interventions to modify the skills. Alexander (1973) compared the interaction of 22 families with a normally functioning adolescent and 20 families with a delinquent adolescent (distressed families). The results indicated that the distressed families demonstrated more defensive and less supportive communications than did the normal families. Additionally, the distressed families tended to reciprocate defensive communications, while the normal families reciprocated supportive communications. Thus, defensive and supportive interaction patterns were identified as communication behaviors which discriminate normal and distressed families (Cell 1).

Next, Alexander and his associates conducted a longitudinal investigation of the effectiveness of alternative family treatment strategies (Cell 2) (Alexander and Parsons, 1973; Klein *et al.*, 1977; Parsons and Alexander, 1973). Distressed families were randomly assigned to either a behavioral family systems treatment program, a no-treatment control group, or one of two alternative treatment programs. The first stage of evaluation (Parsons and Alexander, 1973) included pre–post comparison of the families' interactions in order to document the effectiveness of the treatment program in modifying the interactions of distressed families. The second phase of the study (Alexander and Parsons, 1973) examined the recidivism rates for all four groups of identified delinquents from 6–18 months following treatment (tertiary prevention). Finally, Klein *et al.* (1977) evaluated the primary preventative impact of the behavioral systems intervention. Data were collected on the number of juvenile court referrals between 2½ and 3½ years after family intervention for siblings of the delinquent adolescents. The results showed that the rate of *sibling* referrals for families involved in the behavioral family systems treatment was from 50% to 60% less than the rates for families in the control and alternative treatment groups (Cell 4).

Perhaps the major shortcomings of this program of research, in terms of identifying communication skills associated with family distress and dissolution, is the failure to adequately establish the predictive validity of family interactional behaviors. Ideally, a study is needed demonstrating that family interactional patterns, prior to the development of any family problems, are reliable predictors of future family functioning (Cell 3). Although Alexander and his associates failed to address this issue directly, the data from their longitudinal investigation of family intervention provide some indirect evidence for the predictive validity of family interactional behaviors. The results indicate that positive changes in family interaction are related to more positive family functioning in the future. Nevertheless, it remains to be shown that, in general, families who engage in more supportive interactions function better in the future than do families who engage in more defensive interactions. What is needed is data on the natural course of family interaction and family functioning over the family life-cycle.[4]

Do Prevention and Enhancement Programs Work?

This crucial question has been asked by others (Druckman *et al.*, 1980; Bader *et al.*, 1977; Microys and Bader, 1977) and, as we will see, an answer is hard to come by. Our ignorance is due to a distinct paucity of research focusing on the effectiveness of prevention and enhancement programs. Further, serious conceptual and methodological issues plague the research which has been conducted and this has not allowed a fair test of the

[4]There is an extensive literature in the area of family interactions comparing normal and deviant families (e.g., families with a schizophrenic member). The interested reader is referred to several excellent recent studies (e.g., Blaker, 1980) and reviews (e.g., Doane, 1979).

effectiveness of preventive approaches. Although the *intent* of the prevention and enhancement programs that we have reviewed here is to inoculate couples and families against future relationship problems, there is a notable paucity of well-designed evaluations of the *actual impact* of the interventions on the couples' and families' relationships. To adequately evaluate prevention and enhancement programs, longitudinal studies comparing randomly assigned intervention with appropriate comparison groups are necessary. Longitudinal studies are needed because the goals of primary prevention programs (e.g., preventing dissolution, promoting satisfaction) are necessarily long-term in nature (Markman and Floyd, 1980). The possibility of negative or deterioration effects on couples and families due to participation in prevention or enhancement programs (e.g., Gurman and Kniskern, 1978b; Meadows and Taplin, 1970) underlines the need for well-designed long-term evaluations of our interventions. As we have stated elsewhere,

> "consider the current state of affairs — literally thousands of premarital and married couples are taking advantage of a variety of intervention programs ... and there are virtually no data on the long-term positive or negative effects of these programs".   (Markman and Floyd, 1980, p. 78)

We agree with Price and Cherniss (1977) that social interventionists have an ethical mandate to research the effects of programs which are offered to the consuming public.

Unfortunately the vast majority of studies use either single group designs (e.g., Meadows and Taplin, 1970) or non-random assignment to experimental and comparison groups (e.g., Druckman *et al.*, 1980), both of which are inadequate to evaluate even the short-term (pre–post) effects of these programs. We know of no published study to date with a follow-up longer than one year, therefore precluding a test of the long-term preventive or enhancement effects of the programs. Finally, most studies rely on self-report data which are subject to numerous biases, while few studies use behavioral observation strategies which are needed to adequately evaluate changes in couples and family interaction which are the core of most programs (see Markman *et al.*, 1981, for a review of behavioral observation techniques).

To return to the question, "Do prevention and enhancement programs with couples and families work?", the answer that has emerged is that we do not yet know. However, preliminary results are promising and we are aware of some of the pitfalls of early studies. However, even if prevention programs are shown to be successful, we have to be careful and not make the logical error that Buchwald and Young (1969) refer to as "affirming the consequent". That is, arguing that if skill training prevents problems, then a lack of skill causes problems. For example, people who get frequent headaches may learn that if they take aspirins at the first sign of the headache they can then *prevent* the headache from developing. But this does not mean that lack of aspirin causes headaches. Thus, the need for "basic research" on the etiology of marital and family problems is again highlighted.

In summary, the literature on prevention and enhancement programs highlights three important issues. First, there is a growing awareness of the need for preventive services for couples and families who are not currently experiencing distress. Second, the content of the programs which are currently offered demonstrates that there is a consensus of opinion among professionals that communication, problem-solving, conflict resolution, and related skills are essential elements of these programs. Third, there is a lack of empirical data relating to the short and long-term effectiveness of these programs and a need for methodologically sophisticated outcome research in this area.

Common Problems with Prediction and Prevention Research

We will conclude this chapter by summarizing some of the methodological and practical problems that we have encountered over the years doing prediction and prevention research with couples. The same type of problems will be likely to occur for researchers interested in preventing relationship distress and dissolution with any type of relationship (e.g., friends, families) at any transition period. We will focus on two major issues.

The effects of pre-testing

A major problem with all pre–post follow-up control-group design studies is the effect of the pretest (Campbell and Stanley, 1963). In the case of prediction and prevention studies, the pretest assessment necessarily involves the couple examining their relationship, and thus the assessment itself may serve as a form of intervention (Rubin and Mitchell, 1976; Markman, 1977; Druckman *et al.*, 1980). This phenomenon limits the generalizability of the results of prediction research and operates *against* finding true effects of preventive intervention programs. Thus, the pre–post follow-up designs provide a conservative test of the effectiveness of preventive and enhancement programs. For example, Druckman *et al.*

(1980) found that couples who completed an extensive inventory (i.e. PREPARE; see Fournier, 1979; Olsen et al., 1977) improved almost as much as a group who filled out the inventory and had four premarital counseling sessions. In fact these authors argue that the use of inventories such as PREPARE is a viable alternative to premarital counseling. This conclusion is premature, because as noted earlier, longitudinal studies over a period of years are needed to evaluate prevention studies. Nevertheless, Druckman et al. do highlight the problem of pretest effects and the need for assessing the effects of pretesting through the use of methods like the Soloman-4 group design (Campbell and Stanley, 1963).

Problems with longitudinal studies

The major practical problem with longitudinal studies is the expense and time demands of maintaining contacts with couples or families, and the associated problem of keeping couples (families) interested in the research program. We'd like to offer several suggestions for dealing with these issues that have been useful to us: (1) have research participants provide information on several people that "will always know where to contact you" (e.g., parents, friends); (2) inform the participants about the longitudinal objectives of the study and attempt to establish an alliance with them that gets them reasonably interested in the study (though not to the point of providing biased data); (3) maintain frequent (e.g., yearly) follow-up contacts with participants; (4) provide periodic reports on the progress of the study and general results that are of interest to the participants but do not bias future data collection.

We have had good results using these methods, although in response to one mail follow-up we did receive the following letter:

> "Dear Dr. Markman: I am sorry not to be able to comply with your questionnaire. Somehow your records have gotten confused. My maiden name was _____, but I never participated in a pre-marital research project nor do I know _____. On this basis the questionnaire was good for a laugh, although I had some answering to do to my husband. Good luck with your research."

Conclusion

Despite many problems associated with new research areas, preliminary findings in the area of predicting and preventing marital and family distress and dissolution are promising. Furthermore, the "marriage" of prediction and prevention research that we propose in our model, in the context of systematic research and intervention programs (Gottman and Markman, 1978), will hopefully yield even more fruitful offspring. The basic premise of our model is that the content of primary prevention programs should be based on longitudinal data from studies of marital and family relationships. Additionally, we have attempted to demonstrate the benefits of integrating conceptual and methodological contributions from diverse fields of study. Continued progress rests on systematic efforts to elucidate the empirical and conceptual developmental relationships between (i) couple and family strengths and weaknesses, (ii) attributes of transition periods and (iii) future outcomes such as satisfaction, distress, dissolution, growth and fulfillment. In subsequent articles we examine the clinical issues in developing and delivering primary prevention programs for couples and families (Markman, in press) and describe in more detail the results of our longitudinal research project on couples planning marriage (Markman *et al.*, in press). We look forward to the next decade providing not only valuable longitudinal data but also evaluations concerning the possibilities of understanding and preventing marital and family distress and dissolution.

Acknowledgement

Preparation of this chapter supported in part by grant MH35525–01 from the National Institute of Mental Health. We would like to acknowledge the assistance of Celeste Newman and Janet Kearney in the preparation of this chapter and the helpful comments of our editor, Steve Duck.

References

ABELSON, R.P. (1959). Modes of resolution of belief dilemmas. *Conflict Resolution*, **3**, 343–352.

ABRAHAMS, R.D. (1970). A performance-centered approach to gossip. *Man.* (N.S.), **5**, 290–301.

ADAM, J.H. and ADAM, N.W. (1979). "Divorce: How and When to Let Go", Prentice-Hall: Englewood Cliffs, New Jersey.

AJZEN, I. (1977). Information processing approaches to interpersonal attraction. *In* "Theory and Practice in Interpersonal Attraction", (Ed. S.W. Duck), Academic Press: London and New York.

ALBERT, S. and KESSLER, S. (1978). Ending social encounters. *J. Exper. Soc. Psychol.*, **14**, 541–553.

ALBERTI, R.E. and EMMONS, M.L. (1970). "Your Perfect Right", Impact Publishers: San Luis Obispo, California.

ALBRECHT, S.L. (1980). Reactions and adjustment to divorce: Differences in the experiences of males and females. *Family Rels*, **29**, 59–68.

ALEXANDER, J.F. (1973). Defensive and supportive communication in normal and deviant families. *J. Consult. Clin. Psychol.*, **40**, 223–231.

ALEXANDER, J.F. and PARSONS, B.V. (1973). Short-term behavioral intervention with delinquent families: Impact on family process and recidivism. *J. Abn. Psychol.*, **81**, 219–225.

ALLAN, G.A. (1979). "A Sociology of Friendship and Kinship", Allen and Unwin: London.

ALLEN, B.V., WIENS, A.N., WEITMAN, M. and SASLOW, G. (1965). Effects of warm-cold set of interviewee speech. *J. Consult. Psychol.*, **29**, 480–482.

ALTMAN, I. (1975). "The Environment and Social Behaviour", Brooks/Cole: Monterey, California.

ALTMAN, I. and TAYLOR, D. (1973). "Social Penetration: The Development of Interpersonal Relationships", Holt, Rinehart and Winston: New York.

ANTHONY, J. (1974). The syndrome of the psychological invulnerable child. *In* "The Child in His Family: Children at Psychiatric Risk" (Eds. J. Anthony and C. Koupernik), Wiley: New York.

ARGYLE, M. (1975). "Bodily Communication", International Universities Press: New York.

ARONSON, E. and MILLS, J. (1959). The effect of severity of initiation on liking for a group. *J. Abn. Soc. Psychol.,* **59**, 177–181.

ARONSON, E., WILLERMAN, B. and FLOYD, J. (1966). The effect of a pratfall on increasing interpersonal attraction. *Psychon. Sci.,* **4**, 227–228.

ATKINSON, J.W. (1981). Studying personality in the context of an advanced motivational psychology. *Amer. Psychol.,* **36**, 117–128.

ATKINSON, J.W. and McCLELLAND, D.C. (1948). The projective expression of needs: II. The effect of different intensities of the hunger drive on thematic apperception. *J. Exper. Psychol.,* **38**, 643–658.

AUSTIN, M.C. and THOMPSON, G.G. (1948). Children's friendships: a study of bases on which children select and reject their best friends. *J. Educ. Psychol.,* **39**, 101–116.

AVERY, A., RIDLEY, C., LESLIE, L. and MULHOLLAND, T. (1980). Relationship enhancement with premarital dyads: A six month followup. *Amer. J. Fam. Ther.,* **8**, 23–30.

AYRES, J. (1980). Relationship states and sex as factors in topic dwell time. *Western J. Speech Communication,* **44**, 253–260.

AYRES, J. (1981). Some associations between interpersonal relationship stages and verbal behavior: Theory and research. Paper presented at the Western Speech Communication Association Convention, San Jose, California, February, 1981.

BACKMAN, C.W. and SECORD, P.F. (1959). The effect of perceived liking on interpersonal attraction. *Hum. Rel.,* **12**, 379–384.

BACKMAN, C.W. and SECORD, P.F. (1962). Liking, selective interaction and misperception in congruent interpersonal relations. *Sociometry,* **25**, 321–335.

BADER, E., MICROYS, G., SINCLAIR, C., WILLETT, E. and CONWAY, B. (1977). Do marriage preparation programs really work? Results of recent research in Canada. Unpublished manuscript, Department of Family and Community Medicine, University of Toronto, Canada.

BARNETT, L.R. and NEITZEL, M.T. (1979). Relationship of instrumental and affectional behaviors and self esteem to marital satisfaction in distressed and non-distressed couples. *J. Consult. Clin. Psychol.,* **47**, 946–947.

BARON, R.A., BYRNE, D. and GRIFFITT, W. (1974). "Social Psychology: Understanding Human Interactions", Allyn and Bacon: New York.

BARTELS, B.D. (1977). Nonverbal immediacy in dyads as a function of degree of acquaintance and locus of control. *Dissertation Abstracts International.* **38** (1-B), 387.

BAXTER, L.A. (1979a). Self-disclosure as a relationship disengagement strategy. *Hum. Communication Res.,* **5**, 215–222.

BAXTER, L.A. (1979b). Self-reported disengagement strategies in friendship relationships. Paper presented at the Western Communication Association Convention, Los Angeles, California, February, 1979.

BAXTER, L.A. (1980). Relationship disengagement behavior as a function of perceived mutuality of the desire to end and attributed cause of the relationship's demise. Paper presented at the Western Speech Communication Association Convention, Portland, Oregon, February, 1980.

BAXTER, L.A. (1981). Relationship disengagement: an examination of the reversal hypothesis. Unpublished, Lewis and Clark College, Portland, Oregon.

BAXTER, L.A. and PHILPOTT, J. (1980). Relationship disengagement: A process view. Paper presented at the Speech Communication Association Convention, New York, November, 1980.

BAYES, M.A. (1972). Behavioral cues of interpersonal warmth. *J. Consult. Clin. Psychol.*, **39**, 333–339.

BECK, A.T., WARD, C.H., MENDELSON, M., MOCK, J. and ERBAUGH, J. (1969). An Inventory for measuring depression. *Arch. Gen. Psychiat.*, **9**, 295–302.

BEM, D. (1972). Self-perception theory. *In* "Advances in Experimental Social Psychology", Vol. 6 (Ed. L. Berkowitz), Academic Press: New York and London.

BENGTSON, V.L. and CUTLER, N. (1976). Generations and inter-generational relations: Perspectives on age groups and social change. *In* "Handbook on Aging and the Social Sciences", New York: Van Nostrand Reinhold.

BENTLER, P. and NEWCOMB, M. (1978). Longitudinal study of marital success and failure. *J. Consult. Clin. Psychol.* **46**, 1053–1070.

BERGER, C.R. (1975). Interpersonal communication theory and research: An overview. *In* "Communication Yearbook I" (Ed. B.D. Ruben), Transaction Books: New York.

BERGER, C.R. and CALABRESE, R.J. (1975). Some explorations in initial interaction and beyond: Toward a developmental theory of interpersonal communication. *Hum. Comm. Res.*, **1**, 99–112.

BERGER, C.R., GARDNER, R.R., PARKS, M.R., SCHULMAN, L.S. and MILLER, G.R. (1976). Interpersonal epistemology and interpersonal communication. *In* "Explorations in Interpersonal Communication" (Ed. G.R. Miller), Sage Publishers: Beverley Hills, California.

BERGER, P. (1963). "Invitation to Sociology", Doubleday: New York.

BERGER, P. and KELLNER, H. (1964). Marriage and the construction of reality: An exercise in the micro-sociology of knowledge. *Diogenes,* **46**, 1–25.

BERGER P. and KELLNER, H. (1970). Marriage and the construction of reality. *In* "Recent Sociology #2: Patterns of Communicative Behavior" (Ed. H. Drietzel), Macmillan: New York, pp. 50–72.

BERGER, P.L. and LUCKMANN, T. (1966). "Social Construction of Reality: A Treatise in the Sociology of Knowledge". Doubleday: New York.

BERLYNE, D. (1974). Attention. *In* "Handbook of Perception", Vol. 1 (Eds. E. Carterette and M. Friedman), Academic Press: New York and London.

BERSCHEID, E. (in prep.). Emotion. *In* "The Psychology of Close Relationships (Eds. H.H. Kelley *et al.*). In prep.

BERSCHEID, E., BOYE, D. and DARLEY, J. (1968). Effect of forced association upon voluntary choice of associate. *J. Personal. Soc. Psychol.*, **8**, 13–19.

BERSCHEID, E., BROTHEN, T. and GRAZIANO, W. (1976a). Gain-loss theory and the "law of infidelity": Mr. Doting vs. the admiring stranger. *J. Personal. Soc. Psychol.*, **33**, 709–718.

BERSCHEID, E. and CAMPBELL, B. (in press). The changing longevity of heterosexual close relationships: A commentary and forecast. *In* "The Justice Motive in Social Behavior" (Ed. M.J. Lerner), Plenum: New York.

BERSCHEID, E. and GRAZIANO, W.G. (1979). The initiation of social relationships and interpersonal attraction. *In* "Social Exchange in Developing Relationships" (Eds. R.L. Burgess and T.L. Huston), Academic Press: New York and London.

BERSCHEID, E., GRAZIANO, W., MONSON, T. and DERMER, M. (1976b). Outcome dependency: Attention, attribution and attraction. *J. Personal. Soc. Psychol.*, **34**, 978–989.

BERSCHEID, E. and WALSTER, E.H. (1974). Physical attractiveness. *In*

"Advances in Experimental Social Psychology", Vol. 7 (Ed. L. Berkowitz), Academic Press: New York and London.

BERSCHEID, E. and WALSTER, E.H. (1978). "Interpersonal Attraction" (2nd edn), Addison-Wesley: Reading, Massachusetts.

BIGELOW, B.J. and LA GAIPA, J.J. (1980). The development of friendship values and choice. In "Friendship and Social Relations in Children" (Eds. H.C. Foot, A.J. Chapman and J.R. Smith), Wiley: Chichester and New York.

BILLINGS, A. (1979). Conflict resolution in distressed and non-distressed married couples. J. Consult. Clin. Psychol., 47, 368–376.

BIRCHLER, G. and SPINKS, S. (1980). Behavioral systems in marital and family therapy: Integration and clinical application. Amer. J. Fam. Ther., 8, 6–28.

BIRCHLER, G.R., WEISS, R.L. and VINCENT, J.P. (1975). Multimethod analysis of social reinforcement exchange between maritally distressed and non-distressed spouse and stranger dyads. J. Personal Soc. Psychol., 31, 349–360.

BLAKER, R. (1980). "Studies of Familial Communication and Psychopathology: A Social-Developmental Approach to Deviant Behavior", Columbia University Press: New York.

BLAU, Z.S. (1973). "Old Age in a Changing Society", New Viewpoints: New York.

BLOOM, B.L. (1968). The evaluation of primary prevention programs. In "Comprehensive Mental Health: The Challenge of Evaluation" (Eds. L.M. Roberts, N.W. Greenfield and M.H. Miller), University of Wisconsin Press: Madison.

BLOOM, B.L., ASHER, S.J. and WHITE, S.W. (1978). Marital disruption as a stressor: A review and analysis. Psychol. Bull., 85, 867–894.

BLOOM, B.L. and CALDWELL, R.A. (1981). Sex differences in adjustment during the process of marital separation. J. Marr. Fam., 43, 693–701.

BLUMER, H. (1969). Fashion: From class differentiation to collective selection. Sociol. Quart., 10, 275–291.

BOHANNON, P. (1970a). The six stations of divorce. In "Divorce and After" (Ed. P. Bohannon), Doubleday Anchor: Garden City, NY.

BOHANNON, P. (1970b). "Divorce and After", Doubleday Anchor: Garden City, NY.

BOISSEVAIN, J. (1974). "Friends of Friends: Networks, Manipulators, and Coalitions", Blackwell: Oxford.

BOLLES, R.C. (1967). "Theory of Motivation", Harper and Row: New York.

BOSCO, A. (1973). "A Rediscovery of Love", Abbey Press: St. Meinrad, Indiana.

BOWLBY, J. (1961). Processes of mourning. Int. J. Psychoanalysis, 44, 317–335.

BOWLBY, J. (1979). "Attachment, Separation and Loss; Vol. 3: Loss", Penguin: Harmondsworth.

BOYD, L.A. and ROACH, A.J. (1977). Interpersonal communication skills differentiating more satisfied from less satisfied marital relationships. J. Couns. Psychol., 24, 540–542.

BRADFORD, L. (1977). The death of a dyad. Paper presented at the Speech Communication Association Convention, Washington, D.C., November, 1977.

BRADLEY, G.W. (1978). Self-serving biases in the attribution process: A re-examination of the fact or fiction question. J. Personal. Soc. Psychol., 36, 56–71.

BRECK, B.E. (1978). Restoring the intimacy equilibrium: The compensatory behavior of friends and strangers. Dissertation Abstracts International, 38 (12–B), 6229–6230.

BRIM, O.G., Jr. (1980). Types of life events. J. Soc. Issues, 36, 148–157.

BROCKNER, J. and SWAP, W.C. (1976). Effects of repeated exposure and attitudinal similarity on self-disclosure and interpersonal attraction. *J. Personal. Soc. Psychol.*, **33**, 531–540.

BROWN, C., FELDBERG, R., FOX, E. and KOHEN, J. (1976). Divorce: Chance of a new lifetime. *J. Soc. Issues*, **32**, 119–134.

BRUNER, J.S. and GOODMAN, C.C. (1947). Value and need as organizing factors in perception. *J. Abn. Soc. Psychol.*, **42**, 33–44.

BUCHWALD, A. and YOUNG, R. (1969). Some comments on the foundations of behavior therapy. *In* "Behavior Therapy: Appraisal and Status" (Ed. C. Franks), McGraw-Hill: New York.

BURGESS, E. and COTTRELL, L. (1939). "Predicting Success or Failure in Marriage", Prentice-Hall: New York.

BURGESS, E., LOCKE, J. and THOMAS, M. (1971). "The Family", Van Nostrand Reinhold: New York.

BURGESS, E. and WALLIN, P. (1953). "Engagement and Marriage", Lippincott: Philadelphia.

BURGESS, R.L. (1981). Relationships in marriage and the family. *In* "Personal Relationships 1: Studying Personal Relationships" (Eds. S.W. Duck and R. Gilmour), Academic Press: London and New York, pp.179–196.

BURGESS, R.L. and HUSTON, T.L. (Eds.) (1979). "Social Exchange in Developing Relationships", Academic Press: New York and London.

BURGOON, M., DILLARD, J.P. and DORAN, N.E. (1980). Situational determinants of message strategy selections: An exploratory analysis. Unpublished paper, Department of Communication, Michigan State University, 1980.

BYRNE, D. (1961). The Repression-Sensitization Scale: Rationale, reliability and validity. *J. Personal.*, **29**, 334–349.

BYRNE, D. (1971). "The Attraction Paradigm", Academic Press: New York and London.

BYRNE, D., CLORE, G.L. and WORCHEL, P. (1966). Effect of economic similarity-dissimilarity on interpersonal attraction. *J. Personal. Soc. Psychol.*, **4**, 220–224.

CAIRNS, R.B. (1966). Attachment behavior of mammals. *Psychol. Rev.*, **73**, 409–426.

CAIRNS, R.B. (1979). "Social Development", W.H. Freeman and Company: San Francisco.

CAMPBELL, A. (1981). "The Sense of Well Being in America: Patterns and Trends", McGraw Hill: New York.

CAMPBELL, A., CONVERSE, P.E. and ROGERS, W.L. (1976). "The Quality of American Life", Russell Sage Foundation: New York.

CAMPBELL, D.T. (1974). Evolutionary epistemology. *In* "The Philosophy of Karl Popper" (Ed. P.A. Schilpp), Open Court: Lasalle, Illinois.

CAMPBELL, D.T. and STANLEY, J.C. (1963). "Experimental and Quasi-experimental Designs for Research", Rand McNally: Chicago.

CAMPBELL, E. (1974). The effects of couple communication training on married couples in the childrearing years: A field experiment. Unpublished Doctoral Dissertation, Arizona State University.

CAPPELLA, J.N. (1981). Mutual influence in expressive behavior: Adult-adult and infant-adult dyadic interaction. *Psychol. Bull.*, **89**, 101–132.

CHAIKIN, A.L. and DERLEGA, V.J. (1974). "Self-Disclosure", General Learning Press: Morristown, New Jersey.

CHAPPLE, E.D. (1940). Measuring human relations: An introduction to the study of interaction of individuals. *Genet. Psychol. Monogs., 22*, 3–147.

CHELUNE, G.J. (1979). Measuring openness in interpersonal communication. *In* "Self-Disclosure" (Ed. G.J. Chelune), Jossey-Bass: San Francisco.

CHERLIN, A. (1978). Remarriage as an incomplete institution. *Amer. J. Sociol, 84*, 634–650.

CHILAND, C. (1974). Some paradoxes connected with risk and vulnerability. *In* "The Child in His Family: Children at Psychiatric Risk" (Eds. J. Anthony and C. Koupernik), Wiley: New York.

CHIRIBOGA, D.A. (1979). Marital separation and stress: A life-course perspective. "Alternative Lifestyle", 2(4), 461–470.

CHIRIBOGA, D.A., ROBERTS, J. and STEIN, J.A. (1978). Psychological well-being during marital separation. *J. Divorce, 2*, 21–36.

CIALDINI, R.B., BORDEN, R.J., THORNE, A., WALKER, M.R., FREEMAN, S. and SLOAN, L.R. (1976). Basking in reflected glory: Three (football) field studies. *J. Personal. Soc. Psychol., 34*, 366–375.

CLEVELAND, M. (1979). Divorce in the middle years: The sexual dimension. *J. Divorce, 2*, 255–262.

COHLER, B. (1981). Personal narrative and life course. *In* "Life-span development and behavior", Vol. 4 (Eds. P.B. Baltes and O.G. Brim, Jr.), Academic Press: New York and London.

COLLETT, P. (1977). The rules of conduct. *In* "Social Rules and Social Behavior" (Ed. P. Collett), Rowman and Littlefield: Totowa, New Jersey.

CONDON, W.S. (1975). Multiple response to sound in dysfunctional children. *J. Autism and Childhood Schizophrenia, 5*, 37–56.

COOLEY, C.H. (1902). "Human Nature and the Social Order", Scribner's: New York.

COWEN, E.L., PETERSON, A., BABIGIAN, H., IZZO, L.D. and TROST, M.A. (1973). Long term follow-up of early detected vulnerable children. *J. Consult. Clin. Psychol., 41*, 438–446.

COZBY, P.C. (1973). Self-disclosure: A literature review. *Psychol. Bull., 79*, 73–91.

CRANACH, M. von. (1971). The role of orienting behavior in human interaction. *In* "Behavior and Environment: The Use of Space by Animals and Men" (Ed. A.H. Esser), Plenum Press: New York.

D'AUGELLI, A., DEYSS, C., GUERNEY, B., HERSHENBERG, B. and SBOROFSKY, S. (1974). Interpersonal skill training for dating couples: An evaluation of an educational mental health service. *J. Couns. Psychol.* **21**, 385–389.

DA MATTA, R. (1977). Constraints and license: a preliminary study of two Brazilian national rituals. *In* "Secular Ritual" (Eds. S.F. Moore and B.G. Myerhoff), Van Gorcum, Assen: Amsterdam.

DANISH, S.J., SMYER, M.A. and NOWAK, C.A. (1980). Developmental intervention: Enhancing life event processes. *In* "Life-span Development and Behavior," Vol. 3 (Eds. P.B. Baltes and O.G. Brim, Jr). Academic Press: New York and London.

DARLEY, J. and BERSCHEID, E. (1967). Increased liking as a result of the anticipation of personal contact. *Hum. Rel., 20*, 29–40.

DARLEY, J.M. and COOPER, J. (1972). The "Clean for Gene" phenomenon: The effect of students' appearance on political campaigning. *J. App. Soc. Psychol., 2*, 24–33.

DAVIS, D. (in press). Situational and dispositional determinants of responsiveness in dyadic interaction. *In* "Personality Roles and Social Behavior" (Eds. W. Ickes and E. Knowles), Springer-Verlag: New York.

DAVIS, D. and PERKOWITZ, W.T. (1979). Consequences of responsiveness in dyadic interaction: Effects of probability of response and proportion of content related responses on interpersonal attraction. *J. Personal. Soc. Psychol.*, **37**, 534–550.

DAVIS, J.D. (1976). Self-disclosure in an acquaintance exercise: Responsibility for level of intimacy. *J. Personal. Soc. Psychol.*, **33**, 787–792.

DAVIS, M.S. (1973). "Intimate Relations", Free Press: New York.

DECKERT, P. and LANGELIER, R. (1978). The late divorce phenomenon: The causes and impact of ending a 20-year-old or longer marriage. *J. Divorce*, **1**(4), 381–390.

DENZIN, N.K. (1970). Rules of conduct and the study of deviant behavior: some notes on the social relationship. *In* "Social Relationships" (G.J. McCall, *et al.*), Aldine: Chicago.

DEUTSCH, M. and SOLOMON, L. (1959). Reactions to evaluations by others as influenced by self-evaluations. *Sociometry*, **22**, 93–112.

DION, K.K., BERSCHEID, E. and WALSTER, E. (1972). What is beautiful is good. *J. Personal. Soc. Psychol.*, **24**, 285–290.

DION, K.K. and DION, K.L. (1975). Self-esteem and romantic love. *J. Personal.*, **43**, 39–57.

DION, K.L. and DION, K.K. (1973). Correlates of romantic love. *J. Consult. Clin. Psychol.*, **41**, 51–56.

DOANE, J. (1975). Family interaction and communication deviance in disturbed and normal families. *Fam. Proc.*, **17**, 357–376.

DONOHUE, W.A. (1978). An empirical framework for examining negotiation processes and outcomes. *Communication Monogs.*, **45**, 247–257.

DOUDNA, C. with McBride, F. (1981). "Where are the men for the women at the top?". *In* "Single Life" (Ed. P. Stein), St. Martin's Press: New York.

DRUCKMAN, J.M., FOURNIER, D.M., ROBINSON, B. and OLSON, D.H. (1980). Effectiveness of five types of pre-marital preparation programs. Final report for Education for Marriage, Grand Rapids, Michigan.

DUCK, S.W. (1973). Personality similarity and friendship choice: similarity of what, when? *J. of Personal.*, **41**, 543–558.

DUCK, S.W. (1977). "The Study of Acquaintance", Teakfields: Farnborough.

DUCK, S.W. (1980a). Personal relationships research in the 1980s: Towards an understanding of complex human sociality. *Western J. Speech Communication*, **44**, 114–119.

DUCK, S.W. (1980b). Taking the past to heart: one of the futures of social psychology? *In* "The Development of Social Psychology" (Eds. R. Gilmour and S.W. Duck). Academic Press: London and New York. pp. 211–246.

DUCK, S.W. (1980c). The personal context: Intimate Relationships. *In* "Psychological Problems: The Social Context" (Eds. P. Feldman and J. Orford), Wiley: London, 73–96.

DUCK, S.W. (1981). Toward a research map for the study of relationship breakdown. *In* "Personal Relationships 3: Personal Relationships in Disorder" (Eds S.W. Duck and R. Gilmour), Academic Press. London and New York.

DUCK, S.W. (in prep.) "Personal Relationships 5: Repairing Personal Relationships", Academic Press, London and New York.

DUCK, S.W. and ALLISON, D. (1978). I liked you but I can't live with you: A study of lapsed friendships. *Soc. Behav. and Personal.*, **6**, 43–47.

DUCK, S.W. and GILMOUR, R. (Eds.) (1981a). "Personal Relationships 1: Studying Personal Relationships", Academic Press: London and New York.

DUCK, S.W. and GILMOUR, R. (Eds.) (1981b). "Personal Relationships 2: Developing Personal Relationships", Academic Press: London and New York.

DUCK, S.W. and GILMOUR, R. (Eds.) (1981c). "Personal Relationships 3: Personal Relationships in Disorder", Academic Press: New York and London.

DUCK, S.W. and LEA, M. (1982). Breakdown of relationships as a threat to personal identity. *In* "Threatened Identities" (Ed. G.M. Breakwell), Wiley: London.

DUCK, S.W. and MIELL, D.E. (1981). Charting the development of relationships. Paper presented to one-day International Workshop on Long Term Relationships, Oxford, November, 1981.

DUCK, S.W. and MIELL, D.E. (1982). Toward an understanding of relationship development and breakdown. *In* "The Social Dimension: European Perspectives on Social Psychology" (Ed. H. Tajfel). Cambridge University Press: Cambridge.

DUCK, S.W. and PALMER, J. (in prep.). Patterns of behaviour in dissolving relationships. Unpublished MS, University of Lancaster.

DURKHEIM, E. (1915). "The Elementary Forms of the Religious Life" (translated by J.W. Swain), George Allen and Unwin: London.

DURKHEIM, E. (1951). "Suicide", Free Press: Glencoe, Illinois.

DUTTON, D.G. (1972). Effect of feedback parameters on congruency versus positivity effects in reactions to personal evaluations. *J. Personal. Soc. Psychol.*, **24**, 366–371.

DUVALL, E. (1971). "Family Development", Lippincott: Philadelphia.

EDWARDS, J.N. and SAUNDERS, J.M. (1981). Coming apart: A model of the marital dissolution decision. *J. Marr. Fam.*, **43**, 379–389.

ELDER, G.H., Jr. (1974). "Children of the Great Depression", University of Chicago Press: Chicago.

ELLIS, A. (1948). The Value of Marriage Predictions Tests. *Amer. Soc. Rev.*, **13**, 710–718.

ELLISON, R. (1952). "The Invisible Man", Random House: New York.

EMLER, N. (1981). Gossip and social participation. Paper to Annual Conference of Social Psychology Section, BPS, Oxford, September, 1981.

ERDELYI, M.H. (1974). A new look at the New Look: Perceptual defense and vigilance. *Psychol. Rev.*, **81**, 1–25.

ETZIONI, A. (1961). "A Comparative Analysis of Complex Organizations", The Free Press of Glencoe: New York.

EXLINE, R.V. and WINTERS, L.C. (1965). Affective relations and mutual gaze in dyads. *In* "Affect, Cognition and Personality" (Eds. S. Tomkins and C. Izard), Springer: New York.

FEGER, H. (1981). Analyses of social networks. *In* "Personal Relationships 1: Studying Personal Relationships" (Eds. S.W. Duck and R. Gilmour), Academic Press: London and New York, pp. 91–108.

FERREIRA, A.J. and WINTER, W.D. (1968). Information exchange and silence in normal and abnormal families. *Family Process, 7*, 251–276.

FESTINGER, L. (1957). "A Theory of Cognitive Dissonance", Stanford University Press: Stanford.

FISCHER, C. (Ed.) (1977). "Networks and Places", Free Press: New York.

FISCHHOFF, B. (1976). Attribution theory and judgement under uncertainty. *In* "New Directions in Attribution Research", Vol. 1 (Eds. J.H. Harvey, W.J. Ickes and R.F. Kidd), Lawrence Erlbaum Associates: Hillsdale, New Jersey.

FITZPATRICK, M.A. (1977). A typological approach to communication in relationships. *In* "Communication Yearbook I" (Ed. B. Ruben). Transaction Press: New Jersey.

FITZPATRICK, M.A. and BEST, P.G. (1979). Dyadic adjustment in traditional, independent, and separate relationships: A validation study. *Comm. Monog.,* **46,** 167–178.

FLOYD, F. and MARKMAN, H. (1981). Insiders' and outsiders' assessment of distressed and nondistressed marital interaction. Paper presented to Annual Meeting of the American Association of Behavior Therapy, Toronto, Canada.

FOOT, H.C., CHAPMAN, A.J. and SMITH, J.R. (Eds.) (1980). "Friendship and Social Relations in Children", Wiley: Chichester and New York.

FOURNIER, D. (1979). Validation of PREPARE: A premarital counseling inventory. Unpublished Doctoral Dissertation. University of Minnesota, Minneapolis.

FRANK, J. (1974). "Persuasion and Healing", Schoken: New York.

FREEDMAN, N., O'HANLON, J., OLTMAN, P. and WITKIN, H.A. (1972). The imprint of psychological differentiation on kinetic behavior in varying communicative contexts. *J. Abn. Psychol.,* **79,** 239–258.

FRENCH, J.R.P., Jr. and RAVEN, B. (1960). The basis of social power. *In* "Group Dynamics" 2nd edn (Eds. D. Cartwright and A. Zander), Harper and Row: New York.

FREUD, S. (1900). Die Traumdeutung. Vienna: Deuticke, (The interpretation of dreams). *In* "Selected Works of Sigmund Freud" (Ed. A.A. Brill, 1938), Modern Library: New York.

FROMKIN, H.L. (1972). Feelings of interpersonal undistinctiveness: An unpleasant affective state. *J. Res. In Personal.,* **6,** 178–185.

GARFINKEL, H. (1956). Conditions of successful degradation ceremonies. *Amer. J. Sociol.,* **6,** 420–424.

GIBBINS, K. (1969). Communication aspects of women's clothes and their relation to fashionability. *Brit. J. Soc. Clin. Psychol.,* **8,** 301–312.

GILLIES, J. (1976). "Friends: the Power and Potential of the Company you Keep", Coward, McCann and Geoghegan: New York.

GINSBURG, B. and VOGELSONG, F. (1977). Premarital relationship improvement by maximizing empathy and self-disclosure: The PRIMES Program. *In* "Relationship Enhancement" (Ed. B.G. Guerney, Jr.), Jossey-Bass: San Francisco.

GLASER, B.G. and STRAUSS, A.L. (1971). "Status passages", Chicago: Aldine.

GLASER, B.G. and STRAUSS, A.L. (1975). The ritual drama of mutual pretense *In* "Life as Theater: A Dramaturgical Sourcebook" (Eds. D. Brissett and C. Edgley), Aldine: Chicago.

GLICK, P. (1975). A demographer looks at American families. *J. Marr. Fam.,* **37,** 15–26.

GLICK, P. and NORTON, G. (1979). Marrying, divorcing and living together in the U.S. today. *Pop. Bull.,* **32,** 5.

GLUCKMAN, M. (1963). Gossip and scandal. *Amer. Anthropol.,* **14,** 307–315.

GLUCKMAN, M. (1968). Psychological, sociological and anthropological explanations of witchcraft and gossip: a clarification. *Man* (N.S.), **3,** 20–34.

GOFFMAN, E. (1955). On face-work: an analysis of ritual elements in social interactions. *Psychiatry,* **18,** 213–231.

GOFFMAN, E. (1959). "The Presentation of Self in Everyday Life", Doubleday: New York.

GOFFMAN, E. (1961). "Encounters", Bobbs-Merrill: Indianopolis.

GOFFMAN, E. (1967). "Interaction Ritual", Doubleday Anchor: New York.

GOLDFRIED, M.R. and D'ZURILLA, T.J. (1969). A behavioral analytic model for assessing competence. *In* "Current Topics in Clinical and Community Psychology" (Ed. C.D. Speilberger), Academic Press: New York and London.

GOLDMAN, W. and LEWIS, P. (1977). Beautiful is good: Evidence that the physically attractive are more socially skillful. *J. Exper. Soc. Psychol.,* **13** 125–130.

GOODE, W.J. (1956). "After Divorce", Glencoe: Free Press.

GOODRICH, D. (1961). Possibilities for preventive intervention during initial personality formation. *In* "Prevention of Mental Disorders in Children" (Ed. G. Caplan), Basic Books: New York.

GOTTMAN, J. (1979). "Empirical Investigations of Marriage", Academic Press: New York and London.

GOTTMAN *et al.* (1976a) *i.e.* GOTTMAN, J., NOTARIUS, C., MARKMAN, H., BANK, D., YOPPI, B. and RUBIN, M. (1976a). Behavior Exchange Theory and Marital Decision Making. *J. Personal. Soc. Psychol.* **34,** 14–23.

GOTTMAN *et al.* (1976b) *i.e.* GOTTMAN, J., NOTARIUS, C., GONSO, J. and MARKMAN, H.J. (1976b). "A Couple's Guide to Communication", Research Press: Champaign, Illinois.

GOTTMAN, J.M. and MARKMAN, H.J. (1978). Experimental designs in psychotherapy research. *In* "Handbook of Psychotherapy and Behavior Change" (Eds. S. Garfield and A. Bergin), Wiley: New York.

GOTTMAN, J., MARKMAN, H. and NOTARIUS, C. (1977). The topography of marital conflict: A sequential analysis of verbal and nonverbal behavior. *J. Marr. Fam.* **39,** 461–478.

GRAZIANO *et al.* (1980a) *i.e.* GRAZIANO, W.G., BRODY, G.H. and BERNSTEIN, S. (1980a). Effects of information about future interaction and peer's motivation on peer reward allocations. *Devel. Psychol.,* **16,** 475–482.

GRAZIANO *et al.* (1980b) *i.e.* GRAZIANO, W.G., BROTHEN, T. and BERSCHEID, E. (1980b). Attention, attraction and individual differences in reaction to criticism. *J. Personal. Soc. Psychol.,* **38,** 193–202.

GREENWALD, A.G. (1980). The totalitarian ego: Fabrication and revision of personal history. *Amer. Psychol.,* **35,** 603–618.

GRIFFITT, W., NELSON, J. and LITTLEPAGE, G. (1972). Old age and response to agreement-disagreement. *J. Gerontol.,* **27,** 269–274.

GUERNEY, B. (1977). "Relationship Enhancement", Jossey-Bass: San Francisco.

GURIN, G., VEROFF, J. and FELD, S. (1960). "Americans View Their Mental Health: A Nationwide Survey", Basic Books: New York.

GURMAN, A.S. and KNISKERN, D.P. (1977). Enriching research on marital enrichment programs. *J. Marr. Fam. Couns.,* **3,** 3–11.

GURMAN, A.S. and KNISKERN, D.P. (1978a). Research on marital and family therapy: Progress, perspective, and prospect. *In* "Handbook of Psychotherapy and Behavior Change" (Eds. S.L. Garfield and A.E. Bergin), Wiley: New York.

GURMAN, A.S. and KNISKERN, D.P. (1978b). Deterioration in marital and family therapy: empirical clinical and conceptual issues. *Fam. Proc.,* **17,** 3–20.

HALL, E.T. (1966). "The Hidden Dimension". Doubleday Anchor: New York.

HANNERZ, U. (1967). Gossip, networks and culture in a black American Ghetto. *Ethnos*, **32**, 35–60.

HARPER, R.A. (1952). A pre-marital case: with two years of marital follow-up. *Marr. Fam. Liv.*, **14**, 133–142.

HARPER, R.G., WIENS, A.N. and MATARAZZO, J.D. (1978). "Nonverbal Communication: The State of the Art", Wiley: New York.

HARRÉ, R. (1977a). Friendship as an accomplishment: an ethogenic approach to social relationships. *In* "Theory and Practice in Interpersonal Attraction" (Ed. S.W. Duck), Academic Press: London and New York.

HARRÉ, R. (1977b). Rules in the explanation of social behavior. *In* "Social Rules and Social Behavior" (Ed. P. Collett), Rowman and Littlefield: Totowa, New Jersey.

HARRÉ, R. (1979). "Social Being: a Theory for Social Psychology", Basil Blackwell: Oxford.

HARRÉ, R. (1981). Expressive aspects of description of others. *In* "The Psychology of Ordinary Explanations of Social Behavior" (Ed. C. Antaki), Academic Press: London and New York.

HARRÉ, R. and SECORD, P.F. (1972). "The Explanation of Social Behavior", Blackwell: Oxford.

HARRISON, A.A. (1977). Mere exposure. *In* "Advances in Experimental Social Psychology", Vol. 10 (Ed. L. Berkowitz), Academic Press: New York and London.

HARVEY, J.H., WELLS, G.L. and ALVAREZ, M.D. (1978). Attribution in the context of conflict and separation in close relationships. *In* "New Directions in Attribution Research", Vol. 2 (Eds. J.H. Harvey, W. Ickes, and R.F. Kidd), Lawrence Erlbaum Associates: Hillsdale, New Jersey.

HARVEY, J.H., TOWN, J.P. and YARKIN, K.L. (1981). How fundamental is "the fundamental attribution error"? *J. Personal. Soc. Psychol.*, **40**, 346–349.

HATFIELD, E. and TRAUPMANN, J. (1981). Intimate relationships: A perspective from Equity Theory. *In* "Personal Relationships 1: Studying Personal Relationships" (Eds. S.W. Duck and R. Gilmour), Academic Press: London and New York, pp. 165–178.

HAYNES, S. (1978). Marital effectiveness training: A program for the primary prevention of marital disatisfaction. Unpublished paper, University of Southern Illinois, Carbondale, Illinois.

HEBB, D.O. (1949). "The Organization of Behavior", Wiley: New York.

HEBER, R. and GARBER, H. (1975). Report No. 2: an experiment in the prevention of cultural-familial retardation. *In* "Proceedings of Third Conference of the International Association for the Scientific Study of Mental Deficiency" (Ed. D. Primrose), Polish Medical Publishers: Warsaw.

HEIDER, F. (1958). "The Psychology of Interpersonal Relations", Wiley: New York.

HEIDER, F. (1976). A conversation with Fritz Heider. *In* "New Directions in Attribution Research", Vol. 1 (Eds. J.H. Harvey, W.J. Ickes and R.F. Kidd), Lawrence Erlbaum Associates: Hillsdale, New Jersey.

HELLER, K. (1979). The effects of social support: prevention and treatment implications. *In* "Maximizing Treatment Gains: Transfer Enhancement in Psychotherapy" (Eds. A. Goldstein and F. Kanfer), Academic Press: New York and London.

HELLER, K. and MONAHAN, J. (1977). "Psychology and Community Change", Dorsey Press: Homewood, Illinois.

HELMINGER, T. (1977). "After You've Said Goodbye: How to Recover after Ending a Relationship", Schenckman: Cambridge.

HENDRICK, C. and BROWN, S.R. (1971). Introversion, Extraversion, and interpersonal attraction. *J. Personal. Soc. Psychol., 17,* 250–258.

HETHERINGTON, E.M., COX, M. and COX, R. (1978). The aftermath of divorce. *In* "Mother-child, Father-child Relations" (Eds. J.H. Stevens, Jr. and M. Mathew), National Association for the Education of Young Children: Washington, D.C.

HEWITT, J. (1976). "Self and Society: A Symbolic Interactionist Social Psychology", Allyn and Bacon: Boston.

HILL, C.T., RUBIN, Z. and PEPLAU, L.A. (1976). Breakups before marriage: The end of 103 affairs. *J. Social Issues, 32,* 147–168.

HILL, C.T., RUBIN, Z. and PEPLAU, L.A. (1979). Breakups before marriage: the end of 103 affairs. *In* "Divorce and Separation" (Eds. G. Levinger and O.C. Moles), Basic Books: New York.

HINDE, R.A. (1979). "Towards Understanding Relationships", Academic Press: London and New York.

HINDE, R.A. (1981). The bases of a science of interpersonal relationships. *In* "Personal Relationships 1: Studying Personal Relationships" (Eds. S.W. Duck and R. Gilmour) Academic Press: London and New York.

HOMANS, G.C. (1974). "Social Behavior: Its Elementary Forms" (revised edn), Harcourt Brace Jovanovich: New York.

HUESMANN, L.R. and LEVINGER, G. (1976). Incremental exchange theory: a formal model for progression in dyadic social interaction. *In* "Advances in Experimental Social Psychology", Vol. 9 (Eds. L. Berkowitz and E.H. Walster), Academic Press: New York and London.

HUGHES, E. (1971). "The Sociological Eye", Vol. 1, Aldine-Atherton: Chicago.

HULTSCH, D. and PLEMONS, J. (1979). Life events and life-span development. *In* "Life-span Development and Behavior (Vol. 2)" (Eds. P.B. Baltes and O.G. Brim), Academic Press: New York and London.

HUNT, M. (1973). "The Affair", New American Library: New York.

HUNT, M. and HUNT, B. (1977). "The Divorce Experience", McGraw-Hill: New York.

HUNTER, J.E. and BOSTER, F.J. (1978). Situational differences in the selection of compliance-gaining messages. Unpublished paper, Dept. of Communication, Arizona State University, 1978.

HUSTON, T.L. (1973). Ambiguity of acceptance, social desirability, and dating choice. *J. Exper. Soc. Psychol., 9,* 32–42.

HUSTON, T.L. (1974). A perspective on interpersonal attraction. *In* "Foundations of Interpersonal Attraction" (Ed. T.L. Huston), Academic Press: New York and London.

HUSTON, T.L., SURRA, C., FITZGERALD, N. and CATE, R. (1981). From courtship to marriage: Mate selection as an interpersonal process. *In* "Personal Relationships 2: Developing Personal Relationships" (Eds. S.W. Duck and R. Gilmour), Academic Press: New York and London.

ISEN, A.M. and HASTORF, A.H. (in press). "Cognitive Social Psychology", Elsevier: New York.

JACOBS, L., BERSCHEID, E. and WALSTER, E. (1971). Self-esteem and attraction. *J. Personal. Soc. Psychol.*, **17**, 84–91.

JACOBSON, N.S. (1977). Problem-solving and contingency contracting in the treatment of marital disorder. *J. Consult. Clin. Psychol.* **45**, 52–60.

JACOBSON, N.S. and MARGOLIN, G. (1979). "Marital Therapy: Strategies Based on Social Learning and Behavior Exchange Principles", Brunner/Mazel: New York.

JAMES, W. (1890). "Psychology: The Briefer Course", Holt: New York.

JECKER, J. and LANDY, D. (1969). Liking a person as a function of doing him a favor. *Hum. Relat.*, **22**, 371–378.

JOHNSON, M. (1969). Courtship and commitment: A study of cohabitation on a university campus. Unpublished master's thesis, University of Iowa.

JOHNSON, M. (1973). Commitment: A conceptual structure and empirical application. *Sociol. Quart.* **4**, 359–406.

JOHNSON, M. (1978). Personal and structural commitment: Sources of consistency in the development of relationships. Paper presented at National Council of Family Relations, Philadelphia.

JOHNSON, M. and EWENS, W.L. (1971). Power, personalism and affective style as determinants of impression formation in a game situation. *J. Exper. Soc. Psychol.* **7**, 98–110.

JOHNSON, M. and LESLIE, L. (in press). Couple involvement and network size: A test of the dyadic withdrawal hypothesis. *Soc. Psychol. Quart.*

JONES, E.E. (1964). "Ingratiation: A Social Psychological Analysis", Appleton-Century-Crofts: New York.

JONES, E.E. and DAVIS, K. (1965). From acts to dispositions: The attribution process in person perception. *In* "Advances in Experimental Social Psychology" (Ed. L. Berkowitz), Academic Press: New York and London.

JONES, E.E. and NISBETT, R.E. (1971). "The Actor and the Observer: Divergent Perceptions of the Causes of Behavior", General Learning Press: Morristown, New Jersey.

KAPLAN, R.E. (1976). Maintaining interpersonal relationships: a bipolar theory. *Interpers. Devel.*, **6**, 106–119.

KEISER, G.J. and ALTMAN, I. (1976). Relationship of nonverbal behavior to the social penetration process. *Human Comm. Res.*, **2**, 147–161.

KELLEY, H.H. (1967). Attribution theory in social psychology. *In* "Nebraska Symposium on Motivation", Vol. 15 (ed. D. Levine), University of Nebraska Press: Lincoln.

KELLEY, H.H. (1972). Attribution in social interaction. *In* "Attribution: Perceiving the Causes of Behavior" (Eds. H. Kelley, R. Nisbett, S. Valins and B. Weiner), General Learning Press: Morristown, New Jersey.

KELLEY, H.H. (1979). "Personal Relationships, Their Structures and Processes", Lawrence Erlbaum Associates: Hillsdale, New Jersey.

KELLEY, H.H. and THIBAUT, J.W. (1978). "Interpersonal Relations: A Theory of Interdependence", Wiley: New York.

KELLY, G.A. (1955). "The Psychology of Personal Constructs", Norton, New York.

KELMAN, H.C. (1961). Processes of opinion change. *Public Opinion Quart.* **25**, 57–78.

KENDON, A. (1967). Some functions of gaze direction in social interaction. *Acta Psychologica*, **26**, 22–63.

KENDON, A. (1970). Movement coordination in social interaction: Some examples described. *Acta Psychologica*, **32**, 100–125.

KERCKHOFF, A.C. (1964). Patterns of homogamy and the field of eligibles. *Social*

Forces, **42,** 289–297.

KERCKHOFF, A.C. (1978). Patterns of marriage and family formation and dissolution. *In* "Selected Aspects of Consumer Behavior", U.S. Government Printing Office: Washington, D.C.

KERCKHOFF, A.C. and DAVIS, K.E. (1962). Value consensus and need complementarity in mate selection. *Amer. Soc. Rev.,* **27,** 295–303.

KIESLER, D. (1971). Experimental designs in psychotherapy research. *In* "Handbook of Psychotherapy and Behavior Change" (Eds. A. Bergin and S. Garfield), Wiley: New York.

KLEIN, N.C., ALEXANDER, J.F. and PARSONS, B.V. (1977). Impact of family systems intervention on recidivism and sibling delinquency: A model of primary prevention and program evaluation. *J. Consult. Clin. Psychol.* **45,** 469–474.

KNAPP, M.L. (1978). "Social Intercourse: From Greeting to Goodbye", Allyn and Bacon: Boston.

KNAPP, M.L., HART, R.P., FRIEDRICH, G.W. and SHULMAN, G.M. (1973). The rhetoric of goodbye: Verbal and nonverbal correlates of human leave-taking. *Speech Monographs,* **40,** 182–198.

KNAPP, M.L., ELLIS, D.G. and WILLIAMS, B.A. (1980). Perceptions of communication behavior associated with relationship terms. *Communications Monographs,* **47,** 262–278.

KRAIN, M. (1975). Communication among premarital couples at three stages of dating. *J. Marr. Fam.* **37,** 609–618.

KRANTZLER, M. (1973). "Creative Divorce: A New Opportunity for Personal Growth", Evans: New York.

KRAUS, S. (1979). The crisis of divorce: Growth promoting or pathogenic. *J. Divorce,* **3,** 107–119.

KUHN, M.H. (1964). The reference group reconsidered. *Sociol. Quart.,* **5,** 5–21.

LA GAIPA, J.J. (1977a). Testing a multidimensional approach to friendship. *In* "Theory and Practice in Interpersonal Attraction" (Ed. S.W. Duck). Academic Press: London and New York.

LA GAIPA, J.J. (1977b). Interpersonal attraction and social exchange. *In* "Theory and Practice in Interpersonal Attraction" (Ed. S.W. Duck). Academic Press: London and New York.

LA GAIPA, J.J. (1979). A developmental study of the meaning of friendship in adolescence. *J. Adol.,* **2,** 201–213.

LA GAIPA, J.J. (1980). Life stages and the termination of friendship. Paper presented at symposium "The development and termination of friendship" at the meeting of the Southeastern Psychological Association, Washington, March, 1980.

LA GAIPA, J.J. (1981a). A systems approach to personal relationships. *In* "Personal Relationship 1: Studying Personal Relationships" (Eds. S.W. Duck and R. Gilmour), Academic Press: London and New York.

LA GAIPA, J.J. (1981b). Children's friendships. *In* "Personal Relationships 2: Developing Personal Relationships" (Eds. S.W. Duck and R. Gilmour), Academic Press: London and New York.

LA GAIPA, J.J. (1981c). The meaning of friendship in old age. Paper presented at symposium "Friendship over the life cycle" at the meeting of the Canadian Psychological Association, Toronto, June 1981.

LA GAIPA, J.J. and WOOD, D.H. (1981). Friendship in disturbed adolescents. *In* "Personal Relationships 3: Personal Relationships in Disorder" (Eds. S.W. Duck and R. Gilmour), Academic Press: London and New York.

LANE, C. (1979). Ritual and ceremony in contemporary Soviet society. *Sociol. Rev.*, **27**, 253–278.

LANER, M.R. (1978). Love's Labors Lost: A theory of marital dissolution. *J. Divorce*, **1**, 213–232.

LEMASTERS, E. (1957). Parenthood as a crisis. *Marr. Fam. Liv.*, **19**, 352–355.

LERNER, M. and SIMMONS, C. (1966). Observer's reaction to the innocent victim: Compassion or rejection? *J. Personal. Soc. Psychol.*, **4**, 203–210.

LERNER, R. and SPANIER, G. (Eds.) (1978). "Child Influences on Marital and Family Interaction", Academic Press: New York and London.

LEVINGER, G. (1965). Marital cohesiveness and dissolution: an integrative review. *J. Marr. Fam.*, **27**, 19–28.

LEVINGER, G. (1976). A social psychological perspective on marital dissolution. *J. Soc. Issues*, **32**, 21–47.

LEVINGER, G. (1977). The embrace of lives: Changing and unchanging. *In* "Close Relationships" (G. Levinger and H.L. Raush, Eds.), University of Massachusetts Press: Amherst, Massachusetts.

LEVINGER, G. (1979). A social exchange view on the dissolution of pair relationships. *In* "Social Exchange in Developing Relationships" (Eds. R.L. Burgess and T.L. Huston), Academic Press: New York and London.

LEVINGER, G. and MOLES, O. (Eds.) (1979). "Divorce and Separation", Basic Books: New York.

LEVINGER, G., SENN, D.J. and JORGENSON, B.W. (1970). Progress toward permanence in courtship: a test of the Kerckhoff-Davis hypothesis. *Sociometry*, **33**, 427–443.

LEVINGER, G. and SNOEK, J. (1972). "Attraction in Relationships: A New Look at Interpersonal Attraction", General Learning Press: Morristown, New Jersey.

LEVINSON, D., DARROW, C., KLEIN, E., LEVINSON, M. and McKEE, B. (1978). "The Seasons of a Man's Life", Knopf: New York.

LEWIS, R.A. (1972). A development framework for the analysis premarital dyad formation. *Fam. Proc.*, **11**, 17–48.

LEWIS, R.A. (1973). A longitudinal test of a developmental framework for premarital dyadic formation. *J. Marr. Fam.*, **35**, 16–25.

LEWIS, R. and SPANIER, G. (1979). Theorizing about the quality and stability of marriage. *In* "Contemporary Theories about the Family, Vol. 1" (Eds. W. Burr, et al.), Free Press: New York.

LOPATA, H.Z. (1979). "Women as Widows", Elsevier: New York.

LOPICCOLO, J. and MILLER, V. (1975). A program for enhancing the sexual relationship of normal couples. *J. Couns. Psychol.*, **5**, 41–45.

LOTT, A.J. and LOTT, B.E. (1974). The role of reward in the formation of positive interpersonal attitudes. *In* "Foundations of Interpersonal Attraction" (Ed. T.L. Huston), Academic Press: New York and London.

LUKES, S. (1975). Political ritual and social integration. *Sociology*, **9**, 289–308.

MACE, D.R. (1972). "Getting Ready for Marriage", Abingdon: Nashville, Tennessee.

MACE, D.R. (1979). Marriage and family enrichment: A new field? *Fam. Coord.*, **28**, 3, 409–419.

MADSEN, K.B. (1968). "Theories of Motivation", Kent State University Press: Kent, Ohio.

MAHL, G.F. (1959). Measuring the patient's anxiety during interviews from "expressive" aspects of his speech. *Transact. New York Acad. Sci.*, **21**, 249–257.

MARGOLIN, G. and WEISS, R.L. (1978). Comparative evaluation of theraputic components associated with behavioral marital treatments. *J. Consult. Clin. Psychol.* **46**, 1476–1486.

MARKMAN, H. (1977). A behavior exchange model applied to the longitudinal study of couples planning marriage. Unpublished Doctoral Dissertation, Indiana University, Indiana.

MARKMAN, H. (1979). The application of a behavioral model of marriage in predicting relationship satisfaction of couples planning marriage. *J. Consult. Clin. Psychol.*, **4**, 743–749.

MARKMAN, H. (1981). The prediction of marital distress: a five year follow-up. *J. Consult. Clin. Psychol.*, **49**, 760–762.

MARKMAN, H. (in press). Toward the prevention of marital discord: Issues in program development and delivery. *In* "Marital Interaction: Analysis of Modification" (Eds. N. Jacobson and K. Halweg), Gullfred Press: New York.

MARKMAN *et al.* (1981a) *i.e.* MARKMAN, H., NOTARIUS, C., STEPHEN, T. and SMITH, R. (1981a). Behavioral observation systems for couples. The current status. *In* "Observing Marriage: New Behavioral Approaches" (Eds. E. Elsinger and R. Lewis), Sage Publications: Beverly Hills, California.

MARKMAN *et al.* (1981b) *i.e.* MARKMAN, H., FLOYD, F., STEPHEN, T. and STANLEY, S. (1981b). Pre-marital Preventative Intervention: Conceptual and Research Issues. Paper presented at Annual Meeting of A.P.A. Los Angeles, California, August, 1981.

MARKMAN, H.J. and FLOYD, F. (1980). Possibilities for the prevention of marital distress: a behavioral perspective. *Amer. J. Fam. Ther.* **8**, 29–48.

MARKMAN, H.J., FLOYD, F. and JAMIESON, F. (in prep.). The short-term effects of a cognitive-behavioral primary prevention program for couples planning marriage.

MARKMAN, H.J. and FURMAN, W. (1981). An integration model of communication skills assessment: Illustrations from research with couples and children. Paper presented to 13th Banff International Conference and Behavioral Science: Essentials of behavioral treatment for families. Banff, Canada.

MARKMAN, H.J., JAMIESON, K. and FLOYD, F. (in press). The assessment and modification of premarital relationships: Preliminary findings on the etiology and prevention of marital and family distress. *In* "Advances in Family Interventions, Assessment and Theory Vol. 3" (Ed. J. Vincent), JAI Press: Greenwich, Connecticut.

MARKS, S.R. (1977). Multiple roles and role strain: some notes on human energy, time and commitment. *Amer. Sociol. Rev.*, **42**, 921–936.

MARTIN, D. (1976). "Battered Wives", Glide: San Francisco.

MARWELL, G. and SCHMITT, D.R. (1967). Dimensions of compliance-gaining behavior: An empirical analysis. *Sociometry*, **30**, 350–364.

MASLOW, A. (1970). "Motivation and Personality" (2nd edn), Harper and Row: New York.

MASTERS, W. and JOHNSON, V. (1970). "Human Sexual Inadequacy", Little-Brown: Boston.

MATARAZZO, J.D., WIENS, A.N., SASLOW, G., DUNHAM, R.M. and VOAS, R.B. (1964). Speech duration of astronauts and ground communicators. *Science*, **143**, 148–150.

McALLISTER-JONES, L. and FISCHER, C. (1978). Measuring egocentric networks by mass survey. Working paper, Institute of Urban and Regional Development, University of California, Berkeley.

McCALL, G.J. (1970). The social organization of relationships *In* "Social Relationships" (Ed. G.J. McCall, *et al.*), Aldine: Chicago.

McCALL, G.J. and SIMMONS, J.L. (1978). "Identities and Interactions" (revised edn), Free Press: New York.

McCROSKEY, J.C. (1970). Measures of communication-bound anxiety. *Speech Monographs*, **37**, 269–277.

McDOWALL, J.J. (1978). Interactional synchrony: A reappraisal. *J. Personal. Soc. Psychol.*, **36**, 963–975.

McKEE, J.P. and SHERIFFS, A.C. (1957). The differential evaluation of males and females. *J. Personal.*, **25**, 256–271.

MEAD, G.H. (1934). "Mind, Self and Society", University of Chicago Press: Chicago.

MEADOWS, M.E. and TAPLIN, J.F. (1970). Premarital counseling with college students: a promising triad. *J. Couns. Psychol.* **17**, 516–518.

MEHRABIAN, A. (1971a). "Silent Messages", Wadsworth: Belmont, California.

MEHRABIAN, A. (1971b). Verbal and nonverbal interaction of strangers in a waiting situation. *J. Exper. Res. In Personal.*, **5**, 127–138.

MEHRABIAN, A. (1972). "Nonverbal Communication", Aldine-Atherton: Chicago.

MEHRABIAN, A. and KSIONZKY, S. (1972). Categories of social behavior. *Comparative Group Studies*, **3**, 425–436.

MEHRABIAN, A. and KSIONZKY, S. (1974). "A Theory of Affiliation", Lexington Books: Lexington, Massachusetts.

METTEE, D. and ARONSON, E. (1974). Affective reactions to appraisal from others. *In* "Foundations of Interpersonal Attraction" (Ed. T.L. Huston). Academic Press: New York and London.

MICROYS, G. and BADER, E. (1977). Do pre-marriage programs really help? Unpublished Manuscript, Department of Family Community Medicine, University of Toronto, Canada.

MILARDO, R. (1980). A longitudinal study of social activity among dating partners and their social networks. Paper presented at National Council of Family Relations, Portland.

MILARDO, R. (1982). The social context of developing relationships. Unpublished Ph.D. dissertation, Pennsylvania State University.

MILGRAM, S. (1970). The experience of living in cities. *Science*, **167**, 1461–1468.

MILLAR, E. (1973). A transactional analysis of marital communication patterns: an exploratory study. Unpublished doctoral dissertation, Department of Communication, Michigan State University.

MILLER, G., BOSTER, F., ROLOFF, M. and SEIBOLD, D. (1977). Compliance-gaining message strategies: A typology and some findings concerning effects of situational differences. *Communic. Monogs.*, **44**, 37–50.

MILLER, G.R. and STEINBERG, M. (1975). "Between People: A New Analysis of Interpersonal Communication", Science Research Association, Chicago.

MILLER, S., NUNNALLY, E. and WACKMAN, D. (1975). "Alive and Aware", Interpersonal Communications Program: Minneapolis, Minnesota.

MILLER, S., NUNNALLY, E. and WACKMAN, D. (1976). A communication training program for couples. *Social Casework.* **57**, 9–18.

MILLER, S., NUNNALLY, E. and WACKMAN, D. (1979). "Couples

Communication I: Talking Together", Interpersonal Communication Program: Minneapolis, Minnesota.

MILLER, S.L. (1971). The effects of communication training in small groups upon self-disclosure and openness in engaged couples' systems of interaction: a field experiment. Unpublished doctoral dissertation, University of Minnesota.

MITA, T.H., DERMER, M. and KNIGHT, J. (1977). Reversed facial images and the mere-exposure hypothesis. *J. Personal. Soc. Psychol.*, **35**, 597–601.

MITCHELL, J. (1974). Social networks. *Ann. Rev. Anthropol*, **3**, 279–299.

MOSCOVICI, S. (1972). Society and theory in social psychology. *In* "The Context of Social Psychology" (Eds. J. Israel and H. Tajfel), Academic Press: London and New York.

MOWRER, O.H. (1938). Preparatory set (Expectancy): A determinant in motivation and Learning. *Psychol. Rev.*, **45**, 62–91.

MURRAY, D.C. (1971). Talk, silence and anxiety. *Psychol. Bull.*, **75**, 244–260.

MURSTEIN, B. (1970). Stimulus-value-role: A theory of marital choice. *J. Marr. Fam.*, **32**, 465–481.

MURSTEIN, B. (1971). Critique of models of dyadic attraction. *In* "Theories of Attraction and Love (Ed. B. Murstein), Springer: New York.

MURSTEIN, B.I. (1977). The Stimulus-Value-Role (SVR) Theory of dyadic relationships. *In* "Theory and Practice in Interpersonal Attraction" (Ed. S.W. Duck), Academic Press: London and New York.

MURSTEIN, B.I. and BECK, G.D. (1972). Person perception, marriage adjustment, and social desirability. *J. Consult. Clin. Psychol.* **39**, 396–403.

MUSSEN, P.H. and BARKER, R.G. (1944). Attitudes towards cripples. *J. Abn. Soc. Psychol.*, **39**, 351–355.

NATALE, M. (1975). Convergence of mean vocal intensity in dyadic communication as a function of social desirability. *J. Personal. Soc. Psychol.*, **32**, 790–804.

NATIONAL CENTER FOR HEALTH STATISTICS (1979). "Vital Statistics of the United States for 1975: Volume 3: Marriage and Divorce", U.S. Government Printing Office: Washington, D.C.

NATIONAL CENTER FOR HEALTH STATISTICS (1980). "Annual Summary for the United States for 1979: Births, Deaths, Marriages and Divorces", *Monthly Vital Statistics Report,* **18**(13), November.

NEISSER, U. (1967). "Cognitive Psychology", Appleton-Century-Crofts: New York.

NEUGARTEN, B. (1967). Continuities and discontinuities of psychological issues into adult life. *Hum. Devel.,* **12**, 121–130.

NEUGARTEN, B.L. (1968). The awareness of middle age. *In* "Middle Age and Aging" (Ed. B.L. Neugarten), University of Chicago Press: Chicago.

NEUGARTEN, B.L. (1979). Time, age and the life cycle. *Amer. J. Psychiat.*, **136**, 887–894.

NEUGARTEN, B.L. and HAGESTAD, G.O. (1976). Age and the life course. *In* "Handbook of Aging and the Social Sciences" (Eds. R. Binstock and E. Shanas), New York: Van Nostrand Reinhold Company, (pp. 35–55).

NEUGARTEN, B.L., MOORE, J.W. and LOWE, J.C. (1965). Age norms, age constraints, and adult socialization. *Amer. J. Sociol.,* **70**, 710–717.

NEUGARTEN, B.L. and PETERSON, W.A. (1957). A study of the American age grading system. *Proceedings of the Fourth Congress of the International Association of Gerontology,* **3**, 497–502.

NEWCOMB, M. and BENTLER, P. (1981). Marital breakdown. *In* "Personal Relationships 3: Personal Relationships in Disorder" (Eds. S.W. Duck and R. Gilmour), Academic Press: New York and London.

NEWCOMB, T.M. (1961). "The Acquaintance Process". Holt Rinehart and Winston: New York.

NEWMAN, H. (1981). Communication within ongoing intimate relationships: An attributional perspective. *Personal. Soc. Psychol. Bull.,* **7,** 59–70.

NOCK, S. (1981). Family life-cycle transitions: Longitudinal effects on family members. *J. Marr. Fam.,* **43,** 703–714.

NORTON, A. and GLICK, P. (1979). Marital instability in America: Past, present and future. *In* "Divorce and Separation" (Eds. G. Levinger and O.C. Moles), Basic Books: New York.

NORTON, R.W. and MILLER, L. (1975). Dyadic perceptions of communication style. *Comm. Res.,* **2,** 50–67.

NOVAK, D.W. and LERNER, M.J. (1968). Rejection as a consequence of perceived similarity. *J. Personal. Soc. Psychol.,* **9,** 147–152.

NUNNALLY, E.W. (1971). Effects of communication training upon interaction awareness and empathic accuracy of engaged couples: a field experiment. Unpublished doctoral dissertation, University of Minnesota.

O'DAY, R. (1974). Intimidation rituals: reactions to reform. *J. App. Behav. Sci.,* **10,** 373–386.

OLSON, D. (1978). Insiders' and outsiders' views of relationships: research strategies. *In* "Close Relationships" (Eds. G. Levinger and H.L. Raush), University of Massachusetts Press: Amherst, Massachusetts.

OLSON, D.H., FOURNIER, D. and DRUCKMAN, J. (1977). Premarital, personal and relationship evaluation (PREPARE), Unpublished Research Instrument, University of Minnesota.

OLSON, D.H., RUSSELL, C. and SPRENKLE, J. (1980). Marriage and family therapy: a decade review. *J. Marr. Fam.,* **42,** 973–994.

ORVIS, B.R., KELLEY, H.H. and BUTLER, D. (1976). Attributional conflict in young couples. *In* "New Directions in Attribution Research: 1" (Eds. J.H. Harvey, W. Ickes, and R.F. Kidd), Lawrence Erlbaum Associates: Hillsdale, New Jersey.

OTTO, H.A. (1975). Marriage and family enrichment programs in North America— Report and analysis. *Fam. Coord.,* **24,** 137–142.

OTTO, H.A. (ed.) (1976). "Marriage and Family Enrichment, New Perspectives and Programs", Parthenon Press: Nashville, Tennessee.

PARKER, R.S. (1978). "Living Single Successfully", Franklin Watts: New York.

PARKES, C.M. (1972). "Bereavement: Studies of Grief in Adult Life", International Universities Press: New York.

PARKS, M.R. (in press). Ideology in interpersonal communication: Off the couch and into the world. *In* "Communication Yearbook 5" (Ed. M. Burgoon), Transaction Books, New Brunswick, New York.

PARSONS, B. and ALEXANDER, J. (1973). Short-term family intervention: a therapy outcome study. *J. Consult. Clin. Psychol.,* **41,** 195–201.

PARSONS, T. (1951). "The Social System", Free Press: Glencoe, Illinois.

PARSONS, T. (1963). On the concept of influence. *Public Op. Quart.,* **27,** 37–62.

PEARLIN, L.I. and JOHNSON, J.S. (1977). Marital status, life strains, and depression. *Amer. Sociol. Rev.,* **42,** 704–715.

PERRIN, F.A.C. (1921). Physical attractiveness and repulsiveness. *J. Exp.*

Psychol., 4, 203–217.

PHILLIPS, D. with Judd, R. (1978). "How to Fall out of Love", Fawcett: New York.

PINEO, P. (1961). Disenchantment in the later years of marriage. *Marr. Fam. Liv., 23,* 3–11.

PLEBAN, R. and TESSER, A. (1980). The effects of relevance and quality of another's performance on interpersonal closeness. Unpublished manuscript, University of Georgia.

PREMO, B.E. (1979). Verbal response mode use in married couples versus stranger dyads: Acquaintance and familiarity. *Disser. Abstrs. Internat., 40*(1-B), 498.

PRICE, R. and CHERNISS, C. (1977). Training for a new profession: research as social action. *Prof. Psychol., 8,* 222–231.

PRICE-BONHAM, S. and BALSWICK, J.O. (1980). The noninstitutions: Divorce, desertion, and remarriage. *J. Marr. Fam., 42,* 959–972.

PURRINGTON, B. (1980a). Effects of children on their parents: Parents' perceptions. Unpublished Ph.D. dissertation, Michigan State University.

PURRINGTON, B. (1980b). Reciprocal processes of parent–child influence, Paper presented at National Council of Family Relations, Portland.

RANDS, M. (1980). Social networks before and after marital separation: A study of recently divorced persons. Unpublished Ph.D. dissertation, University of Massachusetts.

RAPOPORT, R. and RAPOPORT, R. (1975). "Leisure and the Life Cycle", Routledge and Kegan Paul: London.

RAPOPORT, R. and RAPOPORT, R.N. (1964). New light on the honeymoon. *Hum. Rels., 17,* 33–56.

RAPAPORT, R.A. (1971). Ritual, sanctity, and cybernetics. *Amer. Anthropol.* **73,** 59–76.

RAPOPORT, R.N. and RAPOPORT, R.V. (1965). Work and family in contemporary society. *Amer. Socio. Rev., 30,* 381–394.

RAPPAPORT, A.F., (1976). Conjugal relationship enhancement program. *In* "Treating Relationships" (Ed. D.H. Olson), Graphic Publishing Company: Lake Mills, Iowa.

RASCHKE, H.J. (1977). The role of social participation in postseparation and postdivorce adjustment. *J. Divorce,* **1,** 129–139.

RAUSH, H.L., BARRY, W.A., HERTEL, R.K. and SWAIN, M.A. (1974). "Communication, Conflict and Marriage". Jossey-Bass: San Francisco.

REESE, H.W. and SMYER, M.A. (1981). The dimensionalization of life events. *In* "Life-span Developmental Psychology: Non-normative Life Events." (Eds. E.J. Callaghan and K. McClusky), Academic Press: New York and London.

REGAN, D.T. (1978). Attributional aspects of interpersonal attraction. *In* "New Directions in Attribution Research", Vol. 2 (Eds. J. Harvey, W. Ickes and R. Kidd), Lawrence Erlbaum Associates: New York.

REIK, T. (1944). "A Psychologist Looks at Love", Farrar and Rinehart: New York.

REIK, T. (1957). "Of Love and Lust", Farrar, Straus: New York.

RICOEUR, P. (1979). The model of the text: Meaningful action considered as a test. *In* "Interpretive Social Science" (Eds. P. Rainbow and W. Sullivan), The University of California Press: Berkeley.

RIDLEY, C. (1980). An interpersonal skills approach to premarital intervention. Unpublished paper, University of Arizona, Phoenix, Arizona.

RIDLEY, C., AVERY, A., HAYNES, L. and HARRELL, J. (1978). Problem-solving training for premarital couples: Six month follow-up. Paper presented to the American Psychological Association meeting, Toronto, Canada.

RILEY, M.W., FONER, A., MOORE, M.E., HESS, B. and ROTH, B.K. (1968). "Aging and Society: An Inventory of Research Findings (Vol. 1)", Russell Sage Foundations: New York.

RILEY, M.W. and WARING, J. (1976). Age and aging. In "Contemporary social problems" (4th edn) (Eds. R.K. Merton and R. Nisbet), Harcourt Press, Brace Jovanovich: New York.

RISKIN, J. and FAUNCE, E.E. (1972). An evaluative review of family interaction research. Family Process, 11, 365–455.

ROBERTS, J.M. (1964). The self-management of cultures. In "Explorations in Cultural Anthropology" (Ed. W.H. Goodenough), McGraw-Hill: New York.

RODIN, J. (1980). Managing the stress of aging: The role of control and coping. In "Coping and Health" (Eds. S. Levine and H. Ursin), Plenum: New York.

RODIN, M.J. (1975). The effect of behavioral context on information selection and differential accuracy in a person perception task. J. Soc. Psychol., 97, 83–94.

RODIN, M.J. (1978). Liking and disliking: Sketch of an alternative view. Personal. Soc. Psychol. Bull., 4, 473–478.

ROGERS, L.E. (1972). Dyadic systems and transactional communication in a family context. Unpublished doctoral dissertation, Department of Communication, Michigan State University.

ROGERS, L.E. and FARACE, R.V. (1975). Analysis of relational communication in dyads: New measurement procedures. Hum. Comm. Res., 1, 222–239.

ROGERS-MILLAR, L.E. and MILLAR, F.E. (1979). Domineeringness and dominance: a transactional view. Hum. Comm. Res., 5, 238–241.

ROKEACH, M. (Ed.). (1960). "The Open and Closed Mind", Basic Books: New York.

ROLLINS, B. and GALLIGAN, R. (1978). The developing child and marital satisfaction of parents. In "Child Influences on Marital and Family Interaction: A Life-span Perspective" (Eds. R. Lerner and G. Spanier), Academic Press: New York and London.

ROLOFF, M.E. (1976). Communication strategies, relationships and relational changes. In "Explorations in Interpersonal Communication" (Ed. G.R. Miller), Sage Publishers: Beverley Hills, California.

ROSENBLATT, P.C. (1974). Cross-cultural perspective on attraction. In "Foundations of Interpersonal Attraction" (Ed. T.L. Huston), Academic Press: New York and London.

ROSENBLUM, L.A., COE, C.L. and BROMLEY, L.J. (1975). Peer relations in monkeys: The influence of social structure, gender, and familiarity. In "Friendship and Peer Relations" (Eds. M. Lewis and L.A. Rosenblum), Wiley: New York.

ROSENFELD, H.M. (1966). Instrumental affiliative functions of facial and gestural expressions. J. Personal. Soc. Psychol., 4, 65–72.

ROSENTHAL, A., FLOYD, F. and MARKMAN, H. (1981). The short-term evaluation of a sexual enhancement program for couples planning marriage. Unpublished manuscript, University of Denver, Denver.

ROSNOW, R.L. (1977). Gossip and marketplace psychology. J. Communic., 27, 158–163.

ROSOW, I. (1974). "Socialization to old age", University of California Press: Berkeley.

ROSOW, I. (1976). Status and role change through the life span. In "Handbook of Aging and the Social Sciences" (Eds. R.E. Binstock and E. Shanas), Van Nostrand Reinhold: New York.

ROSS, L. (1977). The intuitive psychologist and his shortcomings: Distortions in the attribution process. In "Advances in Experimental Social Psychology", Vol. 10 (Ed. L. Berkowitz), Academic Press: New York and London.

ROTH, J.A. (1963). "Timetables", Bobbs-Merrill: Indianapolis.

ROTTER, J.B. (1966). Generalized expectancies for internal versus external control of reinforcement. Psychol. Monog., 80, 609.

RUBIN, L. (1979). "Women of a Certain Age", Harper and Row: New York.

RUBIN, Z. (1970). Measurement of romantic love. J. Personal. Soc. Psychol., 16, 265–273.

RUBIN, Z. (1973). "Liking and Loving", Rinehart and Winston: New York.

RUBIN, Z. (1975). Disclosing oneself to a stranger: reciprocity and its limits. J. Exper. Soc. Psychol., 11, 233–260.

RUBIN, Z. (1980). "Children's Friendships", Harvard University Press: Cambridge, Massachusetts.

RUBIN, Z. and MITCHELL, C. (1976). Couples research as couples counseling. Amer. Psychol. 31, 17–25.

RUTLEDGE, A.L. (1966). "Premarital Counseling", Schenkman Press: Cambridge, Massachusetts.

RUTLEDGE, A.L. (1968a). A systematic approach to premarital counseling. In "Counseling for the Liberal Arts Campus" (Eds. J.C. Heston and W.B Frich), Antioch Press: Yellow Springs, Ohio.

RUTLEDGE, A.L. (1968b). An illustrative look at the history of pre-marital counseling. In "Marriage and Family Counseling: Perspective and Prospects" (Ed. M.P. Peterson), New York Association Press: New York.

SABINI, J.P. and SILVER, M. (1978). Moral reproach and moral action, J. Theory Soc. Behav., 8, 103–123.

SAINT-EXUPERY, A. (1943). "The Little Prince". Harcourt Brace: New York.

SALTS, C.J. (1979). Divorce process: Integration of theory. J. Divorce, 2, 233–240.

SATIR, V. (1967). "Conjoint Family Therapy", Science and Behavior Books: Palo Alto, California.

SATIR, V. (1972). "Peoplemaking", Science and Behavior Books: Palo Alto, California.

SCANZONI, J. (1968). Social system analysis of dissolved and existing marriages. J. Marr. Fam., 30, 451–461.

SCHEFLEN, A.E. (1964). The significance of posture in communication systems. Psychiatry, 27, 316–331.

SCHEFLEN, A.E. (1973). "Communicational Structure: Analysis of Psychotherapy Transaction", Indiana University Press: Bloomington, Indiana.

SCHERER, K.R. (1974). Acoustic concomitants of emotional dimensions: Judging affect from synthesized tone sequences. In "Nonverbal Communication" (Ed. S. Weitz), Oxford University Press: New York.

SCHICKEL, R. (1980). The great second chance. Esquire, 93(3), 40–52.

SCHLEIN, S. (1971). Training dating couples in empathic and open communication: An experimental evaluation of a potential preventive mental health program. Unpublished doctoral dissertation, Pennsylvania State University.

SCHMITT, D.R. (1964). The invocation of moral obligation. *Sociometry,* **27,** 299–310.

SCHNEIDER, D.J., HASTORF, A.H. and ELLSWORTH, P.C. (1979). "Person Perception" (2nd edn), Addison-Wesley Publishing Company: Massachusetts.

SCHOPLER, J. and COMPERE, J.S. (1972). The effects of being kind or harsh to another on liking for him. Unpublished manuscript cited in Tedeschi (1974, q.v.).

SCHULZ, R. (1981). Learned helplessness and aging. *In* "Human Helplessness: Theory and Application" (Eds. M.E.P. Seligman and J. Garber), Academic Press: New York and London.

SCHUTZ, A. (1967). "The Phenomenology of the Social World", North-western University Press: Evanston, Illinois.

SCHUTZ, A. (1970). "Alfred Schutz on Phenomenology and Social Relations" (Ed. H. Wagner), University of Chicago Press: Chicago.

SCHUTZ, W.C. (1958). "FIRO: A Three-Dimensional Theory of Interpersonal Behavior", Holt, Rinehart and Winston: New York.

SCHWARTZ, B. (1968). The social psychology of privacy. *Amer. J. Sociol.,* **73,** 741–752.

SCOTT, M. and POWERS, W. (1978). "Interpersonal Communication: A Question of Needs", Houghton Mifflin: Boston.

SCOTT, M.B. and LYMAN, S.W. (1968). Accounts. *Amer. Sociol. Rev.,* **33,** 46–62.

SELIGMAN, M.E.P. (1975). "Helplessness: On Depression, Development and Death", W.H. Freeman: San Francisco.

SELIGMAN, M.E.P. and GARBER, J. (Eds.) (1981). "Human Helplessness: Theory and Application", Academic Press: New York and London.

SHAKESPEARE, W. (1599/1951). "Hamlet" (Alexander Text), Collins: London.

SIEGMAN, A.W. (1979). The voice of attraction: Vocal correlates of interpersonal attraction in the interview. *In* "Of Speech and Time: Temporal Speech Patterns in Interpersonal Contexts" (Eds. A.W. Siegman and S. Feldstein), Lawrence Erlbaum Associates: Hillsdale, New Jersey.

SIMMEL, G. (1950). "The Sociology of Georg Simmel" (Ed. and Trans. K.H. Wolff), Free Press: New York.

SIMMEL, G. (1971). "On Individuality and Social Forms" (Ed. D.N. Levine), University of Chicago Press: Chicago.

SKINNER, B.F. (1953). "Science and Human Behavior", Macmillan: New York.

SKINNER, B.F. (1975). The steep and thorny way to a science of behavior. *Amer. Psychol.,* **30,** 41–49.

SLATER, P. (1963). On social regression. *Amer. Sociol. Rev.,* **28,** 339–358.

SMITH, L. and SMITH A. (1976). Developing a nation-wide marriage communication labs program. *In* "Marriage Family Enrichment: New Perspectives and Programs" (Ed. H.A. Otto), Parthenon Press: Nashville, Tennessee.

SMYER, M.A. and HOFLAND, B.F. (1982). Divorce and family support in later life: emerging concerns. *J. Fam. Issues,* **3,** (in press).

SNYDER, M. (1974). The self-monitoring of expressive behavior. *J. Personal. Soc. Psychol.* **30,** 526–537.

SNYDER, M. (1979a). Seek, and ye shall find: Testing hypotheses about other people. *In* "Social Cognition: The Ontario Symposium on Personality and Social Psychology", Vol. 1 (Eds. E.T. Higgins and M.P. Zanna), Lawrence Erlbaum Associates: Hillsdale, New Jersey.

SNYDER, M. (1979b). Self-monitoring processes. *In* "Advances in Experimental Social Psychology", Vol. 12 (Ed. L. Berkowitz), Academic Press: New York and London.

SNYDER, M., TANKE, E. and BERSCHEID, E. (1977). Social perception and interpersonal behavior: On the self-fulfilling nature of social stereotypes. *J. Personal. Soc. Psychol.,* **35**, 656–666.

SOLOMON, R.L. (1980). The opponent-process theory of acquired motivation. *Amer. Psychol.,* **35**, 691–712.

SOLOMON, R.L. and CORBIT, J.D. (1973). An opponent-process theory of motivation: II. Cigarette addiction. *J. Abn. Psychol.,* **81**, 158–171.

SOLOMON, R.L. and CORBIT, J.D. (1974). An opponent process theory of motivation: I. Temporal dynamics of affect. *Psychol. Rev.,* **81**, 119–145.

SPANIER, G.B. and CASTO, R. (1979). Adjustment to separation and divorce: An analysis of 50 case studies. *J. Divorce,* **2**, 241–253.

SPANIER, G.B. and LEWIS, R.A. (1980). Marital quality: A review of the seventies. *J. Marr. Fam.,* **42**, 825–839.

SPICER, J.W. and HAMPE, G.D. (1975). Kinship interaction after divorce. *J. Marr. Fam.,* **37**, 113–120.

SROLE, L. LANGNER, T.S., MICHAEL, S.T., OPLER, M.K. and RENNIE, T.A.C. (1962). "Mental Health in the Metropolis: The Midtown Manhattan Study", McGraw-Hill: New York.

STACK, S. (1980). The effects of marital dissolution on suicide. *J. Marr. Fam.,* **42**, 83–92.

STEINER, I.D. (1972). "Group Process and Productivity", Academic Press: New York and London.

STEPHAN, W., BERSCHEID, E. and WALSTER, E. (1971). Sexual arousal and heterosexual perception. *J. Personal. Soc. Psychol.,* **20**, 93–101.

STEPHEN, T.D. (1980). Longitudinal and cross-sectional tests of a theory of symbolic exchange in developing intimate relationships. Unpublished doctoral dissertation, Department of Speech Communication, Bowling Green State University.

STEPHEN, T.D. and MARKMAN, H. (1981). The relationship world index: an instrument for the measurement of symbolic interdependence in developing intimate relationships. Under editorial review.

STINNETT, N., CHESSER, B. and DEFRAIN, J. (1979). "Building Family Strengths: Blueprints for Action", University of Nebraska Press: Lincoln, Nebraska.

STINNETT, N., CHESSER, B., DEFRAIN, J. and KNAUB, P. (1980). "Family Strengths: Positive Models for Family Life", University of Nebraska Press: Lincoln, Nebraska.

STINNETT, F., DEFRAIN, J., KING, K., KNAUB, P. and ROWE, G. (1981). "Family Strengths: The Roots of Well-Being", University of Nebraska Press: Lincoln, Nebraska.

STONE, G. (1962). Appearance and the self. *In* "Human Behavior and Social Processes" (Ed. A. Rose), Houghton Mifflin: Boston.

STRAUS, A.L. (1959) "Mirrors and Masks", Free Press: Glencoe, Illinois.

STRYKER, S. and GOTTLIEB, A. (in press). Attribution theory and symbolic interactionalism: A comparison. *In* "New Directions in Attribution Research", Vol. 3 (Eds. J.H. Harvey, W. Ickes and R.F. Kidd), Lawrence Erlbaum Associates: Hillsdale, New Jersey.

STUART, R.B. (1969). Operant-interpersonal treatment for marital discord. *J. Consult. Clin. Psychol.* **33**, 675–682.

STUEVE, C. and GERSON, K. (1977). Personal relations across the life cycle. *In* "Networks and Places" (Ed. C. Fischer), Free Press: New York.

SULLIVAN, H.S. (1953). "The Interpersonal Theory of Psychiatry", W.W. Norton: New York.

SULS, J.M. (1977). Gossip as social comparison. *J. Communic.* **27**, 164–168.

SUOMI, S.J. and HARLOW, H.F. (1975). The role and reason of peer relationships in rhesus monkeys. *In* "Friendship and Peer Relations" (Eds. M. Lewis and L.A. Rosenblum), Wiley: New York.

SURRA, C. (1980). Dyadic and social network interaction from premarriage to marriage. Paper presented at National Council for Family Relations, Portland.

SUTTLES, G.D. (1970). Friendship as a social institution. *In* "Social Relationships" (Ed. G.J. McCall), Aldine: Chicago.

SUTTON-SMITH, B. and ROSENBERG, B.G. (1970). "The Sibling", Holt, Rinehart and Winston: New York.

TEDESCHI, J.T. (1974). Attributions, liking and power. *In* "Foundations of Interpersonal Attraction" (Ed. T.L. Huston). Academic Press: New York and London.

TERMAN, L. (1938). "Psychological Factors in Marital Happiness", McGraw-Hill: New York.

TERMAN, L. and ODEN, M. (1947). "The Gifted Child Grows up: Twenty-Five Year Follow-up of a Superior Group", Stanford University Press: Palo Alto, California.

TESSER, A. (1978a). Self-esteem maintenance processes in interpersonal behavior. Unpublished research proposal, University of Georgia.

TESSER, A. (1978b). Self-generated attitude change. *In* "Advances in Experimental Social Psychology", Vol. 11 (Ed. L. Berkowitz), Academic Press: New York and London.

TESSER, A. (1980). Self-esteem maintenance in family dynamics. *J. Personal. Soc. Psychol.,* **39**, 77–91.

TESSER, A. and DANHEISER, P. (1978). Anticipated relationship, salience of partner and attitude change. *Personal. Soc. Psychol. Bull.,* **4**, 35–38.

TESSER, A. and PAULHUS, D.L. (1976). Toward a causal model of love. *J. Personal. Soc. Psychol.,* **34**, 1095–1105.

TESSER, A. and REARDON, R. (in press). Perceptual and cognitive mechanisms in human sexual attraction. *In* "The Bases of Human Sexual Attraction" (Ed. M. Cook), Academic Press: New York and London.

TESSER, A. and SMITH, J. (1980). Some effects of task relevance and friendship on helping: You don't always help the one you like. *J. Exper. Soc. Psychol.,* **16**, 582–590.

THARP, R.G. (1963). Psychological patterning in marriage. *Psychol. Bull.* **60**, 97–117.

THIBAUT, J.W. and KELLEY, H.H. (1959). "The Social Psychology of Groups", Wiley: New York.

TRAVIS, P. and TRAVIS, R. (1975). The pairing enrichment program: actualizing the marriage. *Fam. Coord.,* **24**, 161–165.

TRAVISANO, R. (1970). Alternation and conversion as qualitatively different transformations. *In* "Social Psychology Through Symbolic Interaction" (Eds. G. Stone and H. Farberman), Xerox College Publishing: Waltham, Massachusetts.

TROLL, L.E., MILLER, S.J. and ATCHLEY, R.C. (1979). "Families in later life". Wadsworth: Belmont, California.

TURNER, R.H. (1970). "Family Interaction", Wiley: New York.

TURNER, T.S. (1977). Transformation, hierarchy and transcendence. In "Secular Ritual" (Eds. S.F. Moore and B.G. Myerhoff), Van Gorcum, Assen: Amsterdam.

U.S. GOVERNMENT (Department of Health and Human Services). (1981). Monthly vital statistics report, 12, March. U.S. Government Printing Office: Washington, D.C.

VAN GENNEP, A. (1908/1960). "The Rites of Passage", Phoenix Books: New York.

VINCENT, J., COOK, N. and MESSERLY, L. (1980). A social learning analysis of couples during the second postmarital month. Amer. J. Fam. Ther., 8, 2, 49–68.

WADDINGTON, C.H. (1966). "Principles of Development and Differentiation", Macmillan: New York.

WALKER, K.L., MacBRIDE, A. and VACHON, M.L.S. (1977). Social support networks and the crisis of bereavement. Soc. Sci. and Med., 11, 35–41.

WALLER, W. (1930). "The Old Love and the New: Divorce and Readjustment", Liveright: New York.

WALLER, W. (1938). "The Family: A Dynamic Interpretation", Cordon: New York.

WALLER, W. and HILL, R. (1951). "The Family", Dryden: New York.

WALLERSTEIN, J.S. and KELLY, J.B. (1980). "Surviving the break up: How children and parents cope with divorce". Basic Books: New York.

WALSTER, E. (1965). The effect of self-esteem on romantic liking. J. Exper. Soc. Psychol., 1, 184–197.

WALSTER, E., ARONSON, V., ABRAHAMS, D. and ROTTMAN, L. (1966). Importance of physical attractiveness in dating behavior. J. Personal. Soc. Psychol., 4, 508–516.

WALSTER, E., BERSCHEID, E. and WALSTER, G.W. (1973). New directions in equity research. J. Personal. Soc. Psychol., 25, 151–176.

WALSTER, E.H. and WALSTER, G.W. (1978). "A New Look at Love", Addison-Wesley: Reading, Massachusetts.

WALSTER, E.H., WALSTER, G.W. and BERSCHEID, E. (1978). "Equity Theory and Research", Allyn and Bacon: Boston.

WALSTER, E.H., WALSTER, G.W., PILIAVIN, J. and SCHMIDT, L. (1973). "Playing hard to get": understanding an elusive phenomenon. J. Personal. Soc. Psychol., 26, 113–121.

WAMPLER, K. and SPRENKLE, D. (1980). The Minnesota Couple Communication Program: A follow-up study. J. Marr. Fam., 42, 577–580.

WEARY, G. (1979). Self-serving attribution biases: Perceptual or response distortions? J. Personal. Soc. Psychol., 37, 1418–1420.

WEIMAN, J. (1977). Explication and test of a model of communicative competence. Hum. Comm. Res., 3, 195–213.

WEISS, R. (1973). Helping relationships: Relationships of clients with physicians, social workers, priests and others. Soc. Prob. 20, 319–328.

WEISS, R. (1978). The conceptualization of marriage from a behavioral perspective. In "Marriage and Marriage Therapy" (Eds. T. Paolino and B. McCrady), Brunner/Mazel: New York.

WEISS, R. (1980). Strategic Behavioral Marital Therapy: Toward a Model for Assessment and Intervention. In "Advances in Family Intervention, Assessment and Theory Vol. 1'' (Ed. J. Vincent), JAI Press: Greenwich, Connecticut.

WEISS, R.L., HOPS, H. and PATTERSON, G.R. (1973). A framework for conceptualizing marital conflict: A technology for altering it, some data for evaluating it. *In* ''Behavior Change: Methodology, Concepts and Practice'' (Eds. L.A. Hammerlynck, L.C. Handy and E.J. Marsh), Research Press: Champaign, Illinois.

WEISS, R.S. (1968). Materials for a theory of social relationships *In* ''Interpersonal Dynamics'' (revised edn). (Eds. W.G. Bennis *et al.*), Dorsey Press: Homewood, Illinois.

WEISS, R.S. (1975). ''Marital Separation''. Basic Books: New York.

WHEELER, L. (1974). Social comparison and selective affiliation. *In* ''Foundations of Interpersonal Attraction'' (Ed. T.L. Huston). Academic Press: New York and London.

WHEELER, L. and NEZLEK, J. (1977). Sex differences in social participation. *J. Pers. Soc. Psychol.*, **35**, 742–754.

WIENER, M. and MEHRABIAN, A. (1968). ''Language within Language: Immediacy, a Channel in Verbal Communication'', Appleton-Century-Crofts: New York.

WILLS, T.A., WEISS, R.L. and PATTERSON, G. (1974). Behavioral analysis of the determinants of marital satisfaction. *J. Consult. Clin. Psychol.* **42**, 802–811.

WINCH, P. (1971). ''The Idea of Social Science and its Relation to Philosophy'', Routledge and Kegan Paul: London.

WINCH, R.F. (1954). The theory of complementary needs in mate selection: Final results on the test of general hypotheses. *Amer. Soc. Rev.* **19**, 241–249.

WINCH, R.F. (1958). ''Mate Selection: A Study of Complementary Needs'', Harper and Row: New York.

WOLFF, C. (1945). ''A Psychology of Gesture'', Methuen: London.

WOMBLE, D. (1961). Functional marriage course for the already married. *Marr. Fam. Liv.* **23**, 278–283.

WRIGHT, D. (1971). ''The Psychology of Moral Behaviour'', Penguin: Harmondsworth.

YERKOVICH, S. (1977). Gossiping as a way of speaking. *J. of Communic.*, **27**, 192–196.

ZADNY, J. and GERARD, H. (1974). Attributed intentions and informational selectivity. *J. Exper. Soc. Psychol.*, **10**, 34–52.

ZAJONC, R.B. (1968). Attitudinal effects of mere exposure. *J. Personal. Soc. Psychol., Monog. Suppl.*, **9**, Part 2, 1–29.

ZAJONC, R.B. (1980). Feeling and thinking: Preferences need no inferences. *Amer. Psychol.*, **35**, 151–175.

Author Index

A

B

Y

Z

Subject Index